A·N·N·U·A·L E·D·I·T·I·O·N·S

Dying, Death, and Bereavement

Eighth Edition

05/06

EDITOR

George E. Dickinson, Ph.D.

College of Charleston

George E. Dickinson is Professor of Sociology at the College of Charleston in Charleston, South Carolina, where in 2002 he received the Distinguished Teacher-Scholar Award. He earned a B.A. in biology from Baylor University, an M.A. in sociology from Baylor, and a Ph.D. in sociology from Louisiana State University. Dr. Dickinson has been teaching courses in death and dying for over 30 years. His research interests are the role of physicians in relating to terminally ill patients and their families and physicians' attitudes toward physician-assisted suicide and active voluntary euthanasia. He has published over 50 articles in professional journals, and is currently on the international editorial board of *Mortality* in the United Kingdom.

Michael R. Leming, Ph.D.

St. Olaf College

Michael R. Leming is Professor of Sociology and Anthropology at St. Olaf College. He holds degrees from Westmont College (B. A.), Marquette University (M. A.), and the University of Utah (Ph. D.) and has done additional graduate study at the University of California in Santa Barbara. He is the co-author (with George E. Dickinson) of *Understanding Dying, Death, and Bereavement,* Five Editions (ITP, 2002) and *Understanding Families: Diversity, Continuity, and Change,* Two Editions (Harcourt Brace, 1995). He is also the co-editor (with Raymond DeVries and Brendan Furnish) of *The Sociological Perspective: A Value-Committed Introduction* (Zondervan, 1989).

Dr. Leming is the founder and former director of the St. Olaf College Social Research Center, former member of the board of directors of the Minnesota Coalition on Terminal Care and the Northfield AIDS Response, and has served as a hospice educator, volunteer, and grief counselor.

For the past five years he has directed the Spring Semester in Thailand program (www.AmazingSEAsia.com) which is affiliated with Chiang Mai University and lives in Thailand during Minnesota's coldest months.

McGraw-Hill/Dushkin

2460 Kerper Blvd., Dubuque, IA 52001

Visit us on the Internet
http://www.dushkin.com

Credits

1. **The American Way of Dying and Death**
   Unit photo—Courtesy of Health Resources and Services Administration, www.organdonor.gov
2. **Developmental Aspects of Dying and Death**
   Unit photo—© Getty Images/PhotoLink/Kent Knudson
3. **The Dying Process**
   Unit photo—© CORBIS/Royalty-Free
4. **Ethical Issues of Dying, Death, and Suicide**
   Unit photo—© Getty Images/Nick Rowe
5. **Funerals and Burial Rites**
   Unit photo—© CORBIS/Royalty-Free
6. **Bereavement**
   Unit photo—© CORBIS/Royalty-Free

Copyright

Cataloging in Publication Data
Main entry under title: Annual Editions: Dying, Death, and Bereavement. 2005/2006.
1. Dying, Death, and Bereavement—Periodicals. I. Dickinson, George E., and Leming, Michael R., *comp.* II. Title: Dying, Death, and Bereavement.
ISBN 0–07–310204–0   658'.05   ISSN 1096–4223

Eighth Edition

Cover image © Photos.com
Printed in the United States of America   234567890QPDQPD98765   Printed on Recycled Paper

Editors/Advisory Board

Members of the Advisory Board are instrumental in the final selection of articles for each edition of ANNUAL EDITIONS. Their review of articles for content, level, currentness, and appropriateness provides critical direction to the editor and staff. We think that you will find their careful consideration well reflected in this volume.

Preface

In publishing ANNUAL EDITIONS we recognize the enormous role played by the magazines, newspapers, and journals of the public press in providing current, first-rate educational information in a broad spectrum of interest areas. Many of these articles are appropriate for students, researchers, and professionals seeking accurate, current material to help bridge the gap between principles and theories and the real world. These articles, however, become more useful for study when those of lasting value are carefully collected, organized, and reproduced in a low-cost format, which provides easy and permanent access when the material is needed. That is the role played by ANNUAL EDITIONS.

Though dying, death, and bereavement have been around for as long as humankind, as topics of discussion they have been "offstage" for decades in contemporary American public discourse. In the United States, dying currently takes place away from the arena of familiar surroundings of kin and friends, with approximately 80 percent of deaths occurring in institutional settings such as hospitals and nursing homes. Americans have developed a paradoxical relationship with death: We know more about the causes and conditions surrounding death but have not equipped ourselves emotionally to cope with dying, death, and bereavement. The purpose of this anthology is to provide an understanding of dying, death, and bereavement that will assist in better coping with and understanding our own deaths and the deaths of others.

Articles in this volume are taken from professional publications, semiprofessional journals, and popular publications written for both special populations and a general readership. The selections are carefully reviewed for their currency and accuracy. In the current edition, nearly a third of the articles have changed from the previous edition through updating and responding to comments of reviewers.

The reader will note the tremendous range of approaches and styles of the writers from personal, firsthand accounts to more scientific and philosophical writings. Some are more practical and applied, while others are more technical and research-oriented. If "variety is the very spice of life," this volume should be a spicy venture for the reader.

These articles are drawn from many different periodicals, thus exposing the reader to a diversity of publications in the library. With interest stimulated by a particular article, the student is encouraged to pursue other related articles in that particular journal.

This anthology is organized into six units to cover many of the important aspects of dying, death, and bereavement. Though the units are arranged in a way that has some logical order, one can determine from the brief summaries in the table of contents and the cross-references in the topic guide whether another arrangement would best fit a particular teaching situation. The first unit gives an overview of the American way of dying and death. Unit 2 takes a life-span approach and looks at the developmental aspects of dying and death at different age levels. The third unit concerns the process of dying. Unit 4 covers ethical issues of dying, death, and suicide. In the fifth unit, the articles deal with death rituals and funerals. Finally, unit 6 presents articles on bereavement.

Annual Editions: Dying, Death, and Bereavement 05/06 is intended for use as a supplement to augment selected areas or chapters of regular textbooks on dying and death. The articles in this volume can also serve as a basis for class discussion about various issues in dying, death, and bereavement.

Annual Editions: Dying, Death, and Bereavement is revised periodically to keep the materials timely as new social concerns about dying, death, and bereavement develop. Your assistance in the revision effort is always welcome. Please complete and return the postage-paid article rating form at the back of the book. We look forward to your input.

George E. Dickinson
Editor

Michael R. Leming
Editor

Contents

UNIT 1
The American Way of Dying and Death

Five selections discuss definitions of death, various burial customs, the medical aspects of death, and other end-of-life issues.

UNIT 2
Developmental Aspects of Dying and Death

Six articles examine how the experience of watching friends and relatives die can affect individuals at various periods of their lives.

The concepts in bold italics are developed in the article. For further expansion, please refer to the Topic Guide.

UNIT 3
The Dying Process

Seven articles examine the various stages of the dying process, how physicians view dying, spiritual needs of the dying , and the dynamics of hospice.

The concepts in bold italics are developed in the article. For further expansion, please refer to the Topic Guide.

UNIT 4
Ethical Issues of Dying, Death, and Suicide

Nine unit selections discuss active euthanasia, assisted suicide, and other ethical issues one may face at the end of life.

The concepts in bold italics are developed in the article. For further expansion, please refer to the Topic Guide.

UNIT 5
Funerals and Burial Rites

Eight articles discuss pre-planning one's own funeral, the American funeral, cross-
cultural burial rites, and cremation.

The concepts in bold italics are developed in the article. For further expansion, please refer to the Topic Guide.

UNIT 6
Bereavement

Nine articles discuss the grieving process of children, young people, adults, and the loss of a significant other.

The concepts in bold italics are developed in the article. For further expansion, please refer to the Topic Guide.

The concepts in bold italics are developed in the article. For further expansion, please refer to the Topic Guide.

Topic Guide

This topic guide suggests how the selections in this book relate to the subjects covered in your course. You may want to use the topics listed on these pages to search the Web more easily.

On the following pages a number of Web sites have been gathered specifically for this book. They are arranged to reflect the units of this *Annual Edition*. You can link to these sites by going to the DUSHKIN ONLINE support site at *http://www.dushkin.com/online/*.

ALL THE ARTICLES THAT RELATE TO EACH TOPIC ARE LISTED BELOW THE BOLD-FACED TERM.

Advanced directive

1. Technology and Death Policy: Redefining Death
6. Teaching End-of-Life Issues: Current Status in United Kingdom and United States Medical Schools
14. Patients Whose Final Wishes Go Unsaid Put Doctors in a Bind
19. Death and the Law
20. Why Secular Humanism is Wrong: About Assisted Suicide
23. Euthanasia: A Need for Reform
25. End-of-Life Care: Forensic Medicine vs. Palliative Medicine
39. Till Death Do Us Part

AIDS

22. Competent Care for the Dying Instead of Physician-Assisted Suicide

Assisting grievers

10. Helping Teenagers Cope With Grief
12. Placing Religion and Spirituality in End-of-Life Care
31. The Last Thing You Want to Do
32. An Unexpected Kind of Family Foresight
34. Therapist Equates Owner Grief to Family Member Loss: Human-Animal Bond Impacts Physical, Mental Health: Experts Push Pet Bereavement Mainstream
35. Mourning the Loss of a Pet: Coping Strategies to Help Ease Your Grief and Celebrate Their Memory
40. The Increasing Prevalence of Complicated Mourning: The Onslaught Is Just Beginning
41. Listening
42. Grief Takes No Holiday
43. Discussing Tragedy With Your Child
44. Counseling With Children in Contemporary Society

Attitudes toward death

1. Technology and Death Policy: Redefining Death
2. The Unsettled Question of Brain Death
6. Teaching End-of-Life Issues: Current Status in United Kingdom and United States Medical Schools
12. Placing Religion and Spirituality in End-of-Life Care
20. Why Secular Humanism is Wrong: About Assisted Suicide
23. Euthanasia: A Need for Reform
25. End-of-Life Care: Forensic Medicine vs. Palliative Medicine
26. Elisabeth Kübler-Ross's Final Passage
29. Six Feet Under: Thomas Lynch Has Buried 6,000 Of His Neighbors. He Talks About the Business of Death.
31. The Last Thing You Want to Do
32. An Unexpected Kind of Family Foresight
33. Working With Death Was No Way to Live
34. Therapist Equates Owner Grief to Family Member Loss: Human-Animal Bond Impacts Physical, Mental Health: Experts Push Pet Bereavement Mainstream
35. Mourning the Loss of a Pet: Coping Strategies to Help Ease Your Grief and Celebrate Their Memory
39. Till Death Do Us Part
41. Listening
42. Grief Takes No Holiday
43. Discussing Tragedy With Your Child
44. Counseling With Children in Contemporary Society

Bereavement and grief

6. Teaching End-of-Life Issues: Current Status in United Kingdom and United States Medical Schools
9. Terrorism, Trauma, and Children: What Can We Do?
10. Helping Teenagers Cope With Grief
28. The Contemporary American Funeral
29. Six Feet Under: Thomas Lynch Has Buried 6,000 Of His Neighbors. He Talks About the Business of Death.
30. How Different Religions Pay Their Final Respects
31. The Last Thing You Want to Do
32. An Unexpected Kind of Family Foresight
34. Therapist Equates Owner Grief to Family Member Loss: Human-Animal Bond Impacts Physical, Mental Health: Experts Push Pet Bereavement Mainstream
35. Mourning the Loss of a Pet: Coping Strategies to Help Ease Your Grief and Celebrate Their Memory
36. The Grieving Process
37. Disenfranchised Grief
38. Enhancing the Concept of Disenfranchised Grief
39. Till Death Do Us Part
40. The Increasing Prevalence of Complicated Mourning: The Onslaught Is Just Beginning
42. Grief Takes No Holiday
44. Counseling With Children in Contemporary Society

Brain death

1. Technology and Death Policy: Redefining Death
2. The Unsettled Question of Brain Death
17. Hospice Referral Decisions: The Role of Physicians
18. A Commentary: The Role of Religion and Spirituality at the End of Life
19. Death and the Law
25. End-of-Life Care: Forensic Medicine vs. Palliative Medicine

Caregivers

6. Teaching End-of-Life Issues: Current Status in United Kingdom and United States Medical Schools
9. Terrorism, Trauma, and Children: What Can We Do?
10. Helping Teenagers Cope With Grief
12. Placing Religion and Spirituality in End-of-Life Care
13. Dying Words: How Should Doctors Deliver Bad News?
14. Patients Whose Final Wishes Go Unsaid Put Doctors in a Bind
17. Hospice Referral Decisions: The Role of Physicians
18. A Commentary: The Role of Religion and Spirituality at the End of Life
19. Death and the Law
20. Why Secular Humanism is Wrong: About Assisted Suicide
22. Competent Care for the Dying Instead of Physician-Assisted Suicide
23. Euthanasia: A Need for Reform
25. End-of-Life Care: Forensic Medicine vs. Palliative Medicine
32. An Unexpected Kind of Family Foresight
33. Working With Death Was No Way to Live
34. Therapist Equates Owner Grief to Family Member Loss: Human-Animal Bond Impacts Physical, Mental Health: Experts Push Pet Bereavement Mainstream
35. Mourning the Loss of a Pet: Coping Strategies to Help Ease Your Grief and Celebrate Their Memory
39. Till Death Do Us Part
41. Listening
43. Discussing Tragedy With Your Child

World Wide Web Sites

The following World Wide Web sites have been carefully researched and selected to support the articles found in this reader. The easiest way to access these selected sites is to go to our DUSHKIN ONLINE support site at *http://www.dushkin.com/online/*.

AE: Dying, Death, and Bereavement 05/06

The following sites were available at the time of publication. Visit our Web site—we update DUSHKIN ONLINE regularly to reflect any changes.

General Sources

An Introduction to Death and Dying
http://www.bereavement.org/

This electronic book was created to help those who grieve and those who provide support for the bereaved. Sections include Grief Theories, Death Systems, Ritual, and Disenfranchised Grief.

Yahoo: Society and Culture: Death
http://dir.yahoo.com/Society_and_Culture/Death_and_Dying/

This Yahoo site has a very complete index to issues of dying and a search option.

UNIT 1: The American Way of Dying and Death

Agency for Health Care Policy and Research
http://www.ahcpr.gov

Information on the dying process in the context of U.S. health policy is provided here, along with a search mechanism. The agency is part of the Department of Health and Human Services.

Brain Injury and Brain Death Resources
http://www.changesurfer.com/BD/Brain.html

Visit this site to investigate the debate concerning brain death. When is someone dead? Go to the philosophy of life, consciousness, and personhood page to get specifics.

Growth House, Inc.
http://www.growthhouse.org

Growth House is a nonprofit organization working with grief, bereavement, hospice, and end-of-life issues, as well as pain, AIDS/HIV, suicide, and palliative care issues.

Mortality Rates
http://www.Trinity.Edu/~mkearl/b&w-ineq.jpg

This site contains a graphic representation of the U.S. death rates of different social groups to ascertain social inequities.

WWW Virtual Library: Demography and Population Studies
http://demography.anu.edu.au/VirtualLibrary/

A definitive guide to demography and population studies, with a multitude of important links, can be found here.

UNIT 2: Developmental Aspects of Dying and Death

CDC Wonder on the Web—Prevention Guidelines
http://wonder.cdc.gov

At this Centers for Disease Control site, there are a number of papers on suicide prevention, particularly relating to American youth.

Children With AIDS Project
http://www.aidskids.org

This organization's role is to develop fuller understanding of children with and at risk of AIDS, including medical, psychosocial, legal, and financial issues. The mission of the organization is to develop local and national adoptive, foster, and family-centered care programs that are effective and compassionate.

Light for Life Foundation
http://www.yellowribbon.org

The Yellow Ribbon Program of the Light for Life Foundation provides educational material for American youth aimed at preventing youth suicide through the provision of easy access to support services.

National SIDS Resource Center
http://www.sidscenter.org/

The National Sudden Infant Death Syndrome Resource Center (NSRC) provides information services and technical assistance on SIDS and related topics.

Palliative Care for Children
http://www.aap.org/policy/re0007.html

The American Academy of Pediatrics maintains this page, which gives a model for providing palliative care for children living with a life-threatening disease or terminal condition.

UNIT 3: The Dying Process

American Academy of Hospice and Palliative Medicine
http://www.aahpm.org

This is the only organization in the United States for physicians that is dedicated to the advancement of hospice/palliative medicine, its practice, research, and education. There are also links to other Web sites.

Hospice Foundation of America
http://www.hospicefoundation.org

Everything you might need to know about hospice and specific information on the foundation is available at this Web site.

Hospice Hands
http://hospice-cares.com

An extensive collection of links to hospice resources can be found at this site. Try "What's New" to access the *ACP Home Care Guide,* a book whose goal is to support an orderly problem-solving approach in managing care of the dying at home.

National Prison Hospice Association
http://www.npha.org

This prison hospice association promotes care for terminally ill inmates and those facing the prospect of dying in prison.

The Zen Hospice Project
http://www.zenhospice.org

The Zen Hospice Project organizes programs dedicated to the care of people approaching death and to increasing the understanding of impermanence. The project also runs a small hospice in San Francisco. There are links here to related information on the Web.

www.dushkin.com/online/

UNIT 4: Ethical Issues of Dying, Death, and Suicide

Articles on Euthanasia: Ethics
http://ethics.acusd.edu/Applied/Euthanasia/

This site covers biomedical ethics and issues of euthanasia in many ways, including recent articles, ancient concepts, legal and legislative information, selected philosophical literature, Web sites, and a search engine.

Kearl's Guide to the Sociology of Death: Moral Debates
http://WWW.Trinity.Edu/~mkearl/death-5.html#eu

An Internet resource on the ethics of biomedical issues that includes issues of dying and death, such as euthanasia, is found here.

The Kevorkian Verdict
http://www.pbs.org/wgbh/pages/frontline/kevorkian/

This Web site from PBS features two thought-provoking interviews that explore the future for assisted suicide in the United States. What are the dangers and needed safeguards if it is legalized? How should we view Dr. Kevorkian's role in spotlighting this issue?

Euthanasia and Physician-Assisted Suicide
http://www.religioustolerance.org/euthanas.htm

This Web site covers Euthanasia in the United States, as well as status of euthanasia elsewhere in the world and recent developments.

Living Wills (Advance Directive)
http://www.mindspring.com/~scottr/will.html

The largest collection of links to living wills and other advance directive and living will information is available at this Web site.

Not Dead Yet
http://www.notdeadyet.org/

The Americans With Disabilities organization uses this Web site to mobilize Americans against euthanasia and mercy killing. Information about the Hemlock Society is also available here.

Suicide Awareness: Voices of Education
http://www.save.org

This popular Internet suicide site provides information on suicide (both before and after), along with material from the organization's many education sessions.

UNOS: United Network for Organ Sharing
http://www.unos.org/

This Web site of the United Network for Organ Sharing includes facts and statistics, resources, and policy proposals regarding organ transplants.

Youth Suicide League
http://www.unicef.org/pon96/insuicid.htm

International suicide rates of young adults in selected countries are available on this UNESCO Web site.

UNIT 5: Funerals and Burial Rites

Cryonics, Cryogenics, and the Alcor Foundation
http://www.alcor.org

This is the Web site of Alcor, the world's largest cryonics organization.

Funerals and Ripoffs
http://www.funerals-ripoffs.org/-5dProf1.htm/

Sponsored by the Interfaith Funeral Information Committee and Arizona Consumers Council, this Web site is very critical of the funeral industry and specializes in exposing funeral home financial fraud.

The Internet Cremation Society
http://www.cremation.org

The Internet Cremation Society provides statistics on cremations, links to funeral industry resources, and answers to frequently asked questions.

Funeral Consumers Alliance
http://www.funerals.org/

The Funeral Consumers Alliance is the only group that monitors the funeral industry for consumers regarding funeral guides, planning, and issues of social concern.

UNIT 6: Bereavement

Bereaved Families of Ontario Support Center
http://www.bereavedfamilies.net/

The Self-Help Resources Guide at this site indexes resources of the Bereaved Families of Ontario Support Center along with more than 300 listings of other resources and information that are useful to the bereaved.

The Compassionate Friends
http://www.compassionatefriends.org

This self-help organization for bereaved parents and siblings has hundreds of chapters worldwide.

GriefNet
http://rivendell.org

Produced by a nonprofit group, Rivendell Resources, this site provides many links to the Web on bereavement process, resources for grievers, and information concerning grief support groups.

Practical Grief Resources
http://www.indiana.edu/~famlygrf/sitemap.html

Here are lists of Internet and print resources that are available for understanding and coping with grief.

Widow Net
http://www.fortnet.org/WidowNet/

Widow Net is an information and self-help resource for and by widows and widowers. The information is helpful to people of all ages, religious backgrounds, and sexual orientation who have experienced a loss of a spouse or life partner.

We highly recommend that you review our Web site for expanded information and our other product lines. We are continually updating and adding links to our Web site in order to offer you the most usable and useful information that will support and expand the value of your Annual Editions. You can reach us at: *http://www.dushkin.com/annualeditions/.*

UNIT 1

The American Way of Dying and Death

Unit Selections

1. **Technology and Death Policy: Redefining Death**, Robert H. Blank
2. **The Unsettled Question of Brain Death**, Peter Monaghan
3. **Anatomy Lessons, A Vanishing Rite for Young Doctors**, Abigail Zuger
4. **In Science's Name, Lucrative Trade in Body Parts**, John M. Broder, Sandra Blakeslee, Charlie LeDuff, and Andrew Pollack
5. **Deaths Go Unexamined and the Living Pay the Price**, Anahad O'Connor

Key Points to Consider

- Discuss definitions of "death." How is "brain death" defined in different countries? What is the significance of brain death to organ donations? What are other ways to determine death?

- Of what good are dead human remains? Can medical science benefit from an autopsy of an individual whose cause of death was uncertain? Can medical students learn human anatomy without dissecting a human cadaver?

- Medical schools in the U.S. are doing a better job of relating dying and death to the medical school experience than in the past. Yet, hospice and palliative care are only beginning to be an integral part of medical school curricula. In what ways are the British ahead of Americans in this regard? How might hospice and palliative care be of benefit to dying patients? What do you personally know about hospice programs in North America?

DUSHKIN ONLINE **Links: www.dushkin.com/online/**
These sites are annotated in the World Wide Web pages.

Agency for Health Care Policy and Research
http://www.ahcpr.gov

Brain Injury and Brain Death Resources
http://www.changesurfer.com/BD/Brain.html

Growth House, Inc.
http://www.growthhouse.org

Mortality Rates
http://www.Trinity.Edu/~mkearl/b&w-ineq.jpg

WWW Virtual Library: Demography and Population Studies
http://demography.anu.edu.au/VirtualLibrary/

Organ/Tissue Donor Card

I wish to donate my organs and tissues. I wish to give:

☐ any needed organs and tissues

☐ only the following organs and tissues:

_____

Donor
Signature _____ Date _____

Witness _____

Witness _____

Death, like sex, is a rather taboo topic. British anthropologist Geoffrey Gorer's writing about the pornography of death in the mid-twentieth century seemed to open the door for publications on the subject of death. Gorer argued that death had replaced sex as contemporary society's major taboo topic. Because death was less common in the community, with individuals actually seeing fewer corpses and being with individuals less at the time of death, a relatively realistic view of death had been replaced by a voyeuristic, adolescent preoccupation with it. Our modern way of life has not prepared us to cope any better with dying and death. Sex and death have "come out of the closet" in recent decades however, and now are issues discussed and presented in formal educational settings. In fact, end-of-life issues are frequently discussed in the popular media, as evidenced by the popular television show *Six Feet Under* and numerous documentaries and other drama series (e.g., *ER*). Yet, we have a long way to go in educating the public about these historically "forbidden" subjects.

We are beginning to recognize the importance of educating America's youth on the subject of dying and death. Like sex education, death education (thanatology) is an approved topic for presentation in elementary and secondary school curricula in many states, but the topics (especially dying and death) are op-

tional and therefore rarely receive high priorities in the classroom or in educational funding. With a flurry of killings on school grounds across the country, the terrorist attack on the United States on September 11, 2001, the war in Iraq, and terrorist bombings in numerous places in the world, an increased interest on death and dying in the curricula could have a tremendous impact on school curricula.

Physicians obviously deal with dying and death almost on a daily basis. How well are we preparing physicians to relate to terminally ill patients and their families? Traditionally, first-year medical students have taken gross anatomy where they learn about the human body. Yet, in the future, human cadavers may no longer be used in anatomy labs. We have not traditionally emphasized pain control (palliative care) in dealing with patients in the medical sphere. The article on end-of-life issues in the United States and the United Kingdom addresses the current state of death education, hospice, and palliative care in these countries' medical schools. The U.S. is improving in its emphasis on palliative care and hospice orientation, though the UK is well ahead at this point. "Anatomy Lessons, A Vanishing Rite for Young Doctors" discusses the possible vanishing use of human cadavers.

Another issue concerning the American way of dying and death is the question, "When is an individual dead?" Sounds simple enough, but in reality, this is a complex question with a not-so-easy answer. Some states do not have a clear definition as to when an individual is dead. One way of determining death is the "brain death" definition, often used when organ transplants are involved. "Technology and Death Policy: Redefining Death" and "The Unsettled Question of Brain Death" address this question.

Dead human remains have proven useful for medical students in learning anatomy, yet today human body parts compose a lucrative business, as presented in "In Science's Name, Lucrative Trade in Body Parts." What are the ethical issues involved with such business deals? Dead human remains have also been beneficial to medical science in improving knowledge through autopsies. It is from autopsies that the living can benefit from the dead. Yet, fewer autopsies are being done today. "Deaths Go Unexamined and the Living Pay the Price" addresses the whys of this demise in human autopsies.

Technology and death policy: redefining death

ABSTRACT

This paper analyses the policy issues surrounding the definition of death within the context of technological and social changes. Increasingly precise brain imaging techniques, combined with demographic trends and heightened health budget pressures, are bound to accentuate calls for redefining death in terms of partial- or higher-brain criteria. In addition to questioning our notions of consciousness and of what human life entails, a shift toward higher-brain definitions of death have critical public policy implications, which must be thoroughly debated. Adding patients in a persistent vegetative state or with end stage Alzheimer's disease to the ranks of the dead raises many difficult questions, for instance, must the NHS or insurers fund continuing care for a legally dead but still breathing patient whose family cannot let go? The implications for disposal of breathing patients who lack brain functions deemed essential to life are substantial. The public is likely to find it difficult to accept burial or cremation of breathing human forms or the use of lethal injections to ready the 'dead person' for burial.

ROBERT H. BLANK
Department of Government, Brunel University, United Kingdom

Many death-related policy issues, from treatment abatement to physician-assisted suicide, continue to elicit considerable public and professional debate. This is not surprising because they are among the most intensely emotional and ethically fraught issues. One of these social policy issues that will not go away is how we define the death of a human. There are two critical dimensions to this question. The first is the conceptual interpretation of what death means in the context of medical technology, since the traditional understanding of death as the irreversible cessation of cardiopulmonary functions can be "clouded by technological means of prolonging those functions in patients" (Weir, 1989: 292). The second dimension centres on the appropriate clinical tests to be used to determine that a patient is in fact dead, especially when the patient's life has been prolonged by technological means. It is argued here that because the technologies in both of these areas are constantly advancing (in the first instance life-sustaining technologies and in the second diagnostic technologies that measure the presence or absence of specific types of brain activity in particular regions), the definition of death will continue to be a contentious issue and one that cannot be resolved on technical grounds.

The brain death controversy

Until recent decades, death occurred at the moment of permanent cessation of respiration and circulation. Once the heart and lungs ceased functioning they could not be restored. More importantly, once cardiorespiratory function ceased, brain function also ended. Advances in medical technology, which allow for machine regulated breathing and heartbeat even when the capacity to breathe spontaneously is irreversibly lost, however, made the conventional notion of death inappropriate by the late 1970s.

In 1981, the US President's Commission concluded that "in light of ever increasing powers of biomedical science and practice, a statute is needed to provide a clear and socially-accepted basis for making definitions of death" (1981: i). Death would now be linked to direct cessation of brain function rather than to the indirect cessation after shutdown of the heart and lungs. Because the brain cannot regenerate neural cells, once the entire brain including the brain stem has been seriously damaged, spontaneous respiration can never return, even though breathing may be sustained by respirators or ventilators. As discussed in more detail later, the key point is that while machines can maintain certain organic processes in the body, they cannot restore consciousness or other higher brain functioning.

This present situation, in which all bodily functions need not cease when the heart stops pumping spontaneously, has led to the distinction between of social, intellectual, and communicative dimensions. Just what does it mean to be human? In recent decades, a reasonably strong consensus has developed that recognises the possibility of social or cognitive death even though the human organism is kept alive biologically by artificial means. However, some observers remain opposed to the recognition of brain death, and others object specifically to whole-brain death. Others who approve of the brain-death definition are uncomfortable with the dilemmas technology has created.[1]

Brain death

In one sense the brain begins to die early in life as large numbers of redundant neurons are eliminated. Moreover, the normal ageing process includes a gradual loss of sensory capacities. For instance, visual acuity declines linearly between the ages of 20 and 50 and exponentially after age 60. Depth perception declines at an accelerating rate after age 45. By age 80, speech comprehension may be reduced by more than 25% due to extensive neuronal loss in the superior temporal gyrus of the auditory cortex (Ivy, 1996).

"The lack of consensus regarding when a patient would be declared dead limited procurement and led to a public controversy regarding the ethics of organ procurement."

The ageing process, then, is naturally one of decline in the brain, with evidence suggesting a substantial decrease in neuron density as well as in absolute numbers in many of the brain regions, particularly the hippocampus, the subcortical brain regions, and the cerebellum (Selkoe, 1992). As a result, "Total brain mass shrinks by approximately 5 to 10% per decade in the normal aged individual, leading to losses of 5% by age 70, 10% by age 80, and 20% by age 90.... The atrophy is most marked over the frontal lobes, although parietal and temporal lobes suffer considerable losses as well" (Ivy, 1996: 43).

In addition to the gradual process of brain cell death that accompanies normal ageing, an array of neurodegenerative diseases and neurotoxin exposure can cause further death among certain cell types and regions of the brain, as can injury, cancer,

stroke, and other trauma (Morrison & Hoff, 1997). High blood pressure, for example, has been found to shrink the size of the brain in elderly persons. There is also growing evidence that at least some of the changes related to ageing are related to a decline in hormonal activity (Lamberts *et al.*, 1997) with special emphasis recently placed on estrogen. Alcohol and drug abuse can intensify brain cell death at all ages. The concept of brain death, of course, does not refer to this gradual process of cell death, but rather to the cessation of brain activity and function as measured by specific tests, including EEG diagnostics.

The first major step toward defining brain death occurred in 1968, when rising concern by medical practitioners over how to treat respirator-supported patients led to the creation of the 'Harvard criteria' for brain death (Ad Hoc Committee, 1968). These criteria, developed by a Harvard Medical School committee, focused on: (1) unreceptivity and unresponsiveness; (2) lack of spontaneous movements or breathing; and (3) lack of reflexes. Moreover, a flat EEG showing no discernible electrical activity in the cerebral cortex was recommended as a confirmatory test, when available. Before life-support systems could be terminated, all tests were to be repeated at least 24 hours later without demonstrable change. These criteria, with some modifications and revisions due to new knowledge and diagnostic technologies, continue to serve as the standard medical criteria for determining death in most Western nations. Their publication led to the mobilisation of considerable support for legislating policy standards of brain death and thus purportedly eliminating the uncertainties faced by hospitals and physicians.

Another force at work during this period was the emergence of organ transplantation techniques and the growing need for organs [see Singer (1995: 22) for the importance of this factor for the Harvard committee]. For major organ transplants to be successful, a viable, intact organ is needed. The suitability of organs, especially the heart, lungs, and liver, for transplantation diminishes rapidly once the donor's respiration and circulation stop. Therefore, the most desirable donors are otherwise healthy persons who have died following traumatic head injuries and whose breathing and blood flow are artificially maintained until the removal of the organs. Although advocates of the brain-death criterion downplay the extent to which the demand for organs influenced this movement, transplant surgery did give the effort to define brain death a new urgency according to Fox and Swazey (1992). This reluctance to link the two developments is understandable, because the connection could imply that we accepted the revised definition of death only to facilitate use of the 'dead' individual's organs. Certainly, organ-transplant facilities have sought and have benefited from the legal clarity provided by statutes that define brain death. "The lack of consensus regarding when a patient would be declared dead limited procurement and led to a public controversy regarding the ethics of organ procurement", according to Siminoff *et al.* (1996: 52). However, if the only rationale for this new definition of death was to facilitate successful organ transplants, support for brain death would not have been as persuasive.

In response to these issues and pressures from the medical community on the inadequacy of legal definitions of death, many US states in the 1970s passed a number of different laws that tried to incorporate the neurological criteria proposed at Harvard. This proliferation of similar yet variant models and statutes led the President's Commission to propose a "Uniform Definition of Death Act" which presently serves as the accepted standard definition. The Act provides for:

> (Determination of Death.) An individual who has sustained either (1) irreversible cessation of circulatory and respiratory functions, or (2) irreversible cessation of all functions of the entire brain, including the brain stem, is dead. A determination of death must be made in accordance with accepted medical standards.

Before its presentation in the final report, this uniform law was approved by the American Bar Association, the American Medical Association, and the Uniform Law Commissioners as a substitute for their original proposals.

The Commission recommended that uniform state statutes address general physiological standards rather than specific medical criteria or tests, since the latter continue to change with advances in biomedical knowledge and refined techniques. In retrospect, this focus on physiological standards might be used as justification for later moving to partial-brain death criteria. It concluded that "death is a unitary phenomenon which can be accurately demonstrated either on traditional grounds of irreversible cessation of heart and lung functions or on the basis of irreversible loss of all functions of the entire brain" (1981: 1).

Redefining brain death

Although the whole-brain definition of death (or brain stem death) has become the accepted standard of practice in most Western nations, it has always been surrounded in controversy. Veatch (1993), for instance, argues that the whole-brain definition of death has become so qualified it can hardly be referring to the death of the whole brain. For example, isolated brain cells continue to live and emit small electrical potentials measurable by EEG even though super-cellular brain function is irreversibly destroyed. Whole-brain death also ignores spinal cord reflexes, but requires cessation of lower brain stem activity, thus contradicting the definition that "all functions of the entire brain" be dead.

Other observers are even more critical of the current reliance on whole-brain death. Truog contends that the concept is fundamentally flawed, plagued by internal inconsistencies, and confused in theory and in practice (1997). The specific tests for determination of death are inaccurate and do not always meet the required criteria. Furthermore, whole-brain death assumes that the brain is the integrating organ of the body whose functions cannot be replaced, even though intensive care units increasingly have become surrogate brain stems replacing respiratory, hormonal, and other regulatory functions. For Truog: "This gradual development of technical expertise has unwittingly undermined one of the central ethical justifications for the whole-brain criterion of death" (1997: 31).

The major objection to brain death as now defined, however, comes from those who feel it is not inclusive enough. Whether

one believes in life after death or no life after death, there is agreement that when we die we cease to be here, even though our dead bodies remain at least for a while. Furthermore, there is general acceptance that it is necessary and sufficient for one to cease to be here when all possibility of consciousness and mental activity is gone. Until recently this was congruent with heart/lung stoppage, but as seen earlier medical science has separated the two events by providing surrogate blood pumping mechanisms for the brain. It is widely accepted now that death comprises the irreversible cessation of the integrated functioning of the various sub systems of the organism *and*, in humans, the irreversible loss of the capacity for consciousness.

According to McMahan (1998), brain death can be understood to capture both of these dimensions of death: (1) the irreversible cessation of integrated functioning in the organism as a whole; and (2) the irreversible capacity for consciousness and mental activity. This is clear because the brain functions both to regulate and integrate the systemic functioning of the organism and to generate consciousness. When the brain dies, both capacities cease without possibility of restoration. But although respiration and heartbeat can be sustained artificially for some time beyond conventional brain death, the organs normally begin to deteriorate after brain death. According to Singer (1995), brain death was accepted not because of the brain's integrative function, which can be replaced, but because of its association with consciousness or personality. That is why, if our brain is destroyed and we continue to survive as an organism on machine support without any possibility of restoring consciousness, we would normally see our life as over.

One significant problem with a whole-brain death definition is that the two essential capacities of the brain are largely localised in different regions of the brain. Generally consciousness and mental activity are associated with the cerebral cortex while the integration and co-ordination of somatic functions are associated with the brain stem. As a result, the brain stem can survive in a functioning state after the neo-cortex is dead, therefore continuing to integrate somatic functions, including breathing and heartbeat, and permitting the organism to live without life-support systems. According to the conventional whole-brain death definition either of the two capacities alone is sufficient for life—only the loss of both is sufficient for death. If, however, we find it compelling that the capacity for consciousness is necessary for our continued existence, and its loss congruent with ceasing to exist, then the whole-brain death definition must be changed. If death of the neo-cortex is necessary and sufficient for the irreversible loss of consciousness then, according to McMahan, cortical death should be our criterion of death. "A human organism can remain alive even in the absence of life-support following cortical death. It is, rather, we who go out of existence" (McMahan, 1998: 257). What ceases to exist in cerebral death is the mind and this is essentially what in sum and part 'we' are as an entity.

One problem in moving toward a cerebral death definition is the current ambivalence concerning brain death. Many persons, particularly family members, still find it difficult to equate brain death with death. Adopting a higher brain definition would complicate this by declaring dead persons with intact brain

Table 1: Brain Imaging Techniques

Three Vessel Angiography/Digital Subtraction Angiography. Detailed patterns of blood flow or lack thereof in specific areas of the brain.

Computerized Axial Tomography (CAT). Images of brain structure.

Dynamic Computed Tomography (DCT). Trace blood flow throughout brain structure.

Magnetic Resonance Imaging (MRI). Detailed images of brain activity caused by molecular changes in the brain when exposed to a strong magnetic field. Used to detect structural abnormalities and changes in volume of brain issue.

Echo Planar MRI (EPI). Enhanced MRI data using multiple, high power, high speed oscillating field gradients and advanced image processing.

Functional MRI (FMRI). Measures the increases in blood oxygenation that reflect a heightened blood flow to active brain areas (or absence thereof).

Electroencephalograph (EEG). Measures electrical activity or lack thereof in specific regions of the brain.

Magnetoencephalograph (MEG). Real time resolution measurement of small magnetic field patterns in specific regions of the brain.

Positron Emission Tomography (PET). Images created by distribution of radioactively-labelled substances to measure cerebral blood flow and glucose utilisation and neuro-chemical activity.

Single Photon Emission Computerised Tomography (SPECT). Can be designed to attach to specific receptors for precise mapping of brain activity or lack thereof.

BrainSCAN. One of many three-dimensional, spatial imaging systems that combine a series of two-dimensional scans from CAT and MRI into a three-dimensional virtual object.

stems who could breathe on their own. Even if there is agreement that irreversible loss of consciousness represents death, how can we be certain that the capacity for consciousness is lost? And if so, how can we be certain its loss can never be reversed? It is on this point that new technologies and knowledge of the brain become important factors in the debate over defining death.

Brain imaging techniques

One of the major forces that calls for a re-evaluation of the concept of brain death is the rapid advance in the ability to measure activity in very specific regions of the brain. Until recent decades, research on the brain structure was based largely on post-mortem examinations of the brains of normal persons and those individuals who suffered from mental disorders. New techniques which provide vivid images of living brains promise greatly to enhance our understanding of the relationship between the anatomy of the brain and psychological functioning (Blank, 1999). Increasingly, sophisticated use of x-rays, radio-active tracers, and radio waves combined with rapid advances

in computerisation allow for non-invasive and safe investigation of the structure and functioning of the brain. Table 1 illustrates the broad array of imaging and diagnostic techniques now available to measure different forms of activity in increasingly precise regions of the brain.

For Singer (1995) this more precise medical knowledge has "pushed aside" a powerful reason for continuing to treat patients in persistent vegetative state (PVS) as alive, because if we can demonstrate that there is no blood flow to the cortex we know that the capacity for consciousness is irreversibly lost.

> If blood is not flowing to the cortex, then—even though the brain stem might still be functioning and so the patient would not be brain dead—the patient would be 'cortically dead' and would never regain consciousness (Singer, 1995: 43).

The capacity of these techniques to measure levels of activity or lack thereof in specific brain regions, in the whole brain, or in the normal asymmetry of activity between the two sides of the brain, therefore, gives us for the first time the technical means to measure the end of living in precise brain regions. Further advances in software are likely to match hardware improvements and provide even more remarkable and precise imaging of the brain and, thus, more precise measures of the termination of activity in particular regions.

Moves to cerebral definitions of death

As noted earlier, personality, consciousness, memory, and reasoning require a functioning cortex. In cases where there is no evidence of blood flow or electrical or bio-chemical activity in the cortex, some observers feel that a definition of death focusing on the loss of these characteristics is warranted (see McMahan, 1998). Thus cerebral death signals the death of the person when specific higher brain functions cease, not all brain activity. This definition assumes that without consciousness, human life no longer exists. Higher-brain death extends the definition to include patients in PVS and presumably anencephalic babies. Moreover, some observers would also include patients in advanced stages of Alzheimer's disease under partial-brain death, using newer imaging techniques such as FMRI and MEG to make the determination. "As with irreversible coma, the parallel with brain death is plain. And a parallel policy of allowing such patients to perish would seem to be in order" (Churchland, 1995: 307). If it is these higher brain functions that define us as humans, then cerebral death, however narrowly defined, could be a more appropriate standard than whole-brain death.

Extension of brain death to PVS patients would be very problematic. There continues to be widespread technical and conceptual confusion about PVS. Terms such as 'comatose', 'irreversibly comatose', 'patients with locked-in syndrome', 'permanent coma', and so forth complicate the issue (Weir, 1989: 404). Patients with locked-in syndrome, for instance, have such severe paralysis caused by brain stem damage that they appear unconscious though they have a fairly normal level and content of consciousness. Patients with permanent coma have eyes-closed unarousability, which may be caused by extensive damage to the brain stem.

Patients with PVS differ from these other patients in that they have a relatively intact brain stem but massive neurological destruction of the cerebral hemispheres with the complete loss of cerebral cortical functions occurring because of lack of blood flow (ischemia) or oxygen (hypoxia) to the brain over a period of 4–6 minutes. As a result, the patient is left amented, in a transient coma for a few days or weeks, with a transient need for mechanical ventilation for a few days or weeks, then in a prolonged eyes-open unconsciousness that can last for years. They experience no pain or suffering and are completely unaware of themselves or their environment. Patients with PVS, however, do have normal gag and cough reaction and periods of wakefulness and sleep since those are brain stem functions. These latter characteristics, as well as the fact that the state is eyes-open, would make it very difficult to institute a policy defining PVS patients as brain dead. Although some persons object on grounds of potential reversal of loss of mental activity, McMahan concludes that "our long experience with this condition, together with advances in techniques for monitoring blood flow to different parts of the brain, make it possible in most cases to determine with virtual certainty when recovery is impossible" (1998: 258).

While there might be strong economic pressures to terminate treatment for advanced stage Alzheimer's patients, public objections to redefining our definition of death to include such persons will likely be intense.

Similarly, extending brain death to include Alzheimer's and other dementia patients would be extremely controversial, even if it is a logical move based on an irreversible loss of consciousness and mental capacity. People with dementia have a progressive loss of cerebral cortical functions extending over a period of years. In the latter stages of dementia, there is no consciousness of oneself or the environment, though brain stem activity might be unaffected. Redefining death to include Alzheimer's patients, however, would not resolve the problem of doctor-assisted euthanasia. Although Pabst-Battin views the permitting of active euthanasia of advanced Alzheimer's patients in "conjunction with an antecedently executed living will or personal directive requesting it" as the best possible compromise, she sees problems arising between public perception and philosophical reflection (Pabst-Battin, 1994: 160). Cerebral brain death of course would undermine the voluntariness that Pabst-Battin and others who support euthanasia demand, unless it allowed for antecedent personal choice as to one's acceptance of the official definition.

While there might be strong economic pressures to terminate treatment for advanced stage Alzheimer's patients, public ob-

jections to redefining our definition of death to include such persons will likely be intense. This despite McMahan's conclusion that even if there is a possibility that some "dim, flickering rudimentary mode of consciousness" might survive cerebral death, this is not a viable objection because it would be hard to show that whatever "shadowy, semi-conscious mental activity" we imagine might remain would contribute to the good life of that person (1998: 259).

Truog suggests that higher-brain death is bound to remain the domain of philosophers rather than policy makers because of the implications of treating breathing patients as if they were dead.

Moreover, reliance on cerebral death has been criticised because of the difficulty of measuring with precision the loss of higher brain functions and because it focuses on the end of personhood rather than the death of the organism. It is argued that despite advances, diagnostic tests for PVS are unreliable as evidenced by anecdotal cases of the recovery of some patients wrongly diagnosed as being in a PVS. Some critics have also charged that if we accept the notion of cerebral brain death, we are vulnerable to sliding down the slippery slope into finding as dead an ever-widening range of marginally functional humans, such as less advanced dementia patients or persons with very low IQs.

Truog suggests that higher-brain death is bound to remain the domain of philosophers rather than policy makers because of the implications of treating breathing patients as if they were dead (1997). The public is unlikely to accept the burial or cremation of yet breathing humans or the use of lethal injections to terminate cardiorespiratory functions of the brain dead person prior to burial. This objection is congruent with the President's Commission rejection of any form of partial-brain death on the grounds that to declare dead a person who is spontaneously breathing yet has no higher brain functions would too radically change our definition of death. Despite these concerns, many observers feel that we are now at the stage technologically to move from whole to cerebral brain death. Veatch recommends changes in the wording to replace "all functions of the entire brain" with references to either higher brain functions, cerebral functions, or his preferred "irreversible cessation of the capacity for consciousness" (1993: 23). Veatch would, however, incorporate a conscience clause, which allows a person to choose through advance directive his/her preferred option based on personal, religious or philosophical beliefs. Likewise, Emanuel (1995) proposes a "bounded-zone" definition of death where individuals are allowed to choose higher levels including PVS, but where traditional cardiorespiratory death would be the lower bound for all persons.

Although cerebral death has strong supporters, Truog rejects any movement in that direction and argues instead for a return to the cardiorespiratory standard. He contends that while whole-brain death served a useful transition function, brain death is no longer needed to justify withdrawal of life support, has little significance regarding resource allocation, and is not crucial for organ transplantation as it was in the 1970s. Advance directives and sympathetic court decisions now allow withdrawal without reliance on brain death, although Truog fails to mention the vast inconsistencies of court decisions in this area. For Truog, organ transplantation could be decoupled from brain death by shifting attention from brain death to the principles of consent (or prior consent) of donor and of doing no harm to the PVS patients and anencephalic infants. It is unlikely, I believe, that the courts or public would take this well because as Truog notes: "The process of organ procurement would have to be legitimized as a form of justified killing, rather than just as a dissection of a corpse" (Truog, 1997: 34). Truog is correct, however, that return to cardiorespiratory death would eliminate the objections some groups have with brain death and would serve as the common denominator that it represented before technology altered the context of death.

Issues in the redefinition of death

It must be emphasised that however we define death, whether whole or cerebral, it offers no benefit for the dead person, but rather for the family, society, and potential recipients of organs. Moreover, if we accept the assumption that consciousness is necessary for the human experience, then we cannot harm the person who lacks it by defining them as dead. Both harm and benefits accrue to the yet living, to the values of society and to culture. As such, whatever definition is selected, it must be a matter of public policy, not a medical or technological one even though the changes in medical science introduced here might have influence on how the public and the experts view death.

As noted above, some observers question the necessity or desirability of having a single standard of death. Should there be a legal right to choose the criterion of death based on the religious, cultural, or philosophical beliefs of the individual or family (see Younger *et al.,* 1999)? Would it create medical and legal chaos to honour this diversity through inclusion of conscience clauses in death statutes or must society come to full agreement on a standard? Gervais notes that we have ourselves generated these issues surrounding the definition of death "because we decided to use brain death as a signal that organ donation may begin" and because we decided to use the brain-death criterion in the absence of an agreed on definition (2000: 45).

Whatever standards for determining death are used, they will remain troublesome as a matter of public policy. Despite the widespread policy of brain death across the jurisdictions, thousands of cortically brain-dead persons are kept alive by artificial means, usually at the request or demand of the family. The difficulty of letting go, the false hope for a miracle, and the confusion of values resulting from the new technologies, cause many persons to refuse to authorise unplugging the artificial life-support machines. There is current debate in the UK as to whether brain dead transplant donors should be anaesthetised because of

the social acceptability of a still death. It might be assumed that it is also done for the benefit of some operating room staff who find reflex movements disturbing. For Giles Morgan, president of the Intensive Care Society, "In simple terms, if you are dead, you are dead and so dead people don't require anaesthesia… If you aren't dead, you shouldn't be having your organs taken away" (Boseley, 2000). Many others disagree, however, and the issue is expected to intensify.

Under these circumstances, other difficult practical questions arise. Can third-party payers, including public funding sources, refuse to pay for care of a person who is legally dead? On what grounds can insurers justify such coverage? Veatch suggests incorporation of a clause that standard health insurance not be required to cover medical costs to maintain any person who is "alive with a dead brain" (1993: 22). Can wills be probated in such a case? How can patients be protected from premature termination of helpful treatment under the guise of declaring death? What mechanisms are needed to maintain proper respect for the dignity of a brain-dead person when the various transplant teams need organs to save other patients who are brain-alive?

Although a few short years have powerfully transformed the meaning of death, many questions remain. Our very conception of what it means to be human is challenged by these rapid advances in medical technology. In light of the expanded knowledge of the brain and its functions, it is likely that some variation of higher-brain death will become the centre of debate in the future. The growing financial and psychological burden on the living and the increase in neurodegenerating diseases due to an ageing population will press in that direction despite strong protests. Although it is tempting to resolve these problems with a simple solution, as noted by Singer "Solving problems by redefinition rarely works, and this case [brain death] was no exception" (1995: 51). The solutions to difficult problems of today from abortion and euthanasia cannot be discovered by medical science, nor by defining them away. They require significant dialogue, debate, and utilisation of that unique and remarkable human characteristic of consciousness.

Note

1. The definition of brain death is inconsistent in the literature. Brain death generally refers to brain stem death or whole brain death where there is no discernible brain activity including autonomic functioning. In situations where there remains brain stem or other non-cortical activity, the terms partial, higher, neo-cortical, and cortical death are used interchangeably.

REFERENCES

AD HOC COMMITTEE OF THE HARVARD MEDICAL SCHOOL TO EXAMINE THE DEFINITION OF DEATH (1968). A definition of irreversible coma. *JAMA, 205,* 337–340.

BLANK, R. H. (1999). *Brain policy.* Washington, DC: Georgetown University Press.

BOSELEY, S. (2000). Transplant now over pain rule. *The Guardian,* 19 August.

CHURCHLAND, P. M. (1995). *The engine of reason, the seat of the soul: a philosophical journey into the brain*. Cambridge: MIT Press.

EMANUEL, L. L. (1995). Re-examining death: the asymptotic model and a bounded zone definition. *Hastings Center Report, 25* (4), 27–35.

FOX, R. C. & SWAZEY, J. P. (1992). *Spare parts: organ replacement in American society*. New York: Oxford University Press.

GERVAIS, K. G. (2000). The interdeterminancies of death. *Hastings Center Report, 30* (4), 45.

IVY, G. O. (1996). The aging nervous system. In A. BASKYS & G. REMINGTON (Eds), *Brain mechanisms and psychotropic drugs*. Boco Raton: CRC Press.

LAMBERTS, S. W. J., VAN DEN BELD, A. W. & VAN DER LAY, A. -J. (1997). The endocrinology of aging. *Science, 278*, 419–421.

MCMAHAN, J. (1998). Brain death, cortical death and persistent vegetative state. In H. KUHSE & P. SINGER (Eds.), *A companion to bioethics* (pp. 250–260). Oxford: Blackwell.

MORRISON, J. H. & HOFF, P. R. (1997). Life and death of neurons in the aging brain. *Science, 278*, 412–418.

PABST-BATTIN, M. (1994). *The least worst death: essays in bioethics at the end of life*. New York: Oxford University Press.

PRESIDENT'S COMMISSION FOR THE STUDY OF ETHICAL PROBLEMS IN MEDICINE AND BIOMEDICAL AND BEHAVIORAL RESEARCH (1981). *Defining death*. Washington, DC: Government Printing Office.

SELKOE, D. J. (1992). Aging brain, aging mind. *Scientific American* (September), 135–142.

SIMINOFF, L. A., ARNOLD, R. M. & SEAR, M. (1996). Death. In R. H. BLANK (Ed.), *Encyclopedia of biomedical policy* (pp. 51–53). Westport, CT: Greenwood Press.

SINGER, P. (1995). *Rethinking life and death: the collapse of our traditional ethics*. Oxford: Oxford University Press.

TRUOG, R. D. (1997). Is it time to abandon brain death? *Hastings Center Report, 27* (1), 29–37.

VEATCH, R. M. (1993). The impending collapse of the whole-brain definition of death. *Hastings Center Report, 23* (4), 18–24.

WEIR, R. F. (1989). *Abating treatment with critically ill patients*. New York: Oxford University Press.

YOUNGER, S. J., ARNOLD, R. M. & SHAPIRO, R. (Eds) (1999). *The definition of death: contemporary controversies*. Baltimore: Johns Hopkins University Press.

Robert H. Blank is Chair of Public Policy at Brunel University. Previously he was Chair of Political Science at the University of Canterbury in Christchurch, New Zealand. He has published over 25 books in the field of medical policy, most recently *The Price of Life* (Columbia University Press, 1997) and *Brain Policy* (Georgetown University Press, 1999).

Correspondence to: Robert H. Blank, Chair of Public Policy, Department of Government, Brunel University, Uxbridge, UK.

From *Morality*, Vol. 6, No. 2, July 2001. © 2001 by Robert H. Blank.

The Unsettled Question of Brain Death

Cultural views differ of a notion with broad importance in a technological age

By PETER MONAGHAN

IT IS A RATHER unnerving fact that whether you are dead or alive may depend on where you live. In most developed nations, once your brain stops functioning, you are considered "brain dead," and "brain dead" means dead, even if your heart is still beating and a ventilator keeps your lungs going. In 1968, the medical arguments for that diagnosis, which had been emerging since the late 1950s, were captured in "A Definition of Irreversible Coma," a report from the Ad Hoc Committee of the Harvard Medical School to Examine the Definition of Brain Death.

Nowadays, in the United States and Canada, organs can be removed for transplant from a brain-dead body if there is reasonable certainty that the individual would have wished to donate them, while in several European countries, "presumed consent" allows transplant surgeons to take organs unless the expiring individual specifically forbade it.

Still, writes Margaret Lock in *Twice Dead: Organ Transplants and the Reinvention of Death* (University of California Press), the idea that brain death is the end of life holds sway not thanks to revelation, medical or divine, but as a matter of cultural convention.

If Ms. Lock, a professor of anthropology at Montreal's McGill University, has her way, policy makers and members of the public will reconsider brain death with those cultural conventions in mind, as well as the legal, medical, and political considerations. Her book is the first in a new Public Anthropology series from California, intended to transform "received, accepted understandings of social issues."

Revisiting the concept of brain death is all the more timely, she suggests, now that advances in critical-care technology, at least in the developed world, make the line between life and death a matter of consequence to more people.

BEYOND NORTH AMERICA

It is easy to see that the idea of brain death is merely a convention when you consider its status outside the United States and Canada, Ms. Lock suggests. In Japan, despite the availability of equivalent medical technologies, "brain death" did not achieve legal standing until 1997, after three decades of fierce public and legal debate. It remains limited and contested today, with the result that organ transplants are few. Brain-dead individuals are not considered legally dead unless they have indicated that they want to become organ donors.

Similarly, Germany in 1999 reversed its earlier recognition of brain death; Sweden made it legal only in the late 1980s but still debates it; and Denmark in the early 1990s recognized brain death as a concept, but decided to retain the existing standard—heart and lung cessation—as the determinant of legal death.

A powerful discourse has led modern Americans to believe that brain death is scientifically deducible and verifiable, Ms. Lock suggests in an interview. "We feel so strongly that death is just a matter of biology. And we also feel strongly that it's something that can be measured in the body, one way or another." But shuffling off this mortal coil is not so simple, she argues. Sophisticated measurements of brain activity, or the lack of it, are one thing, but when doctors decide that someone whose heart is still beating is dead, they enter "the whole social and cultural sphere."

Much of the issue is, of course, that the organs of the brain dead are coveted for transplants. One explicit goal of the Harvard committee, back in 1968, was to facilitate more organ transplants—and the fresher the corpse, the better. Brain death seems tailored to foster organ donations, suggests Robert

Borofsky, a professor of anthropology at Hawaii Pacific University, and the editor of the Public Anthropology series. The idea that the moment of death is something "that we should simply leave to professionals," he says, "has come in 'on little cat feet,'" like the fog in Carl Sandburg's famous poem.

MEDICAL CHOICE OR MURDER?

Ms. Lock began to think about brain death in the 1980s, while in Japan to work on her book *Encounters With Aging: Mythologies of Menopause in Japan and North America* (California, 1993). "I noticed that in the media there were a good number of articles talking about it," she says. In some high-profile court cases, doctors had faced murder charges for taking brain-dead patients off of life support. "Clearly it was a major bioethical issue in Japan that was disturbing people. But it wasn't being talked about back home."

She considered the Japanese anxiety warranted. "Here we are redefining the concept of death, and it would seem reasonable that there should be some public interest in this," she says. But in the United States, Canada, and much of Europe, religious and legal debate had to catch up with medical technologies that were already producing a "new death" and a shifting idea of when it was acceptable to remove organs for donation. Meanwhile, her research shows, doctors and other medical professionals still feel "considerable anxiety" about the question of brain death.

Ms. Lock spent several years interviewing Japanese and North American physicians working in intensive-care units, transplant surgeons, organ recipients, donor families, and average citizens, as well as Japanese activists opposed to the recognition of brain death. She also observed, and in her book vividly describes, a "procurement" procedure—the hooking up to monitors of a woman determined to be dead, and the snipping free of the liver, kidneys, and other organs from her still-breathing body. The "donor was merely a container that must be handled with care," she writes.

As advances in medical technology encourage more people to seek new organs to compensate for the failure or poor upkeep of their originals, the pressure on supply mounts, as does the social pressure not to be so "selfish" as to decline to donate. In developed countries, the supply of organs has become more pinched as safety measures like seatbelts mean that fewer accidents produce likely donors. In this brave new world, public attention has been drawn away from complex conundrums by the heroics of doctors and a cultural determination to keep patients alive at all costs.

"I'm not opposed to organ transplants," says Ms. Lock, "and I'm very sympathetic to people who are suffering from horrible diseases and can have a lot of help through transplants."

Had Ms. Lock been intent on sensationalizing the debate, she could have emphasized cases like that of the American woman who became brain dead in an accident when 22 weeks pregnant but was kept on life-support machinery for nine weeks, until the fetus could be delivered. Ms. Lock's focus is, however, on analyzing what constitutes death, today. "What matters, to most of us, is the [irreversible] loss of consciousness," she notes. "There

is obviously this rather strong sentiment in North America and probably much of Europe. But quite clearly, many Japanese don't feel the same way."

The sources of that difference run deep. The Enlightenment philosopher René Descartes established the brain as the crux of the living person (placing the West at odds, still, with most of the world), and encouraged dualistic thinking: mind or body, self or other, society or the individual—and alive or dead. "All of these dichotomies are absolutely characteristic of Enlightenment thinking," says Ms. Lock.

Those constructions are present in Japan, despite the country's different philosophical and religious traditions, "but they're more muddy there because they don't fit with more intuitive kinds of thinking there that lead people to feel that you cannot make these separations easily, at all." Beyond medical and legal issues, she says, lie metaphysical ones, such as: Does the person cease to exist when the physical body dies? And perhaps the most fundamental, most obdurate question of all: What exactly is death?

A key question, which lacks professional medical consensus, is whether death is an event or a process. The law prefers the former, but "decentralists" argue for the latter on the grounds that different organs conk out at different times.

The conception of death as dispersed through the body accords with the predominant Japanese understanding of death, as "more than the extinction of individual bodies," as "above all a familial and social occasion," says Ms. Lock. Intent on properly seeing family members off and not desecrating bodies, they leave the boundary between life and death "fuzzy."

In that context, the social significance of death continues to override medical authority. Even Japanese neurologists, Ms. Lock notes, hesitate to think of brain-dead patients as dead and to cooperate with organ procurers.

DEATH IN THE WEST

The West has its own cultural history of death, Ms. Lock notes. Death became a medical rather than religious matter only in the 19th century, as medicine became an influential profession. Then, doctors stopped leaving the room during last rites, and the belief faded that one was not dead until putrefaction set in.

Once "individual death was stripped of much of its social significance and remade as a biological event," she writes in *Twice Dead*, "anxieties abounded about premature pronouncement of death and burial alive." That age-old fear increased in the 19th century to the point that wealthy Europeans built "waiting mortuaries," where their bodies could be monitored to ensure they really were dead. Devices were placed in many coffins to permit the not-dead-after-all to communicate from the grave with lights, flags, and noisemakers. Just enough cases of grisly premature burial emerged that such remedies seemed warranted. The West, Ms. Lock says, has seen "a long and tortuous history of vivisection, cadaver dissection, and commodification of the human body." That history has helped create a sense that "organs that are not retrieved go to waste, that sick people have a right to organs for transplant."

How Do Doctors Decide?

BY LILA GUTERMAN

Although lawyers, ethicists, and a few physicians are still debating what constitutes death, most Western neurologists will tell you, "Brain death *is* death." the obvious question, then, is, How do physicians determine when someone's brain has stopped functioning? Differences in standards persist from one country to the next, but they are relatively minor.

To determine if a patient's brain has ceased to function, physicians generally look for three signs: the patient must be in a deep coma with a known cause; the patient must have no reflexes associated with a part of the brain called the brainstem; and the patient must not be able to breathe independently. Physicians must also rule out conditions that can mimic the effects of brain death, such as hypothermia or a drug overdose.

'AWARENESS OF LIFE'

The brainstem, an area at the base of the brain, controls breathing, blood pressure, and the capacity for consciousness. Without a working brainstem, a person can't regain consciousness. "We've realized that awareness of life, and life itself, is emanating from the brainstem," says Merlin D. Larson, an anesthesiologist at the University of California at San Francisco. "If there's no brainstem, then there's no life."

Physicians conduct a battery of tests of brainstem reflexes, including checking whether pupils are sensitive to light, whether the patient has a gag reflex, and whether the patient's eyes move when his head is turned quickly. To check if the patient can still breathe, physicians must take her off a ventilator. They temporarily give the patient some carbon-dioxide gas to inhale. In a normal person, the gas would trigger the brainstem to direct the body to begin breathing again.

Even if all of those conditions are satisified, and the physicians pronounce the patient dead, a brain-dead person may behave on the operating table as though she were alive—moving around during the breathing test or when she is operated on. According to Eelco F. M. Wijdicks, a neurologist at the Mayo Clinic who wrote a review on diagnosing brain death in *The New England Journal of Medicine* last year, the spinal cord produces those movements, not the brain.

A survey by Dr. Wijdicks of 80 countries, published last month in *Neurology*, showed that all 70 countries with guidelines require irreversible coma and lack of brainstem reflexes for a diagnosis of brain death. But not all countries require the breathing test, and countries differ on how long a patient needs to be monitored and how many physicians must diagnose brain death. In the United States, patients must be monitored for at least six hours, and all but eight states allow the diagnosis to be made by only one physician. Some countries require further confirmation that the brain has stopped functioning, such as an electroencephalogram, or EEG, which should show no electrical activity in the brain. Such tests are optional in the United States.

Michael Swash, a professor of neurology at Royal London Hospital at Queen Mary, part of the University of London, says the differences are "subtle" and shouldn't lead to the possibility that a patient could be declared dead in one country and alive in another.

'OVERWHELMING AGREEMENT'

Following Dr. Wijdicks's review article last year, *The New England Journal of Medicine* published five letters questioning various aspects of the diagnosis. Some took issue with the idea that brain death is death, while others clarified points having to do with diagnosis. Alexander M. Capron, an expert on brain death, says that "overwhelming agreement among [Western] neurologists" exists on the tests necessary to diagnose brain death. Mr. Capron, a professor of law and medicine at the University of Southern California, notes that the standards have hardly changed since the first guidelines were designed, in the late 1960s. But, he says "there is lingering controversy."

One bone of contention has to do with whether brain-dead patients should receive anesthesia when their organs are removed for transplants. Basil F. Matta and Peter J. Young, anesthesiologists at Addenbrooke's Hospital, in Cambridge, England, wrote in *Anaesthesia* in 2000 that anesthesia should be required. Some patients with dead brainstems still have electrical activity in other parts of their brains, and there is no way to test whether the pain-perceiving area of the brains still funciton. The authors note that giving anesthesia and muscle relaxants may do more good for the physicians around the operating table than the patient on it, because the brain-dead patient would not move when being operated on.

Other concerns about residual brain function exist. Some brain-dead patients still have electrical activity in their EEG's or produce hormones from their pituitary glands, "Not only does this represent brain funciton, but it represents a fairly sophisticated brain function in terms of the brain's role in maintaining the body's homeostasis," or stable internal environment, writes Robert D. Truog, a professor of anesthesia, pediatrics, and medical ethics at Harvard Medical School, in the *Annals of the New York Academy of Sciences*. The hormones regulate salt and water balances in the body. "People can live fine without pupils constricting," a brainstem reflex, he says. "But you can't live at all if your brain doesn't regulate salt and water balance."

Those issues lead some, like Dr. Truog, to question the larger issue of whether brain-dead patients are really dead. "There isn't any underlying biological fact that we're trying to diagnose," he says. "In a very fundamental way, there's no such thing as... the correct tests for brain death."

Long before the development of powerful immunosuppressants permitted transplants to become routine, in the late 1970s, the artificial ventilator, a relatively simple invention of the 1950s, had forced the issue of whether death was located in the brain rather than the heart and lungs. More-sophisticated machinery pitched in, such as defibrillation, which jump-starts a stopped heart, and the electrocardiogram, which revealed that the heart remains partly active for up to half an hour after death. In the early 1990s, neurologic data showed that residual physiological activity persists in brain cells even when integrated brain functioning stops.

Developments in life-support technologies complicate the issues further. What, for example, to make of the "living cadaver," the human-machine hybrid that a brain-dead body on life support becomes? In Japan, both neurologists and the public are relatively accepting of it. But in the West, "the very existence of such hybrids is a potential threat to the moral order," she suggests. "A living cadaver, exhibiting many signs of life, is redolent with ambiguity."

And yet, she says, it is characteristic of the ambivalence about brain death that the number of "living cadavers" will soar, because of the dictates of medical heroism and "a vision of death as scandal, as failure."

With such developments in the offing as producing human tissues and organs from cloned cells, the time does appear to be ripe for a fresh appraisal of brain death, says Stuart J. Youngner, director of the Center for Biomedical Ethics at Case Western Reserve University, where he is a professor of bioethics, medicine, and psychiatry. In a 1989 study, he demonstrated that doctors and nurses were quite confused about the legal determinants of death. Now, he is completing an extensive study of public views of death. "There's tremendous variation and confusion," which will continue, he believes, "because it doesn't have to do just with information; it has to do with people's personal and religious views about these issues."

He advocates a decisive step to deal with the confusion: Pause to reflect. "I don't think we should go backwards, but we should be careful about further gerrymandering the line between life and death so that we can get more organs," he says. He would put temporary bans on taking organs from anencephalic infants (born without brains and debatably not "alive"), a practice that has been legal since 1995 in the United States; on declaring patients in a persistent vegetative state to be dead; and on hastening their deaths by administering drugs or withholding treatment.

'LEGITIMATE QUESTIONS'

Most American neurologists don't share Dr. Youngner's and Ms. Lock's sense that brain-dead people aren't clinically or philosophically the same as people who die in other ways, according to James L. Bernat, a professor of medicine at Dartmouth Medical School. "It isn't really a big controversy among practicing neurologists," he says. "There are legitimate questions being raised by intellectually honest, caring people who just think this is wrong, but those particular positions have not swayed public opinion or professional opinion to the point of being taken seriously enough to change laws anywhere."

He says that for him, brain-dead people are dead because the central control that keeps a person whole, as a single functioning unit, has stopped working. "With increasing technology, doctors and scientists will be able to keep portions of the body going, but the organism is dead when the central organizing influence is dead," he says.

But Dr. Youngner insists on different types of the dead. "The brain dead are not the same as dead dead people. Phenomenologically, they are not. I think at this point it would be better to say, Well, they're not dead, but is it OK to take their organs? and deal with the issue as a moral issue, rather than as an ontological issue, which is, Are they dead?" he says. Organs might still be taken in cases where, for example, "the person feels no pain, they're on a trajectory to be dead soon anyway, and this is what they would have wanted."

Ms. Lock agrees. "If organs are going to be procured, then this activity must be justified on the basis of something other than complete biological death," she writes. But after three decades of assurance that brain death is a settled question, the American public may feel it has been deceived. Resulting "queasiness" may discourage dying people from agreeing to donate organs, she says.

Yes, when people sign organ-donor cards, they do agree to a form of depersonalization. "There are no easy alternatives at present to the commodification of living organs," she writes, "but I hope that transplants procured from brain-dead bodies will in the end prove to be a stopgap measure."

For now, she writes, "my donor card is signed." But she has suggestions for how donation should be regulated and construed to make it more publicly acceptable. For example, while she does not think human organs should be placed on the open market, she questions why the families of those who make gifts of their organs should receive no compensation or recognition. And she suggests that donation should be construed not as a social obligation, but as a form of social participation, or ritual.

All those issues, Ms. Lock adds in an interview, should be placed in perspective—as accouterments of wealth, largely in the West. "It seems really inappropriate to me," she says with evident disgust, "to be plunging on with enhancement technologies to get longer and longer life spans when one out of four children are dying in the rest of the world for want of clean water and all the rest of it. It's just ridiculous."

Lila Guterman contributed to this article.

Anatomy Lessons, a Vanishing Rite for Young Doctors

By ABIGAIL ZUGER

Over the centuries, dissecting the human body has evolved from a criminal offense to a vehicle of mass entertainment to an initiation rite.

In the Middle Ages, human dissections were forbidden. In 17th century Europe, medical school dissections were open to the public and often attracted unruly crowds cracking obscene jokes. By the 20th century, dissection had become the exclusive purview of scientists and a mandatory rite of passage for all doctors.

The scandals reported this month with donated cadavers at the University of California, Los Angeles and Tulane University are simply the most recent in a field long beset by abuses.

In 18th and early 19th century America, the public repeatedly rioted against doctors and medical institutions accused of dishonoring the dead. In 1878, the body of Senator John Scott Harrison (the son of President William Henry Harrison) disappeared from its Cincinnati crypt, only to surface in the dissection laboratory of a local medical school.

Now, though, the place of dissection in medical education is changing in ways that have not been seen before.

The hours devoted to formal anatomy training are sharply down in medical schools. Anatomy instructors are in short supply. Computerized scans and three-dimensional recreations of the human body provide cleaner, more colorful teaching tools than the time-consuming dissections of the past.

Some educators say that dissection, as taught to medical students since the Renaissance, is on its way out. Others maintain it is becoming more important than ever, not only for teaching the structure of the human body but also for the more subtle lessons it can impart on the meaning of being a doctor.

"It is always difficult to decide how much anatomy should be learned by a doctor," said Dr. Frank Gonzalez-Crussi, a retired pathologist in Chicago who has written extensively on the history and philosophy of human dissection.

Much of the traditional anatomy curriculum is irrelevant to medical practice and might easily be eliminated, Dr. Gonzalez-Crussi said, but there is still no substitute for dissection, which forces the student, willy-nilly, to confront human mortality.

Through the mid-20th century, medical students typically spent hundreds of hours dissecting. Working in small groups with scalpels and scissors, they would tease out every major structure in the body, including tendons, arteries and nerves, memorizing dozens of tortuous pathways and hundreds of Latin names in the process.

But as the focus of medical science has shifted from whole organs to cells and molecules, more and more teaching hours are consumed by molecular biology and genetics.

"Something has to give somewhere," said Dr. Arthur F. Dalley II, director of medical gross anatomy at the Vanderbilt School of Medicine.

That something has been anatomy. Surveys show that today's medical students may spend more than 80 percent less time in dissections than did students in the 1950's. The personnel to teach anatomy courses have declined in parallel:

anatomy faculty members are aging, Dr. Dalley said, and fewer classically trained graduate students are available to replace them. In many universities, anatomy departments have been engulfed by other departments in the biological sciences.

A shortage of donated cadavers is not the big problem. Most medical schools receive enough to meet their teaching needs. Anatomical research continues to have practical applications, for example, in the design of new implants or prosthetic devices. Still, startling new discoveries in anatomy are uncommon, and money for research is sparse.

"It seems that anatomy has fewer and fewer advocates," Dr. Dalley said.

To supplement dissections, medical schools now routinely use computer-based tools, most often C.T. and M.R.I. scans of living patients. Some programs take advantage of the National Library of Medicine's Visible Human Project, which provides radiologic scans and actual digitalized photographs of cross sections of a male and female cadaver.

Computer-generated models — like one program that gives the viewer the illusion of flying through the nooks and crannies of a human skull — can clarify tiny, convoluted anatomical structures in a way that actual preserved specimens cannot.

A handful of schools now pare down anatomy courses by sparing students all hands-on contact with a cadaver. At the University of California at San Francisco, for instance, students learn anatomy by inspecting important structures in cadavers that have already been dissected by an instructor.

Studies have shown that students who learn anatomy from professionally prepared dissections, called prosections, perform about as well on standardized tests as those who do the dissection themselves. But anatomists bristle at any suggestion that either prosections or computer models will make them obsolete.

"It is very definitely not a trend," Dr. Dalley said.

Dr. Todd Olson, a professor of anatomy at Albert Einstein College of Medicine in the Bronx, noted, "There are some excellent computer-based resources, but they are not a replacement for the cadaver."

Dr. Carol Scott-Conner, a professor of surgery at the University of Iowa who is president of the American Association of Clinical Anatomists, said she was not sure "that every medical student needs an intensive anatomy course."

"But everybody needs to learn anatomy," she said, adding that actively participating in a dissection is a better way to learn than looking at an exhibit or a computer screen.

Even when the details of anatomy and the Latin names fade from a doctor's memory, memories of the experience remain vivid, Dr. Scott-Conner said.

Further, drawings and models ignore the huge variability in human anatomy, in which duplicated, misshapen or aberrant structures are common. Students who spend time searching for an important nerve or a blood vessel that surfaces nowhere near where it is supposed to be learn a hands-on lesson about the huge range of normal in medicine.

Anatomists also emphasize that working with a cadaver elicits a sense of reverence that pictures and models do not.

Medical attitudes toward human specimens have varied over the years. Apocryphal stories from the 19th and early 20th centuries describe medical students jumping rope with the intestines of cadavers, and playing lewd practical jokes with cadavers' genitalia.

As recently as 30 years ago, medical students who expressed any fear or squeamishness about human dissection were often told they were "weak" and in the wrong field, Dr. Olson of Einstein said.

Now, however, schools uniformly encourage students to work through their emotions, he said, and also make sure they understand the gravity of the proceedings.

"Students are informed at the beginning of the course that gross anatomy is a solemn endeavor and disrespect will not be tolerated," said Dr. Charles Maier, who directs the anatomy course at Case Western Reserve University Medical School.

Dr. Maier, like many other course directors, tells students the cadavers are their "first patients," to be treated with all the respect that living patients would command.

Funeral services held at the end of anatomy courses emphasize this point.

"Many if not most schools have memorial services of one sort or another" Dr. Maier said.

The nondenominational service at Case is held at a local cemetery and is similar to a standard graveside ceremony. Family members of the deceased are invited, and afterward, they mingle with the dozens of students who attend. Dr. Maier said he routinely received letters of thanks from families after the events.

Medical students at the State University of New York at Stonybrook keep a two-month diary of their time in the dissection laboratory as a part of a course on medicine in society.

"Some say they're not affected by it and it hasn't changed them at all," said Dr. Jack Coulehan, a professor of preventive medicine there, but a majority record a cascade of emotions, which the class then discusses.

At the Yale School of Medicine, practicing doctors periodically visit the first-year anatomy course to describe some of their dying patients to the students and to talk about the doctor's role in dealing with terminal illness and death.

"In medicine now there's a big emphasis on teaching students professionalism," said Dr. Lawrence J. Rizzolo, the director of the Yale course. "In anatomy we begin the discussion — how the student will function as a professional, learning how to react to an uncomfortable situation, facing death and dying. We get them in touch with their feelings."

When the anatomy course ends, the Yale students thank their donors, as they call the cadavers, in a ceremony that includes original poems and musical compositions. Every first-year student attends, Dr. Rizzolo said, and the service has come to celebrate not only the rite of passage of the anatomy course but also the students' immersion in medicine.

"Studying medicine is a privilege, and the service paid homage to that," said Zach Goldberger, a Yale student who performed an original piano elegy at the ceremony his class held three years ago.

Two years ago, Yale students created a colorful quilt to commemorate the anatomy course, with panels dedicated to each cadaver in their course.

Asked to contemplate medical education without cadaver dissection, Yale students were unenthusiastic.

"It's not just about the information," said Dagan Coppock, a fourth-year medical student. "It's about the process."

Mr. Coppock called the anatomy class "a powerful, sacred experience."

Without dissection, students would never get to see "how it all fits together," said his classmate Kavita Mariwalla.

"It gives you a real appreciation for the beauty of the human body," she said. "It's amazing. You are so thankful for it. It made me stand in awe."

In Science's Name, Lucrative Trade in Body Parts

By JOHN M. BRODER

LOS ANGELES, March 11 — About 10,000 Americans will their bodies to science each year, choosing a path that, in the popular imagination at least, leads to the clinical dignity of the medical school or teaching hospital, where the dead help to unveil the wonders of human anatomy or the mysteries of disease.

Few donors, it is safe to say, imagine the many other ways corpses give their all for science: mangled in automobile crash tests, blown to bits by land mines or cut up with power saws to be shipped in pieces around the country or even abroad. Few see themselves ending up in a row of trunks, limbless and headless, arrayed on gurneys in the ballroom of a resort hotel for a surgical training seminar.

Nor do many people suspect that corpses are precious raw material in a little-known profit-making industry, and that they are worth far more cut up than whole.

A scandal at the cadaver laboratory at the University of California, Los Angeles, has thrown back a heavy curtain that has kept this business largely hidden from public view.

The university suspended its Willed Body Program this week, and university police arrested the program's director and a man the university accuses of trafficking in as many as 800 cadavers in a six-year body-parts-for-profit scheme.

The accused middleman, Ernest V. Nelson, who has cut up and carted away hundreds of cadavers from the U.C.L.A. medical school since 1998, said the university had been fully aware of what he was doing. He transferred the human parts, for sizable fees, to as many as 100 research institutions and private companies, including major companies like Johnson & Johnson, his lawyer said.

There is little controversy in the medical community about the use of donated bodies in teaching and research, although few discuss the topic openly and many prefer not to ask where the body parts they use come from.

The parts are supplied by a largely invisible network of brokers who make handsome profits for processing and transporting human remains. Selling body parts is illegal, but there is no prohibition on charging for shipping and handling. Research doctors say the demand for bodies and parts far outstrips the supply, raising prices and encouraging a growing number of body-parts entrepreneurs. Some of these are companies that promote their "facilitator" services on Web sites emphasizing the great benefit to humanity a willed body provides.

These sites do not mention that a human body, particularly one in pieces, is also of considerable benefit to a broker. Delivery of an intact cadaver costs as little as $1,000, but different specialists seek out specific pieces of anatomy for their work, and individual parts can be expensive. A head can cost $500 in processing fees, according to brokers who handle such parts. A torso in good condition can fetch $5,000. A spine goes for as much as $3,500, a knee $650, a cornea $400. In 2002, a pharmaceutical company paid $4,000 for a box of fingernails and toenails.

"Until pretty recently, it was something everybody kind of knew about but didn't want to talk about," said Dr. Stuart J. Youngner, chairman of the department of bioethics at Case Western Reserve University in Cleveland. "It's icky. It's upsetting. The people who handle these things have been able to get away with stuff because nobody really wants to get into it."

Dr. Youngner added that the interests of medicine and the people who handle the dead, legally or not, have intersected for hundreds of years and have led to recurring scandals. He cited the case of William Burke and William Hare, two Scotsmen of the 19th century whose trade in corpses was so profitable that they graduated to murder to provide fresh bodies to anatomists and university students.

Mistreatment of the Dead

In the last five years, authorities have uncovered numerous instances of mistreatment of the dead. In 1999, the director of the Willed Body Program at the University of California, Irvine, was fired for selling six spines to a Phoenix hospital for $5,000. An investigation discovered that hundreds of bodies were unaccounted for.

The director of the cadaver laboratory at the University of Texas Medical Branch at Galveston was fired in 2002 for selling body parts to a pharmaceutical company and other entities. In 2003, Michael Francis Brown, the owner of a crematory in Riverside County, Calif., was convicted of embezzlement and mutilation of corpses. He received 20 years in prison for illegally removing and selling heads, knees, spines and other parts from bodies he was supposed to cremate. Prosecutors say he made more than $400,000 in the body trade.

Doctors and medical device manufacturers say the use of human remains is indispensable to advancing medical science. There is no substitute, they say, for unembalmed flesh in teaching a doctor how to perform laparoscopic or arthroscopic surgery, or how to repair a heart valve.

But even those who benefit from the knowledge gleaned from work on cadavers say they are troubled by the black market in body parts and the cavalier way many donated bodies are handled.

"The problem is the insensitive and illegal treatment of remains of bodies obtained for medical education and research," said Dr. Todd R. Olson, a professor of anatomy at the Albert Einstein College of Medicine in New York and director of its anatomical donations program.

"A lot of money is changing hands," Dr. Olson said, and there is virtually no regulation of the interstate traffic in body parts. "It is easier to bring a crate of heads into California than a crate of apples. If it's produce, authorities want to know all about it."

Dr. Olson said he believed the majority of university-based cadaver programs were properly run and served a vital function in medical education. But those seeking body parts for profit constantly approach others involved in handling corpses, including licensed funeral directors and morgue workers, and many succumb to temptation. "Whatever you call it, it is theft," he said.

Fresh Cadavers for Training

Many aspects of this tale are chillingly described in an article by Annie Cheney in the current issue of Harper's Magazine. Books, movies and urban myths have explored this grisly trade for years. But the business is rapidly growing and changing.

One of the largest suppliers of bodies and body parts for medical experimentation is the Medical Education and Research Institute in Memphis. The institute conducted 478 seminars last year; 90 percent of them used fresh cadaver specimens.

Janice Hepler, the institute's executive director, said each part of a cut-up cadaver was tagged with a number so that the remains could be reassembled for cremation when research was complete. Staff members accompany body parts to seminars around the country, where they are treated as surgical patients who "are asleep and not dead," she said. The body parts are returned to Memphis, where they are ultimately cremated as a whole person.

The institute works closely with the Methodist Church, funeral directors and hospices to seek donations, Ms. Hepler said. It collects the bodies of 200 donors a year. It charges medical societies $6,000 to $35,000 for training seminars, and the societies pass the costs on to the doctors who attend them.

Last weekend, the institute sent six torsos with heads to a Marriott hotel in Phoenix for a training course purchased by the International Spinal Injection Society, a San Francisco organization that teaches physicians how to inject painkillers into the upper spine. Staff members accompanied the bodies, conducted the training and brought the bodies back, Ms. Hepler said.

The society conducts 14 such cadaver courses a year and requires 90 specimens, a spokeswoman said.

The Memphis operation and several like it, including a Philadelphia company called Innovations in Medical Education and Training and a cadaver transport company called National Anatomical Services, on Staten Island, are the aboveground sector of the industry.

But there is a thriving underground market as well, practitioners say, a direct descendant of the grave robbers who supplied cadavers to doctors and researchers.

'It's No Secret'

The society of those who deal in black-market body parts is a small one, said Vidal Herrera, who has logged more than 30 years in the business of death and dissection. It occasionally comes to light, as it did last November when Federal Express employees at a depot near St. Louis noticed a package leaking what looked like blood. Inside were a human arm and two legs packed in dry ice. The parts were addressed to a freelance body broker, Richard Leutheuser, who operated from his home in suburban Kirkwood, Mo.

"It's no secret," Mr. Herrera said while sitting at a dissection table in his gray, windowless storefront morgue in the San Fernando Valley, north of Los Angeles. "Everybody knows who to call — the buyers, the sellers, the disarticulators, the schools, the crematoriums. It's a lucrative business."

Mr. Herrera described the business as a world of thugs, hacksaws and back-alley body pickups. He would know. His résumé includes two years with the Los Angeles County morgue; eight years with the Los Angeles medical examiner's office, where he was an investigator; 16 years as autopsy technician with the veterans hospital in Westwood; and 16 years as a freelance dissectionist, performing autopsies and procuring organs and tissue for universities.

For two years, he was the director of the U.C.L.A. Willed Body Program. The world of death is an insular one, he said.

Mr. Herrera, 51, was embroiled in an earlier scandal at the U.C.L.A. body program. In 1993, he was accused of illegally disposing of human remains that were mixed with medical instruments and animal parts. Though he was the director of the program, hired to come in and clean it up, he was never charged with a crime and the university eventually settled with him for an undisclosed amount for wrongful termination.

In the black market, there are generally three places where tissue, organs and bone can be illegally procured, he said: university programs like U.C.L.A.'s; hospitals and county morgues that perform autopsies; and crematories and funeral homes.

In Southern California, Mr. Herrera said, there are about a dozen middlemen mining these institutions. These go-betweens play on the worst impulses of technicians who are underpaid, undereducated and often underappreciated, he said.

"It's not a market created by guys like Ernie; he's only serving the medical companies and medical societies," Mr. Herrera said, referring to Mr. Nelson, the accused middleman. "When I started at U.C.L.A., I got at least a dozen calls from these very same guys telling me how the game is played and what the prevailing prices are."

The movement of supermarket beef is "better monitored than human parts," he said. "The demand is greater than the supply, and so the researchers and the doctors at the other end of things don't want to know. They want to have their conference in the hotel, take off their gloves, throw them in a bucket and go home."

A great many ways have been found to supply the growing demand for body parts, Mr. Herrera and others in the funerary business say. With the cost of burial exploding, the next of kin are generally responsive to the pitch of signing over loved ones' remains to disarticulators for medical study.

When legitimate ways cannot be found, Mr. Herrera said, men like Mr. Nelson come calling. Many times, a man with a van is dispatched in darkness to a crematory to pick up boxes of arms and legs and heads. Days or weeks later, he said, "someone is handed an urn of ashes. Who's going to know?"

Relatives of some of those who have donated bodies have been surprised to learn what happened after death. In a class-action lawsuit dating back to 1996, dozens of families are suing U.C.L.A. over how the university handled remains.

Sidney Liroff, who died two years ago this month, willed his body to U.C.L.A. as a gift to science. His widow, Selma, 81, said that she had planned to follow him, even though they are both Jewish and, according to custom, must be buried intact within 24 hours of death.

"We just wanted quietly to do a good thing," Mrs. Liroff said in an interview this week. "We are kept alive by science. Research is a good thing. That's why we did it."

But having learned of the scandal at U.C.L.A., she said, she has no idea what happened to her husband, and she is devastated. "It's ghoulish," she said, her voice hoarse and crackling. "Imagine the pictures that come up in my mind."

Mrs. Liroff said she had been promised that her husband would be returned to her after research was completed. She wanted to scatter his ashes in a rose garden. But when she called the university she was told by a technician that her wishes could not be accommodated.

"We were married for 57 years," she said. "I just wanted him back."

Sandra Blakeslee reported from Santa Fe, N.M., for this article, John M. Broder and Charlie LeDuff from Los Angeles, and Andrew Pollack from San Francisco

Deaths Go Unexamined and the Living Pay the Price

By ANAHAD O'CONNOR

Dr. Gregory Davis hunched over an autopsy table last Thursday morning and cut into the lifeless body of a 52-year-old man. Days earlier, the man, who had no real health problems other than a smoking habit, had been found dead in his apartment, the victim of a heart attack, a coroner determined.

But Dr. Davis, a forensic pathologist at the University of Kentucky, opened him up and found something startling. The actual cause of death was bacterial meningitis, a severe infection that could have spread to others before the man died.

Dr. Davis left the autopsy room to call the coroner and local health department, urging them to alert the man's family. "We had to ensure that the family and other contacts got treated with antibiotics," he said. "It was a major finding."

Autopsies were once routine, performed in more than half of hospital deaths and, in some parts of the country, in a majority of deaths that occurred elsewhere. But over the last few decades, the number of such procedures in the United States and several other countries has sharply dropped.

Hospitals, afraid of being sued over mistaken diagnoses, increasingly forgo autopsies, experts say. The advent of sophisticated imaging techniques like C.T. scans and M.R.I.'s have created an illusion among doctors that the procedure is unnecessary. Grieving relatives, too, are often unwilling to shoulder the cost or wait for autopsies to be completed.

The decline, researchers say, may be gradually eroding the quality of care. A growing number of missed or mistaken diagnoses are going unchecked, depriving doctors of a learning tool. And studies, including one published last week, find that autopsies uncover missed or incorrect diagnoses in up to 25 percent of hospital deaths. Medical examiners once relied on autopsies to pinpoint diagnostic mistakes, so doctors could know what pitfalls to avoid in the future.

Autopsies unmasked diseases that once baffled scientists, allowing researchers, for example, to link cigarette smoking to lung cancer and providing the first glimpses of AIDS, tuberculosis and heart disease. In some cases, autopsies have also detected hereditary illnesses, providing essential information for surviving relatives.

But autopsies are no longer a fixture. "The culture has come to accept the fact that they aren't happening any more," said Dr. George D. Lundberg, a pathologist who is editor in chief of Medscape General Medicine, an online journal. "Large numbers of medical students go through school without ever seeing one. It's a self-fulfilling prophecy. It feeds on itself."

In the mid-1940's, about half of Americans who died were autopsied. In 1984, the rate was about 13 percent; by 1994 it had dropped to 9.4 percent. A year later, the National Center for Health Statistics stopped collecting national autopsy statistics altogether, but most experts agree that the rate is now probably less than 5 percent. Many newer hospitals, Dr. Davis said, no longer have autopsy rooms or the stainless-steel tables for the procedure.

As the number of autopsies has dropped, the percentage of accurate diagnoses also appears to have slipped. A study in 2001 of a hospital intensive care unit in Cleveland found a 20 percent rate of incorrect diagnoses. In more than 40 percent of those cases, the researchers said, the patients would have received different treatments if the correct diagnoses had been made.

Another study, published in 1998, examined autopsy records at a hospital in New Orleans, finding that 44 percent of cancer cases were undetected or misdiagnosed. In about half the patients, the cancer had spread and, in many cases, was probably the cause of death, the researchers found.

For such patients, the information that autopsies yield is obviously too late. But it can help prevent the illness or premature deaths of others.

"It's really an issue of quality control," said Dr. Alejandro C. Arroliga, head of the section of critical care medicine at the Cleveland Clinic Foundation and an author of the 2001 study.

"It's not realistic to expect that doctors will always be right," Dr. Arroliga said, "especially when a lot of patients come in with several coexisting medical conditions. But autopsies tell you where you're having problems. They are educational tools."

The discrepancy between diagnosis and cause of death, Dr. Arroliga and other researchers found, is not always a result of negligence. In many cases, particularly in intensive care units, one disorder may go undetected because it is obscured by another.

A staple of television crime shows but now rare in real life

In a study published last week, French researchers autopsied 53 percent of 315 patients who had died in an I.C.U. in Paris, and found more than 25 percent of the diagnoses questionable. The researchers discovered 171 missed illnesses, including cancer and infections, and 33 incorrect diagnoses.

A large number of the patients in the study had compromised immune systems and were taking a number of drugs for different infections, making the diagnoses hard, said Dr. Alain Combes, an internist at the hospital and the study's lead author.

"We think it's important to continue doing autopsies on I.C.U. patients, because they're sicker, have more pathologies and often die from unclear causes," said Dr. Combes, whose study appeared in the Feb. 23 issue of The Archives of Internal Medicine. "It's a difficult science, and you always learn from your mistakes. That is particularly true in the I.C.U., where deaths occur very frequently and very rapidly."

Financial constraints have clearly played a role in putting autopsies on the endangered procedures list. A typical autopsy can last several hours and cost $2,000 to $3,000 or more. Arrogance has also contributed: with C.T. scans and other imaging techniques, some doctors assume that they will be able to see whatever is wrong, even though studies show that such diagnostic tools do occasionally err.

Another factor, some experts said, is the risk of malpractice suits if a mistake or a missed diagnosis is exposed. In most wrongful-death cases against a hospital or physician, an autopsy is critical to establishing negligence, said Wayne Grant, a lawyer in Atlanta who has won many malpractice suits over 25 years.

"Of the potential death cases that we have turned down, well over 50 percent are cases in which there has not been an autopsy," Mr. Grant said. "When a patient dies and there's no autopsy, the doctor can bury his mistakes along with the patient."

In some cases, Dr. Davis said, doctors actually do themselves a disservice when no autopsy is performed. In those cases, they are burying the proof of their innocence. In one, he recalled, a family contended that a doctor had sewn a relative's transplanted liver in backward, a medical impossibility. The patient was exhumed, autopsied and was eventually shown to have died from other complications.

"It's a nightmare scenario, one that could have been avoided if the autopsy was done in the first place," Dr. Davis said.

Some hospitals that once performed autopsies on 60 percent of patients or more have now stopped entirely. Many that still do autopsies, often only at the behest of survivors, no longer cover the costs. In much of the country, it is up to the coroner or medical examiner to order an autopsy when a person dies outside a hospital, but state laws vary.

In the past, the Joint Commission on Accreditation of Healthcare Organizations required that hospitals perform autopsies in at least 20 percent of all deaths. But the commission dropped the requirement in 1970, when it suspected that hospitals were performing the procedure at random simply to meet the quota.

Still, some experts argue that because autopsies are expensive, do not always turn up new findings and can take away time that doctors might better spend obtaining biopsy results for living patients, it does not make sense to require them.

"On a relative value base, they have fallen down the scale," said Dr. Dennis O'Leary, president of the accreditation commission. "And the fact that you do an autopsy and find something there that you didn't see before the patient died may not necessarily be significant."

The commission's change in policy, others say, has speeded the decline of autopsies.

Dr. Lundberg said that restoring the old policy could result in an immediate increase in the autopsy rate and that even randomly performed autopsies could be useful.

"It's the random ones that uncover the surprises," he said. "That is what makes them epidemiologically valid."

Autopsies may be more acceptable to the public now than in the past. Traditionally, doctors have been reluctant to bring up the topic with grieving family members. But television programs like the "X-Files," "C.S.I.: Crime Scene Investigation" and "Crossing Jordan" have made autopsies more familiar, Dr. Davis said, though such fictional portrayals often create unrealistic expectations.

"Sometimes people will ask things like, 'What was he thinking when he died?'" Dr. Davis said. "They're confusing autopsies with forensic investigations. I call it the 'X-Files' phenomena."

UNIT 2

Developmental Aspects of Dying and Death

Unit Selections

Key Points to Consider

- With children experiencing death situations at an average age of eight years, what societal steps can be taken to help children better cope with the death of a person or a pet?

- What do you recall from your own childhood experiences with fairy tales and death? Do you remember any death themes in children's literature and how you reacted at the time? Describe.

- With the events of September 11, 2001, what impact has that had on your own views toward dying and death? How should we relate to small children regarding questions of war and terrorism?

- Discuss the pros and cons of taking small children to a funeral. Recall your own childhood experiences with death. Were they positive or negative?

- Adolescents are at a vulnerable age—still not adults, yet expected to act like adults. How can we help teens to cope with dying and death and know when to refer them to a support group?

- Are the elderly in America "warehoused" and put away to die? Can you present evidence of such "warehousing"? How might the image of the elderly be improved in our society? Is growing old "the best is yet to be" or is growing old "hell"?

DUSHKIN ONLINE **Links: www.dushkin.com/online/**
These sites are annotated in the World Wide Web pages.

CDC Wonder on the Web—Prevention Guidelines
http://wonder.cdc.gov
Children With AIDS Project
http://www.aidskids.org
Light for Life Foundation
http://www.yellowribbon.org
National SIDS Resource Center
http://www.sidscenter.org/
Palliative Care for Children
http://www.aap.org/policy/re0007.html

Death is something we must accept, though no one really understands it. We can talk about death, learn from each other, and help each other. By better understanding death conceptualization at various stages and in different relationships within the life cycle, we can better help each other. It is not our intent to suggest that age should be viewed as the sole determinant of one's death concept. Many other factors influence this cognitive development such as level of intelligence, physical and mental well-being, previous emotional reactions to various life experiences, religious background, other social and cultural forces, personal identity and self-worth appraisals, and exposure to or threats of death. Nonetheless, we will discuss death and death perceptions at various stages from the cradle to the grave or, as some say, the womb to the tomb.

Research on very young children's conceptions of death does not reveal an adequate understanding of their responses. A need exists to look more carefully at the dynamics of the young and to their families relating to the concept of death. Adults, several decades later, recall vivid details about their first death experiences, and for many it was a traumatic event filled with fear, anger, and frustration.

In "Communication Among Children, Parents, and Funeral Directors," Daniel Schaefer, a funeral director, encourages parents to talk to their children about death. As parents, we need to recognize the insecurity often found in children at the time of a death and to deal with the situation accordingly. Children can generally accept many of life's experiences; the problem is that we adults are often inept in our dealing with dying and death and thus may practice avoidance in relating to children. As psychologist and former priest Robert Kavanaugh noted, children are not unlike adults in many ways—they are simply smaller. Kavanaugh likens children to subcompact automobiles, whereas we adults are the big cars, each with four tires, an engine, and a steering wheel, yet, one is larger than the other. Children can "take" much more than we adults often realize. We do not give enough credit and try to protect them. We must remember that children, too, have feelings and especially need emotional support during a crisis such as death.

Children's exposure to death may come through children's literature. "Children, Death, and Fairy Tales" explores death themes in fairy tales and examines the evolution of these themes in children's literature. Following the events of September 11, 2001, we realize in the United States that we are no longer immune from terrorist attacks. Just how should we handle questions that children may ask regarding sudden massive deaths? "Terrorism, Trauma, and Children" addresses this topic and gives practical suggestions about how adults can assist children in coping with the fear of terrorism.

In relating to adolescents who are in the springboard of life, vivacious and ready to conquer the world though still not prepared, how can we help them to adjust to the death of a significant other? Clinical thanatologist Alan Wolfelt gives solid advice regarding the do's and don'ts of trying to help a teenager deal with a death in "Helping Teenagers Cope with Grief."

As individuals move into "the autumn" of their lives and are classified as "elderly" (65 years of age and beyond), death surrounds them, and they are especially made aware that they are reaching the end of the tunnel. Though old age is often pictured as gloom and doom ("growing old is hell"), it can also be viewed as "the best is yet to be." As poet Robert Browning said, you are "as old as you feel" and aging is really "mind over matter." As long as you do not mind, it does not matter, as aging professional athlete Satchel Paige noted years ago. In June of 2004, former President George Bush parachuted out of an airplane on his 80th birthday, not something typically thought of for 80-year-olds. You are as old (young) as you feel! Research suggests that the elderly tend to be accepting of death, having lived a normal life span, and are grateful for the life they have had. A statistical profile of death etiology (causation) of the elderly is provided in "Trends in Causes of Death Among the Elderly."

Teaching end-of-life issues: Current status in United Kingdom and United States medical schools

Abstract

Our objective was to determine how broadly end-of-life issues are represented in the undergraduate medical school curricula of the United Kingdom (UK) and the United States (US). Mailed surveys yielded response rates of 100 percent in the UK and 92 percent in the US. With one exception, all medical schools in the survey offered some exposure to dying, death, and bereavement and most addressed the topic of palliative care. Hospice involvement was found in 96 percent of UK medical schools but in only 50 percent of US schools. Overall, the UK appears to provide more exposure to end-of-life issues in medical schools, although the US appears to be moving in that direction.

Key words: end of life, death and dying, palliative care, medical school curriculum, Great Britain, United States, hospice

George E. Dickinson, PhD
David Field, PhD

Introduction

End-of-life issues in medical schools in the UK and US have not historically held a pivotal place in the curriculum. For instance, in 1968 the UK Todd Report on undergraduate medical education[1] contained no reference to teaching about death and dying, and it was not until 1980 that the Wilkes Report[2] recommended that a terminal care element be included in undergraduate medical training in the UK. Likewise, in 1975 in the US, only seven medical schools offered a course on death and dying, and only five percent had at that time offered anything on death and dying within the previous 10 years.[3] In 1972, H. S. Olin[4] proposed a model course to be offered in US medical schools to teach students about the care of the dying patient. The Association for Palliative Medicine in Great Britain and Ireland produced its curriculum in 1993.[5] Thus, death and dying offerings in medi-

cal schools in the UK and US are new to the last quarter of the 20th century.

Longitudinal studies[6,7] by the authors in UK and US medical schools, however, have ascertained that the emphasis on dying, death, and bereavement has increased in recent years. Certainly, the topic of death and dying has maintained a high profile with issues such as Dr. Jack Kevorkian and his "suicide machine," active voluntary euthanasia, physician assisted suicide, organ transplants, advance directives, and medicine's ability to prolong life through artificial means. Because of public opinion and media pressure, medical schools have been more or less forced to address end-of-life issues. With the UK as one of the leaders in the world in palliative care and end-of-life issues and the US rapidly making advancements in this area, the authors decided to survey medical schools jointly in these two countries to determine their offerings in dying, death,

and bereavement as we enter the 21st century. This collaborative report outlines the broadly conceived provisions for palliative care in the undergraduate medical curriculum in UK and US medical schools in 2000–2001.

Methods

In the fall of 2000, a brief questionnaire was sent to 24 UK and 122 US medical schools asking for information about their dying, death, and bereavement educational provisions. The names and addresses of the UK schools were taken from the web site of the Council of Heads of Medical Schools, and the US names and addresses came from the Association of American Medical Colleges' *Medical School Admissions Requirements, 2001–2002*. In the UK, the surveys were addressed to clinical and preclinical deans or directors of

Table 1. Methods used in teaching about dying, death, and bereavement		
	UK* (%)	US** (%)
Lecture	21 (88)	91 (81)
Role-play	22 (92)	44 (39)
Hospice visit	22 (92)	55 (49)
Video/film	19 (79)	50 (45)
Seminar/small group discussion	23 (96)	94 (84)
Simulated patients	5 (21)	37 (33)
Clinical case discussions	23 (96)	77 (69)
*N = 24; ** N = 112		

medical education and initially were mailed in November. In addition, questionnaires were posted to people known by the researchers to be involved with delivering such teaching. In the US, the questionnaires initially were mailed in November and addressed to the academic dean at the medical schools, who then typically forwarded them to the education or curriculum dean. Follow-up mailings (a total of three in the US) to those schools not responding were sent out in the last quarter of 2000 and in the early part of 2001.

Information sought through the questionnaire included the following:

- extent of offerings on palliative care;
- end-of-life topics covered in the curriculum;
- percentage of students participating;
- teaching methods used;
- background of the instructor(s);
- whether a terminally ill patient addressed the class;
- whether students had a continuing relationship with a terminally ill patient; and
- extent to which students spend time with hospice patients.

Results

Response rate to the questionnaires was 100 percent (24 out of 24) in the UK and 92 percent (112 out of 122) in the US. In the UK, St. Andrews medical school provides preclinical education only and had no provision of formal ed-

ucation in the subject area; results are thus based on the remaining 23 schools. The recently combined University College London (UCL) and Royal Free Medical School introduced a new common curriculum in September 2000; however, as information about this new course was not available, the pre-existing UCL and Royal Free courses are treated as separate in this analysis. Thus, 24 programs provide the basis for information about UK offerings.

The question as to the extent to which the topics of dying, death, and bereavement are represented in the curriculum yielded the following results. In both the UK and the US, *all* schools responding, except St. Andrews, offer some exposure to this topic. In both the UK and US, the percentage of medical schools offering death and dying as a separate course is about the same: Three programs in the UK (13 percent) and 20 programs in the US (18 percent). Likewise, the percentage of programs covering the subject in only one or two lectures was roughly equal between countries (three programs or 13 percent in the UK and 16 programs or 13 percent in the US). However, death and dying offered as a module of a larger course was more frequent in US schools (55 programs, or 49 percent) than in UK programs (six programs, or 26 percent).

The cafeteria-type response choice, "other," was a popular selection for both UK and US respondents. Overall, these programs could be summarized as having death and dying offerings integrated throughout the curriculum, in addition to clerkships and clinical placements re-

lated to the topic. Indeed, some schools had several sessions on death and dying for each year a student attended. The mean number of teaching hours reported was 20 in UK and 14 in US, although this does not reflect the range of variation in teaching time. In the UK programs, *all* the students had some exposure to dying, death, and bereavement; in the US, the total was 96 percent of students.

Teaching methods

Medical schools in the UK used a greater variety of teaching methods in their dying, death, and bereavement courses (Table 1). The most popular methods in both countries were the seminar and small-group discussion (96 percent in the UK and 84 percent in the US); the lecture (86 percent UK and 81 percent US); and clinical case discussions (96 percent UK and 69 percent US). The least popular teaching method in both countries was simulated patients (21 percent and 33 percent, respectively, in the UK and US). Other methods used, with much more frequency in the UK than in the US, were role-playing, hospice visits, and video or films.

Professional background of instructors

A multidisciplinary team approach is used to present material in both the UK and the US (Table 2). The overwhelming majority of instructors in both countries are physicians (> 90 percent). In the UK, *all* the programs surveyed had a physician who was a palliative medicine specialist, whereas in the US such a specialty is just coming into existence.

Table 2. Professional background of instructors for the dying, death, and bereavement offerings

	UK*	US**
Physician/general practitioner***	20 (83)	105 (94)
Palliative medicine specialist	24 (100)	—
Psychiatrist	10 (42)	34 (30)
Social worker	11 (46)	35 (31)
Nurse	3 (13)	40 (36)
Nurse specialist in palliative care	15 (63)	—
Psychologist	7 (29)	29 (26)
Sociologist	6 (25)	9 (8)
Philosopher	—	17 (15)
Theologian/religious minister	11 (46)	49 (44)
Ethicist	4 (17)	8 (7)

* n = 24; ** n = 112; *** (includes all specialists except palliative medicine (UK only) and psychiatrists.

Psychiatrists are represented in approximately one-third of the programs in both countries. A nurse specialist in palliative care is found in over half of the UK programs, while nurse specialists are found in only about one-third of US offerings. Professionals with a background in religion are represented in nearly half of all programs on death and dying in both the UK and the US, while social workers, psychologists, sociologists, and ethicists are used to a lesser extent in both countries.

Exposure to dying patients

Schools were asked if a terminally ill patient addressed the students or if the students had a relationship with such a patient that extended for at least several weeks. In both the UK and the US, approximately one-fourth of the respondents (25 percent and 29 percent, respectively) indicated that a terminally ill patient addressed the class. Only one school in the UK (4 percent) reported including extended relationships for *all* students, although six UK schools (25 percent) reported that some or most students would do so. Twenty-seven US medical schools (24 percent) said that students had a continuing relationship with a patient lasting several weeks, although not all students had this exposure. The medical schools surveyed were also asked the extent to which students

spent time with hospice patients. In the UK, all but two of the programs (92 percent) included hospice participation as part of the program, whereas only about half of US schools (56 percent) did so. In nine UK programs (37 percent), students visited a hospice patient for "a few hours"; the same was true for 33 US schools (29 percent). Schools where students visited a hospice patient for a day or longer (up to a month in some cases) numbered 9 (37 percent) in the UK and 23 (21 percent) in the US. In the remaining programs, participation occurred on a voluntary basis and thus was not easily accounted for.

In cases where hospice involvement was not part of the curriculum, respondents were asked whether it would be instituted in the future. Thirty-five US medical schools answered in the affirmative, 12 said no, and five were undecided. Thus, hospice participation appears to have an integral role to play in US medical schools in the future (two-thirds of those not currently including it in the curriculum were planning to do so). In the UK, involvement has already been established.

Palliative care

In responding to the question, "do you directly address the topic of palliative care in your curriculum?" all of the UK schools and 97 of the US schools (87 percent) answered in the affirmative.

Palliative care was offered as a separate course in only seven UK schools and in 12 US schools (Table 3). The topic was most frequently presented as a module of a larger course or was scattered throughout the curriculum and in clerkships in a combination of presentations. Other than "through a separate course," the least popular way of teaching aspects of palliative care was through one or two lectures. In the UK, all students participated in the palliative care offerings, whereas in the US 88 percent of students participated.

Topics covered in the curriculum

End-of-life care topics was presented to each school to determine the extent of their coverage on these issues (Table 4). Of the 19 topics listed, over 70 percent of the schools in both the UK and the US included the following in their curricula:

- attitudes toward dying and death;
- communication with dying patients and their families;
- grief and bereavement;
- psychological aspects of dying;
- analgesics for chronic pain;
- analgesics for cancer pain; and
- advance directives.

Topics least covered in both countries were physical therapy and neonatal issues. The topic with the most discrepancy between countries was death

Table 3. Mode of delivery for palliative care education		
	UK* (%)	US** (%)
Separate course	7 (29)	12 (11)
Module of a larger course	6 (25)	46 (41)
Covered in "one or two lectures"	1 (4)	28 (25)
Other (primarily scattered in curriculum)	10 (42)	25 (22)
* n = 24; ** n = 112.		

certificates, with 83 percent of UK medical programs covering the topic as opposed to only 26 percent in the US. In addition, euthanasia was represented much more often in UK schools (89 percent) than in the US (46 percent), as was symptom relief in advanced terminal disease (100 percent in the UK and 66 percent in the US). More emphasis on relating to AIDS patients was found in US medical schools (52 percent) than in the UK (37 percent).

Discussion

Moving into the 21st century, both UK and US medical schools show marked improvement in emphasizing end-of-life issues in the curriculum when compared to the last quarter of the 20th century. Indeed, results of these surveys are encouraging. Coursework on death and dying, although limited in many medical schools, is ubiquitous today. In addition, all but one UK medical school (which did not teach clinical students) and 87 percent of US schools addressed the topic of palliative care in the curriculum. It is true that in many schools the exposure is not extensive; while hospice exposure was found in all UK medical schools, only 50 percent of US medical schools had such participation. Still, the majority (66 percent) of US medical schools not currently involving students in hospice programs have plans to do so in the future.

Of the 19 end-of-life topics listed in the survey, eight were covered in at least 70 percent of the medical schools in both the UK and the US while 13 were covered in at least 75 percent of UK medical schools. UK medical

schools also emphasized euthanasia and symptom relief in advanced terminal diseases much more frequently than US medical schools. Thus, the UK seems to emphasize end-of-life issues in the current medical school curriculum more than the US.

Separate courses on dying, death, bereavement, and palliative care did not seem to be the direction that medical schools wish to go. Though the authors have limited comparative historical data on palliative care courses, separate course offerings had not increased significantly over the past decade or two. The integrated approach seemed the best fit for the current medical school curriculum. If such exposure is offered consistently throughout the years of medical school, the integrated approach should give more depth to end-of-life issues than a single isolated course.

The discrepancy between end-of-life offerings in UK versus US medical schools is not surprising. Weissman and Griffie[8] observed that US medical schools "have been slow to develop clinical, education, and research programs in end-of-life care" and have never adequately integrated hospice care into US medical schools. Recent studies of clinical outcomes in the US reported by Ross and colleagues[9] suggest that the current level of physician training in palliative medicine and the care of the terminally ill has "significant shortcomings." Likewise, Meekin and colleagues[10] state that "few [US] schools have devised and implemented effective means to incorporate formal palliative care education into medical school curricula." The prevailing US medical culture continues to view death as a medical failure, and palliative

care, despite its scientific basis, is often perceived as "low-tech."[11]

Limited knowledge of and negative attitudes toward pain control tend to prevail in US medical schools. Grossman and Sheidler[12] reported on the ability of medical students and house officers to calculate the equianalgesic doses of various opioids and found that only 8 percent of answers were within the acceptable range, even though appropriate references were supplied. First-year medical students in Wisconsin[13] displayed many negative attitudes toward cancer pain, indicating the need for deliberate educational efforts. The process of medical education, known as *professionalization,* may even reinforce negative orientation to patients with complex biopsychosocial problems and may contribute to erroneous beliefs and irrational attitudes about pain, note Weinstein and colleagues.[14] They also suggest instituting pain curricula for medical students developed by cancer health care teams, since various studies suggest such specialists are more successful with chronic pain management. With cancer specialists teaching about pain management, medical students' negative attitudes may be improved. Since medical educators acknowledge that students' attitudes, behavior, and clinical knowledge of pain therapy and palliative care can be positively influenced by education, the logical solution would be to add mandatory rotations in pain therapy and palliative care in the nation's medical schools.[15] The limited number of US medical schools with academic faculty positions in palliative medicine should also be addressed.[16]

Table 4. End-of-life topics covered in the curriculum		
	UK* (%)	US** (%)
Attitudes toward death and dying	24 (100)	90 (80)
Communication with dying patients	21 (89)	97 (87)
Communication with family members of dying patients	23 (96)	85 (76)
Grief and bereavement	22 (92)	81 (72)
Social contexts of dying	21 (89)	71 (63)
Psychological aspects of dying	22 (92)	80 (71)
Religious and cultural aspects of dying	16 (67)	74 (66)
The experience of dying	19 (79)	68 (61)
Analgesics for chronic pain	23 (96)	87 (78)
Analgesics for cancer pain	23 (96)	83 (74)
Symptom relief in advanced terminal disease	24 (100)	74 (66)
End-of-life hydration	16 (67)	55 (49)
End-of-life nutrition	14 (58)	57 (51)
Other physical therapy	8 (33)	5 (4)
Neonatal issues	8 (33)	29 (26)
Relating to patients with AIDS	9 (37)	58 (52)
Euthanasia	21 (89)	51 (46)
Advance directives	18 (75)	91 (81)
Death certificates	20 (83)	29 (26)
* N = 12; ** N = 112		

Changes in the professional background of death and dying course instructors in contrast to earlier surveys by the authors are worth noting. In the UK, the increased use of nurse specialists in palliative care and the decreased involvement of psychologists and sociologists were the most notable changes. Likewise, in the US, psychologists, sociologist, theologians, and philosophers were presenting death and dying courses less frequently in 2000–2001 than in the previous 25 years. On the other hand, US nurses and social workers are teaching much more than in previous years, and the same is true for attorneys. This last change might reflect the concern over lawsuits in the event of possible wrongdoing. The dying patient serves as "teacher" through relationships with students in approximately one-fourth of UK and US medical schools today. This approach is an excellent way for the new physician to learn, with empathy and immediacy, about the dying process.

More emphasis on end-of-life issues in medical schools will enhance the physician's role as a health care professional and allow for better rapport with dying patients. The evidence from medical literature overwhelmingly supports the fact that physicians need to be compassionate and knowledgeable in their care of the dying, and that they should possess these skills upon graduation from medical school. Our survey suggests that US and UK programs are on the way toward accomplishing these skills. Though we have a way to go, especially in US medical schools, changes over the last 25 years have been for the better. Ultimately, when end-of-life issues have been fully incorporated into medical school curricula, both physi-

cians and dying patients will be the benefactors.

References

1. Royal Commission on Medical Education, 1966–1968: *The Todd Report.* London: HMSO, 1968.
2. Wilkes E: *Report of the Working Group on Terminal Care* (The Wilkes Report). HMSO, 1980.
3. Dickinson, GE: Death Education in US medical schools. *J Med Educ.* 1976; 51 (2): 134–136.
4. Olin HS: A proposed model to teach medical students the care of the dying patient. *J Med Edu.* 1972; 47: 564–567.
5. Association for Palliative Medicine: *Palliative Medicine Curriculum.* Southampton, England: APM, 1993.
6. Field D: Education for palliative care: Formal education about death, dying, and bereavement in UK medical schools in 1983 and 1994. *Med Educ.* 1995; 29: 414–419.

7. Dickinson GE, Mermann AC: Death education in US medical schools, 1975–1995. *Acad Med.* 1996; 71 (12): 1348–1349.

8. Weissman DE, Griffie J: Integration of palliative medicine at the medical college of Wisconsin 1990–1996. *J Pain Symptom Manage.* 1998; 15: 195–201.

9. Ross DD, O'Mara A, Pickens N, *et al.:* Hospice and palliative care education in medical school: A module on the role of the physician in end-of-life care. *J Cancer Educ.* 1997; 12: 152–156.

10. Meekin SA, Klein JE, Fleishman AR, *et al.:* Development of a palliative education assessment tool for medical student education. *Acad Med.* 2000; 75: 662–665.

11. Fins JJ, Nilson EG: An approach to educating residents about palliative care and clinical ethics. *Acad Med.* 2000; 75: 662–665.

12. Grossman SA, Sheidler VR: Skills of medical students and house officers in prescribing narcotic medications. *J Med Educ.* 1985; 60: 552–557.

13. Weissman DE, Dahl JL: Attitudes about cancer pain: A survey of Wisconsin's first-year medical students. *J Pain Symptom Mange.* 1990; 5: 345–349.

14. Weinstein SM, Laux LF, Thornby JI, *et al.:* Medical students' attitudes toward pain and the use of opioid analgesics: Implications for changing medical school curriculum. *Southern Med J.* 2000; 93: 472–478.

15. Benedetti C, Dickerson D, Nichols LL: A barrier to pain therapy and palliative care. *J Pain Symptom Manage.* 2001; 21: 360–361.

16. Oneschuk D, Hanson, J, Bruera E: An international survey of undergraduate medical education in palliative medicine. *J Pain Symptom Manage.* 2000; 20: 174–179.

George E. Dickinson, PhD, Professor of Sociology, Department of Sociology and Anthropology, College of Charleston, Charleston, South Carolina.

David Field, PhD, Visiting Professor of Sociology, Department of Epidemiology and Public Health, University of Leicester, Leicester, United Kingdom. The UK study was conducted while Dr. Field was at the Centre for Cancer and Palliative Care Studies, The Institute of Cancer Research, London, United Kingdom.

From *American Journal of Hospice & Palliative Care,* May/June 2002, pp. 181-186. © 2002 by Prime National Publication Corporation. Reprinted by permission.

Communication Among Children, Parents, and Funeral Directors

Daniel J. Schaefer

I have been a funeral director for the last twenty-five years. My family has been in the funeral service for one hundred and seven years. We have buried our friends; I have buried parents of my friends and children of my friends. Over the last ten years or so, I have found that something is missing: there have been fewer children attending funerals than I knew were in my friends' families. I began to ask parents, very simply, "What are you saying to your kids about this death in your family?" The replies of 1,800 sets of the parents of more than 3,600 children proved that they were basically unprepared to talk with their children about death and terribly uneasy about doing so, but not unwilling to say something once they were prepared by someone or given appropriate information.

The bits of information that I am going to present are not a standard message. They are building materials. The blueprint is individual to each family, so what we do is to take the family's blueprint, which has their particular death circumstance, then take the building materials, and build a message that parents can give to their children. For the families that I serve, I do this on an individual basis.

TALKING TO CHILDREN ABOUT DEATH

Thinking about talking to children about death is upsetting. It makes many parents anxious. It has been helpful for parents to know how many other parents feel. On Memorial Day two years ago, at three in the morning, I received a call that my brother had been killed in an automobile accident. I have five children, and I knew that four hours from then I was going to have to explain to them about their uncle. I said to my wife, "It's unusual—I've done this with hundreds of families, but I have this thing in the pit of my stomach. I *know* what to say to these

kids; I know exactly what I'm going to do. Can you imagine how it must be for somebody who doesn't know what to say?"

What do people say about speaking to children about death? Some are sure that they do have to talk to their children and some say they are not sure that it is necessary. Some parents who believe that something should be said are told by others that they should avoid upsetting their children. Parents naturally tend to build a protective wall around their children. What I say to them is "Let's look at the wall, let's see if it works, and if it does work, who is it working for? Is it working for you, to protect you from your child's grief? If we look over the wall, what do we see on the other side? Do we see a kid who is comfortable or do we see, in fact, a kid who is a solitary mourner?"

When parents plan to speak to their children about death, they have to understand that what they are about to do is not easy, that they are going to be upset and stressed, that they are probably going to lack energy, and that they are going to feel unable to concentrate. They are going to be afraid of their own emotions and the effect that these emotions will have on their children. They are not going to know what their children understand, and basically they have to realize that they want to protect their children from pain. It is important that parents know ahead of time that they are going to feel this way.

What do other people say to them? They say, "Your kids don't know what's going on," "Wait until later," "Tell them a fairy tale," "Don't say anything," "Send them away until the funeral is over," or "Do you really want to put your kids through all this?" implying that no loving parent would. It is almost frightening to talk with one's children on this subject, but I believe that it is dangerous not to.

Almost all parents will agree that children are surprisingly perceptive. They overhear conversations, read emotions and responses around them, and ask questions, directly and indirectly. They *will* receive messages; it is impossible not to communicate. No matter how hard parents try not to, they are going to communicate their grief to their children. Without some explanation, the children will be confused and anxious. What I say to parents is, "Since you're going to be sending a message out anyway, why don't you try to control the message?" A message is controlled by making sure that the information is true, geared for the age of the child, and, if possible, delivered in surroundings that make the child's reception of the message a little easier to handle.

For parents, feeling in control is important at a time when feeling out of control is routine and common, and when helping the child—the most dependent person in the family at that time—is also critical. The discussion between parent and child may be the child's only chance to understand what is happening. Sometimes, however, the pressure and enormity of this task, along with the advice of others, really proves too great for parents. They choose a short-term covering for themselves, without realizing the long-term effect on their children.

Explaining the How and Why of Death

Children have to know from the beginning what sad is. They have to know why their parents are sad and why they themselves are sad. So parents can begin with, "This is a very sad time," or "A very sad thing has happened," or "Mommy and Daddy are sad because...." Children have to know that it is a death that has made the parents sad: with no explanation, they may think that they have caused the sadness. They also have to know that it is appropriate to feel sad.

The next stage involves an explanation of death and what it means. Death basically means that a person's body stops working and will not work any more. It won't do any of the things it used to do. It won't walk, talk, or move; none of its parts work; it does not see and it does not hear. This foundation is what parents feel comfortable referring back to when children ask questions like "Will Grandpa ever move again?" "Why can't they fix him?" "Why isn't he moving?" "Is he sleeping?" "Can he hear me?" "Can he eat after he's buried?" If parents come up with different answers to all of these questions, it becomes confusing, but when they have a foundation, they can come back to it repeatedly. The notion that something has stopped working is a firm foundation for children, and parents feel comfortable in not lying or deceiving in using this type of explanation.

Because death is a form of abandonment, the words "passed away," "gone away," or "left us," that many people use hold out to the child the hope that the deceased will return, which of course causes tremendous frustration while they wait for the person to return. Appropriate explanations to children of why a particular death happened might be, for example, in a case of terminal illness, "Because the disease couldn't be stopped. The person became very, very sick, the body wore out, and the body stopped working"; in a case of suicide, "Some people's bodies get sick and don't work right, and some people's minds don't work right. They can't see things clearly, and they feel that the

only way to solve their problems is to take their own life"; in a case of miscarriage, "Sometimes a baby is just starting to grow; something happens and makes it stop. We don't know what it was—it wasn't anything that anyone did."

CHILDREN'S REACTIONS TO DEATH

When people start to take this information and relate it to their own family situations in preparation for confronting their families, they want to know what they need to be concerned about and what to look for. Even newborn infants and toddlers know when things are different. The smaller they are, the less likely it is that they will be able to figure out why. Children respond to changes in behavior; they sense when life patterns change. Infants may alter their nursing patterns; toddlers become cranky, and change their sleeping and eating patterns. Excitement at home, new people around, parents gone at odd times, a significant person missing, a sad atmosphere—children know that something is different and react accordingly. When parents expect these changes in their children, they can respond to them more sensibly.

Piaget says that children between the ages of three and six years see death as reversible. The way this translates for parents (and for children) is that people will come back, that dead is not forever. Parents have said to me, "How could a child think that somebody will return?" From a child's point of view, ET returns, Jesus and Lazarus returned, and Road Runner returns constantly. And children may misinterpret the rise-again eulogies often given by clergy.

Several years ago (1978), "Sesame Street" produced a program dealing with the death of Mr. Hooper. The program was written up in newspapers and other publications as being an advance for the education of children. The problem is that Mr. Hooper has returned in reruns of the show, so that children who experienced his death now find that Mr. Hooper is back again.

People may say, "My child isn't affected by his grandfather's death—he's only four years old." I say, "Why should he be affected? As far as he's concerned, Grandpa's only going to be dead for a little while." Knowing how children perceive death helps parents to understand their children better, so that they will not become upset when a child continues to ask questions. They know that children in that age range can be expected to ask more questions.

Children also tend to connect events that are not connected. Does this death mean that someone else is going to die? "Grandpa died after he had a headache. Mommy has a headache. Does that mean that she is going to die?" "Old people die. Daddy is old [he is thirty]. Is he going to die?" This means that we have to explain the difference between being very, very sick and just sick like Mommy or Daddy might be; the difference between being very, very old and over twenty; and the difference between being very old and very sick and being very old but not very sick.

Children ages six to nine know that death is final, but they still think about return. They need a more detailed explanation of why a person has died than younger children do. With these children, it is much more important to distinguish between a fatal illness and just being sick—to say, "It's not like when you get sick, or when Mommy or Daddy get sick." If a parent tells a child, "Grandpa had a pain in his stomach, went to the hospital, and died," what is the child to think the next time that Mommy has menstrual cramps? What are children to think when a grandparent dies from lung cancer after a tremendous bout of coughing and then find that their father has a cough? It is normal for children in that situation to start to cling to the father and ask, "Are you okay?"

Children of this age may not want to go to a house where a person has died because "it's spooky." They also have to deal with and understand their emotions, to know that crying, feeling bad, and being angry are all acceptable behaviors.

Children ages nine to twelve move much closer to an adult sense of grieving. They are more aware of the details of an illness and more aware of the impact of a death on them. Consequently, they need more emotional support. They need to know that their feelings are acceptable and that someone is supportive of those feelings.

Teenagers also need support with their new feelings. Parents may find it better to share their own feelings with their adolescent children. Teenagers also have to understand why a person has died.

At the funeral of a friend, I met a man I used to know, another funeral director. He said to me, "It's strange. When I grew up in Queens with my grandfather, we lived in a two-family house for ten-and-a-half years. When my parents had enough money, they bought a house on Long Island, and we moved there. That was in the summer. On my birthday, in October, Grandpa didn't send me a card. I was a little concerned about that, but when Grandpa didn't come for Thanksgiving, and then when he didn't come for Christmas, I asked my mother where Grandpa was. She said he couldn't come." My friend went on: "I couldn't think what I could possibly have done to this dear man that I had spent my childhood with that would cause him not to like me any more. Then it went on again. Grandpa never came in the summer, then it was another Thanksgiving and another Christmas. It wasn't until I was thirteen that they told me that my grandfather had died. I thought that was bizarre until a woman came into my funeral home three weeks ago and when I said to her, as I say to everybody, 'What did you say to your kids about the death of your mother?' she said, 'I haven't told them. I just told them she went on vacation in Vermont.'" So the difference between ten years ago, or fifteen, or twenty years ago and today is not so great for uninformed parents.

Responsibility

People say, "How can a child feel responsible for the death of another person?" Yet, they will say to their children, "You're driving me crazy," "You'll be the death of me yet," or "Don't give me a heart attack!" Adults may say such things as figures of speech, but children do not always see it that way. "If only I had prayed harder," they may say. Children basically see God as a rewarder or punisher; He rewards good behavior and punishes bad. Therefore, if a child does a bad thing that only he or she knows about, God may punish the child by the death of someone in the child's family. If illness or death follows a misdeed, the child can feel really responsible for this. For example, when a parent leaves the home, a child may say, "If I had cleaned my room (done my chores, hadn't wet my pants, done better in school), maybe he (or she) wouldn't have left." This is what happens when no explanation is given to a child about why a person has died. When a grandparent stops visiting, the child again may say, "What did I do?"

Magical Thinking

Some children believe that by wishing that a person will die, they can cause the person's death. They sometimes also believe that if they think about the death of a person who is dying, they themselves may die.

Anger

This is a common response at the time of a death and one that is extremely damaging to families. Understanding it and anticipating its presence helps families deal with anger from both sides, the parent's and the children's. Children can be angry at parents for not telling them that the deceased was sick, for having spent so much time with the deceased and not enough time with them, for not allowing them to attend the funeral, or just because they need someone to be angry at.

I offer two examples of children's anger at parents. When my brother died, two days after the funeral there was a tremendous downpour. There were two inches of water in the back yard, and my ten-year-old son came to me and said, "I want to pitch my tent in the back yard." I said, "David, you can't pitch a tent. There are two inches of water in the yard!" He became angry, threw the tent down, and walked away. I said to him, "Look, I'll tell you why you're angry: you don't have anyone to be angry at. You can't be angry at your uncle because he was in an automobile accident. He wasn't drunk and he wasn't driving fast. It was a wet road, he didn't know it, and the car turned over and he was killed. You can't be angry at the doctors or the hospital because he was dead when he arrived there." I said, "There's nobody else to be angry at, so the next possibility is to be angry at me. As long as you understand that, it's okay." He came back a while later and said, "You know, after thinking about it, I don't know why I ever wanted to pitch my tent in the yard."

The second example came a few days ago when I spoke to a woman about coming to a funeral. She said, "You know, I was seven years old when they took me to my grandfather's funeral. I could go to the funeral, I could sit outside—my parents even bought me a brand new dress—but I was not allowed to go in and say goodbye to Grandpa. So you know what? I never wore the dress again and I never talked about Grandpa again."

Children can also be angry at themselves for wishing that a person would die or for not visiting or helping a dying person. One young boy had seen his grandfather walking down the street carrying some packages and noticed that his grandfather was not doing so well. But Grandfather did not do well a lot of the time, so the boy helped his grandfather take the packages inside, went on home, and did not say anything to his father about his grandfather. The grandfather died of a heart attack in the house. Later, the boy's father came to me and asked, "What am I going to say? My son said, 'If only I'd told you this time that Grandpa didn't look well, maybe we could have done something.'" Two weeks ago a mother came to me and said, "My daughter thinks that my mother may have died because she failed to send her a get-well card. She thought that maybe it would have saved her if she had sent it."

The driver of a car, the doctor at a hospital, the deceased for putting themselves in dangerous situations, even the event that caused a death—these are just a few examples of the legitimate targets of children's anger. When parents know that children are responding with anger or that they may do so, the parents will do best if they address it directly with the children. The important point for parents is that they feel much more in control when they can anticipate this kind of anger. They know the historical background of their old circumstances, their own blueprint, and if they consider these they can help their children through their anger.

Guilt

This is another aspect of grief and grieving. Knowing that a child may feel guilt, or having it pointed out, lets parents know that their children can, on one hand, be angry at the deceased and, on the other, feel guilty about being angry. Children may express their guilt in statements such as "I didn't do enough," "I should have visited him before he died," and "If only I hadn't gone to the movies last week instead of going to see Grandpa, I would have been able to say goodbye before he died." All of these "shoulds" and "if onlys" can have a tremendous impact on a family if they are not directed, if nobody anticipated them, and if nobody explains them to the children.

CHILDREN AND FUNERALS

People feel the need to know how to explain what is going to happen next: "After I've explained to my children that this person has died, what do I say to them about what's going to happen now?" I have some material in script form that I offer to families, but basically parents have to start from the beginning with a child. They can say, "Grandpa will be taken from where he died to a funeral home; it's a place where they'll keep him for a few days until he's buried. He'll be dressed in clothes he liked and put into a casket—that's a box we use so that no dirt gets on him when he's buried. People will come to the funeral home to visit and say how sorry they are that Grandpa has died. Because his body isn't working any more, it won't move or do any of the things it used to do, but if you want to come and say some prayers, you can."

The basic premise here is that people will ask whether or not they should bring a child to the funeral home. People are surprised when I say, "Never! Don't ever bring children to a funeral home if you're not going to prepare them for it ahead of time." My son had cardiac surgery a year and a half ago. Before his operation, they showed him the operating room, the recovery room, and the intensive care unit. He knew everything that was going to happen to him before he went into the hospital for the surgery. His doctor even drew a diagram of the operation for him and made a model of the surgical repair out of clay for him. But people will still waltz children into a funeral home and say, "We're just going to see Grandma." Then they wonder why the children are upset when they walk in and find out that Grandma is lying down in a casket and not moving.

Children should be treated like people and given the same concern we give anyone else. They should hear an explanation of what will happen and then be given the opportunity to come to the funeral home or not, but they cannot make that decision without information. If children decide to come, they should be prepared further. They should be told the color of the rugs and walls, whether there are plants or paintings, whether there are flowers, what color the casket is, what color clothing the deceased is wearing, and that the deceased is lying down and not moving. The children should be informed so completely that when they walk into the funeral home it is almost as if they have been there before. Does it work? Children have walked into my funeral home and checked off exactly the points that I covered with their parents three hours before— "Oh, there's a green rug, there's the painting on the wall, there are the flowers." When this happens, I know that the parents have used the information I have provided, and I know that the children are comfortable because the place is not strange to them. All of this draws a child into the family support network on the same side of the wall, rather than putting the child alone on the other side of the wall.

We cannot assume that parents speak to their children about death or that they know how to do so. We cannot assume that if a death occurs suddenly in the middle of the night the parents will be prepared to talk to their children about it at seven o'clock in the morning when they get up. We cannot assume that "user-friendly" information is available, that if parents were given a booklet it would apply, or even that they would read it. I used to think that talking to children about death was only the concern of parents, but another funeral director who is using my program told me that a senior citizen came to him and said, "I'm here because I want to make sure that when I die my children will provide my grandchildren with this type of information."

We cannot assume that children are not talking or thinking about a death, that they are not affected when a family pet dies or by the deaths they see every day on television, or by the death of a neighbor or classmate. We cannot assume that children are prepared in any way to come to a funeral. We cannot assume that their parents have answered their questions or that the children have asked questions. For example, I have found that about 85 percent of the children between the ages of four and twelve who come to a funeral home and see a half-closed casket do not realize or believe that the deceased's legs are in the bottom of the casket. How do I know? Because I have said to parents, address that issue with children: Walk into the funeral home and up to the casket, and say, "You know, some kids think that the whole person isn't there, so if you want us to, we'll show you the rest of the person." Some parents respond by saying "No, I don't want to do that, I don't want to deal with that." But I have found that their children will accept my invitation to have the bottom part of the casket opened so that they can look inside. I have been putting a family into a limousine and heard a child ask, "Why did they cut Grandma up?" and heard the mother say, "What do you mean they cut Grandma up?" So I have said, "She only saw half of Grandma; let's go back inside." We have gone back in, opened the bottom of the casket, and the child has said, "Oh, yes, she is all there."

Children constantly ask for this type of information. A mother said to me, "Why does my child ask if that's a dummy inside the casket? And why does she ask me how they got the dummy to look so much like Grandpa?" And I say, "What did you say to your child? And she says that she told the child that her grandfather had died and gone to heaven. So I say, "If Grandpa died and went to heaven, who's inside the casket?"

A psychiatrist told me that he had one patient, a five-year-old boy who had been very close to his grandmother. When she died, the boy was told that Grandma had gone right up to heaven. His mother later found the boy standing on the windowsill of the apartment, about to jump out. After the boy was safely on the floor again, his mother asked him why he had been going to jump and what he thought would happen if he did. The boy said, "I would go up, just like Grandma."

So many of the points that seem like separate, discrete bits of information are actually the building materials to be fitted into a family blueprint. When I present this information to parents, they ask, "How do you expect us to put all of this together in our grief? How do you expect us to do that?" I say, "I don't expect you to do that; I expect your funeral director to do it."

Daniel J. Schaefer is a funeral director, Brooklyn, NY.

From *Loss, Grief, and Care* by Daniel J. Schaefer, 1988, Chapter 5, pp. 131-142. © 1988 by Haworth Press, Inc., 10 Alice Street, Binghamton, NY. Reprinted by permission.

Children, Death, and Fairy Tales

Abstract
"Children, Death and Fairy Tales" examines the evolution and transformation of themes relating to death and dying in children's literature, using illuminating parallels from historical demographics of mortality and the development of housing. The classic fairy tale "Little Red Riding Hood" is used to draw these trends together.

Elizabeth P. Lamers, M.A.
Malibu, California

Historical Background

There is a history behind each of the familiar stories that parents read at their children's bedsides. Many of what have now become common fairy tales had their origin in an oral tradition intended as adult entertainment, replete with ribald humor and sensational events. As these tales began to be transcribed and considered more specifically as material intended for children, they began to contain incidents and behavior that reflected the customs of the place and period in which they were written down and that were intended to provide children with a moral education. Especially in the earliest versions, death had a place in children's stories because of its ubiquity and drama. There have been significant transformations to fairy tales, and to the content of children's stories in general, since a literature for children first appeared. Until recently, topics that have come to be considered disturbing to young people, concerning issues that adults would wish to protect them from, have been diluted, softened, and removed from the literature for children. In our modern generations, children have been insulated from an awareness of mortality.

Particularly in the last hundred years, a significant movement away from issues of morality and mortality has taken place. This has reflected the tremendous changes in attitudes concerning children and death over the last century. These changes have coincided with the shifting of the demographics of death in this time period and with the changing of attitudes toward children and their upbringing.

Up to the end of the nineteenth century, the highest mortality rate was to be found in children under the age of fifteen; today the highest rate is found in adults of far more advanced years. In the past, children were exposed to dying because it occurred almost exclusively at home after a short illness; death now occurs almost exclusively in some sort of health care institution following a prolonged illness. Although in recent years hospice programs have sought to return dying to the home, the majority of elderly persons still die either in a rest home or a hospital. As a result, children and even young adults today are commonly separated from the reality of death.[1] This isolation is reinforced by a paucity of material that would introduce children to the universal experiences of dying and death.

The changing composition and structure of the modern family has also had an isolating effect on the young person's awareness of mortality. At the end of the last century, it was common for children to grow up as a member of an extended family consisting of parents, grandparents, aunts and uncles who all lived in the same rural area. A child today is more likely a member of a "nuclear" or one parent family, living in an urban area, often separated from relatives by hundreds of miles. Children in rural areas once were exposed to dying and death in their families, in their communities, and among farm animals. They had repeated opportunities to be close to death, to ask questions about death, and to participate in healing religious and social bereavement ceremonies and rituals.

While once the loss of a relative was an occasion for ceremonies that emphasized and reinforced family coherence, today the death of a relative, especially an elderly or distant one, may pass with little or no observance. Many parents have come to believe that children should be shielded from dying and the facts of death, and it is common today for children to not attend funeral services.[2]

Although children may be exposed to literally hundreds of deaths in television programs and cartoons, these are a different kind of death, typically of a "bad" person, who, because of some evil actions, "deserved" to die. Children's cartoons consistently present a distorted view of mortality, even fostering the especially erroneous conclusion that death is somehow "reversible." With little contradiction, beliefs like these can continue to influence and pervade perceptions of death.[3] They come to stand in place of substantial experiences with dying and death, giving rise to difficulties and misunderstandings in later years, when the child, as an adult, has real experiences with mortality. Beliefs like these have been fostered by the isolation of the child from the experience of death as a part of life, an isolation that can be traced in the transformation that has occurred in the stories and fairy tales that have been read to children since such tales first appeared in written form in the early 1700s.

Books about Death for Children

The removal and glossing over of incidents of dying and death from material that children are exposed to has been occurring regularly since about the 1920s. At the same time religion was being removed from school books. It is only in the last twenty years that this tendency has begun to be reversed, and children's books now often contain topics that were previously taboo, including, feelings, divorce, sex and even death. Religion is still taboo in school books.

From the early 1800s until the 1920s, American children were commonly taught to read with a series of textbooks, such as those by Lyman Cobb, Worcester, Town, Russell, Swan or McGuffey. In *McGuffey's Eclectic Readers,*[4] the subject of many of the selections and poems was the death of a mother or child. These deaths were typically presented as a tragic but an inevitable part of life. The manner in which death was portrayed can be found in such representative examples as William Wordsworth's poem "We Are Seven,"[5] in which a little girl describes her family as having seven children, even though two are dead and buried in the churchyard near their house. The experience of the death of an older sister is also described in this poem. Other selections from the Readers in which death is a theme are: *Old Age and Death*[6] by Edmund Waller, *The Death of Little Nell*[7] by Charles Dickens, *Elegy in a County Churchyard*[8] by Thomas Gray, and *He Giveth His Beloved Sleep*[9] by Elizabeth Barrett Browning.

A selection in the Fourth Reader by an anonymous author, entitled "My Mother's Grave,"[10] provides an emotional account of a young girl's experience with her dying mother. The story aims to make children polite and obedient to their parents, by giving the example of a young girl who didn't realize how fleeting life can be. The author of the story recaptures her thoughts while revisiting the grave of her mother, who had died thirteen years previously. She remembers how she had been unkind to her mortally-ill mother after coming home from a trying day at school. Realizing her lapse in manners later in the evening, she returns to her mother's room to ask forgiveness, to find her mother asleep. The little girl vows to awaken early to

"tell how sorry I was for my conduct," yet when she rushes to her mother's room in the brightness of morning she finds her mother dead, with a hand so cold "it made me start." The author relates how, even thirteen years later, her remorse and pain are almost overwhelming. This is not the type of subject matter and emotional content that is generally considered appropriate for today's basal readers.[11] The basal readers commonly used today in classrooms rarely contain any references to death or dying. They might contain a chapter from a book such as *Charlotte's Web,* by E. B. White,[12] but the chapter would not be the one in which Charlotte dies.

Insight into the fashion in which scenes of death and dying were typically portrayed in the nineteenth century can be found in the book *Little Women,* written by Louisa May Alcott in 1869, and still widely read by young readers today. Alcott wrote of the death of young Beth in a straightforward manner that was especially uncommon for her day. Recognizing that her depiction was at odds with the melodramatic scenes that were current in more romantic literature, Alcott added in the paragraph following Beth's death: "Seldom, except in books, do the dying utter memorable words, see visions, or depart with beatified countenances...."[13]

The elements that Alcott took exception to were all common in death scenes in the literature of 1830 to 1880, where they reflected the expectations of an audience that was accustomed to being given a romanticized picture of death and its consequent "final reward" in what was known as "consolation literature." A preoccupation with death and a glorification of the afterlife was evident in popular literature from both England and America in this period. Much of this literature was written either by Protestant clergy (especially Congregationalists and Unitarians), their wives, or other pious women of the congregation.[14]

Between 1940 and 1970 only a few children's books contained references to death. Two that have become classics are *The Dead Bird* by Margaret W. Brown[15] and *Charlotte's Web* by E. B. White.[16] White's publisher initially refused to publish *Charlotte's Web* unless the ending was modified to allow Charlotte to live. White refused.[17] The book was criticized by reviewers who said that death was not "an appropriate subject for children." *Charlotte's Web* is still a best-seller, and often is one of the books which second or third grade teachers choose to read to their classes.

The separation of children from death has diminished somewhat in the last twenty years. Elizabeth Kubler-Ross'[18] early work helped make death a subject that could be discussed and studied. Children's books in the late sixties began to discuss subjects that had previously been neglected, such as death and divorce. During the nineteen seventies and eighties over 200 fiction books were written for children with death as a major theme. Unfortunately very few measured up to the standard set by *Charlotte's Web, Little Women, The Yearling* or *The Dead Bird.* During the same period some very good non-fiction books about death were written for children of various ages. (See resource list at end of chapter.)

This cornucopia of books on death has helped to begin to make death a more acceptable topic for discussion. The hospice movement has also helped by reintroducing home care for dying persons to many communities. Even so, many children are still insulated from death and often are discouraged from attending funerals. It is not unusual to find adults in their forties who have never attended a funeral.[19] The diminished awareness of mortality that begins in childhood is often carried on into adulthood.

The Development of Children's Literature

Prior to the development of a literature intended specifically for children in the middle of the seventeenth century, there were two characteristic ways in which children were considered. The first was a holdover from the age of the Greeks and Romans, in which children were perceived as miniature adults. Another manner of perceiving children, as something infra-human, was distinguished by Michel de Montaigne, the French humanist and essayist of the sixteenth century. It is difficult, however, from a modern perspective, to be sympathetic to Montaigne's assertion that children possessed "neither mental activities nor recognizable body shape."[20]

Authors writing children's literature in the eighteenth century were primarily interested in educating children and assisting them to become socially acceptable human beings. Beyond providing just a certain amount of book learning, they also sought to teach the correct ways to behave. For this reason, all the tales of Charles Perrault had an emphatic moral at their end. They were cautionary tales of what could happen to a child if he or she didn't act in a proper fashion. Some of Perrault's titles were: La Belle au Bois Dormant (Sleeping Beauty),[21] Le Petit Chaperon Rouge (Little Red Riding Hood)[22] and Les Fées (Toads and Diamonds).[23] As pointed out by Maria Tartar in *Off With Their Heads!*:

> From its inception, children's literature had in it an unusually cruel and coercive streak—one which produced books that relied on brutal intimidation to frighten children into complying with parental demands. This intimidation manifested itself in two very different forms, but both made examples of children. First, there were countless cautionary tales that managed to kill off their protagonists or make their lives perpetually miserable for acts of disobedience. Then there were stories about exemplary behavior which, nonetheless, had a strange way of also ending at the deathbeds of their protagonists."[24]

In 1658, John Amos Comenius's *Orbis Sensualium Pictus* (A World of Things Obvious to the Senses Drawn in Pictures), a Latin school book, was published. This teaching device was the first picture book for children,[25] and it was also the first to respond to the recognition that children needed their own literature because they were not scaled-down adults. It was still almost a century later, however, before children's literature began to come into its own. In 1744, John Newbery wrote *A Little Pretty Pocket Book*[26] for children. This book is credited as signifying the "real" start of children's literature in England.

Fairy Tales

Fairy tales provide an excellent example of the fashion in which themes that came to be considered distressing to children have been moderated over time, and insulation of children from an awareness of mortality can be traced through the progression of different versions of typical stories. A generalization can be made about fairy tales as they came to be thought of specifically as children's stories: the sexual content was diminished, and the amount of violence tended to be increased. This process can be seen in successive editions of the Brothers Grimm's Fairy Tales. To understand this evolution, it is necessary to have a picture of the environment in which it took place. According to the perception of children's needs current at the time that the Brothers Grimm were writing, children did not need to be protected from portrayals of violence.

William Jordan in *Divorce Among the Gulls* provides a dramatic context for the state of life that was not untypical for children in London a mere one hundred years after the time that a children's literature came into being:

> "I doubt that any of us can comprehend how brutal the fight for survival has been throughout evolution. We ignore our prehistoric, evolutionary legacy, a world in which most children died in infancy or childhood, where teeth rotted out by the age of twenty, where gangrene took the lives of the injured, where thirty-five was foul old age. Even as recently as 1750 in London, the toll of disease staggers the mind: of 2,239 children born that year, only 168 were still alive five years later."[27]

From its inception, literature for children has been motivated by a belief that children needed written material, not so much for entertainment, but to prepare them for life. The majority of books published and intended for children up through the 1800s can be compared to James Janeway's *A Token for Children: Being an Account of the Conversion, Holy and Exemplary Lives, and Joyful Deaths of Several Young Children* (1671–72).[28] The London Bills of Mortality for the period shortly following the publication of Janeway's book show that the mortality rate of children age five and under was running as high as 66 percent.[29] Writers of this era commonly concurred with Janeway's position that they held a sacred duty to salvage the souls of those who were "not too little to go to Hell." The exemplary stories in *A Token for Children* were also designed to provide comfort to children faced with the tragedy of a sibling's death or confronted with their own mortality when visited by some dread disease.[30]

The violence and death in stories written for children takes on a different light when put in the context of such high rates of mortality. The practice of abandoning unwanted children either at the Foundlings' Hospital or on church steps was increasing in the seventeen hundreds. It was not just the poor but all classes who contributed to the ranks of abandoned children. The foundling institution was established to make it possible to dispose of infants without leaving any record. Buffon noted in 1772 that about one-third of all children born in Paris that year were abandoned. Jean-Jacques Rousseau (1712–1778) claimed to have turned his five children over to the state, leaving them at the Foundlings' Hospital at birth.[31]

A high mortality rate for children was reflected in children's literature. As Freud noted in *The Interpretation of Dreams,* half the human race failed to survive the childhood years.[32] The characteristically romanticized depiction of an afterlife, that was superior to the life of this world, was seen as a way to help children cope with the brutal facts of the life they had no choice but to lead. In the seventeenth and eighteenth centuries, children were routinely required—not just encouraged—to attend public executions so that they could see the price of criminal behavior. This says much about the methods of child rearing believed appropriate in this era.[33]

The Brothers Grimm's story "Aschenputtel," or "Cinderella," shows an emphasis on punishment that was lacking in the earliest oral versions, and that increased in intensity in subsequent editions. In the early version, taken by Perrault from the oral tradition, Cinderella forgave her stepsisters for mistreating her and introduced them at court. Grimm's first version has Cinderella's sisters turning pale and being horrified when Cinderella becomes a princess, but in the second edition the sisters are punished by being blinded by pigeons that peck out their eyes.[34]

In the Brothers Grimm's "Hansel and Grethel" there is a description of how horribly the witch howled when Grethel pushed her into her own oven and how "… Grethel ran away, and therefore she was left to burn, just as she had left many poor little children to burn."[35] The use of violence as punishment for bad behavior is typical in fairy stories. And violent occurrences were frequently shown to be the result of even minor misdeeds. This tendency is evident in the collection of stories found in *Struwwelpeter.* In these short tales Little Pauline plays with matches and goes up in flames, and Conrad the Thumbsucker gets his thumbs sliced off. As Tartar observes the interesting point here is that "… the weight is given to the punishment (often fully half the text is devoted to its description) and the disproportionate relationship between the childish offense and the penalty for it make the episode disturbing."[36]

The removal of sexuality from books intended for children was a development that paralleled the evolution of housing in Europe. In the Middle Ages houses were rarely more elaborate than was necessary. Few homes had more than one room. The poor had hovels which were little more than a shelter for sleeping. Family life tended to be compromised. Because there was no room for children, only for infants, the older children were commonly sent away to work as apprentices or servants.

The living quarters of the bourgeoisie would typically be above a store or artisan's shop. It generally consisted of a single, large room in which the household cooked, ate, transacted business, entertained and slept. Households of up to twenty-five people were not uncommon. Privacy was unknown,[37] and children were not sent to bed in their own rooms so that racy stories could be told to adults only. Beds were generally large because they were intended to hold more than one or two people. Children lived and worked alongside adults and listened to the same stories. Since children were in the company of adults who were not their parents, but were employers or other servants, there

was not the same concern then about what children were exposed to that parents of today have.

By the seventeenth century, living arrangements had evolved so that there tended to be greater segregation between quarters allocated to working, food preparation and sleeping. There still tended to be a main room used for dining, entertaining and receiving visitors, but servants and children began to be separated into smaller rooms adjacent to the central, common areas.[38] It was at this time that fairy stories began to be transformed into works intended more strictly for children. This transformation of living spaces coincides with other changes that had great impact on children, including attitudes about how children should be taught about proper behavior, and about death and dying.

By looking at the changes in one fairy tale, Little Red Riding Hood, we can observe the changes in attitudes toward death, children and their education. The earliest known oral version of the tale of Little Red Riding Hood, for example, would not generally be considered suitable entertainment for children today. In the version of the story traditionally told in Brittany, Little Red is unwittingly led by the wolf to eat her grandmother's flesh and drink her blood, and she performs a provocative striptease for the disguised wolf before climbing into bed with him. Little Red later escapes from the wolf when she goes outside to relieve herself. As this tale was originally told, its primary purpose was to entertain adults, so it was not as heavily encumbered with the admonitions and advice that later came to distinguish versions of this tale intended for children.

The earliest written version of Little Red Riding Hood was recorded in French by Charles Perrault in 1696–97. The title of the story in French was 'Le Petit Chapeon Rouge.' The 'chapeon' was a hat worn in the Middle Ages, which suggests an even earlier oral tradition.[39] One of the fullest texts faithful to the traditional, oral versions of "Little Red Riding Hood" was also recorded in France at the end of the nineteenth century.[40]

Perrault's first version of the tale was published in *Histoires ou Contes du Temps Passé* (Stories [Tales] of Times Passed), subtitled *Contes de Ma Mère L'Oye* (Tales of My Mother Goose). Perrault included seven other tales along with the tale of Little Red Riding Hood. Each of these tales had a moral in verse at the end. In this version of Little Red's tale, the grandmother and Little Red are both eaten by the wolf, and both perish. Although Perrault did not have Little Red's mother giving her any initial warnings before she departed for her grandmother's house, he did conclude the story with a moral suitable for the intended audience of children: Do not speak to strangers or you, too, may provide a wolf with his dinner. The violence of this story is later moderated in the Brothers Grimm's retelling, by the introduction of an additional character, a hunter or woodcutter, who is able to rescue Little Red and her grandmother by slicing open the wolf and letting them out.

The version of Little Red's tale as told by the Brothers Grimm also gives an expanded role to Little Red's mother, who gives Little Red many warnings and much advice before sending her off through the forest to her grandmother's house. Little Red is admonished to "make haste… go straight… behave prettily and modestly… do not run… and do not forget to curtsy and say 'good morning' to everyone who knows you."[41] These initial admonitions served to educate the young audience of the story in the manners that were expected of them, and they provided a framework in which the resulting action of the story would be played out. The Brothers Grimm vividly portrayed the consequences of not heeding mother's advice. Interestingly, in this version, the hunter refers to the wolf as "old sinner,"[42] perhaps as an oblique reference to risqué incidents excised from the children's version but remembered from the oral tradition.

In a popular nineteenth century retelling of Little Red's tale the grandmother still gets eaten by the wolf, but Little Red survives and learns to pay closer attention to her mother's words: "For she saw the dreadful end to which/ A disobedient act may lead."[43] This version of the tale has an interesting emphasis on avoiding any unnecessary suffering of the characters. Here is the depiction of the wolf putting an end to the grandmother:

"He jumped up on the bed, and ate her all up. But he did not hurt her so much as you would think, and as she was a very good old woman it was better for her to die than to live in pain; but still it was very dreadful of the wolf to eat her."[44]

The editor of *Old Favorite Fairy Tales* was apparently undecided about whether the grandmother's fate was good or bad. When the woodcutter arrives on the scene to rescue Little Red, he advises her that one shouldn't "tell one's affairs to strangers, for many a wolf looks like an honest dog,"—an interesting way of warning a young girl that looks can be deceiving!

In later versions, the hunter arrives in time to shoot the wolf before he eats either Little Red or her grandmother, and in still other versions, even the wolf is spared to escape through an open window, or to become Little Red's pet. The moral or message of the story also evolves with the transformation of the events depicted in the tale. In the traditional, oral version of Little Red Riding Hood, Little Red was not forewarned by her mother about the dangers of talking to strangers, therefore Little Red cannot be seen as naughty or disobedient. In Perrault's original written version, the mother does not give Little Red any cautions, either, while in later versions the mother often gives many instructions and admonitions to her daughter. Upon rescuing Little Red from the dire misfortune she brings upon herself, the hunter/woodcutter inevitably gives her a lecture on obedience and points out to her that she now knows what can happen if she disobeys her mother's warnings. The role that mortality plays in the changing tale of Little Red Riding Hood is seen to diminish as the tale evolves. Rather than being the graphic and unmourned event as Perrault depicted it, it becomes unrealistically softened in the later versions, eventually being banished to the periphery of the young audiences' attention.

What Is a Fairy Tale?

To better understand the significance of the place that fairy tales, and other tales told to children, have in determining the formation of attitudes relating to death and dying, it is helpful to become familiar with some of the different definitions that these tales have been given. Fairy tales have been defined in various ways by different people. Rollo May considered fairy tales to be "…our myths before we become conscious of ourselves."[45] Bruno Bettelheim wrote,

"The figures and events of fairy tales… personify and illustrate inner conflicts, but they suggest ever so subtly how these conflicts may be solved, and what the next steps in the development toward a higher humanity might be… presented in a simple homely way…. Far from making demands, the fairy tale reassures, gives hope for the future, and holds out the promise of a happy ending."[46]

Madonna Kolbenschlag writes:

"Fairy tales are the bedtime stories of the collective consciousness. They persist in cultural memory because they interpret crises of the human condition that are common to all of us. They are shared wish fulfillments, abstract dreams that resolve conflicts and give meaning to experience."[47]

Edwin Krupp makes a distinction between fairy tales and the rest of children's literature:

"The term 'fairy tale' is sometimes used for all children's stories, but the fairy tale really has its own special character. It involves or takes place in another realm or world, not in the one in which we usually reside. Fairy tales are really stories of the supernatural. Other laws prevail in them, and the creatures that inhabit them do not belong to ordinary reality."[48]

All of these definitions are good and even have merit in their own context, yet they are unsatisfying in their failure to consider the origin of these tales in adult entertainment and the purposeful manner in which they were converted into tales intended for children.

There is an easily confusing overlap between fairy tales, folk tales and myths. Myths are the most easily distinguishable, as they are mainly stories intended to provide explanations for the occurrence of natural phenomenon, generally by personifying a natural effect as an animistic or anthropomorphic deity. The depiction of the sun in its course as Apollo driving his fiery chariot, and winter being caused by Demeter mourning for the six months of Persephone's captivity in Hades, are typical of mythological stories. Even though, in their later elaborations, myths might come to deal with models of behavior and other topics commonly found in fairy tales, their origins can be found in the earliest explanations of natural phenomena. Broad definitions like Rollo May's seem to apply more clearly to myths than to fairy tales.

Folk tales and fairy tales are not as easily distinguished, as indicated by the fact that published collections of folk tales and fairy tales may very well contain some of the same stories.

A characteristic of fairy tales is the flexible way that they have been perceived by authors. Authors in different times and places have recognized that fairy tales are capable of carrying a message that can be tailored to fit their particular needs. Existing as they do in the common domain, fairy tales and their characters provide an easily accessible medium for both writers and their audience. The task of the audience is eased by the familiarity of the characters and situations with which they are presented, and the writer's burden is lightened as he brings stories from an earlier time into conformity with the standards he is trying to represent. The subtle or obvious manner in which a fairy tale departs from its audiences' expectations, while still fulfilling their desires, is a measure of its successful telling. A current example of this phenomenon is the bestseller *Women Who Run With the Wolves*,[49] in which many fairy tales are retold with an emphasis on their pertinence to the modern female experience.

Fairy tales are also significant in the wide range of characters and situations that may be found in them. Children are presented characters that they can identify with in fairy tales—commonly in the guise of a child not unlike him or herself—who is faced with an adverse situation in which he or she is called upon to make new judgments and exhibit mature behaviors. Children can be exposed to a range of novel situations through the fairy tale, and exposed to models for their own behavior to fit a variety of needs. The most popular fairy tales, especially, have always adapted as adult perceptions of children's needs have changed, and adult needs to communicate various lessons to children have changed.[50]

In distinction to fairy tales, folk tales often concern the actions of pseudo-historical or typical personages who are engaged in activities that represent cultural standards that children are expected to aspire to. The unerring accuracy of William Tell is related in a folk tale, as is George Washington's chopping down of the cherry tree and his precocious, unwavering honesty. The adventures of Paul Bunyan and his gigantic blue ox, Babe, are folk tales that recast popular stories from the era of the westward expansion of the United States as "tall tales" with a common, main character.

It cannot be maintained, as Bettelheim's definition suggests, that a fairy tale invariably holds the promise of a happy ending. The Little Mermaid, which is a definite fairy tale, has been subjected to a great of distortion, or "artistic license," to produce a happy ending. At the conclusion of the tale as Hans Christian Andersen originally wrote it, the Little Mermaid chooses death for herself rather than murdering the Prince, which would have enabled her to regain her form as a mermaid. The only consolation for the Little Mermaid, who had already sacrificed her home, family, and voice to pursue her love for the mortal, human Prince, is, that after performing deeds of kindness for three hundred years as a "daughter of the air," she might gain a human soul and join the Prince in heaven. The very morning that the Little Mermaid sacrifices herself and spares the Prince, he marries a princess from another land whom he mistakenly believes had rescued him from drowning, when actually the Little Mermaid had saved him. Only in Disney's version does the Little Mermaid manage to displace the "other woman" and

marry the Prince. Disney justifies this alteration by casting the evil sea-witch in disguise as the other princess.

The classic fairy tale "Bluebeard" also presents a problematic ending. In this fairy tale, one of three sisters marries a wealthy but mysterious man, distinguished primarily by a beard of blue color. After the wedding, the wife is given access to all Bluebeard's possessions, but she is forbidden to use one small golden key. When she inevitably opens the door the key unlocks, she discovers the bloody bodies of Bluebeard's previous wives. When Bluebeard discovers his wife's transgression, he prepares to add her to his collection. At the last moment, the wife is saved by the sudden appearance of her brothers, who hack her husband into pieces before her eyes. The happiness of the ending of this tale must be considered more one of degree; although the latest wife did not meet the fate of her predecessors, is it really a happy ending to have your brothers murder your husband? This tale also leaves unresolved the dilemma of the wife's part in the action. Her disobedience is a necessary part of the story, yet there is no clear resolution to this issue. The fast and easy way to conclude a fairy tale is to recite "and they lived happily ever after," yet when one takes a close look at fairy tales there are many which do not have a "perfect" ending.

The Future of Fairy Tales

When folk and fairy tales existed solely in an oral medium, every storyteller was able to tell a version of a story that was personalized by the demands of his or her time, place and audience. When stories came to exist more exclusively in printed form, they began to reflect more enduringly the nature of the time and place in which they were recorded. For this reason, it is especially odd that we continue to read to our children—often without the slightest degree of critical reflection—unrevised versions of stories that are imbued with the values of a different time and place. L. Frank Baum, the originator of the tales of the Land of Oz (1900), recognized this predicament, and recommended that it was time for a new set of 'wonder tales,' and that previous fairy tales should be classed as 'historical.'[51]

There is a growing perception that children are capable of having an understanding of dying and death as natural processes, and that the lifelong relationship a person has to dying and death is based in no small measure on the experiences of childhood. In the last twenty years, there has been a revolution in the practices and perceptions surrounding dying and death, yet little has been effectively done to transmit these changes to children. Adults are beginning to recognize the difficulties they have experienced as a result of being sheltered from an awareness of mortality and the need is felt for a way to transmit a realistic awareness of mortality to children.

Denoting traditional fairy tales as 'historical' would help distinguish the changes in values and behaviors that have occurred in the many years since they were recorded, and would encourage parents and teachers to more critically examine just what they are presenting to children. Modern editions of fairy tales have enormous appeal, demonstrated by the lavishly illustrated editions that have been offered recently by some of the large publishing houses. It is interesting to note that reviews of these books have concentrated on the beauty of the illustrations, the size of the book, the quality of the paper… in other words on everything but the content. The assumption seems to be that the buying public already knows what the content is and that no explanation is necessary.

But it is important to consider the implications of fairy tales in our modern world. Perhaps it is time to begin transforming them to reflect the tremendous changes that have occurred in a world increasingly forced to accept the limits of medical technology, where death is being acknowledged again as a necessary and inevitable counterpart to life.

Reading with a child is a wonderful activity; introducing someone to the world of books is to offer them the promise of a greater and better world. Fairy tales can be an important part of this process, because their "real" existence is in the imagination of a child. Through the action of a fairy tale a child can learn that he or she can confront circumstances that are new or frightening and be able to do the right thing. It is important that the tales we tell to our children reflect what we ourselves believe. Rather than continuing to insulate children from the realities of death and dying—especially by providing the unsuitable types of messages that Saturday morning T.V. provides—fairy tales can provide a medium for children to be introduced to the types of situations that they will encounter all their lives.

One of the few activities that haven't changed since the eras of our parents and grandparents is tucking a child into bed with a story, even down to the story we might choose to read. There is a comfort in this nostalgia, and a sense of continuity to this activity that can make all involved believe in the truth of the final "… and they lived happily ever after." A cartoon in a recent edition of *the New Yorker* magazine illustrated this, while also showing the capacity fairy tales have to portray facets of the world that are not necessarily easy to explain. The cartoon showed a mother reading a bedtime story to her daughter with the caption, "She married and then divorced, and then she married and divorced, and then she married and lived happily ever after."

Although this cartoon was certainly intended to be ironic, it still points out the purpose of providing moral instruction that fairy tales can fulfill. With the expanding use of hospice programs and the corresponding increase in opportunities for children to be exposed to meaningful death experiences, and the increase of the awareness of the lethalness of AIDS, it is important that even the tales told to children come to reflect current perceptions of dying and death.

Notes

1. De Spelder, Lynne A. & Strickland, Albert L. 1983. *The Last Dance*. Palo Alto, CA: Mayfield Publishing.

2. Lamers, E. P. 1986. The dying child in the classroom. In G. H. Paterson (Ed.), *Children and Death* (pp. 175–186). London: King's College.

3. Lamers, E. P. 1986. The dying child in the classroom. In G. H. Paterson (Ed.), *Children and Death* (pp. 175–186). London: King's College.

4. *McGuffey's Eclectic Readers* (Vols. 2–6) (1920). New York: Van Nostrand.

5. Wordsworth, William. We Are Seven, *McGuffey's Eclectic Readers* (Vols. 2–6) (1920). New York: Van Nostrand, Third Reader, p. 163.

6. Waller, Edmund. Old Age and Death, *McGuffey's Eclectic Readers* (Vols. 2–6) (1920). New York: Van Nostrand. Sixth Reader, p. 95.

7. Dickens, Charles. The Death of Little Nell, *McGuffey's Eclectic Readers* (Vols. 2–6) (1920). New York: Van Nostrand. Sixth Reader, p. 96.

8. Gray, Thomas. Elegy in a County Churchyard, *McGuffey's Eclectic Readers* (Vols. 2–6) (1920). New York: Van Nostrand. Sixth Reader, p. 108.

9. Browning, Elizabeth Barrett. He Giveth His Beloved Sleep, *McGuffey's Eclectic Readers* (Vols. 2–6) (1920). New York: Van Nostrand, Sixth Reader, p. 195.

10. Anonymous, My Mother's Grave. *McGuffey's Eclectic Readers* (Vols. 2–6) (1920). New York: Van Nostrand, Fourth Reader, p. 253.

11. A basal reader is a text with which reading is taught. There are many different series, each usually having one book per grade level.

12. White, E. B. 1952. *Charlotte's Web*. New York: Harper & Row.

13. Alcott, Louisa M. 1947. *Little Women*. New York: Grosset & Dunlop, (originally pub. 1869), p. 464.

14. Douglas, Anne. 1988. *The Feminization of American Culture*. New York: Anchor Press. "The Domestication of Death," p. 200–226.

15. Brown, Margaret W. 1965. *The Dead Bird*. Reading, MA: Addison-Wesley.

16. White, E. B. 1952. *Charlotte's Web*. New York: Harper & Row.

17. Guth, D. L. 1976. *Letters of E. B. White*. New York: Harper & Row, p. 531.

18. Kubler-Ross, E. 1969. *On Death and Dying*. New York: Macmillan.

19. Newton, F. I. 1990. *Children and the Funeral Ritual: Factors that Affect Their Attendance and Participation,* Masters Thesis, California State University, Chico.

20. Encyclopaedia Britannica. 1976. Children's Literature, Macropaedia, Vol. 4, p. 229.

21. Perrault, Charles. *La Belle au Bois Dormant* (Sleeping Beauty). In Mulherin, Jennifer (Ed.). 1982. *Favorite Fairy Tales*. London: Granada Publishing, p. 12.

22. Perrault, Charles. *Le Petit Chapeon Rouge* (Little Red Riding Hood). In Mulherin, Jennifer (Ed.). 1982. *Favorite Fairy Tales*. London: Granada Publishing, p. 22.

23. Perrault, Charles. *Les Fees* (Toads and Diamonds). In Mulherin, Jennifer (Ed.). 1982. *Favorite Fairy Tales*. London: Granada Publishing, p. 52.

24. Tatar, Maria. 1992. *Off With Their Heads! Fairytales and the Culture of Childhood.* Princeton, NJ: Princeton University Press. p. 9.

25. Johnson, Clifton. 1963. *Old-Time Schools and School Books.* New York: Dover (reprint of the Macmillan 1904 edition), p. 16.

26. Newbery, John. 1744. *A Little Pretty Pocket Book.* Encyclopaedia Britannica (1976), Children's Literature, Macropaedia, Vol. 4, p. 231.

27. Jordan, William. 1991. *Divorce Among the Gulls,* New York: Harper Collins, p. 169.

28. Janeway, James. *A Token for Children: Being an Account of the Conversion, Holy and Exemplary Lives, and Joyful Deaths of Several Young Children* (1671–72). In Tatar, Maria. 1992. *Off With Their Heads! Fairytales and the Culture of Childhood.* Princeton, NJ: Princeton University Press, p. 14.

29. Tatar, Maria. 1992. *Off With Their Heads! Fairytales and the Culture of Childhood.* Princeton, NJ: Princeton University Press, p. 14–15.

30. Tatar, Maria. 1992. *Off With Their Heads! Fairytales and the Culture of Childhood.* Princeton, NJ: Princeton University Press, p. 87.

31. Boorstin, D. J. 1992. *The Creators.* New York: Random House, p. 573.

32. Freud, S. The Interpretation of Dreams, Vol. 4 of the Standard Edition, trans. James Strachery (London: Hogarth, 1953), p. 254. In Tatar, *Off With Their Heads! Fairytales and the Culture of Childhood.* Princeton, NJ: Princeton University Press, p. 46.

33. Tatar, Maria. 1992. *Off With Their Heads! Fairytales and the Culture of Childhood.* Princeton, NJ: Princeton University Press, p. 46.

34. Tatar, Maria. 1992. *Off With Their Heads! Fairytales and the Culture of Childhood.* Princeton, NJ: Princeton University Press, p. 7.

35. Owens, L. 1981. *The Complete Brothers Grimm Fairy Tales.* New York: Avenel, p. 57.

36. Tatar, Maria. 1992. *Off With Their Heads! Fairytales and the Culture of Childhood.* Princeton, NJ: Princeton University Press, p. 34.

37. Rybcznski, Witold. 1987. *Home: A Short History of an Idea.* New York: Penguin, p. 28.

38. Rybcznski, Witold. 1987. *Home: A Short History of an Idea.* New York: Penguin, p. 38.

39. Mulherin, Jennifer (Ed.). 1982. *Favorite Fairy Tales.* London: Granada Publishing, p. 22.

40. Tatar, Maria. 1992. *Off With Their Heads! Fairytales and the Culture of Childhood.* Princeton, NJ: Princeton University Press, p. 37.

41. Owens, Lily. (Ed.) 1981. *The Complete Brothers Grimm Fairy Tales.* New York: Avenel Books, p. 109.

42. Owens, Lily. (Ed.) 1981. *The Complete Brothers Grimm Fairy Tales.* New York: Avenel Books, p. 112.

43. Tatar, Maria. 1992. *Off With Their Heads! Fairytales and the Culture of Childhood.* Princeton, NJ: Princeton University Press, p. 39.

44. 1933. *Old Favorite Fairy Tales,* National Publishing Co., p. 20.

45. May, Rollo. 1992. *The Cry for Myth.* New York: Delta, p. 196.

46. Bettelheim, Bruno. 1977. *The Uses of Enchantment.* New York: Vintage Books, p. 26.

47. Kolbenschlag, Madonna. 1981. *Kiss Sleeping Beauty Good-Bye.* New York: Bantam, p. 2.

48. Krupp, Edwin C. 1991. *Beyond the Blue Horizon: Myths and Legends of the Sun, Moon, Stars, and Planets.* New York: Harper Collins, p. 11.

49. Estés, Clarissa P. 1992. *Women Who Run With the Wolves.* New York: Ballantine Books.

50. Tucker, Nicholas. 1982. *The Child and the Book.* New York: Cambridge, p. 80.

51. Tatar, Maria. 1992. *Off With Their Heads! Fairytales and the Culture of Childhood.* Princeton, NJ: Princeton University Press, p. 19.

Books about Death for Children and Young Adults

The following list of books is a sample of general books (fiction and non-fiction) about death available for children.

Non-fiction:

Bernstein, Joanne, & Gullo, Stephen J., *When People Die,* New York: Dutton, 1977.
Le Shan, Eda J., *Learning to Say Good-by: When a Parent Dies,* New York: Macmillan, 1976.
Richter, Elizabeth, *Losing Someone You Love. When a Brother or Sister Dies,* New York: Putnam's, 1986.
Rofes, Eric E. & The Unit at Fayerweather Street School, *The Kids' Book About Death and Dying,* Boston: Little, Brown & Co., 1985.
Segerberg, Osborn, Jr., *Living With Death,* New York: Dutton, 1976.
Stein, Sara B., *About Dying,* New York: Walker, 1974.
Zim, Herbert, & Bleeker, Sonia, *Life and Death,* New York: Morrow, 1970.

Fiction:

Alcott, Lousia M., *Little Women,* New York: Grosset & Dunlop, 1947. (originally pub. 1869) (sister—illness)
Alexander, Sue, *Nadia the Willful,* New York: Pantheon, 1983. (brother—accidental)
Aliki, *Two of Them,* New York: Greenwillow, 1979. (grandfather—old age)
Bartoli, Jennifer, *Nonna,* New York: Harvey House, 1975. (grandmother—natural death)
Blume, Judy, *Tiger Eyes,* Scarsdale, NY: Bradbury, 1981. (father—murdered in robbery)
Brown, Margaret W., *The Dead Bird,* Reading, MA: Addison-Wesley, 1965. (wild bird—natural death)
Bunting, Eve, *The Empty Window,* New York: Frederick Warne, 1980. (friend—illness)
Coerr, Eleanor, *Sadako and the Thousand Paper Cranes,* New York: Putnam, 1977. (Hiroshima—leukemia caused by radiation)
Craven, Margaret, *I Heard the Owl Call My Name,* New York: Doubleday, 1973. (young priest—illness)

de Paola, Tomie, *Nana Upstairs and Nana Downstairs,* New York: Putnam, 1973. (great-grandmother and grandmother—natural death)

Douglas, Eileen, *Rachel and the Upside Down Heart,* Los Angeles: Price, Stern, Sloan, 1990. (father—heart attack)

Gerstein, Mordicai, *The Mountains of Tibet,* New York: Harper & Row, 1987. (reincarnation)

Hermes, Patricia, *You Shouldn't Have to Say Good-bye,* New York: Harcourt, 1982. (mother—illness)

Hickman, Martha W., *Last Week My Brother Anthony Died,* Nashville, TN: Abingdon, 1984. (infant brother—congenital heart condition)

Kantrowitz, Mildred, *When Violet Died,* New York: Parent's Magazine Press, 1973. (pet bird—natural death)

Mann, Peggy, *There Are Two Kinds of Terrible,* New York: Doubleday, 1977. (mother—illness)

Miles, Miska, *Annie and the Old One,* Boston: Little, Brown, 1971. (Navajo Indians—grandmother—natural death)

Paterson, Katherine, *Bridge to Terabithia,* New York: Crowell, 1977. (friend—accidental death)

Saint Exupery, Antoine de, *The Little Prince,* New York: Harcourt, 1943. (death—general)

Smith, Doris B., *A Taste of Blackberries,* New York: Crowell, 1973. (friend—bee sting allergy)

Talbert, Marc, *Dead Birds Singing,* Boston: Little, Brown, 1985.(mother, sister—car accident)

Tobias, Tobi, *Petey,* New York: Putman, 1978. (gerbil—illness)

Varley, Susan, *Badger's Parting Gifts,* New York: Lothrop, Lee & Shepard, 1984. (personified animals—remembering someone after death)

Viorst, Judith, *The Tenth Good Thing About Barney,* New York: Atheneum, 1971. (pet cat—natural death)

Warburg, Sandol Stoddard, *Growing Time,* Boston: Houghton Mifflin, 1969. (pet dog—natural death)

White, E. B., *Charlotte's Web,* New York: Harper & Row, 1952. (death as a natural consequence of life)

Wilhelm, Hans, *I'll Always Love You,* New York: Crown, 1985. (pet dog—natural death)

Williams, Margery, *The Velveteen Rabbit,* New York: Holt, Rinehart & Winston, 1983 edition. (life and death—general)

Zolotow, Charlotte, *My Grandson Lew,* New York: Harper & Row, 1974. (grandfather—remembering him)

This article also appeared as a chapter in *Awareness of Mortality,* J. Kauffman (ed.), Baywood, Amityville, New York, 1995.

Edited version of an article originally appearing in *Omega,*. Vol. 31, No. 2, 1995 © by Elizabeth P. Lamers. Reprinted by permission of the author.

Terrorism, trauma, and children: What can we do?

By Linda Goldman

"I never knew grief could feel so much like fear."

—C. S. LEWIS

On September 11, 2001, our children, either directly or vicariously, witnessed the terrorist assault upon our nation, watching over and over again as fanatics crashed American planes into the World Trade Center, the Pentagon, and the fields of Pennsylvania. Our young people witnessed adults running frantically out of control, jumping blindly out of windows, screaming, crying, and appearing bewildered—through black smoke-filled skies and burning buildings—as an insidious and non-locatable enemy emerged to wreak pandemonium and panic upon their lives. The media acted as a surrogate parent and extended family *before* this horrific event, and shared with our children *during* this event visually, aurally, and viscerally. These were sounds and images so graphic that they will forever be imprinted upon their psyche and ours. This unprecedented horror is now a traumatic overlay, potentially triggering all of the pre-existing grief-related issues that our children were carrying before September 11.

Death-related tragedies involving suicide, homicide, and AIDS, and non-death-related traumas such as bullying and victimization, divorce and separation, foster care and abandonment, violence and abuse, drugs and alcohol, and sexuality and gender identification had left many youth living their lives with overwhelmed feelings and distracted thoughts. After September 11, these issues still prevail, infused with the paradigm of terrorism, war, biological destruction, and nuclear annihilation—ideas that are entirely new for our children, for whom "war" is part of a history lesson. In the adult world our children look to for security and comfort, they now see or sense a world of terror, panic, and anxiety, with too many questions and too few answers about their future.

Children processing their grief and trauma may not necessarily progress in a linear way through typical grief phases. The four phases of grief are shock and disbelief, searching and yearning, disorganization and despair, and rebuilding and healing (*Life and Loss,* 2002). These phases may surface and resurface in varying order, intensity, and duration. Grief and trauma work can be messy, with waves of feelings and thoughts flowing through children when they least expect them to come. Kids can be unsuspectingly hit with "grief and trauma bullets" in the car listening to a song or the news, seeing or hearing an airplane overhead, or watching the video of the New York devastation or the Pentagon crash. A fireman's siren, a jet fighter, a soldier in military uniform, a letter in the mailbox, or a balloon bursting can trigger sudden intense feelings without any warning.

Children's voices

Children's reactions to terrorism, war, anthrax, and the perceived loss of safety and protection provide a window into their psyches and help suggest ways the adults around them can help. Our ability to listen to questions, thoughts, and feelings is paramount in creating a safe zone for our children to process these life-changing times.

Children normally assume they live in a friendly, safe, and caring world. The terrorist attacks of September 11 amplified the pre-existing signs that their world is unprotected, scary, and contains an uncertain future. This deepened loss of the assumptive world of safety for our children creates a new set of voices that all parents, educators, and health professionals must heed.

Five-year-old Tommy, after sitting and listening to his Mom's careful explanation about the terrorist attack, explained why he was really upset about the terrorism: "This is a real tragedy, because I kept searching and searching all day and couldn't find any of my cartoons on TV."

Talking to children about terrorism, trauma, and war

One question weighing heavily on the minds of parents, educators, and mental health professionals is "How do we talk to our children about war, terrorism, prejudice, biochemical attack, and nuclear destruction?"

Sometimes it may help to ask children if they have been "thinking about world events" and if they are, open a dialogue. Some children don't want to talk about it. Some live in fear they will be killed, others say there is nothing to worry about. Some may want to know the facts; therefore we need to choose words

"If the terrorists can crash into the World Trade Centers and the Pentagon, they can crash into a regular house like mine!"

Darian, age 6, illustrates his fear for his own safety after September 11.

mize the scope of the tragedy, without contemplating with them what did or may happen.

Keeping explanations developmentally appropriate allows children to process this experience at their own level. Young elementary school children need simple information balanced with reassurance that trustworthy adults are bringing stability to their day-to-day life. Middle school children may seek out more facts and want to know more about what is being done to keep them safe and healthy at home, school, and in the community. High school students may outspokenly voice opinions about what happened and why, and may need to develop ways to combat terrorism, rationalize war, and prevent world annihilation. (Adapted from National Association of School Psychologists, NASP, www.nasponline.org.)

Telling children the truth in an age-appropriate way is very important. They often have a conscious or unconscious knowledge of events happening around them and can sense the impact of the terrorist trauma on the adult world. One mom shared just such an experience in the car with her four-year-old son, Andy. She was "sneaking" a listen to the news on the day of the attack. As the reporter began talking about the destruction of the World Trade Center, she quickly turned it off so Andy couldn't hear. Andy immediately explained his level of awareness: "Mommy, they are talking about the plane crash that blew up buildings today."

He just knew about it. If Andy had then been told his experience wasn't real, he may have begun to doubt himself and/or the adult world and question his mother's truthfulness. If Andy felt his mom was hiding the truth about what happened, he might worry more, thinking his mom was too afraid to tell him what really happened. Either way, Andy may have another loss—the loss of the trust in the adult world. Teachable moments for all children can evolve with teachers and parents on subjects such as bullying, violence, prejudice, sexual discrimination, and conflict resolution.

It's OK to let children know you are upset and worried too. Using mature modeling of this upset and worry can create examples for children to follow. It's often hard for them to reconcile a message of "Don't worry; everything is fine" with the enormity of anxiety they may feel coming from the adult world. Find out what they may know about the traumatic event, remembering that they may process what they see and hear inaccurately. Search for faulty perceptions and replace these with simple truths. Young children usually worry about their immediate environment, their family and friends and pets, and their ongoing day-to-day routine. Kids may worry something will happen to their dog, their home, or their friend.

that will help them understand what is happening around them. Because so many of us feel "it's just too big," we need to be able to discuss each piece of this huge experience a little at a time. The following are examples of definitions helpful to initiate dialogue with children.

Terrorism is an act or acts of violence, abuse, murder, or devastation against unsuspecting people and countries by a person or group of people that believe their cause is more important than human life or property. Their feeling of "being right" is sometimes more important to them than their own lives. Terrorists can be big or small, black or white, or any color, American or foreign. Their goal is to create terror, disruption, and vulnerability.

Trauma is an experience that can be scary and difficult. It may create feelings of fear, anger, rage, and revenge. A trauma can be a death of someone close to use, caused by a car accident or a terrorist bombing. It can also be from knowing something scary that happened on TV, or to someone we know, or even to a stranger we see on a news video.

Creating dialogues

When creating dialogues with children, use accurate, real, and age-appropriate language, avoiding clichés or denial of their experience. Concentrate on giving the facts, and keep responses to questions simple and age-appropriate. This helps adults follow the lead of children as to how much information they choose to take in. Especially with young children, mini-

Prepare children for dialogue

Reassure children that what they are feeling is very common. Emphasize to them that adults are feeling the same things that they are. Remind them that everyone has different ways of showing their feelings and that is OK. Restore confidence by reassuring them that problems are being handled, people who were hurt are being cared for, buildings are being cleared, and that things are getting a little better each day.

Helping our children grieve can only help the grieving child in each one of us.

Mature modeling guides children to create responsible ways to be helpful during the crisis. Emphasize ways that adults can help. Parents can volunteer to give blood, food, time, and money. Relief agencies such as the Red Cross issued appeals for help. Contributions of needed goods and family money can be taken to needy areas. Children can be included in planning ways families can help and joining in delivering food and clothing. Families and schools may want to join together in saying a prayer for the victims that were attacked, for their families, and for world leaders to bring about peace.

Accept children's reactions

While there are several commonly seen reactions to trauma in children, these reactions range widely. Some children will listen to your explanation and then go out to play. Others will want to stay near you and talk about it for a length of time, or maybe ask you to drive them to school instead of taking the bus. Still others may be angry that adults can't immediately fix the problem.

Children can use many activities to safely tell their story. Props like firefighter and police hats, doctor kits, toy soldiers, and hand puppets can be used to reenact the tragedy and war. Toys, puppets, art, clay modeling, collage, letter writing, journaling, and other projective play can be used for role-play and expression of emotions. Positive visualizations and breathing exercises can help kids to relax.

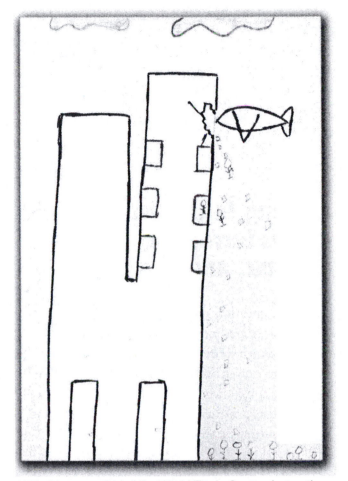

With this recreation of the World Trade Center destruction, 13-year-old Tiara illustrates her grief over the horrific footage she viewed on TV.

Activities to help children participate in world events

Children can create rituals that allow commemoration and avenues to voice feelings. Lighting candles, planting flowers, writing letters, raising money for victims, or saying prayers for survivors or world peace allow children to be recognized mourners. Thirteen-year-old Helen lived in a New Jersey community where many families, especially those of firefighters and police, had been deeply affected by the World Trade Center disaster. "Let's make brownies," she told her younger brother and sister, "and sell them to raise money for the firefighters. Everybody likes brownies."

Communities can involve children in participating in fundraisers for the survivors of terrorist attacks. Making patriotic pins and selling them to raise money to help victims and survivors, creating Web sites for world peace, or having a poster contest at school on "What We Can Do to Feel Safe" are ways to give children back a sense of control and participation in their own lives.

What kids can do about terrorism

1. Talk about their feelings. Allow children ways to tell their story as much as they need to. Draw pictures, create poems, write letters, or offer suggestions about ways to help.

2. Make a fear box. Cut out pictures from newspapers and magazines about what frightens them and paste these around the box. Write down their fears and put them inside.

3. Create a worry list. Make a list of worries from 1 to 5; number 1 is the biggest. Suggest that children talk about this list with someone they trust, like their mom or dad, their sister or brother, their guidance counselor, or a good friend.

4. Put together a "peaceful box." Ask kids to find toys, stuffed animals, and pictures that make them feel safe and peaceful, and keep these items in the box.

5. Help others. Help boys and girls give food or clothing to people who need it. Suggest that the family donate money to a good cause, like the Red Cross, the fund for victims and survivors of terrorist action, or the children in Afghanistan.

6. Display an American flag and create an original global flag. Children can place these flags together outside their house to remind everyone of their support for their country and their hope for world peace.

7. As a family, say a nightly prayer and light a candle for world peace.

Helping our children grieve

We are now a nation and a world of grieving, traumatized children, and the terror of bullying lives inside most of us on this planet and threateningly looms over our everyday life. Our children fear terrorism from foreign strangers and bullying from well-known classmates, siblings, and adult figures. If we can help our kids to see the relationship between terrorist attacks, bullying behaviors, and issues of power and control, we can begin rooting out the behaviors that create oppression, prejudice, misguided rage, and destruction of people and property as a justification for a cause or self-serving purpose.

Responsible adults need to help children cope with trauma and loss and grief from the terrorists outside their country and the bullying within their homes, schools, and community. Providing information, understanding, and skills on these essential issues may well aid them in becoming more compassionate, caring human beings and thereby increase their chances of living in a future world of inner and outer peace.

When the crisis interventions have passed, we will need extensive training in schools and universities to prepare to work with kids in the context of a new paradigm of trauma and grief. Educators, parents, health professionals, and all caring adults must become advocates in creating understanding and procedures to work with our children facing a present and future so different from their past. Our task is to help our children stay connected to their feelings during the continuing trauma of terrorism and war.

The terrorist attack has transformed us all into a global community joining together to re-instill protection and a sense of safety for America and for the world. Helping our children grieve can only help the grieving child in each one of us.

Read more about children and complicated grief issues in Linda Goldman's book Breaking the Silence: A Guide to Help Children With Complicated Grief/Suicide, Homicide, AIDS, Violence, and Abuse *(Taylor and Francis, 2002). To contact Linda Goldman, e-mail her at lgold@erols.com or visit her Web site at www.erols.com/lgold.*

From *Healing*, Spring 2002, pp. 1-4. © 2002 by Linda Goldman. Reprinted by permission of the author.

Helping Teenagers Cope with Grief

Each year thousands of teenagers experience the death of someone they love. When a parent, sibling, friend or relative dies, teens feel the overwhelming loss of someone who helped shape their fragile self-identities. And these feelings about the death become a part of their lives forever.

Caring adults, whether parents, teachers, counselors or friends, can help teens during this time. If adults are open, honest and loving, experiencing the loss of someone loved can be a chance for young people to learn about both the joy and pain that comes from caring deeply for others.

Many Teens Are Told To "Be Strong"

Sad to say, many adults who lack understanding of their experience discourage teens from sharing their grief. Bereaved teens give out all kinds of signs that they are struggling with complex feelings, yet are often pressured to act as they are doing better than they really are.

When a parent dies, many teens are told to "be strong" and "carry on" for the surviving parent. They may not know if they will survive themselves let alone be able to support someone else. Obviously, these kinds of conflicts hinder the "work of mourning".

Teen Years Can Be Naturally Difficult

Teens are no longer children, yet neither are they adults. With the exception of infancy, no developmental period is so filled with change as adolescence. Leaving the security of childhood, the adolescent begins the process of separation from parents. The death of a parent or sibling, then, can be a particularly devastating experience during this already difficult period.

At the same time the bereaved teen is confronted by the death of someone loved, he or she also faces psychological, physiological and academic pressures. While teens may begin to look like "men" or "women", they will still need consistent and compassionate support as they do the work of mourning, because physical development does not always equal emotional maturity.

Teens Often Experience Sudden Deaths

The grief that teens experience often comes suddenly and unexpectedly. A parent may die of a sudden heart attack, a brother or sister may be killed in an auto accident, or a friend may commit suicide. The very nature of these deaths often results in a prolonged and heightened sense of unreality.

Support May Be Lacking

Many people assume that adolescents have supportive friends and family who will be continually available to them. In reality, this may not be true at all. The lack of available support often relates to the social expectations placed on the teen.

They are usually expected to be "grown up" and support other members of the family, particularly a surviving parent and/or younger brothers and sisters.

Many teens have been told, "now, you will have to take care of your family." When an adolescent feels a responsibility to "care for the family", he or she does not have the opportunity—or the permission to mourn.

Sometimes we assume that teenagers will find comfort from their peers. But when it comes to death, this may not be true. It seems that unless friends have experienced grief themselves, they project their own feelings of helplessness by ignoring the subject of loss entirely.

Relationship Conflicts May Exist

As teens strive for their independence, relationship conflicts with family members often occur. A normal, though trying way in which teens separate from their parents is by going through a period of devaluation.

If a parent dies while the adolescent is emotionally and physically pushing the parent away, there is often a sense of guilt and "unfinished business". While the need to create distance is normal we can easily see how this complicates the experience of mourning.

Signs a Teen May Need Extra Help

As we have discussed, there are many reasons why healthy grieving can be especially difficult for teenagers. Some grieving teens may even behave in ways that seem inappropriate or frightening. Be on the watch for:

- symptoms of chronic depression, sleeping difficulties, restlessness and low self esteem
- academic failure or indifference to school-related activities
- deterioration of relationships with family and friends
- risk-taking behaviors such as drug and alcohol abuse, fighting, and sexual experimentation
- denying pain while at the same time acting overly strong or mature.

To help a teen who is having a particularly hard time with his or her loss, explore the full spectrum of helping services in your community. School counselors, church groups and private therapists are appropriates resources for some young people, while others may just need a little more time and attention from caring adults like you. The important thing is that you help the grieving teen find safe and nurturing emotional outlets at this difficult time.

Caring Adult's Role

How adults respond when someone loved dies has a major effect on the way teens react to the death. Sometimes adults don't want to talk about the death, assuming that by doing so, young people will be spared some of the pain and sadness. However, the reality is very simple: teens grieve anyway.

Teens often need caring adults to confirm that it's all right to be sad and to feel a multitude of emotions when someone they love dies. They also usually need help understanding that the hurt they feel now won't last forever. When ignored, teens may suffer more from feeling isolated than from the actual death itself. Worse yet, they feel all alone in their grief.

Be Aware of Support Groups

Peer support groups are one of the best ways to help bereaved teens heal. They are allowed and encouraged to tell their stories as much, and as often, as they like. In this setting most will be willing to acknowledge that death has resulted in their life being forever changed. You may be able to help teens find such a group. This practical effort on your part will be appreciated.

Understanding the Importance of the Loss

Remember that the death of someone loved is a shattering experience for an adolescent. As a result of this death, the teen's life is under reconstruction. Consider the significance of the loss and be gentle and compassionate in all of your helping efforts.

Grief is complex. It will vary from teen to teen. Caring adults need to communicate to children that this feeling is not one to be ashamed of or hide. Instead, grief is a natural expression of love for the person who died.

For caring adults, the challenge is clear: teenagers do not choose between grieving and not grieving; adults, on the other hand, do have a choice—to help or not to help teens cope with grief.

With love and understanding, adults can support teens through this vulnerable time and help make the experience a valuable part of a teen's personal growth and development.

Dr. Alan D. Wolfelt is a noted author, educator and practicing clinical thanatologist. He serves as Director of the Center for Loss and Life Transition in Fort Collins, Colorado and is on the faculty at the University of Colorado Medical School in the Department of Family Medicine. As a leading authority in the field of thanatology, Dr. Wolfelt is known internationally for his outstanding work in the areas of adult and childhood grief. Among his publications are the books, *Death and Grief: A Guide For Clergy, Helping Children Cope With Grief and Interpersonal Skills Training: A Handbook for Funeral Home Staffs*. In addition, he writes the "Children and Grief" column for Bereavement magazine and is a regular contributor to the journal Thanatos.

Trends in Causes of Death Among the Elderly

By Nadine R. Sahyoun, Ph.D., RD
  Harold Lentzner, Ph.D.
  Donna Hoyert, Ph.D.
  Kristen N. Robinson, Ph.D.

Highlights

The leading causes of death among the elderly are chronic diseases, notably cardiovascular disease and cancer. Other major causes of death include:

- Chronic respiratory diseases such as emphysema and chronic bronchitis
- Diseases common among the elderly such as Alzheimer's and renal diseases
- Infectious diseases and injuries

Significant trends in mortality among the elderly have emerged:

- Death from heart disease and atherosclerosis has declined dramatically for all groups.
- Death from cancer decreased for men in the 1990's after increasing in the previous 2 decades.
- Hypertension declined among older white men, but drastically increased among older black men.
- Biomedical advances, public health initiatives, and social changes may reduce mortality and increase longevity.

Overview

Since 1900, life expectancy in the United States has dramatically increased, and the principal causes of death have changed. At the beginning of the 20th century, many Americans died young. Most did not live past the age of 65, their lives often abruptly ended by one of a variety of deadly infectious diseases. But over time, death rates dropped at all ages, most dramatically for the young. By the dawn of the 21st century, the vast majority of children born in any given year could expect to live through childhood and into their eighth decade or beyond.

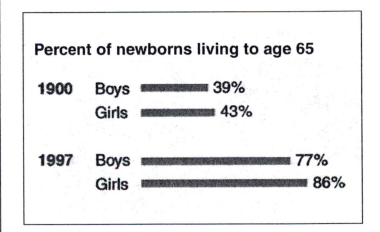

Percent of newborns living to age 65

1900 Boys 39%
      Girls 43%

1997 Boys 77%
      Girls 86%

Life expectancy has increased, but will the expansion continue?

For those born in the second half of the 20th century, chronic diseases replaced acute infections as the major causes of death. Today, death in the United States is largely reserved for the elderly. Roughly three-fourths of all deaths are at ages 65 and older.

Will we see major advances in life expectancies in the 21st century? Experts disagree. Some say we cannot continue to reduce mortality at the oldest ages without making dramatic and unforeseen medical advances against such major killers as cardiovascular disease and cancer.[1-3] But others counter that it is not only possible—other societies like Japan have already achieved significantly higher life expectancies—but likely as we reap the benefits of a more robust, better educated population taking better care of themselves and using modern medical technologies and therapies.[4-7]

Top 3 leading causes of death in the United States

1900's
Pneumonia & Influenza
Tuberculosis
Diarrhea & Enteritis

30% of all deaths

1990's
Heart Disease
Cancer
Stroke

60% of all deaths

Countries with highest life expectancy, 1995

Men		Women	
Japan	76.4 yrs.	Japan	82.9 yrs.
Sweden	76.2	France	82.6
Israel	75.3	Switzerland	81.9
Canada	75.2	Sweden	81.6
Switzerland	75.1	Spain	81.5
Greece	75.1	Canada	81.2
Australia	75.0	Australia	80.9
Norway	74.9	Italy	80.8
Netherlands	74.6	Norway	80.7
Italy	74.4	Netherlands	80.4

Life expectancy in the U.S. was 72.5 yrs. for men and 78.9 yrs. for women.

Quality of life is an important concern

Perhaps a more pressing question is this: If we succeed in extending life expectancy, what will these added years bring? Will they be spent in active, productive, fulfilling endeavors, or will they be overshadowed by declining health, loss of memory, and lingering illness? How valuable is a longer life if we simply increase the time we spend functionally limited by such debilitating ailments as heart disease, osteoporosis, or Alzheimer's disease?

As we face the challenge of extending and improving life, we must be aware of trends in important measures of health, so that we identify the most effective ways to use resources to achieve these goals. Specifically, we should be familiar with trends in:

- Elderly mortality and the leading causes of death
- Quality of life including measures of illness and disability
- Factors associated with healthy aging
- The cost of illness

This new series of reports features information to help monitor the health of our aging population

Older Americans can expect to live longer than ever before. Under existing conditions, women who live to age 65 can expect to live about 19 years longer, men about 16 years longer. Whether the added years at the end of the life cycle are healthy, enjoyable, and productive depends, in part, upon preventing and controlling a number of chronic diseases and conditions.

This report is one of a series undertaken by the National Center for Health Statistics, with support from the National Institute on Aging, to help meet the challenge of extending and improving life. By monitoring the health of the elderly, using information compiled from a variety of sources, we hope to help focus research on the most effective ways to use resources and craft health policy.

What are the leading causes of death?

Chronic diseases are the leading causes of death

Heart disease and cancer have been the two leading causes of death among persons 65 years of age and older for the past 2 decades, accounting for nearly a million deaths (995,187) in 1997. Over one-third (35 percent) of all deaths are due to heart disease, including heart attacks and chronic ischemic heart disease. Cancer accounted for about one fifth (22 percent) of all deaths.

Other important chronic diseases among persons 65 years of age and older include stroke (cerebrovascular disease), chronic obstructive pulmonary diseases, diabetes, and pneumonia and influenza.

The leading causes of death are the same for different age-race-sex groups, but their ranking order varies. Heart disease remains the leading cause of death for most of the groups. Cancer is as common as heart disease within the youngest age group, 65–74 years of age, but decreases in importance with age, ranking third among women 85 years of age and older.

The third leading cause of death is most often stroke. However, among white men and women 65–74 years old, the third leading cause is chronic obstructive pulmonary diseases and allied conditions (COPD), which includes chronic bronchitis, emphysema, asthma, and other chronic respiratory diseases. Deaths from COPD are believed to be caused primarily by cigarette smoking. COPD ranks as the fourth or fifth cause of death for almost all other age-race-sex groups. The remaining leading causes vary in rank among different age, race, and sex groups.

Elderly decedents frequently suffer from more than one life-threatening condition at the time of death. It is sometimes difficult for the attending physician or other official charged with filling out the death certificate to

Leading causes of deaths for persons 65 years of age and older

White	Black	American Indian	Asian or Pacific Islander	Hispanic
1. Heart Disease	Heart Disease	Heart Disease	Heart Disease	Heart Disease
2. Cancer	Cancer	Cancer	Cancer	Cancer
3. Stroke	Stroke	Diabetes	Stroke	Stroke
4. COPD	Diabetes	Stroke	Pneu/Influenza	COPD
5. Pneu/Influenza	Pneu/Influenza	COPD	COPD	Pneu/Influenza

identify the initiating cause among several grave conditions. While a single cause, known as the underlying cause of death, is used in nearly all statistical reporting systems, the death certificate also allows for the listing of other causes in addition to a single underlying cause—up to 20 diseases and conditions.

Other major causes of death among the elderly include Alzheimer's disease and renal diseases

Alzheimer's disease and several important renal diseases (including nephritis, nephrotic syndrome, and nephrosis) have gained importance as causes of death among the elderly over the past 2 decades. Alzheimer's disease is now among the 10 leading causes of death for older white persons, but not for other racial groups. This cause of death increased significantly from 1979 to 1988, stabilized for a few years, and gradually increased after 1992.[8] The increase may be due to improvements in diagnosis and reporting of Alzheimer's disease, wider knowledge of the condition within the medical community, and other unidentifiable factors. This disease became a ranked condition in 1994.

Nephritis, nephrotic syndrome, and nephrosis ranks between sixth and tenth as a cause of death. It is a relatively more common cause of death among black than among white persons.

Older adults are vulnerable to common infectious diseases

Although infectious diseases are no longer the most common causes of death, pneumonia, influenza, and septicemia remain among the top causes of death. They were responsible for 5.5 percent or 95,640 deaths of people 65 years of age and older in 1997. However, the role infectious diseases play in declining health and mortality is not fully apparent. This is because several other medical conditions caused by infectious diseases, such as endocarditis and rheumatic heart disease, are classified as diseases of the heart despite their infectious origins. A study of deaths attributed to diseases known to be caused by infectious organisms showed a 25 percent increase in mortality between 1980 and 1992 for persons 65 years of age and older.[9]

The combined death rate from pneumonia and influenza has increased in recent years for all age-race-sex groups. This increase may be partly due to the higher tendency by medical certifiers to record pneumonia as the underlying cause of death with advancing age. But it also may reflect an increase in the severity of pneumonia, attributed to changes in the population at risk of contracting pneumonia or other respiratory pathogens, the increasing occurrence of drug-resistant microorganisms, and the detection of new respiratory infections.[10]

Pneumonia is now one of the most serious infections in elderly persons, especially among women and the oldest old. In a study of nursing home-acquired pneumonia patients, pneumonia resulted in death among 40 percent of individuals who required hospitalization.[11]

Septicemia ranks as the sixth leading cause of death for black women 85 years of age and older, but is less important for other demographic groups. This disease is nonspecific and often occurs as a consequence of other bacterial infections of the urinary tract, skin, or respiratory system.

Injuries remain a major cause of death well into old age

Death from injury is the leading cause of death among children and young adults. And although its relative importance decreases among the elderly, it remains a frequent cause of death among people 65 years of age and older (2 percent, or 31,400 deaths in 1997). Injuries from motor vehicle crashes, firearms, suffocation, and falls account for most deaths.

What are the significant trends?

Important changes in mortality have occurred over 2 decades

Between 1979–81 and 1995–97, the death rate from all causes decreased among persons 65–74 years of age (by 6 percent for women and 19 percent for men) and those 75–84 years of age (by 8 percent for women and 16 percent for men). The death rate increased slightly for women 85 years of age and older, but declined by about 3 percent for men of the same age. Among all three age groups, the decrease has been much greater for men.

Circulatory diseases have declined

A primary reason for the overall decline in mortality is the decrease in the death rate for heart disease and stroke. Heart disease declined by 30–40 percent for both women and men ages 65–74 and 75–84; stroke declined by about 35–40 percent for men and women in the same two age groups. Declines at the oldest age group for heart disease and stroke were more modest, but still significant (heart disease, 14 percent for women and 19 percent for men; stroke, 27 percent for women and 29 percent for men).

For the two racial groups examined, diseases of the heart decreased at a slower rate for black than for white persons (20 vs 37 percent for ages 65–74; 16 vs 32 percent for ages 75–84; and 8 vs 18 percent for ages 85+). The decline in stroke followed a similar pattern with the reduction more modest among the black population.

The decrease in mortality from atherosclerosis is striking

Death from atherosclerosis, which includes arteriosclerosis or "hardening of the arteries," has dropped over 2 decades for all age, sex, and racial groups. In 1979, atherosclerosis ranked as one of the top five causes of death, especially within the oldest age group. As an underlying cause, this disease declined over the years so that today it does not even rank among the top 10 leading causes of death for most age groups.

Such a drastic decline in atherosclerosis may reflect both a decrease in incidence over time and a change in reporting practice. Atherosclerosis is now frequently regarded as a preclinical process or a risk factor so the condition may have been recorded less frequently over time as physicians choose a more specific cause of death.[12]

Cancer rates among men decreased in the 1990's

Since 1990, there has been an overall downward trend among white men 65–74 (3 percent decline) and 75–84 years of age (6 percent) and among black men 65–74 (9 percent) and 75–84 years of age (2 percent), although the trend varies greatly by type of cancer. This decrease does not hold among women or the oldest old. For example, respiratory and intrathoracic cancer (largely lung cancer) increased until 1990 and then decreased among white men 65–84 years of age. But it continued to increase among black men, the oldest old, and all women. Breast cancer increased until 1990 and then stabilized among white women 65–84 years old; it continued to increase among the oldest group of white women and among black women over 75 years of age.

Chronic bronchitis, emphysema, and other COPD conditions increased as causes of death, especially among women

Nonspecific or undifferentiated chronic lung disease is the largest contributor to the increase in COPD; emphysema has also increased among women. The increase is more pronounced among older age groups, particularly women, and among black persons. Although research points to a true increase in COPD over time, a portion of this increase may be artificial and could be the result of changes in reporting practices.

Deaths from motor vehicle injuries and suicide

Deaths from motor vehicle injuries decreased over time for white men except the oldest old, but there was no common trend among older black men. Motor vehicle deaths increased for older white women, but remained the same for black women. The number of deaths from suicide and homicide has remained relatively small, although suicides increased by about 25 percent from 4,500 in 1981 to 5,700 in 1997. The rate of suicide is higher for elderly white men than for any other age group, including teenagers.

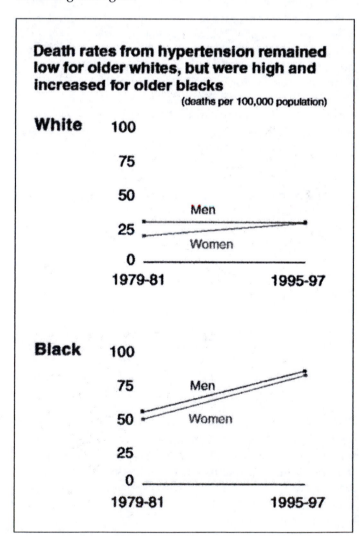

Death rates from hypertension remained low for older whites, but were high and increased for older blacks

(deaths per 100,000 population)

Hypertension mortality declined among white men, but drastically increased among older black men of all ages

When we examine the data by race and age, the differences are striking. Between 1979–81 and 1995–97, mortality from hypertension decreased among older white men (75–84 and 85+ years particularly), but dramatically increased among older black men. Similarly, although mortality from hypertension increased among older white women, the increase was much greater among older black women.

What are the possibilities for future progress?

Biomedical breakthroughs, technological advances, public health initiatives, and social changes may reduce mortality and increase the length of life

While most advances in life expectancy are the measured consequence of advances in social and economic well-being, biomedical science, and public health, scientific and medical breakthroughs have, at times, brought impressive gains over a short period. For example, in the late 19th and early 20th centuries, death from infectious diseases plummeted after the discovery of the germ theory of disease and the broad public health initiatives that followed. Could we be entering such a breakthrough period today? Could emerging medical technologies drawn from new scientific discoveries dramatically reduce or postpone deaths at older ages from such major killers as heart disease, cancer, and respiratory diseases and thus increase life expectancy? Or will the move toward a longer life expectancy be more deliberate?

Since mortality from any one cause of death may fluctuate from year to year, we averaged the death rate over 3 years and compared rates for 1979–81 to those for 1995–97 to obtain the percent change.

For heart disease, advances in prevention and treatment offer the hope that death rates will continue to decline. Adopting healthy lifestyles (such as reasonable physical activity, a balanced diet, and stable lean body weight) that are known to reduce risk factors for heart disease may not be magic bullets, but should reduce the onset of circulatory problems, particularly if all segments of the population accept them. Developments in treating heart disease, including aspirin therapies, antibiotics, and more effective emergency and surgical procedures, may well reduce or delay deaths from heart disease.

For cancer, a better understanding of the genetics of cancer (the goal of the Cancer Genome Anatomy Project) may lead eventually to new prevention strategies, targeted screening, or better treatment regimes.[13] Recently approved hormonal treatments for breast cancer may reduce or delay mortality,[14] and gene therapies offer hope that prostate cancer can be effectively treated.[15]

In general, we may expect real changes to continue to come through broader and slower avenues. As knowledge of disease etiology and medical technology progresses at a rapid pace, the multi-pronged approach of public health education, screening, and early intervention and treatment of disease could yield positive results. Because chronic diseases are the result of a long process, it takes time to reap the benefits of efforts made now.

But unbroken progress toward lengthening our life span is not inevitable. Elderly persons, like children, are particularly vulnerable to epidemics. A major epidemic such as influenza or disease-resistant strains of gastrointestinal infections could produce a sharp increase in mortality among the frail elderly and at least temporarily halt the progress in life expectancy. Public health surveillance of known and emerging infections is critical to the long-term health of our aging population.

Moreover, meaningful reductions in mortality, even at the older ages, require reductions in the racial, class, and rural/urban disparities that influence health and well-being.

Improved quality of life?

There is concern that extending life will merely increase the number of years in declining health. Many wonder, for example, whether an improvement in treating potentially fatal heart attacks or strokes will simply lengthen the survival of persons who are physically incapacitated, cognitively impaired, or emotionally distraught. This unhappy scenario, coupled with an unparalleled growth in the population of older persons (projected to reach 70 million by the year 2030), would place severe demands on our health care system as more people spend more years of life chronically disabled.

However, recent findings on levels of disability obtained from several large national surveys suggest that in addition to living longer lives, our noninstutionalized elderly may now be stronger, healthier, and better able to care for themselves.[16,17]

More about the multiple-cause-of-death system

Good public health policies depend on complete information. By considering not just the single underlying cause of death listed on the death certificate, but also the other accompanying health problems listed on the certificate—the comorbid conditions—we arrive at a much more complete picture of the true cause of death. These comorbid conditions may play as important a role in contributing to death as the underlying cause, especially among the elderly. Understanding their role is necessary if additional advances if life expectancy are to be made.

What happens when we switch to this approach? A number of diseases are more likely to be identified as comorbid conditions present at the time of death rather than as the underlying cause. Of these, the most important are:

Diabetes: In 1996 the multiple-cause death rate for diabetes was about 3.3 times higher than the underlying cause rate for older decedents. This means that while approximately 153,000 decedents had diabetes on their death certificate, only about 46,400 had the disease listed as the underlying cause. Many adults develop noninsulin-dependent diabetes mellitus (NIDDM) as they age; the disease can cause weight loss, vision deficits, increased susceptibility to infections, and coma leading to death if the diabetes is not controlled. According to death certificates, roughly 70 percent of all elderly diabetics who died also had heart disease, and in about half of those deaths, heart disease was listed as the underlying cause of death.

COPD: The conditions categorized as COPD (chronic obstructive pulmonary diseases) are more likely to be listed as contributing conditions than as the underlying cause of death; the multiple cause of death rate is over twice the underlying cause rate. In 1996, approximately 203,300 elderly decedents had a chronic respiratory disease listed on the death certificate. Nearly 40 percent of these decedents had heart disease or malignant neoplasms listed as the underlying cause of death.

Atherosclerosis: Atherosclerosis is now rarely mentioned as the underlying cause of death, although the disease is a precursor of circulatory diseases that are the major causes of death. Over 71,000 elderly persons had atherosclerosis listed as a cause of death, more than 4.5 times the number who had the disease listed as the underlying cause.

About the data

Information on mortality comes from death certificates collected by the States and forwarded to NCHS for processing and publishing. Geographic coverage has been complete since 1933, and the high quality and availability of the data (and variety of social, economic, and health factors) have made death rates the best barometer of the health and well-being of a population. However, all data collection systems have limitations, and some of these limitations must be considered when using information to estimate levels and trends of cause-specific mortality in older persons. Here are three examples.

First, changes in coding conventions, in the death certification format or in the training of those who fill out the death certificates may lead to discontinuities in trends in cause of death. For example, when attending physicians, coroners, and funeral home directors began using the new international coding conventions (ICD-9) in 1979,

the number of deaths attributed to septicemia jumped abruptly. The level eventually stabilized after these certifiers received instructions to record more specific causes of death as the underlying cause. As another example, in 1989, after the format was changed to include more space to encourage certifiers to provide more complete information, a study found that the mortality trend for some causes of death changed significantly.[18] Similarly, diabetes as a cause of death rapidly increased after instructions on the death certification included diabetes as an example. This may have reminded certifiers to include this disease on the death certificate.

Second, death certificates for the elderly are often incomplete. The completeness of the death certificate depends on the thoroughness of the certifier and of the amount of information available. Studies show that the quality of the decedent's medical history and thus the physicians' report of underlying cause of death diminishes with the age of the deceased. This may be because medical conditions of younger decedents are more acute and directly associated with death. The incompleteness for the elderly decedents may be a particular problem for those dying in long-term care institutions where medical certification is handled with less precision, less is known about the decedents' medical histories, and less diagnostic information is available from laboratory tests and autopsy results.[19]

Third, the age on the death certificate is often incorrect for older persons. Misreporting the age of decedents has been documented (both under- and over-reporting), particularly among black decedents, and reported that the errors were greater for women than for men.[20] This results in rates that are either too high or too low.

These factors need to be considered when using mortality data, which remain the most reliable and favored indicator of public health researchers.

Notes

1. Fries JF. Aging, natural death and the compression of morbidity. New Engl. J Med. 303: 130–5, 1980.
2. Fries JF. Strategies for reduction of morbidity. Am J Clin Nutr. 55: 1257S–62S, 1992.
3. McCormick J, Skrabanek P. Coronary heart disease is not preventable by population interventions. Lancet. ii: 839–41, 1988.
4. Rothenberg R, Lentzner HR, Parker RA. Population aging patterns: the expansion of mortality. J Gerontol. 46 (2): S66–70, 1991.
5. Manton KG, Stallard E, Corder L. Changes in morbidity and chronic disability in the U.S. elderly population: evidence from the 1982, 1984, and 1989 National Long Term Care Surveys. J Gerontol. 50B (4): S194–S204, 1995.
6. Manton KG, Vaupel JW. Survival after the age of 80 in the United States, Sweden, France, England and Japan. New Engl J Med. 333 (18): 1232–5, 1995.
7. Schneider EL, Brody JA. Aging, natural death and the compression of morbidity: another view. New Engl J Med. 309 (14): 854–6, 1983.
8. Hoyert DL. Mortality trends for Alzheimer's disease, 1979–91. National Center for Health Statistics. Vital Health. 20 (28), 1996.
9. Pinner RW, Teutsch SM, Simonsen L, Klug LA, Graber JM, Clarke MJ, Berkelman RL. Trends in infectious diseases mortality in the United States. J Am Med Assoc. 275 (3): 189–93, 1996.

10. CDC. Pneumonia and influenza death rates, United States, 1979–1994. MMWR Morb Mortal Wkly Rep. 44 (28): 535–7, July 21, 1995.

11. Marrie TJ. Pneumonia. Clin Geriatr Med. 8: 721–34, 1992.

12. Hoyert DL, Rosenberg H, MacDorman MF. Effect of changes in death certificate format on cause-specific mortality trends, United States, 1979–92. Office for National Statistics. Studies on Medical and Population Subjects. 64: 47–58, 2000.

13. Sandhu JS, Keating A, Hozumi N. Human gene therapy. Crit Rev Biotechnol. 17 (4): 307–326, 1997.

14. Thurlimann B. Hormonal treatment of breast cancer: new developments. Oncology. 55 (6): 501–507, 1998.

15. Brinkmann U, Vasmatzis G, Lee B, Yerushalmi N, Essand M, Pastan I. PAGE-1 and X chromosome-linked GAGE-like gene that is expressed in normal and neoplastic prostate, testis, and uterus. Proc Natl Acad Sci USA. 95 (18): 10757–62, 1998.

16. Manton KG, Corder L, Stallard E. Chronic disability trends in elderly United States populations: 1982–1994. Proc Natl Acad Sci. 94: 2593–2598, 1997.

17. Freedman VA, Martin LG. Understanding trends in functional limitations among older Americans. Am J Public Health, 88: 1457–1462, 1998.

18. Hoyert DL, Rosenberg H, MacDorman MF. Effect of changes in death certificate format on cause-specific mortality trends. United States, 1979–82. Office for National Statistics. Studies on Medical and Population Subjects. 64: 47–58, 2000.

19. Feinlieb MF, ed. Proceedings of 1988 International Symposium on data on aging. National Center for Health Statistics. Vital Health Stat. 5 (6), 1991.

20. Elo IT, Preston SH. Estimating African-American mortality from inaccurate data. Demography. 31: 427–58, 1994.

UNIT 3
The Dying Process

Unit Selections

Key Points to Consider

- How can spirituality benefit an individual who is dying? What roles do religion and spirituality play in hospice's treatment of the dying? Religious and spiritual aspects of the dying process could not only be helpful to the dying person and family but to health care providers as well.

- Probably no one really likes to give bad news, yet physicians often must do this. Imagine you suspect that you are dying. How would you want your medical doctor to share information about your prognosis, if diagnosed with a terminal illness? Or would you prefer to not be told the bad news?

- An advanced directive informs the physician of a terminally-ill patient's wishes regarding prolonging life. What are the advantages to the patient, physician, and family members if the patient has an advanced directive? What are the advantages of having a power of attorney for health care?

- Who are the influential players in decision-making regarding hospice referrals? What part does the patient play? How pivotal is the role of physicians in suggesting hospice for their patients? Do family members have much influence on these decisions?

 **Links: www.dushkin.com/online/**
These sites are annotated in the World Wide Web pages.

American Academy of Hospice and Palliative Medicine
http://www.aahpm.org

Hospice Foundation of America
http://www.hospicefoundation.org

Hospice Hands
http://hospice-cares.com

National Prison Hospice Association
http://www.npha.org

The Zen Hospice Project
http://www.zenhospice.org

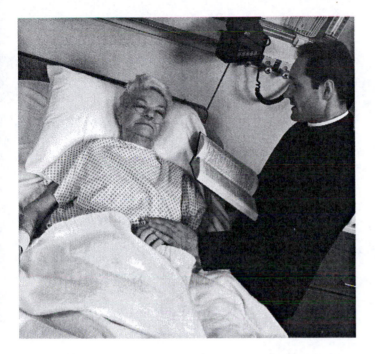

While death comes at varied ages and in differing circumstances, for most of us there will be time to reflect on our lives, our relationships, our work, and what our expectations are for the ending of that life. This is called the dying process. In recent decades, a broad range of concerns has arisen about that process and how aging, dying, and death can be confronted in ways that are enlightening, enriching, and supportive. Efforts have been made to delineate and define various stages in the process of dying so that comfort and acceptance of our inevitable death will be eased. The fear of dying may heighten significantly when actually given the prognosis of a terminal illness by one's physician. Just how physicians should inform patients of a terminal prognosis is addressed in "Dying Words." Awareness of approaching death allows us to come to grips with the profound emotional upheaval that will be experienced. Fears of the experience of dying are often more in the imagination than in reality. Yet, when the time comes and death is forecast for the very near future, it is reality, a situation that may be more fearful for some than others.

There are many and varied social, religious, and psychological responses that constitute and inform the process of dying and the supports sought can be studied and used to the benefit of all. Spiritual questions and dilemmas are significant issues, as life comes to a close, and should be focused on as we learn to care for others. Such is highlighted in "Placing Religion and Spirituality in End-of-Life Care" and "A Commentary: The Role of Religion and Spirituality at the End of Life." Key players in the drama that will unfold are physicians and nurses. The intensely personal aspects of spiritual issues, and commonly observed ignorance of them, can produce uneasiness in caregivers, both professionals and friends. Their personal attitudes and their professional roles are being examined by their professions, by the courts and legislatures, and by the public as increasingly serious attention is paid to the dying process. How do we decide on the care of the incompetent person who is dying? How do we delegate authority for end-of-life decisions and provide the comfort and assurance so needed as the end of life comes? Such dilemmas are addressed in "Patients Whose Final Wishes Go Unsaid Put Doctors in a Bind."

The process of dying can be profoundly influenced by the compassion and support of those trained to be with the dying. It is important for professional caregivers to learn the ways of comfort and compassion. It is also a challenge for family and friends to learn to be attentive to the demanding needs of those who are dying. Sensitivity to the needs we all have for love and consolation, awareness of the exquisitely personal nature of death, and willingness to attend to the difficult tasks at hand will greatly enhance the experience for all. There is also the rich reward received when the dying teach us about the richness of living for others. "Start the Conversation" explains what the dying individual will experience physically and emotionally. Moreover, the inevitable caregiving choices that must be made are clearly outlined. Quality end-of-life concerns are addressed from patients' perspectives in "Quality End-of-Life Care."

The development, since the early 1970s, of the hospice movement in the United States offers an alternative to the impersonal aspects of hospitalization. Hospice offers both home care and institutional care for the dying in a quiet environment with personal attention to the extremely intimate process of dying aa well as assurance of the relief of pain. Overwhelmingly, home care is the type hospice found in the U.S. today, yet free standing hospices are increasing, though not to the degree as in the UK. The article entitled "Hospice Referral Decisions: The Role of Physicians" discusses how hospice referrals are made and by whom. Hospice programs help the individual to have control of the process of dying, something missing in the sterile environments of hospitals.

Placing Religion and Spirituality in End-of-Life Care

Timothy P. Daaleman, DO; Larry VandeCreek, DMin

In 1995, THE SUPPORT (STUDY TO UNDERSTAND PROGNOSES and Preferences for Outcomes and Risks of Treatment) trial stimulated a reexamination of systems of care for seriously ill and dying patients.[1] This study has indirectly promoted a rapprochement among religion, spirituality, medicine, and health care.[2] The goal of a quality comfortable death is achieved by meeting a patient's physical needs and by attending to the social, psychological, and the now recognized spiritual and religious dimensions of care.[3,4] This perspective is highlighted in a recent consensus statement that includes the assessment and support of spiritual and religious well-being and management of spiritual and religious problems as core principles of professional practice and care at the end of life.[5] Yet multiple ethical and pragmatic issues arise. For example, should physicians identify patients' spiritual and religious needs and intervene in clinical settings? The roles and responsibilities of patients and physicians in this scenario are unclear. An understanding of religion and spirituality within the context of end-of-life care, quality of life, and patient-clinician interactions may illuminate the problems and potentialities for both patients and clinicians.

Religion: The Provision of Belief and the Establishment of an Ethic

The distinction between religion and spirituality is an important and nuanced one. From its Latin roots (*religio*), religion has been associated with various connotations: the totality of belief systems, an inner piety or disposition, an abstract system of ideas, and ritual practices.[6] In end-of-life care, religion and religious traditions serve 2 primary functions: the provision of a set of core beliefs about life events and the establishment of an ethical foundation for clinical decision making.[7] Religious doctrine and belief systems provide a framework for understanding the human experience of death and dying for patients, family members, and health care professionals. Intuitively, strong religious beliefs, whether expressed or privately held, should be associated with a decreased fear of death and greater acceptance of death. However, research that has examined the interaction between religious belief and attitudes toward death has produced controversial results that generally do not support this assumption.[8]

In addition, religious traditions include substantial normative and ethical issues in end-of-life care.[7] Ethics in this context spans a wide range of human interaction from interpersonal to organizational levels and represents the moral response to approaching and encountering death. Religion-based ethics provides a point of reference for clinical decision making and many religious groups, such as the National Conference of Catholic Bishops,[9] the Unitarian Universalist General Assembly,[10] and the Conservative Movement's Committee on Jewish Law and Standards,[11] actively participate in public discourse about issues that accompany the end of life (eg, palliative care, withdrawal of advanced life support, advance care planning). Although these sources provide an ethical framework for decisions at the end of life,[12] religion-based ethics can both facilitate and impede clinical decision making,[13] which reflects a dynamic interplay among patients, family members, clinicians, and institutions.

The issues of physician-assisted suicide (PAS) and euthanasia exemplify the complex interaction between religious belief and ethical decision making in end-of-life care. Recent studies have found an inverse association between measures of religiousness and attitudes toward PAS. A survey of physicians, nurses, and social workers in New York City found that respondents who had lower levels of religious belief were more willing to endorse assisted suicide than those who reported higher levels of belief.[14] This finding is consistent with a national study by Emanuel et al[15] who found that oncologists who report high or moderate levels of religious belief were less likely to perform euthanasia or PAS than those who reported no religious belief. In a national survey of US physicians representing specialties most likely to receive patient requests for assistance with suicide or euthanasia, Meier et al[16] reported that physicians who have no religious affiliation were more likely to be willing to provide assistance and to have complied with a patient request for PAS than those with a religious affiliation.

These findings parallel those from patient populations as well. A study of patients with amyotrophic lateral sclerosis living in Oregon and Washington found that respondents who scored higher on a scale measuring the importance of religion were less likely to consider assisted suicide than those with lower scores.[17] In 2 studies of older adults, the degree of self-reported strength of religious beliefs or role of religion in life was inversely proportional with more permissive attitudes toward assisted suicide.[18,19] For both patients and physicians, these studies suggest that religious belief may have a significant effect on ethical decision making at the end of life.

Spirituality: Resources for Personal Meaning

Spirituality may or may not be linked to religious beliefs, religious practices, or communities that support those practices and beliefs.[20] Terminally ill patients acknowledge a greater spiritual perspective and orientation than both nonterminally ill hospitalized patients and healthy patients.[21] Although there are multiple interpretations of spirituality within health care settings,[22] constructs of meaning or a sense of life's purpose have been suggested as primary components.[23] For example, in women with advanced breast cancer, maintaining a purpose or meaning in life has been identified as an important aspect of self-transcendence and spiritual well-being.[24,25] The coping literature delineates 2 forms of meaning: implicit meaning and found meaning.[26] Implicit meaning is an appraisal process that involves the gathering and processing of medical information.[27] Found meaning, or meaningfulness, interprets and places this information into a larger life context.[26] Antonovsky[28] describes this generally positive, pervasive way of seeing the world, and one's life in it, as a "sense of coherence," lending comprehensibility and manageability.

Psychological states and quality-of-life outcomes have been the primary end points in end-of-life care studies that have incorporated a measure of spirituality. For example, among oncology patients, modest correlations have been found between spirituality and lower levels of anxiety and psychosocial distress.[29,30] Additional studies suggest that spirituality is also positively associated with subjective well-being[21] and quality of life to the same degree as physical well-being.[31]

Quality of Life

In clinical and research settings, quality-of-life assessment examines the social, physical, and psychological influences on patient illness, health, and well-being.[32] Measures of religiousness and spirituality that are specific to end-of-life care vary in their content, validity, and reliability, which reflect the developmental state of work in this area. The McGill Quality of Life Questionnaire[33] incorporates items to assess achievement of life goals and personal meaning, while the Functional Assessment of Chronic Illness Therapy-Spiritual Well-Being[31] scale contains questions that measure the comfort and strength derived from religious faith, in addition to a sense of meaning, purpose, and peace in life. The Systems of Belief Inventory,[34] which was designed for use in quality-of-life and psychosocial research examining illness adjustment, measures religious and spiritual beliefs and practices and the social support that accompanies those beliefs and practices.

Religion and spirituality potentially can mediate quality of life by enhancing patient subjective well-being through social support and stress and coping strategies. Theoretically, religious and spiritual beliefs may enhance subjective well-being in 4 ways: promoting a salubrious personal lifestyle that is congruent with religious or personal faith traditions, providing systems of meaning and existential coherence, establishing personal relationships with a divine other, and ensuring social support and integration within a community.[35] Social support has been suggested as an intervening factor between quality of life and religion and spirituality. The positive impact of social support and support groups on survival in cancer patients generated considerable interest in the early 1990s,[36] although follow-up studies have failed to replicate earlier findings.[37] Religious and spiritual beliefs have been found to be beneficial when examined within theoretical models of stress and coping.[38] Research on religious approaches to coping and problem solving have been predictive of successful psychological adjustment to stressful life events.[39] For example, Jenkins and Pargament[40] report that cancer patients who attribute more control over their illness to God have higher self-esteem and are more adjusted to their disease state than those who do not attribute such control to God.

Patient-Clinician Interactions and Interventions

Assessment of quality of life raises some practical and ethical issues regarding the clinician's role in spiritual and religious support during end-of-life care. How do physicians and nurses frame religious and spiritual concerns within health care settings? Are religious and spiritual concerns subsumed within social and psychological constructs and domains that comprise an individual's experience of illness and disease, or are spirituality and religion conceptualized and viewed a priori? This tension is highlighted by recommendations and initiatives that incorporate religion and spirituality in plans to improve care at the end of life. For example, assessment guidelines for palliative care plans developed by the Institute of Medicine embed spiritual assessment within measures of emotional status.[41] However, a report from the Commonwealth-Cummings project lists spiritual and existential beliefs as an independent modifiable dimension of the patient's dying experience.[4]

The inconsistent orientation and lack of conceptual clarity that accompany religion and spirituality raise several secondary questions relative to the operationalization of any guideline or recommendation. Who is responsible for assessing and meeting the spiritual and religious needs of dying patients: physicians, nurses, social workers, psychologists, or clergy and health care chaplains? Some have advocated that physicians or other members of the health care team should address these issues.[42] Yet within the patient-physician relationship, physicians wield a power that is largely positive and salutary, and this power may result in a loss of patient autonomy if left unchecked or unguarded.[43] In the development of treatment goals and care plans, patient autonomy can be threatened when physicians' religious convictions are dissonant with those of patients and family members. For example, studies that measured physician religiousness and PAS support the assumption that physicians' religious belief may influence the patient-physician relationship. In light of these concerns, data from a US national survey suggest that clergy and professional pastoral care providers assume a primary role for religious and spiritual concerns in clinical settings.[44] In this survey, more than 80% of family physicians reported that they refer to these clergy and pastoral care providers in conditions associated with end-of-life care. However, if quality of life is enhanced by the search for personal meaning, should physicians and other health care professionals also incorporate these aspects in care? Would physicians' approaches differ from those of professional pastoral care providers tied to religious or faith traditions? These issues are fertile ground for future research.

Future Directions: Hospice as a Sentinel Model

The hospice movement provides a case study to examine the development of religion and spirituality within end-of-life care. The foundation of the modern hospice movement was grounded in a Western Christian religious tradition.[45] This faith tradition served a primary function for hospice by providing an ethical foundation and a set of core beliefs, initially for a small committed group of people in the United Kingdom in the 1960s. Saunders, who pioneered the hospice movement, provided much of the philosophical framework that still underlies contemporary hospice,[46] and the mission statement for one of the original hospices, St Christopher's, remains rooted within this religious tradition.[45] But as the hospice movement grew and encountered patients and health care professionals who often did not share this tradition, hospice had to accommodate and

modify its mission or risk alienating a constituency that it was founded to serve. Today hospice maintains a global approach to patient care with an emphasis on relieving suffering, but the religious basis and foundation for this care are conspicuously absent.

Religious traditions provide a framework for both individual and organizational ethics, and it is uncertain how loosening the ties of hospice to a specific religious tradition may affect the hospice ethos. For example, although the place of euthanasia and PAS is often minimized and discouraged in hospice settings,[46] recent research suggests that these organizational values may not be pervasive. In one survey of US oncologists, approximately 40% of patients were receiving hospice care at the time of euthansia or PAS,[15] while an additional study found that 32% of patients in Oregon enrolled in a hospice program requested a prescription for lethal medications.[47] Although these studies do not imply that hospice care has a waning emphasis on religious and spiritual concerns, it is unclear whether these findings represent a limitation of hospice care in individual cases, a compassionate response to the control of pain and suffering in these settings, or the fact that most hospice care is only one, albeit important, component of the patient's life and decision-making contribution.

Hospice considers the religious or spiritual dimension of the person as independent and not subsumed within social or psychological domains. The World Health Organization also holds a similar perspective and defines palliative care as

> the active total care of patients whose disease is not responsive to curative treatment... [when] control of pain, of other symptoms, and of psychological, social, and spiritual problems is paramount.[48]

The understanding of spirituality has also evolved. For example, hospice's original religious definition of spirituality as a relationship with God or a Divine Other has been replaced by a definition of spirituality as the personal and psychological search for meaning.[45] This trend is part of a larger cultural movement in the United States in which there is a transition from a traditional membership in a faith community to a spirituality of seeking.[49] The increase in quality-of-life research that includes measures of spirituality and the spiritual resources in hospice care are manifestations of the widespread acceptance of a spirituality that is uprooted from its religious sources. The distancing of religious beliefs from spirituality has facilitated a greater and necessary acceptance of hospice into a multicultural world, one in which hospice workers may move about among many different faith traditions.

Yet religion and faith traditions still occupy a substantial place in end-of-life care. From a social constructionist perspective, social determinants such as social support, education, gender, and religion are primary elements that facilitate the interpretation and understanding of death and dying.[50] In this context, religious and faith traditions may be part of the scaffolding in the construction of meaning as death approaches. Spirituality may be viewed as the actions and interactions of an embodied human actor who is facing death and creating a personally meaningful social world, a constructed world that can be either a resource or an encumbrance.[50] For hospice and palliative care this has several implications: a richer appreciation of the social and demographic determinants of a quality care at the end of life, a greater understanding of the psychological and theological processes involved in "meaning making," and an emphasis on assessment strategies and interventions that are inclusive of these factors.

When viewed from either a constructionist or phenomenological perspective, the ties that bind hospice to palliative care in the assessment and management of spiritual concerns are best understood by examining the locus of care at the end of life. Multiple connotations of hospice exist, yet many associate this term with a physical place of respite and care. In the evolution of end-of-life care and the emergence of the disciplines of palliative care, there has been a shift in the common understanding of hospice from an institution that provides care of the individual.[51] Hospice and palliative care have negotiated much of the difficult terrain that accompanies religion and spirituality and medicine, and they have done so by moving the locus of care out of biomedical institutions back into the community. By offering a health care delivery model that incorporates a community-based approach while emphasizing the uniqueness of the individual, regardless of the importance of religion or spirituality in the individual's life, hospice and palliative care provide a structure for and facilitate the processes that are involved in this most basic of human experiences, that of dying.

Funding/Support: Dr Daaleman is supported by the Robert Wood Johnson Foundation Generalist Faculty Scholars Program and the John A. Hartford Foundation. **Acknowledgment:** We thank Sarah A. Forbes, RN, PhD, for her review of the manuscript.

REFERENCES

1. SUPPORT Principal Investigators. A controlled trial to improve care for seriously ill hospitalized patients: the Study to Understand Prognoses and Preferences for Outcomes and Risks of Treatment (SUPPORT). *JAMA*. 1995;274:1591–1598.

2. Daaleman TP. A cartography of spirituality in end-of-life care. *Bioethics Forum*. 1997;13:49–52.

3. Byock R. *Dying Well: The Prospect for Growth at the End of Life*. New York, NY: Riverhead; 1997.

4. Emanuel EJ, Emanuel LL. The promise of a good death. *Lancet*. 1998;351 (suppl 2):521–529.

5. Cassel CK, Foley KM. *Principles for Care of Patients at the End of Life: An Emerging Consensus Among the Specialties of Medicine*. New York, NY: Millbank Memorial Fund; 1999.

6. Wulff DM. *Psychology of Religion: Classic and Contemporary*. New York, NY: John Wiley & Sons; 1997.

7. O'Connell LJ. Religious dimensions of dying and death. *West J Med*. 1995;163:231–235.

8. Neimeyer RA, ed. *Death Anxiety Handbook, Research, Instrumentation, and Application*. Washington, DC: Taylor & Francis; 1994.

9. National Conference of Catholic Bishops. *Ethical and Religious Directive for Catholic Health Care Services*. Washington, DC: United States Catholic Conference; 1994.

10. General Assembly of Unitarian Universalists. *The Right to Die with Dignity: Proceedings of General Assembly*. Boston, Mass: Unitarian Universalist Association; 1988.

11. Dorff E. A Jewish approach to end-stage medical care. *Conservative Judaism*. 1991;43:3–51.

12. Dubose ER. *Physician Assisted Suicide, Religious and Public Policy Perspectives*. Chicago, Ill: The Park Ridge Center; 1999.

13. Posts SG. Medical futility and the free exercise of religion. *J Law Med Ethics*. 1995;23:20–26.

14. Portenoy RK, Coyle N. Kash KM, et al. Determinants of the willingness to endorse assisted suicide, a survey of physicians, nurses, and social workers. *Psychosomatics*. 1997;38:277–287.

15. Emanuel EJ, Daniels ER, Fairclough DL, Clarridge BR. The practice of euthanasia and physician-assisted suicide in the United States. *JAMA*. 1998;280:507–513.

16. Meier DE, Emmons CA, Wallenstein S. et al. A national survey of physician-assisted suicide and euthanasia in the United States. *N Engl J Med*. 1998;338:967–973.

17. Ganzini L, Johnston WS, McFarland BH, Tolle SW, Lee MA. Attitudes of patients with amyotrophic lateral sclerosis and their care givers toward assisted suicide. *N Engl J Med*. 1998;339:967–973.

18. Seidlitz L, Duberstein PR, Cox C, Conwell Y. Attitudes of older people toward suicide and assisted suicide: an analysis of Gallup Poll findings. *J Am Geriatr Soc*. 1995;l43:993–998.

19. Sullivan M, Ormel J, Kempen GUM, Tymstra T. Beliefs concerning death, dying, and hastening death among older, functionally impaired Dutch adults: a one-year longitudinal study. *J Am Geriatr Soc*. 1998;46:1251–1257.

20. Van Ness PH. *Spirituality and the Secular Quest*. New York, NY: Continuum;1996.

21. Reed PG. Spirituality and well-being in terminally ill hospitalized adults. *Res Nurs Health*. 1987;10:335–344.

22. Larson DB, Swyers JP, McCullough ME, eds. Scientific research on spirituality and health: a consensus report. Rockville, Md: National Institute of Healthcare Research; 1998.

23. Fitchett G, Handzo G, Spiritual assessment, screening, and intervention. In: Holland JC, ed. *Psycho-oncology*. New York, NY: Oxford University Press; 1998:790–808.

24. Coward DD. The lived experience of self-transcendence in women with advanced breast cancer. *Nurs Sci Q*. 1989;3:162–169.

25. Hassey Dow K, Ferrell BR, Leigh S, et al. An evaluation of the QOL among long-term survivors of breast cancer. *Breast Cancer Res Treatment*. 1996;39:261–273.

26. Thompson SC, Janigian AS. Life schemes: a framework for understanding the search for meaning. *J Soc Clin Psychol*. 1988;7:260–280.

27. Lazarus RS, Folkman S. *Stress, Appraisal, and Coping*. New York, NY: Springer;1984.

28. Antonovsky A. *Unraveling the Mystery of Health: How People Manage Stress and Stay Well*. San Francisco, Calif: Jossey-Bass; 1987.

29. Kaczorowski JM. Spiritual well-being and anxiety in adults diagnosed with cancer. *Hospice J*. 1989;5:105–116.

30. Smith ED, Stefanek ME, Joseph MV, et al. Spiritual awareness, personal perspective on death, and psychosocial distress among cancer patients: an initial investigation. *J Psychosoc Oncol*. 1993;11:89–103.

31. Brady MJ, Peterman AH, Fitchett G, Mo M, Cella D. A case for including spirituality in quality of life measurement in oncology. *Psychooncology*. 1999;8:417–428.

32. Testa MA, Simonson DC. Assessment of quality of life outcomes. *N Engl J Med*. 1996;334:835–840.

33. Cohen SR, Mount BM, Tomas J, Mount L. Existential well-being is an important determinant of quality of life: evidence from the McGill Quality of Life Questionnaire. *Cancer*. 1996;77:576–586.

34. Holland JC, Kash KM, Passik S. et al. A brief spiritual beliefs inventory for use in quality of life research in life-threatening illness. *Psychooncology.* 1998;7:460–469.

35. Ellison CG. Religious involvement and subjective well-being. *J Health Soc Behav.* 1991;32:80–99.

36. Spiegel D, Bloom JR, Kraemer HC, Gottheil E. Effects of psychosocial treatment on survival of patients with metastatic breast cancer. *Lancet.* 1989;2:888–891.

37. Cunningham AJ, Edmonds CV, Jenkins GP, et al. A randomized controlled trail of the effects of group psychological therapy on survival in women with metastatic breast cancer. *Psychooncology.* 1998;7:508–517.

38. Krause N, Tan TV. Stress and religious involvement among older blacks. *J Gerontol.* 1989;44:S4–S13.

39. Pargament KI. *The Psychology of Religion and Coping, Theory, Research, and Practice.* New York, NY: Guilford Press; 1997.

40. Jenkins RA, Pargament KI. Cognitive appraisals in cancer patients. *Soc Sci Med.* 1988;26:625–633.

41. Institute of Medicine. *Approaching Death: Improving Care at the End-of-Life.* Washington, DC: National Academy Press; 1997.

42. Lo B, Quill T, Tulsky J, for the ACP-ASIM End-of-Life Care Consensus Panel. Discussing palliative care with patients. *Ann Intern Med.* 1999;130:744–749.

43. Brody H. *The Healer's Power.* New Haven, Conn: Yale University Press; 1992.

44. Daaleman TP, Frey B. Prevalence and patterns of physician referral to clergy and pastoral care providers. *Arch Fam Med.* 1998;7:548–553.

45. Bradshaw A. The spiritual dimension of hospice: the secularization of an ideal. *Soc Sci Med.* 1996;43:409–419.

46. Mathew LM, Scully JH. Hospice care. *Clin Geriatr Med.* 1986;2:617–634.

47. Ganzini L, Nelson HD, Schmidt TA. et al. Physician's experiences with the Oregon Death with Dignity Act. *N Engl J Med.* 2000;342:557–563.

48. World Health Organization. *Cancer Pain Relief and Palliative Care.* Geneva, Switzerland: World Health Organization; 1990. Technical Report Series 804.

49. Wuthnow R. *After Heaven: Spirituality in America Since the 1950's.* Berkeley: University of California Press; 1998.

50. Seale C. *Constructing Death, the Sociology of Dying and Bereavement.* Cambridge, England: Cambridge University Press; 1998.

51. Doyle D, Hanks G, MacDonald N, eds. *Oxford Textbook of Palliative Medicine.* Oxford, England: Oxford University Press; 1999.

Author Affiliations: Departments of Family Medicine and History & Philosophy of Medicine, Center on Aging, University of Kansas Medical Center, Kansas City (Dr Daaleman); and The Healthcare Chaplaincy, New York, NY (Dr VandeCreek). **Corresponding Author and Reprints:** Timothy P. Daaleman, DO, Department of Family Medicine, University of Kansas Medical Center, 3901 Rainbow Blvd, Kansas City, KS 66160–7370 (e-mail: tdaalema@kumc.edu).

From the *Journal of the American Medical Association,* November 15, 2000, pp. 2514-2517. © 2000 by the American Medical Association. Reprinted by permission.

ANNALS OF MEDICINE

DYING WORDS

How should doctors deliver bad news?

BY JEROME GROOPMAN

Not long ago, I had an appointment with a patient who was likely to die within a year and a half. Maxine Barlow was a twenty-eight-year-old teacher in Boston. The only child of a middle-class family, she had recently become engaged to a financial analyst, Peter Wayland (all names have been changed). One morning in the shower, Maxine found a small lump in her breast, a little larger than a pea. A biopsy showed that it was breast cancer. Further tests revealed that the cancer had spread to Maxine's spine and liver, which meant that surgery could not fully remove it, and Maxine's surgeon referred her to me for chemotherapy.

Maxine and I met on a brisk autumn afternoon. Her appointment was my last of the day, since our conversation was likely to extend beyond the hour usually allotted to new patients. I had to explain the gravity of her condition and the possible choices she could make.

After I had examined Maxine, we were joined in my office by her parents and by Peter. They sat in a semicircle facing me, with Maxine between them. I moved my chair out from behind my desk.

"Let's review what was found at surgery," I began. Maxine reached for Peter's hand. Although I addressed Maxine, I also briefly met the gaze of her parents and of Peter, in order to engage everyone." The cancer in the breast measured one and a half centimetres, about half an inch, and under the microscope the cancer cells were actively dividing,"

I said. "They should be treated aggressively. The tests we did on the tumor showed that it is not sensitive to hormones"—which ruled out Tamoxifen, a common hormone-blocker. "The scan showed that several deposits of tumor had spread from the breast to the bones in the neck. There also are four deposits in the liver. We can treat them with chemotherapy, which destroys the cancer cells wherever they might be lurking. The good news is that you stand a very strong chance of going into remission."

"So that means that she'll be O.K.?" Maxine's mother asked.

My stomach tightened in a familiar way. This part never got any easier.

"Remission does not mean cure," I said. "Remission means that all the cancer we can measure disappears. Therapy is palliative."

"What do you mean, 'palliative'?" Peter asked in a panicked voice.

"She has to be cured," Maxine's father said.

This distinction was important, and I needed to make sure, gently but unequivocally, that they understood. "There is a very good chance that we will see the metastatic deposits in your bones and liver shrink significantly, or completely melt away. But the most intensive chemotherapy or radiation available—even bone-marrow transplant—is not enough to destroy every cancer cell in your body. That is why, currently, we cannot say the cancer can be cured."

Maxine sat without speaking. Her eyes filled with tears, and I gave her some tissues.

"What is the point of treatment, then?" I asked. "Palliation. That means that even if the cancer cannot be cured it can be controlled. The best-case scenario is that the cancer becomes like a parasite," I said, purposefully invoking a stark image. "We knock it down with the therapy, and hope that it stays down for many, many months or years. You can live an active life—work, jog, travel, whatever. The bones and liver can heal. And when the cancer returns we work to knock it down again. All the while, we hold on to the hope that an experimental treatment will be found that is able to eradicate the cancer—to truly cure you."

Like Maxine, Mrs. Barlow was fighting back tears. Her husband stared at me. I paused before broaching a second critical issue.

"We talked about the best-case scenario. But we also have to acknowledge that there is a worst-case scenario."

I had found that this part of the discussion was best completed rapidly, as if removing an adhesive bandage.

"The worst-case scenario is that ultimately the cancer becomes resistant to all the treatments we have, and even experimental therapies are no use. Most people say that if they reach a point in the illness when their brain is impaired, and there is no likelihood of improving their quality of life, then nothing should be done to keep them artificially alive, through machines like respirators.It's essential, Maxine, that I know what you want done if we reach that point."

"I—I don't think I would want that," she said, haltingly.

"You mean that you would want only comfort measures to alleviate pain, and nothing done to prolong your life, like a respirator or cardiac resuscitation?"

"Yes, I think so," Maxine whispered.I nodded. This was her "end-of-life directive." I would put it in writing in her medical chart.

"We have a plan of therapy and an understanding. Now let's look on the positive side," I said, trying to spark some of the determination she would need in order to endure the months of chemotherapy ahead. "You are young, your organ function is excellent—despite the deposits of tumor, your liver is still working well, and your blood counts are fine—so there is every reason to think that you will tolerate the drugs and we will make real progress."

I smiled confidently. Maxine struggled to do the same.

"But what are the exact odds for a remission?" Peter Wayland asked. "I mean, how many patients like Maxie stay in remission and for how long, on average?"

Maxine looked at him sharply. "Dr. Groopman said that there is every reason to think I'll go into remission," she said. "What more do we need to know now?"

She turned to me, her face full of uncertainty.

This was a crucial moment in our interview. There were several ways that I could answer Peter's question. I could give the bald statistics—that more than fifty per cent of people with cancer like Maxine's die within two years—or I could put it more gently, and say that she had a chance, if a low one, of surviving for more than two years. I could even say, somewhat vaguely, that she was young and strong and had as good a chance as anyone of surviving, on the principle that she would benefit more from encouragement than from statistics. As I looked at Maxine, I sensed that she preferred neither the extreme of ignorance nor the extreme of excruciating detail but some middle ground.

"Statistics don't say anything about any particular individual, only about groups," I said. "There can be wide variability in the behavior of any cancer in each person, because each of us is different—different genetically, living in a different environment—and we metabolize the treatments differently.

"I want my patients to be informed," I said, looking now at Peter. "When Maxine said she understood there is a very good chance of remission, that is accurate. It could last months or it could last years. Putting precise numbers on it at this point doesn't really tell us anything more about Maxine. In the meantime, we need to plan for the best while acknowledging the worst."

Oncologists give bad news to patients some thirty-five times per month on average, telling a patient that he has cancer, that his tumor has come back, that his treatment has failed, that no further treatment would be helpful. And yet there is no agreement among specialists about how to deliver such news. More than forty per cent of oncologists withhold a prognosis from a patient if he or she does not ask for it or if the family requests that the patient not be told. A similar number speak in euphemisms, skirting the truth.Today, in most of Europe doctors often do not tell patients that they are dying.

Until recently, many doctors rarely informed their patients that there was nothing to be done for them; conventional wisdom had it that patients ought to be spared the anguish of knowing that they were going to die. The renowned physician Sir William Osler, who, at the turn of the last century, wrote the seminal textbook "The Principles and Practice of Medicine," emphasized the importance of keeping the patient optimistic. "It wasn't the style to be specific," Dr. David Golde, a former physician-in-chief at Memorial Sloan-Kettering Cancer Center, said of his medical training, which began in 1962. "The patient's questions and the doctor's answers—both avoided detail. And doctors never volunteered to give more information. Of course, there were no formalized end-of-life directives. The

doctor's duty to ease the path was unspoken." When I asked him what he meant by not being specific, he said, "The doctor would say, 'Yes, you have a serious disease.'"

In 1969, a book called "On Death and Dying," by Elisabeth Kübler-Ross, which later became a best-seller, made death an acceptable subject for discussion between patients and doctors for the first time. In the nineteen-eighties, cultural and political changes in America—some precipitated by AIDS—introduced the notion that a patient had a right to know everything his doctor knew. In 1993, Sherwin Nuland's book "How We Die," which won the National Book Award, described in detail the psychology and physiology of death.

As medical practice grows more sophisticated more people are living longer with the knowledge that they may be dying. Decisions made in the late stages of illness are increasingly an aspect of treatment. Dying requires emotional and physical stamina from the individual and his family. And the difficulty of negotiating all this has an effect on doctors as well as patients. A recent article reported that more than half of the oncologists interviewed say that the frequent witnessing of death leads to an overwhelming sense of fatigue and futility; the profession has one of the highest burnout rates in medicine.

Despite this, during my nine years of medical school and professional training in the nineteen-seventies, I was never instructed in how to speak about dying to a gravely ill patient and the patient's family. It was presumed that, as medical students, we learned how to deliver bad news through careful observation of our mentors, just as we learned how to lance a deep abscess by watching doctors and then trying it ourselves. But most physicians preferred to speak to their patients in private. And the subject was never raised in our classrooms.

As an oncology fellow, I began my career believing that it was essential to provide details to my patients. Sharing statistics seemed like the obvious thing to do: surely a patient should have access to everything I knew. Early on, I had a case somewhat similar to Maxine's. Claire Allen was a small, straw-haired librarian in her forties with breast cancer; she was married, with two young children. Like Maxine, she had multiple metastases to bone and liver. We met in my clinic office, and she looked at me expectantly.

"Claire, with this disease, a remission would ordinarily last three to six months," I told her bluntly. "A person could expect to survive between one to two years."

She appeared to take the news stalwartly, but I later learned from her husband that she had left the appointment deeply shaken. She told her children that she had only one Christmas left. Her face was full of despair whenever I saw her. And yet Claire lived for nearly four years. She was able to travel, work part time, and take care of her children, but was unable to stop thinking that she could die at any moment.

Chastened, I tried a different approach. Henry Gold, a short-order cook in his sixties, had acute leukemia that had resisted all treatment. At one point, he asked me what else could be done. I reassured him that there were drugs that had not yet been tried, even though I knew they were unlikely to help. When Henry started to bleed around his lungs, I had the interns drain the hemorrhage with chest tubes; I insisted that he be intubated, supported on a respirator in the I.C.U., and given numerous blood transfusions. His heart developed a dangerous arrhythmia, so I gave orders for cardiac medications and electroshock. I never asked Henry what he wanted. He stayed alive for more than a week on the respirator, a catheter in his heart, tubes in his throat, unable to speak to family and friends who had come to his bedside.

On a chilly morning two days after our first meeting, Maxine returned to the clinic for her first round of chemotherapy. She had insisted on coming alone; Peter would pick her up afterward. The chemotherapy suite is a large, open space that holds twenty or so patients receiving intravenous drugs, some behind curtains, others talking or watching television. Maxine looked at the patients she passed. Most were wearing hats or kerchiefs to cover their bald heads. Several reclined in their chairs, thin and pale, too weak to sit up. It was clear that some of them would soon die.

A half hour after Maxine's chemotherapy treatment, Peter still had not arrived. Maxine's cell phone rang. "He's tied up," she explained to me, and we arranged for a car service to take her home. When I called Maxine later that evening to see how she was doing, Peter answered the phone and told me that she was sleeping.

"She's going to die, isn't she?" he said. He explained that he had been searching the Internet, and had read that in cases like Maxine's patients survived on average eighteen months, and that a remission lasted three to six months at best.

"Peter, as I said when we met, statistics don't tell you what is going to happen to any one person, just groups."

I got off the phone as quickly as I could. There could be no "back channel" discussions with friends or family; if Maxine had wanted to, she could have logged on to the Internet.

Over the next seven months, the metastases in Maxine's bones and in her liver decreased significantly. Although she was frequently tired and lost her hair, she was able to work part time, and even took a weekend trip to Manhattan with her parents and went to Newport for a friend's wedding. Then, on a routine visit at the end of May, after her eighth month of therapy, I noticed that one of her eyes wandered, and she seemed to be tilting her head to the right.

"Are you having any trouble seeing?"

She said that sometimes it was difficult to read.

"Any double vision?"

Yes, she said, on a few occasions that week, when she was walking down stairs.

Movement of the eyes is controlled by a set of cranial nerves at the base of the skull. An initial MRI scan of the brain did not turn up anything abnormal, but scans do not always detect small deposits on the cranial nerves. I explained that a spinal tap was the best way to determine if the cancer had spread to the brain; it would allow us to search for tumor cells in the spinal fluid.

Maxine lay on her side as a medical resident performed the procedure. I tried to distract her. We talked about the Red Sox, who had started the season strong, and whether, as usual, they would end up losing games in the home stretch. After sterilizing and anesthetizing the area between the fourth and fifth lumbar vertebrae, the resident passed a fine trocar into the spinal canal. Maxine twitched. Drops of fluid fell from the trocar into a test tube that he held under it. Normal spinal fluid is clear; Maxine's was cloudy.

"It's over," I said. "Stay down for an hour, so you don't get a headache."

She asked what it meant if the cancer had gone to her cranial nerves.

I was almost certain, based on the cloudiness of the spinal fluid, that this was the case. How much did Maxine want to know?

"It is a major setback," I said.

"I'm not sure I want to ask how long a remission lasts if the cancer is in my brain," she said.

"Are you sure you want to talk about this now?"

Maxine closed her eyes and nodded.

"People usually live several weeks to a few months without any treatment," I said. "But that represents the average. There are people who live longer. Treatment with radiation and chemotherapy instilled into the spinal fluid may or may not extend life, but it can reduce some of the most annoying complications, like the double vision."

Maxine was silent. "Is it even worth being treated?" she finally asked.

"You are the only one who can answer that question," I said. "If we don't treat it, it will quickly spread to other cranial nerves and parts of the brain and spinal cord. The quality of your life would be markedly impaired. I want to help sustain as much quality of life for as long as possible."

Maxine opened her eyes.

"I don't want to die," she said, beginning to sob. "I didn't think it would happen so fast, so soon. I'm not ready to die."

"I don't want to lose you," I said. There was nothing more I could say now that would help. "Let's go step by step, and talk after the results from the spinal tap."

Later that day, I went to the pathology laboratory. Under the microscope, numerous large cells, with distorted nuclei, filled what should have been an empty field. "Carcinoma," the pathologist said.

Over the next few weeks, we began radiation treatment and a new round of chemotherapy, infused into her spinal fluid. At first, Maxine's double vision improved. But after three weeks or so she found that she couldn't move her left eye, and we put a patch over it. Shortly thereafter, the left side of her face began to droop. A second MRI showed that the cancer had spread to the membranes lining the cerebral cortex and spinal cord. It was evening when I came into Maxine's hospital room. She was watching television.

She turned to me as I switched off the TV.

"Peter left me."

I nodded, saying that I had noticed that he was not around the past few days.

"He's been seeing someone else the past three months."

I remained silent.

"I always felt, deep inside, that he was weak." Maxine paused. "No, not just weak. He's a schmuck. A real schmuck."

"Do you know what that word literally means in Yiddish?" I asked.

Maxine laughed.

I took her hand. She tried to press back, but had little force. The nerves from the cervical spinal cord were being compressed by the deposits of cancer.

"I'm not sure how much strength I have left," Maxine said. She was in a fragile condition. It was time to assess clinical issues.

"Remember once I asked you what your wishes were if we reached a point when further therapy would not improve the quality of your life?"

Maxine nodded. "So you think it's just a few days?" she asked. Her voice was hollow.

"Probably more than just a few days," I said. "Probably weeks. Or maybe longer—I've been wrong before."

"And really nothing can be done?"

Like all patients, Maxine was finding it almost impossible to give up hope.

"Nothing that I know of," I said. "And to continue to give you chemotherapy would not improve the time we have left. But anything I can do to make the time that we have left good for you, I'll do."

Maxine turned away. "How do I actually die from the cancer?"

"You lose consciousness, go into a coma, and either you stop breathing or your heart stops. But you're not aware of any of it."

She was silent as I sat holding her hand.

The first time I witnessed death was in my second year of medical school. My father had had a massive, unexpected heart attack, and I went to meet my mother at the hospital in Queens. The sheets were drenched with sweat. His eyes were filmy and repeatedly rolled upward. Coarse, grunting noises punctuated his breathing, and his chest heaved. His limbs jerked wildly. This went on for nearly half an hour, as a large clock on the wall ticked off the minutes. Then, after a last convulsion, a pink foam poured from his mouth, his head snapped back, the little color remaining in his skin drained away, and he was still.

I held my mother, numb with disbelief. The doctor on call, whom we did not know and who had stood by as we watched, closed the curtain around the bed. He looked at me holding my mother, and said weakly, "It's tough, kid."

Although I later learned that the flailing movements of my father's limbs were the result of neurological reflexes, and that he had not been conscious, I could not stop wondering if he had suffered. The ugliness of these final minutes often invades otherwise comforting memories of times we spent together. When I became a physician, I vowed that I would do everything I could to temper such gruesome experiences for the patient and for the family.

During the Middle Ages and the Renaissance, death was supposed to be met with words of welcome. This was the core of *ars moriendi*—"the art of dying." The "art" prepared and purified the person by linking his experience to Jesus' death on the Cross. Treatises like

William Caxton's, printed in 1491, instructed laymen to think about the end of life, even when they were healthy, and dictated what words they should expect to hear and say when death was near: "This time of your departing shall be better to you than the time of your birth, for now all sickness, sorrow, and trouble shall depart from you forever. Therefore be not aggrieved with your sickness and take it not with grutching but take it rather all by gladness."

Today, the physician frequently finds himself assuming a role that was once the exclusive province of religious authorities. Yet the palliative care he offers is primarily meant to ease physical suffering; he is not trained to alleviate emotional pain. In medical terms, a "good death" is a death with the least physical suffering possible. As *ars moriendi* suggests, though, there is a historical notion of a "good death" that is more complicated; it is as much about a cultivated attitude toward leaving life as it is about the physical act. Is there more, then, that physicians should do to make dying in a hospital after illness less emotionally taxing?

Last January, one of the first academic studies of how effectively oncologists communicate critical information to their patients was published. A hundred and eighteen patients cared for by nine oncologists participated in the research. The doctor-patient interactions were recorded on audiotape. The study tried to determine two things: whether the information disclosed to the patients was sufficient for them to make an informed decision about further treatment, and whether the doctor encouraged the patient's participation in choosing among treatments.

Although the oncologists knew that they were being taped, in more than a quarter of the consultations the patients were not told that their disease was incurable; a similar percentage were not informed of the side effects associated with the proposed anti-cancer therapy. Only five patients of the hundred and eighteen—some four per cent—received what the researchers considered adequate information. In nearly ninety per cent of the taped discussions, the oncologists failed to ask the patients if they understood the information being presented to them. These results are in keeping with prior research indicating that more than a third of patients with incurable metastatic cancer believe that the treatment offered by their doctors will actually cure them.

Suffering is not the only cost. Many in the medical profession have speculated that doctors' uncertainty in guiding patients through the end of life is one of the primary causes of rising health-care costs. More money is spent on care during the last weeks of life than on the months or years of care that precede it. The kinds of interventions that are routine in an intensive-care unit—pumps to sustain circulation, respirators to ventilate the lungs—cost hundreds of thousands of dollars. Some physicians don't want to acknowledge that a patient is going to die, and regularly order tests and procedures at a point when no reasonable gain can come of them. Studies show that a doctor does not shorten the life of the patient when he chooses to provide palliative rather than intensive care.

All of this is reason to change the profession's approach to end-of-life care. But change has been slow in coming. "There is every institutional barrier to palliative care," Dr. Kathleen Foley, a neuro-oncologist at Sloan-Kettering, told me. "Traditionally, oncologists are paid to give chemotherapy, not to have long conversations. In the early nineteen-nineties, a review by the American Board of Internal Medicine of training of medical residents concluded that there was a very low level of competency in dealing with these issues. And yet the National Cancer Institute has been unresponsive to the issue of palliative care. Although sixty percent of Americans who have cancer will die from it, the National Cancer Institute allocates only one per cent of its budget for research and training in palliative care. It's not welcome to talk about dying."

Dr. Diane Meier, the director of the Center to Advance Palliative Care at the Mount Sinai School of Medicine, in New York, which is funded by the Robert Wood Johnson Foundation, has been working to institutionalize palliative care for nearly a decade. When I called her in her office, she told me that there are currently seven studies showing that palliative care saves money. "It's always been the right thing to do, of course," she said, referring to the integration of palliative care into treatment.

But it was only after her foundation and others demonstrated that palliative care saves money that hospitals and insurance companies began to institutionalize such policies. According to Meier, even today what happens to people at the end of life has less to do with their wishes than with the available resources of the particular hospital and how health care is funded in this country. Many hospitals don't have palliative-care programs, for example, and so patients are often kept in an acute-care setting until the end of their lives.

The motivation to change medical practice is finally in place. Is there actually a "best approach" to telling a patient that the end of her life is near? In March, *The Journal of Clinical Oncology* published several scenarios illustrating how a doctor might handle such a situation. The article makes it clear that, until now, the medical profession, which is built on the notion of improving and refining its practices, has been painfully inept in its efforts to improve palliative care. The scenarios were based on a case similar to Maxine's. A woman treated for breast cancer that had spread to bone and liver now had regrowth of the cancer. She was married, with two young children, and her medical record did not contain an end-of-life directive.

SCENARIO ONE:

MD (*with unusual somberness*): Mrs. M, I don't think there is anything more we can do for you. I think it's time for hospice.

MRS. M (*looking frightened*): What? You mean there's nothing else?

MD: I'm sorry.

The oncologist leaves the room.

SCENARIO TWO:

MD: Mrs. M, umm, uhhh, how are you feeling?

MRS. M (*tentatively, after a pause*): I'm a bit better, thank you.

MD (*speaking quickly and cheerfully*): Well, I'd like to have the team that helps with comfort come see you. Is that all right?

MRS. M: Sure, if you think they can help.

MD: Great, I'll tell them to come by.

The physician leaves the room.

Not surprisingly, the article criticizes both approaches—the first for bluntly abandoning the patient, and the second for skirting the truth. It goes on to suggest that the physician choose a comfortable, private place, and then offers an idealized script, in which the doctor summarizes the situation ("The cancer is getting worse.... The scans showed the tumors in the liver are bigger")and asks Mrs. M what she expects will happen:

MRS. M (*thoughtful, and a bit teary*): Well, I guess I'm going to die of this cancer. (*Starting to cry more*)

MD (*sitting quietly, moves box of tissues closer to patient*):... What have you been thinking?

MRS. M: Well, I'd like it to be peaceful. I'd like to just fall asleep. And I want my husband to be able to cope, and for my children to grow up and remember me.... (*Brightening a bit*) And I'd like to go to Las Vegas one more time!

MD (*laughing*): It sounds like what you are saying is you want to make the most of the time that is left.

MRS. M: That's right.

The "successful" discussion from the oncology journal points to the obvious problem of trying to codify such practice. Today, after caring for patients with advanced cancers for more than twenty-five years, I have told nearly five hundred people that they were going to die; rarely has such a conversation gone as smoothly or the conclusion been as tidy as the journal's model. But "How not to" scenarios, like the first two in the article, may at least help prevent the kinds of blunders I made early in my career. And, as the study showed, doctors can do much more to insure that patients and their families receive sufficient information to make important decisions.

Work is now being done to identify the key problems. In 1995, the Open Society Institute sponsored an initiative called the Project on Death in America; Kathleen Foley, the neuro-oncologist from Sloan-Kettering, is its director. "The purpose is to educate physicians, nurses, and social workers who will provide leadership in academic hospitals," she told me. It's not clear what "leadership" means in this context, and when I asked how effective such measures were, she said, "We know that the current generation doesn't know how to do this well. But if the role models know it we hope for a domino effect that will make it easier for the next generation."

The Open Society Institute will have spent forty-five million dollars on education by the end of next year, and the palliative-care center supported by the Robert Wood Johnson Foundation, where Diane Meier works, has spent a hundred and forty million dollars on advancing palliative care over the past decade. These efforts have resulted in changes to the profession. Since the late nineteen-nineties, Foley told me, "the American Board of Internal Medicine has required demonstration of a level of competency in palliative care and symptom management." As part of medical training, an actor will go through a script with a resident, who must demonstrate his or her ability to guide the person through decision-making—such as coming to an end-of-life directive and coming up with a plan for pain management.

After I talked with Maxine, I arranged for her to be transferred to a special hospice unit, and soon she began to drift in and out of consciousness. The cancer pressing on the cranial nerves connected to the back of her throat and her tongue had made it difficult for her to swallow. The nurses had to suction her saliva to prevent her from choking. Shortly before noon a week later, I was paged and told that Maxine's death appeared imminent.

Maxine's parents were sitting by her bed when I came in. They stood up, and Mrs. Barlow hugged me, crying. Mr. Barlow's face was frozen with grief.

Maxine was no longer conscious. Every few seconds, her chest heaved, and she gasped. She was entering what is called the agonal phase—taken from the Greek agon, which means struggle—a period that precedes death and can last from a few minutes to hours.

I warned Maxine's parents that this was usually harrowing, and that sometimes family members preferred not to witness it.

"I want to be with my baby," Maxine's mother said.

Maxine's hands began to twitch and her breathing moved into a syncopated pattern called Cheyne-Stokes, a short set of staccato breaths bracketing a long pause.

Mrs. Barlow raised her head.

"Maxie, we love you, and God loves you."

Mr. Barlow sat straight, his hands clasped in his lap.

Sometimes as a patient dies there is a convulsive burst of muscular activity, like a grand-mal seizure. I braced myself for it when Maxine's fingers began to twitch, as if she were grasping for an invisible object. These muscle contractions continued for some forty minutes. Then a harsh rattling sound came from her chest. I glanced at the nurse, who was next to the morphine infusion. There was a single explosive jerk of Maxine's body, a sharp arching of her chest, followed by a series of fluttering movements in the muscles of her neck.

The Barlows stood up. Maxine's skin was already changing to an ashen hue. I placed my stethoscope over her heart. "I am sorry," the nurse said. I reached over and took Mr. Barlow's hand, and then turned and embraced Mrs. Barlow as she cried.

I left the Barlows and went to the nurses' station to fill out Maxine's death certificate. I designated the primary cause as respiratory failure due to metastatic breast cancer to the brain and handed the chart with the death certificate to the floor clerk. The time of death was 12:57 P.M.

Originally appeared in *The New Yorker,* October 28, 2002, pp. 62-70. © 2002 by the William Morris Agency, Inc. Reprinted by permission.

Patients Whose Final Wishes Go Unsaid Put Doctors in a Bind

By N. R. KLEINFIELD

"Do you know your name?" the doctor asked.

The man knew his name.

"How old are you?" the doctor said.

He thought and thought, then offered, "About 59."

He was in his 80's.

"What month is it?"

"February." It was late June, in the 90's, so sweltering that someone had just arrived with heat stroke.

"Do you know where you are?"

"In New York City," he said. "Across from South Ferry."

He was in the Bellevue Hospital Center emergency room, a long way from South Ferry, amid a bleating chorus of voices. He had been brought in from a nursing home because of a seizure scare. Quickly, he was swallowed up by the constellation of procedures necessary to assess his condition—needles in his veins, an EKG, a CAT scan, anti-seizure medication. On and on.

Patients like the elderly man show up virtually every day in the Bellevue emergency room, and with increasing frequency at hospitals throughout the country, sometimes in even more dire condition, unable to speak or move. Doctors find themselves wrestling with what to do with such damaged individuals. The marvels of modern medicine have generated a swelling population of nursing home patients in demented states, riddled with disease, not competent to decide what more they want from doctors and their machines.

As was true of this man, few have done planning to specify what, if any, additional care they desire as their lives tick away, and they can no longer be reached. Many have no close relatives to speak on their behalf.

As the country ages and the ranks of the demented expand, the problem looms ever larger. It is particularly persistent in New York, which has a poor record of persuading people to adopt advance health care directives and has one of the strictest laws in the country on when doctors can stop healing.

"They send these patients to us to treat, and we do them a disservice," said Dr. Lewis R. Goldfrank, the director of the Bellevue emergency room. "We do things for them I wouldn't do for my own mother. The problem is, we don't know how to die in America."

Dr. Goldfrank was dismayed that the elderly man was there. "There's nothing I can offer this man," he said. "But when he gets here, I have to do something." Of the broader problem, he said, "This is not illegal, but it's abuse. It's legal abuse of patients."

The man that day had severe dementia, existing in some ghostly nether land between life and death. He had arrived from the Coler-Goldwater nursing home on Roosevelt Island. If many patients like this could communicate their wishes, Dr. Goldfrank says, they would just want to be left alone, spared further suffering and the indignity of grueling procedures to assure their health.

These cases feed end-of-life futility debates among doctors and those who care for the elderly.

Joan M. Teno is a professor of community health and medicine at Brown University Medical School whose research focus is how older, frail people who are dying are cared for in this country. "What happens to the unrepresented person in the nursing home is a humongous problem that we haven't really dealt with," she said.

Ms. Teno said that government numbers for 1999, the latest available, indicate that nationwide only 35 percent of people with severe cognitive impairment have an advance directive. Kentucky has the best record, she said, with about two-thirds of its severely impaired population with advance directives, and Mississippi is worst, with 12 percent. New York State stands at 26 percent.

State law varies and is often murky on how much flexibility doctors have in treating ailments of demented or vegetative patients whose desires are unknown. New York law requires that doctors have "clear and convincing" evidence of a patient's wishes before withholding treatment. Doctors say that in practice, this means that if someone has done no advance planning, they usually feel compelled to do all they can.

Many doctors would like New York law relaxed so they have more say in situations they deem futile. But that enters immensely complex and controversial territory. When is care futile? What are the features of a life worth prolonging? As Dr. Maureen A. Gang, an attending doctor in the Bellevue emergency department, put it, "Grandma might have profound dementia. But a relative might say, 'Grandma seems very happy when she watches Mister Rogers. She giggles.' How do you decide what value to put on that life?"

Both doctors and advocates for the elderly agree that if more people specified their desires earlier, then significantly more people would get only the care they want at life's end. Ms. Teno said doctors do a poor job of discussing advance directives with patients, and said she feels the country would benefit from a sizable public awareness campaign.

Dr. Eric Manheimer, Bellevue's medical director, said: "There is a wide recognition in the medical community that it's a large and urgent problem that's not going to go away. It's sometimes hidden from people until it happens to someone in their family."

This tension is lived out every day at Bellevue. A close relationship exists between Bellevue and Coler-Goldwater Specialty Hospital & Nursing Facility, both part of the Health and Hospital Corporation. Bellevue is the primary emergency room that serves the patients of Coler-Goldwater, an acute care facility on Roosevelt Island that has 1,400 nursing home beds filled with the very ill.

Dr. Goldfrank estimates that his emergency room averages two patients a day from Coler-Goldwater for which care is given that he feels is futile and harmful.

"In the old days, we used to say that pneumonia was the friend of the old man," Dr. Goldfrank said. "It would get him out of this mess."

In the modern world, an advance directive is the friend of the old person. But most don't have one.

For Dr. Wendy Huang, the case that really got to her was the old woman and the legs.

Last August, a woman in her 80's arrived at Bellevue from Coler-Goldwater. She had severe dementia, was bedbound, had no relatives or advance directive. She had been sent over because of a fever. Her feet had developed gangrene.

Dr. Huang, a third-year resident in emergency medicine, treated her. Dr. Goldfrank was the attending physician. He recognized that she would die without surgery on her legs. But he also concluded she would die soon even with the surgery. He saw no point. But he felt he had no choice but to refer her to the surgery department. It decided to amputate both her legs below the knee. Several days later, while still in the hospital, she died.

"I didn't see how we were going to improve anything by amputating her legs," Dr. Huang said. "I thought it was more humane to just give her antibiotics. I thought the outcome would have been the same."

She talked to Dr. Goldfrank about the experience, and that led to conversations between Bellevue and Coler-Goldwater about these end-of-life cases. Both places want to increase the number of advance directives. Paperwork itself, the doctors said, was sometimes erratically transmitted, and directives that did exist were not updated.

Susi Vassallo, another attending doctor in the E.R., said, "Going to the hospital is not necessarily a humane activity." She mentioned that almost all of these elderly patients are "hard sticks," meaning it is difficult to get a needle into a vein to draw blood. Sometimes, doctors have to do a deeper stick in the neck or chest—a riskier and more painful procedure.

Dr. Gregory Mints, who is in Bellevue's medicine department, mentioned a man who is treated frequently. He had tried to hang himself and wound up in a vegetative state, unable to move or talk. He has no family or advance directive. He arrives with infections, gets treated, goes back, returns.

"He can't communicate," Dr. Mints said. "For all practical purposes, he is dead. Rats, you know, die of kidney failure. Humans die of heart attacks. That's the common way we die. We have the technology to fix the heart, so as a result

we rot. We just rot away. These people come here and, in many cases, we have to torture some of them."

Dr. Yolanda Bruno, the medical director at Coler-Goldwater, said that she and the Coler-Goldwater doctors feel the same as the Bellevue doctors—frustrated.

Roughly half of the Coler-Goldwater patients have cognitive dysfunction, and the vast majority have no advance directive and often no close relative.

About a year and a half ago, Dr. Bruno said, Coler-Goldwater systematically tried to raise the number of advance directives among its lucid patients. She said the proportion was significantly increased. Most of these, though, were Do Not Resuscitate orders that stop doctors from trying to revive them if they go into cardiac arrest. But those orders do not otherwise allow doctors to withhold medical care. Only a small fraction would agree to broader directives.

"Most of the people in the nursing facility who have decision-making capability don't want advance directives," Dr. Bruno said. "We found they didn't want to think about it."

Getting people to draft advance directives is a formidable undertaking. It compels people to imagine what state of life they would accept, to contemplate debilitating illness and damaged minds, in essence, to address the unthinkable.

Even when you assign a surrogate, the complexity does not end. For cultural reasons, some people are unwilling to give up on life, no matter what. Doctors speak of relatives who keep demented individuals alive to collect pensions. One doctor told of the ex-wife of a demented man who was his health care proxy. The divorce had been bitter. It was clear to the doctor that she wanted him subjected to all the care that was available—stick him all you wish. She wanted him to suffer as long as possible.

And so the ambulances wheel in the patients. Their bodies get worked over so they can live another day or another month or another year in a world most people can not reach or fathom.

As was the case of the elderly man who arrived at the emergency room thinking it was a hot day in February.

Dr. Goldfrank discussed the case with a neurology resident, who said there was nothing to do for him and suggested that they "load him and send him back."

Dr. Goldfrank admitted to the resident that there was little to do for "this human being with this amount of brain. We allow D.N.R.'s. We need to adopt Do Not Do Furthers." But he said he had already discussed the man with Coler-Goldwater, and they weren't comfortable accepting him back without further observation.

"There's nothing to preserve," the resident said.

"You're right," Dr. Goldfrank said. "There's nothing to preserve."

He was admitted to the hospital.

The man's closest relative lives in another city and has not seen him since 1995. Now and then she sends him candy. No one had discussed establishing a care plan for him. Dr. Alexis A. Halpern, a third-year resident in the E.R., spoke to her and suggested that she think about the subject.

While the man was still in the E.R., saliva got into his lungs, and a tube had to be inserted through his mouth for him to breathe. His blood pressure dropped. A central line was inserted through his neck to provide fluids and medication and to take blood samples.

He was transferred to an intensive care unit, connected to a ventilator. He developed pneumonia. He was swept up into the regimens of hospital stay. X-rays were taken, medications administered, a catheter inserted, blood samples drawn multiple times a day.

"There's no question we did too much for him, in his fragile state, that we made him worse," Dr. Goldfrank said. "With someone like this, it becomes a question of what is doing good?"

Three weeks later, he was still hospitalized, just lying there. A feeding tube was being put in.

What if he had never come? Who knows. He might have died, perhaps mercifully. His condition might have stabilized without his having to endure the ordeal in the hospital. It is clear what happened to him. What no one knows is what he would have wanted.

Start the Conversation

The MODERN MATURITY guide to end-of-life care

The Body Speaks

Physically, dying means that "the body's various physiological systems, such as the circulatory, respiratory, and digestive systems, are no longer able to support the demands required to stay alive," says Barney Spivack, M.D., director of Geriatric Medicine for the Stamford (Connecticut) Health System. "When there is no meaningful chance for recovery, the physician should discuss realistic goals of care with the patient and family, which may include letting nature take its course. Lacking that direction," he says, "physicians differ in their perception of when enough is enough. We use our best judgment, taking into account the situation, the information available at the time, consultation with another doctor, or guidance from an ethics committee."

Without instructions from the patient or family, a doctor's obligation to a terminally ill person is to provide life-sustaining treatment. When a decision to "let nature take its course" has been made, the doctor will remove the treatment, based on the patient's needs. Early on, the patient or surrogate may choose to stop interventions such as antibiotics, dialysis, resuscitation, and defibrillation. Caregivers may want to offer food and fluids, but those can cause choking and the pooling of dangerous fluids in the lungs. A dying patient does not desire or need nourishment; without it he or she goes into a deep sleep and dies in days to weeks. A breathing machine would be the last support: It is uncomfortable for the patient, and may be disconnected when the patient or family finds that it is merely prolonging the dying process.

The Best Defense Against Pain

Pain-management activists are fervently trying to reeducate physicians about the importance and safety of making patients comfortable. "In medical school 30 years ago, we worried a lot about creating addicts," says Philadelphia internist Nicholas Scharff. "Now we know that addiction is not a problem: People who are in pain take

pain medication as long as they need it, and then they stop." Spivack says, "We have new formulations and delivery systems, so a dying patient should never have unmet pain needs."

In Search of a Good Death

If we think about death at all, we say that we want to go quickly, in our sleep, or, perhaps, while fly-fishing. But in fact only 10 percent of us die suddenly. The more common process is a slow decline with episodes of organ or system failure. Most of us want to die at home; most of us won't. All of us hope to die without pain; many of us will be kept alive, in pain, beyond a time when we would choose to call a halt. Yet very few of us take steps ahead of time to spell out what kind of physical and emotional care we will want at the end.

The new movement to improve the end of life is pioneering ways to make available to each of us a good death—as we each define it. One goal of the movement is to bring death through the cultural process that childbirth has achieved; from an unconscious, solitary act in a cold hospital room to a situation in which one is buffered by pillows, pictures, music, loved ones, and the solaces of home. But as in the childbirth movement, the real goal is choice—here, to have the death you want. Much of death's sting can be averted by planning in advance, knowing the facts, and knowing what options we all have. Here, we have gathered new and relevant information to help us all make a difference for the people we are taking care of, and ultimately, for ourselves.

In 1999, the Joint Commission on Accreditation of Healthcare Organizations issued stern new guidelines about easing pain in both terminal and nonterminal patients. The movement intends to take pain seriously:

to measure and treat it as the fifth vital sign in hospitals, along with blood pressure, pulse, temperature, and respiration.

The best defense against pain, says Spivack, is a combination of education and assertiveness. "Don't be afraid to speak up," he says. "If your doctor isn't listening, talk to the nurses. They see more and usually have a good sense of what's happening." Hospice workers, too, are experts on physical comfort, and a good doctor will respond to a hospice worker's recommendations. "The best situation for pain management," says Scharff, "is at home with a family caregiver being guided by a hospice program."

The downsides to pain medication are, first, that narcotics given to a fragile body may have a double effect: The drug may ease the pain, but it may cause respiratory depression and possibly death. Second, pain medication may induce grogginess or unconsciousness when a patient wants to be alert. "Most people seem to be much more willing to tolerate pain than mental confusion," says senior research scientist M. Powell Lawton, Ph.D., of the Philadelphia Geriatric Center. Dying patients may choose to be alert one day for visitors, and asleep the next to cope with pain. Studies show that when patients control their own pain medication, they use less.

Final Symptoms

Depression This condition is not an inevitable part of dying but can and should be treated. In fact, untreated depression can prevent pain medications from working effectively, and antidepressant medication can help relieve pain. A dying patient should be kept in the best possible emotional state for the final stage of life. A combination of medications and psychotherapy works best to treat depression.

Anorexia In the last few days of life, anorexia—an unwillingness or inability to eat—often sets in. "It has a protective effect, releasing endorphins in the system and contributing to a greater feeling of well-being," says Spivack. "Force-feeding a dying patient could make him uncomfortable and cause choking."

Dehydration Most people want to drink little or nothing in their last days. Again, this is a protective mechanism, triggering a release of helpful endorphins.

Drowsiness and Unarousable Sleep In spite of a coma-like state, says Spivack, "presume that the patient hears everything that is being said in the room."

Agitation and Restlessness, Moaning and Groaning The features of "terminal delirium" occur when the patient's level of consciousness is markedly decreased; there is no significant likelihood that any pain sensation can reach consciousness. Family members and other caregivers may interpret what they see as "the patient is in pain" but as these signs arise at a point very close to death, terminal delirium should be suspected.

Hospice: The Comfort Team

Hospice is really a bundle of services. It organizes a team of people to help patients and their families, most often in the patient's home but also in hospice residences, nursing homes, and hospitals:

• Registered nurses who check medication and the patient's condition, communicate with the patient's doctor, and educate caregivers.
• Medical services by the patient's physician and a hospice's medical director, limited to pain medication and other comfort care.
• Medical supplies and equipment.
• Drugs for pain relief and symptom control.
• Home-care aides for personal care, homemakers for light housekeeping.
• Continuous care in the home as needed on a short-term basis.
• Trained volunteers for support services.
• Physical, occupational, and speech therapists to help patients adapt to new disabilities.
• Temporary hospitalization during a crisis.
• Counselors and social workers who provide emotional and spiritual support to the patient and family.
• Respite care—brief noncrisis hospitalization to provide relief for family caregivers for up to five days.
• Bereavement support for the family, including counseling, referral to support groups, and periodic check-ins during the first year after the death.

Hospice Residences Still rare, but a growing phenomenon. They provide all these services on-site. They're for patients without family caregivers; with frail, elderly spouses; and for families who cannot provide at-home care because of other commitments. At the moment, Medicare covers only hospice services; the patient must pay for room and board. In many states Medicaid also covers hospice services (see How Much Will It Cost?). Keep in mind that not all residences are certified, bonded, or licensed; and not all are covered by Medicare.

Getting In A physician can recommend hospice for a patient who is terminally ill and probably has less than six months to live. The aim of hospice is to help people cope with an illness, not to cure it. All patients entering hospice waive their rights to curative treatments, though only for conditions relating to their terminal illness. "If you break a leg, of course you'll be treated for that," says Karen Woods, executive director of the Hospice Association of America. No one is forced to accept a hospice referral, and patients may leave and opt for curative care at any time. Hospice programs are listed in the Yellow Pages. For more information, see Resources.

The Ultimate Emotional Challenge

A dying person is grieving the loss of control over life, of body image, of normal physical functions, mobility and strength, freedom and independence, security, and the illusion of immortality. He is also grieving the loss of an earthly future, and reorienting himself to an unknowable destiny.

At the same time, an emotionally healthy dying person will be trying to satisfy his survival drive by adapting to this new phase, making the most of life at the moment, calling in loved ones, examining and appreciating his own joys and accomplishments. Not all dying people are depressed; many embrace death easily.

Facing the Fact

Doctors are usually the ones to inform a patient that he or she is dying, and the end-of-life movement is training physicians to bring empathy to that conversation in place of medspeak and time estimates. The more sensitive doctor will first ask how the patient feels things are going. "The patient may say, 'Well, I don't think I'm getting better,' and I would say, 'I think you're right,' " says internist Nicholas Scharff.

At this point, a doctor might ask if the patient wants to hear more now or later, in broad strokes or in detail. Some people will need to first process the emotional blow with tears and anger before learning about the course of their disease in the future.

"Accept and understand whatever reaction the patient has," says Roni Lang, director of the Geriatric Assessment Program for the Stamford (Connecticut) Health System, and a social worker who is a longtime veteran of such conversations. "Don't be too quick with the tissue. That sends a message that it's not okay to be upset. It's okay for the patient to be however she is."

Getting to Acceptance

Some patients keep hoping that they will get better. Denial is one of the mind's miracles, a way to ward off painful realities until consciousness can deal with them. Denial may not be a problem for the dying person, but it can create difficulties for the family. The dying person could be leaving a lot of tough decisions, stress, and confusion behind. The classic stages of grief outlined by Elisabeth Kübler-Ross—denial, anger, bargaining, depression, and acceptance—are often used to describe post-death grieving, but were in fact delineated for the process of accepting impending loss. We now know that these states may not progress in order. "Most people oscillate between anger and sadness, embracing the prospect of death and unrealistic episodes of optimism," says Lang. Still, she says, "don't place demands on them

Survival Kit for Caregivers

A study published in the March 21, 2000, issue of **Annals of Internal Medicine** shows that caregivers of the dying are twice as likely to have depressive symptoms as the dying themselves.

No wonder. Caring for a dying parent, says social worker Roni Lang, "brings a fierce tangle of emotions. That part of us that is a child must grow up." Parallel struggles occur when caring for a spouse, a child, another relative, or a friend. Caregivers may also experience sibling rivalry, income loss, isolation, fatigue, burnout, and resentment.

To deal with these difficult stresses, Lang suggests that caregivers:

• Set limits in advance. How far am I willing to go? What level of care is needed? Who can I get to help? Resist the temptation to let the illness always take center stage, or to be drawn into guilt-inducing conversations with people who think you should be doing more.

• Join a caregiver support group, either disease-related like the Alzheimer's Association or Gilda's Club, or a more general support group like The Well Spouse Foundation. Ask the social services department at your hospital for advice. Telephone support and online chat rooms also exist (see Resources).

• Acknowledge anger and express it constructively by keeping a journal or talking to an understanding friend or family member. Anger is a normal reaction to powerlessness.

• When people offer to help, give them a specific assignment. And then, take time to do what energizes you and make a point of rewarding yourself.

• Remember that people who are critically ill are self-absorbed. If your empathy fails you and you lose patience, make amends and forgive yourself.

to accept their death. This is not a time to proselytize." It is enough for the family to accept the coming loss, and if necessary, introduce the idea of an advance directive and health-care proxy, approaching it as a "just in case" idea. When one member of the family cannot accept death, and insists that doctors do more, says Lang, "that's the worst nightmare. I would call a meeting, hear all views without interrupting, and get the conversation around to what the patient would want. You may need another person to come in, perhaps the doctor, to help 'hear' the voice of the patient."

What Are You Afraid Of?

The most important question for doctors and caregivers to ask a dying person is, What are you afraid of? "Fear aggravates pain," says Lang, "and pain aggravates fear." Fear of pain, says Spivack, is one of the most common problems, and can be dealt with rationally. Many people do not know, for example, that pain in dying is not inevitable. Other typical fears are of being separated from loved ones, from home, from work; fear of being a burden, losing control, being dependent, and leaving things undone. Voicing fear helps lessen it, and pinpointing fear helps a caregiver know how to respond.

How to Be With a Dying Person

Our usual instinct is to avoid everything about death, including the people moving most rapidly toward it. But, Spivack says, "In all my years of working with dying people, I've never heard one say 'I want to die alone.' " Dying people are greatly comforted by company; the benefit far outweighs the awkwardness of the visit. Lang offers these suggestions for visitors:

• Be close. Sit at eye level, and don't be afraid to touch. Let the dying person set the pace for the conversation. Allow for silence. Your presence alone is valuable.

• Don't contradict a patient who says he's going to die. Acceptance is okay. Allow for anger, guilt, and fear, without trying to "fix" it. Just listen and empathize.

• Give the patient as much decision-making power as possible, as long as possible. Allow for talk about unfinished business. Ask: "Who can I contact for you?"

• Encourage happy reminiscences. It's okay to laugh.

• Never pass up the chance to express love or say goodbye. But if you don't get the chance, remember that not everything is worked through. Do the best you can.

Taking Control Now

Sixty years ago, before the invention of dialysis, defibrillators, and ventilators, the failure of vital organs automatically meant death. There were few choices to be made to end suffering, and when there were—the fatal dose of morphine, for example—these decisions were made privately by family and doctors who knew each other well. Since the 1950s, medical technology has been capable of extending lives, but also of prolonging dying. In 1967, an organization called Choice in Dying (now the Partnership for Caring: America's Voices for the Dying; see Resources) designed the first advance directive—a document that allows you to designate under what conditions you would want life-sustaining treatment to be continued or terminated. But the idea did not gain popular understanding until 1976, when the parents of Karen Ann Quinlan won a long legal battle to disconnect her from respiratory support as she lay for months in a vegetative state. Some 75 percent of Americans are in favor of advance directives, although only 30–35 percent actually write them.

Designing the Care You Want

There are two kinds of advance directives, and you may use one or both. A Living Will details what kind of life-sustaining treatment you want or don't want, in the event of an illness when death is imminent. A durable power of attorney for health care appoints someone to be your decision-maker if you can't speak for yourself. This person is also called a surrogate, attorney-in-fact, or health-care proxy. An advance directive such as Five Wishes covers both.

Most experts agree that a Living Will alone is not sufficient. "You don't need to write specific instructions about different kinds of life support, as you don't yet know any of the facts of your situation, and they may change," says Charles Sabatino, assistant director of the American Bar Association's Commission on Legal Problems of the Elderly.

The proxy, Sabatino says, is far more important. "It means someone you trust will find out all the options and make a decision consistent with what you would want." In most states, you may write your own advance directive, though some states require a specific form, available at hospital admitting offices or at the state department of health.

When Should You Draw Up a Directive?

Without an advance directive, a hospital staff is legally bound to do everything to keep you alive as long as possible, until you or a family member decides otherwise. So advance directives are best written before emergency status or a terminal diagnosis. Some people write them at the same time they make a will. The process begins with discussions between you and your family and doctor. If anybody is reluctant to discuss the subject, Sabatino suggests starting the conversation with a story. "Remember what happened to Bob Jones and what his family went through? I want us to be different…." You can use existing tools—a booklet or questionnaire (see Resources)—to keep the conversation moving. Get your doctor's commitment to support your wishes. "If you're asking for something that is against your doctor's conscience" (such as prescribing a lethal dose of pain medication or removing life support at a time he considers premature), Sabatino says, "he may have an obligation to transfer you to another doctor." And make sure the person you name as surrogate agrees to act for you and understands your wishes.

Filing, Storing, Safekeeping…

An estimated 35 percent of advance directives cannot be found when needed.

• Give a copy to your surrogate, your doctor, your hospital, and other family members. Tell them where to find the original in the house—not in a safe deposit box where it might not be found until after death.

Five Wishes

Five Wishes is a questionnaire that guides people in making essential decisions about the care they want at the end of their life. About a million people have filled out the eight-page form in the past two years. This advance directive is legally valid in 34 states and the District of Columbia. (The other 16 require a specific state-mandated form.)

The document was designed by lawyer Jim Towey, founder of Aging With Dignity, a nonprofit organization that advocates for the needs of elders and their caregivers. Towey, who was legal counsel to Mother Teresa, visited her Home for the Dying in Calcutta in the 1980s. He was struck that in that haven in the Third World, "the dying people's hands were held, their pain was managed, and they weren't alone. In the First World, you see a lot of medical technology, but people die in pain, and alone." Towey talked to MODERN MATURITY about his directive and what it means.

What are the five wishes? Who do I want to make care decisions for me when I can't? What kind of medical treatment do I want toward the end? What would help me feel comfortable while I am dying? How do I want people to treat me? What do I want my loved ones to know about me and my feelings after I'm gone?

Why is it so vital to make advance decisions now? Medical technology has extended longevity, which is good, but it can prolong the dying process in ways that are almost cruel. Medical schools are still concentrating on curing, not caring for the dying. We can have a dignified season in our life, or die alone in pain with futile interventions. Most people only discover they have options when checking into the hospital, and often they no longer have the capacity to choose. This leaves the family members with a guessing game and, frequently, guilt.

What's the ideal way to use this document? First you do a little soul searching about what you want. Then discuss it with people you trust, in the livingroom instead of the waiting room—before a crisis. Just say, "I want a choice about how I spend my last days," talk about your choices, and pick someone to be your health-care surrogate.

What makes the Five Wishes directive unique? It's easy to use and understand, not written in the language of doctors or lawyers. It also allows people to discuss comfort dignity, and forgiveness, not just medical concerns. When my father filled it out, he said he wanted his favorite afghan blanket in his bed. It made a huge difference to me that, as he was dying, he had his wishes fulfilled.

For a copy of Five Wishes in English or Spanish, send a $5 check or money order to Aging With Dignity, PO Box 1661, Tallahassee, FL 32302. For more information, visit www.agingwithdignity.org.

- Some people carry a copy in their wallet or glove compartment of their car.
- Be aware that if you have more than one home and you split your time in several regions of the country, you should be registering your wishes with a hospital in each region, and consider naming more than one proxy.
- You may register your Living Will and health-care proxy online at uslivingwillregistry.com (or call 800-548-9455). The free, privately funded confidential service will instantly fax a copy to a hospital when the hospital requests one. It will also remind you to update it: You may want to choose a new surrogate, accommodate medical advances, or change your idea of when "enough is enough." M. Powell Lawton, who is doing a study on how people anticipate the terminal life stages, has discovered that "people adapt relatively well to states of poor health. The idea that life is still worth living continues to readjust itself."

Assisted Suicide: The Reality

While advance directives allow for the termination of life-sustaining treatment, assisted suicide means supplying the patient with a prescription for life-ending medication. A doctor writes the prescription for the medication; the patient takes the fatal dose him- or herself. Physician-assisted suicide is legal only in Oregon (and under consideration in Maine) but only with rigorous preconditions. Of the approximately 30,000 people who died in Oregon in 1999, only 33 received permission to have a lethal dose of medication and only 26 of those actually died of the medication. Surrogates may request an end to life support, but to assist in a suicide puts one at risk for charges of homicide.

Good Care: Can You Afford It?

The ordinary person is only one serious illness away from poverty," says Joanne Lynn, M.D., director of the Arlington, Virginia, Center to Improve Care of the Dying. An ethicist, hospice physician, and health-services researcher, she is one of the founding members of the end-of-life-care movement. "On the whole, hospitalization and the cost of suppressing symptoms is very easy to afford," says Lynn. Medicare and Medicaid will help cover that kind of acute medical care. But what is harder to afford is at-home medication, monitoring, daily help with eating and walking, and all the care that will go on for the rest of the patient's life.

"When people are dying," Lynn says, "an increasing proportion of their overall care does not need to be done by doctors. But when policymakers say the care is nonmedical, then it's second class, it's not important, and nobody will pay for it."

Bottom line, Medicare pays for about 57 percent of the cost of medical care for Medicare beneficiaries.

Another 11 percent is paid by Medicaid, 20 percent by the patient, 10 percent from private insurance, and the rest from other sources, such as charitable organizations.

Medi-what?

This public-plus-private network of funding sources for end-of-life care is complex, and who pays for how much of what is determined by diagnosis, age, site of care, and income. Besides the private health insurance that many of us have from our employers, other sources of funding may enter the picture when patients are terminally ill.

• **Medicare** A federal insurance program that covers health-care services for people 65 and over, some disabled people, and those with end-stage kidney disease. Medicare Part A covers inpatient care in hospitals, nursing homes, hospice, and some home health care. For most people, the Part A premium is free. Part B covers doctor fees, tests, and other outpatient medical services. Although Part B is optional, most people choose to enroll through their local Social Security office and pay the monthly premium ($45.50). Medicare beneficiaries share in the cost of care through deductibles and co-insurance. What Medicare does not cover at all is outpatient medication, long-term nonacute care, and support services.

• **Medicaid** A state and federally funded program that covers health-care services for people with income or assets below certain levels, which vary from state to state.

• **Medigap** Private insurance policies covering the gaps in Medicare, such as deductibles and co-payments, and in some cases additional health-care services, medical supplies, and outpatient prescription drugs.

Many of the services not paid for by Medicare can be covered by private long-term-care insurance. About 50 percent of us over the age of 65 will need long-term care at home or in a nursing home, and this insurance is an extra bit of protection for people with major assets to protect. It pays for skilled nursing care as well as non-health services, such as help with dressing, eating, and bathing. You select a dollar amount of coverage per day (for example, $100 in a nursing home, or $50 for at-home care), and a coverage period (for example, three years—the average nursing-home stay is 2.7 years). Depending on your age and the benefits you choose, the insurance can cost anywhere from around $500 to more than $8,000 a year. People with pre-existing conditions such as Alzheimer's or MS are usually not eligible.

How Much Will It Cost?

Where you get end-of-life care will affect the cost and who pays for it.

• **Hospital** Dying in a hospital costs about $1,000 a day. After a $766 deductible (per benefit period), Medicare reimburses the hospital a fixed rate per day, which varies by region and diagnosis. After the first 60 days in a hospital, a patient will pay a daily deductible ($194) that goes up (to $388) after 90 days. The patient is responsible for all costs for each day beyond 150 days. Medicaid and some private insurance, either through an employer or a Medigap plan, often help cover these costs.

• **Nursing home** About $1,000 a week. Medicare covers up to 100 days of skilled nursing care after a three-day hospitalization, and most medication costs during that time. For days 21–100, your daily co-insurance of $97 is usually covered by private insurance—if you have it. For nursing-home care not covered by Medicare, you must use your private assets, or Medicaid if your assets run out, which happens to approximately one-third of nursing-home residents. Long-term-care insurance may also cover some of the costs.

• **Hospice care** About $100 a day for in-home care. Medicare covers hospice care to patients who have a life expectancy of less than six months. (See Hospice: The Comfort Team.) Such care may be provided at home, in a hospice facility, a hospital, or a nursing-home. Patients may be asked to pay up to $5 for each prescription and a 5 percent co-pay for in-patient respite care, which is a short hospital stay to relieve caregivers. Medicaid covers hospice care in all but six states, even for those without Medicare.

About 60 percent of full-time employees of medium and large firms also have coverage for hospice services, but the benefits vary widely.

• **Home care without hospice services** Medicare Part A pays the full cost of medical home health care for up to 100 visits following a hospital stay of at least three days. Medicare Part B covers home health-care visits beyond those 100 visits or without a hospital stay. To qualify, the patient must be homebound, require skilled nursing care or physical or speech therapy, be under a physician's care, and use services from a Medicare-participating home-health agency. Note that this coverage is for medical care only; hired help for personal nonmedical services, such as that often required by Alzheimer's patients, is not covered by Medicare. It is covered by Medicaid in some states.

A major financial disadvantage of dying at home without hospice is that Medicare does not cover out-patient prescription drugs, even those for pain. Medicaid does cover these drugs, but often with restrictions on their price and quantity. Private insurance can fill the gap to some extent. Long-term-care insurance may cover payments to family caregivers who have to stop work to care for a dying patient, but this type of coverage is very rare.

Resources

MEDICAL CARE

For information about pain relief and symptom management: **Supportive Care of the Dying** (503-215-5053; careofdying.org).

For a comprehensive guide to living with the medical, emotional, and spiritual aspects of dying:
Handbook for Mortals by Joanne Lynn and Joan Harrold, Oxford University Press.

For a 24-hour hotline offering counseling, pain management, downloadable advance directives, and more:
The Partnership for Caring (800-989-9455; www.partnershipforcaring.org).

EMOTIONAL CARE

To find mental-health counselors with an emphasis on lifespan human development and spiritual discussion:
American Counseling Association (800-347-6647; counseling.org).

For disease-related support groups and general resources for caregivers:
Caregiver Survival Resources (caregiver911.com).

For AARP's online caregiver support chatroom, access **America Online** every Wednesday night, 8:30–9:30 EST (keyword: AARP).

Education and advocacy for family caregivers:
National Family Caregivers Association (800-896-3650; nfcacares.org).

For the booklet,
Understanding the Grief Process (D16832, EEO143C), e-mail order with title and numbers to member@aarp.org or send postcard to AARP Fulfillment, 601 E St NW, Washington DC 20049. Please allow two to four weeks for delivery.

To find a volunteer to help with supportive services to the frail and their caregivers:
National Federation of Interfaith Volunteer Caregivers (816-931-5442; nfivc.org).

For information on support to partners of the chronically ill and/or the disabled:
The Well Spouse Foundation (800-838-0879; www.wellspouse.org).

LEGAL HELP

AARP members are entitled to a free half-hour of legal advice with a lawyer from **AARP's Legal Services Network.** (800-424-3410; www.aarp.org/lsn).
For **Planning for Incapacity,** *a guide to advance directives in your state,* send $5 to Legal Counsel for the Elderly, Inc., PO Box 96474, Washington DC 20090-6474. Make out check to LCE Inc.
For a **Caring Conversations** booklet on advance-directive discussion:

Midwest Bioethics Center (816-221-1100; midbio.org).

For information on care at the end of life, online discussion groups, conferences:
Last Acts Campaign (800-844-7616; lastacts.org).

HOSPICE

To learn about end-of-life care options and grief issues through videotapes, books, newsletters, and brochures:
Hospice Foundation of America (800-854-3402; hospice-foundation.org).

For information on hospice programs, FAQs, and general facts about hospice:
National Hospice and Palliative Care Organization (800-658-8898; nhpco.org).

For **All About Hospice: A Consumer's Guide** (202-546-4759; www.hospice-america.org).

FINANCIAL HELP

For **Organizing Your Future,** *a simple guide to end-of-life financial decisions,* send $5 to Legal Counsel for the Elderly, Inc., PO Box 96474, Washington DC 20090-6474. Make out check to LCE Inc.

For **Medicare and You 2000** *and a* **2000 Guide to Health Insurance for People With Medicare** (800-MEDICARE [633-4227]; medicare.gov).

To find your State Agency on Aging: **Administration on Aging, U.S. Department of Health and Human Services** (800-677-1116; aoa.dhhs.gov).

GENERAL

For information on end-of-life planning and bereavement: (www.aarp.org/endoflife/).

For health professionals and others who want to start conversations on end-of-life issues in their community:

Discussion Guide: On Our Own Terms: Moyers on Dying, based on the PBS series, airing September 10–13. The guide provides essays, instructions, and contacts. From PBS, www.pbs.org/onourownterms Or send a postcard request to On Our Own Terms Discussion Guide, Thirteen/WNET New York, PO Box 245, Little Falls, NJ 07424-9766.

Funded with a grant from The Robert Wood Johnson Foundation, Princeton, N.J. *Editor* Amy Gross; *Writer* Louise Lague; *Designer* David Herbick

Quality End-of-Life Care
Patients' Perspectives

Peter A. Singer, MD, MPH, FRCPC
Douglas K. Martin, PhD
Merrijoy Kelner, PhD

BECAUSE EVERYONE DIES, END-of-life care is among the most prevalent issues in health care. Both health care professionals and patients see room for improvement.[1] Encouragingly, major initiatives, such as the American Medical Association's Education for Physicians on End-of-Life Care project, Open Society Institute's Project on Death in America, and Robert Wood Johnson Foundation's Last Rites Campaign, are under way to improve the quality of end-of-life care.

A necessary scientific step to focus these efforts is the development of a taxonomy or conceptual framework for quality end-of-life care.[2] However, what end-of-life care means and how to measure it is still a matter of debate and ongoing research. Three expert groups have recently published frameworks for quality end-of-life care (**TABLE 1**).[3-5] These taxonomies derive from the medical expert perspective rather than the perspective of patients and families.[6] We are unaware of any descriptions of quality end-of-life care from the patient perspective, from which quality end-of-life care is arguably most appropriately viewed. This is the perspective that clinicians and health care organizations will need to understand to improve the quality of care they deliver to dying patients. Therefore, the purpose of this study was to identify and describe elements of quality end-of-life care as identified by those most affected: patients.

Context Quality end-of-life care is increasingly recognized as an ethical obligation of health care providers, both clinicians and organizations. However, this concept has not been examined from the perspective of patients.

Objective To identify and describe elements of quality end-of-life care from the patient's perspective.

Design Qualitative study using in-depth, open-ended, face-to-face interviews and content analysis.

Setting Toronto, Ontario.

Participants A total of 126 participants from 3 patient groups: dialysis patients (n = 48), people with human immunodeficiency virus infection (n = 40), and residents of a long-term care facility (n = 38).

Outcome Measures Participants' views on end-of-life issues.

Results Participants identified 5 domains of quality end-of-life care: receiving adequate pain and symptom management, avoiding inappropriate prolongation of dying, achieving a sense of control, relieving burden, and strengthening relationships with loved ones.

Conclusion These domains, which characterize patients' perspectives on end-of-life care, can serve as focal points for improving the quality of end-of-life care.

JAMA. 1999;281:163–168
www.jama.com

METHODS

Design

This study used a qualitative research method called *content analysis*, in which "standardized measurements are applied to metrically defined units [of text] and these are used to characterise and compare documents."[7]

Participants

We analyzed data from interviews with patients who participated in 3 recent studies.[8-10] Participants from the 3 studies were dialysis patients, persons infected with the human immunodeficiency virus (HIV), and residents of a long-term care facility. In this study, we examined all participant interviews from the dialysis (n = 48) and long-term care (n = 38) studies, and a random selection of 40 participant interviews (from a total of 140 participants) from the HIV study.

Dialysis patients were a sample of individuals receiving hemodialysis at all 6 units serving adults in metropolitan Toronto, Ontario. They were originally enrolled in a study examining the acceptability of generic vs. dialysis-specific advance directive (AD) forms[11] and interviewed 6 months later.[8] Participants were excluded if they were younger than 18 years, were unable to understand written English, were incapable of completing an AD form, would experi-

Table 1. Domains of Quality End-of-Life Care

Journal of the American Geriatrics Society Statement[3]	Institute of Medicine Committee[4]	Emanuel and Emanuel[5*]	Patient Perspectives[†]
• Physical and emotional symptoms • Support of function and autonomy • Advance care planning • Aggressive care near death • Patient and family satisfaction • Global quality of life • Family burden • Survival time • Provider continuity and skill • Bereavement	• Overall quality of life • Physical well-being and functioning • Psychosocial well-being and functioning • Spiritual well-being • Patient perception of care • Family well-being and perceptions	• Physical symptoms • Psychological and cognitive symptoms • Social relationships and support • Economic demands and caregiving needs • Hopes and expectations • Spiritual and existential beliefs	• Receiving adequate pain and symptom management • Avoiding inappropriate prolongation of dying • Achieving a sense of control • Relieving burden • Strengthening relationships

*"Modifiable dimensions of patient's experience" from Emanuel and Emanuel.[5]
[†] Patient perspectives are from the current study.

ence undue emotional distress from completing an AD form, had received dialysis for less than 3 months, or refused to participate in the research. Of 532 patients receiving hemodialysis, 310 were excluded, 81 refused, 43 withdrew, 7 died, 43 were not approached, and 48 completed the study.

Participants with HIV were a sample of persons who responded to the study advertisements or posters distributed by the AIDS Committee of Toronto and placed in the waiting rooms of the Toronto Hospital Immunodeficiency Clinic. They were originally enrolled in a previous study that examined the preference for either an HIV-specific or generic AD form[12] and interviewed 6 months later.[9] Participants were excluded if they were younger than 16 years, were not fluent in English, could not read, were incapable of completing an AD form (as measured by a Standardized Mini-Mental State Examination test score <23), would experience undue emotional distress from completing an AD form, resided outside metropolitan Toronto, or refused to participate in the research. Of 587 possible participants, 200 were not approached for the study, 85 were excluded, 52 refused, 93 withdrew, 17 died, and 140 were interviewed (of whom 40 were randomly selected for this analysis).

Long-term care residents were a sample of persons from a 398-bed hospital in Toronto that provides both rehabilitative and long-term care for adults who are chronically ill and disabled by neurological problems, respiratory conditions, amputations, and age-related disorders.[10] The purpose

of the original study was to examine residents' views about control at the end of life. Three criteria were established for selecting participants: patients had to be 65 years or older, capable of understanding and answering questions in English, and healthy enough, both physically and mentally, to take part in a short interview. Nurse managers recruited participants in each unit of the hospital in which appropriate patients could be identified. No patients refused. The 38 participants represent the total population of eligible patients during the data collection period.

Data Collection

Data were gathered by in-depth, open-ended, face-to-face interviews. The interviewer asked open-ended questions, followed up participants' responses, pursued themes as they arose, and sought clarification or elaboration as required. In the dialysis and HIV studies, the interviews were audiotaped and transcribed; in the long-term care study, the interviewer wrote down the participants' comments. Opportunities were consistently made available for participants to express unsolicited opinions and recount their clinical experiences and life histories. As the interviews proceeded and ideas were suggested by patients' reflections and clarifications, new questions were added and others were refined. The interview guide was modified to follow up issues emerging from the data as the interviews and analysis progressed.

The initial interview guide for dialysis patients covered 3 themes: (1) had the participant completed an AD form? (2) if not, why not? and (3) if so, what was the process and was it acceptable?

In the HIV study, participants were asked about their reasons for engaging in advance care planning (ACP), the process and content of their ACP discussions, their perspective on the importance of ACP, and their evaluation of the ACP process.

Long-term care residents were asked the following questions about patient control at the end of life: (1) had they previously thought about it? (2) what were their general views on control over decision making at the end of life? (3) what would be their personal preference "when the time comes"? (4) did they see any potential obstacles to having their wishes honored? and (5) what were their personal views about withdrawal or termination of treatment, as well as euthanasia and physician-assisted suicide?

Data Analysis

The data were read and participants' views regarding quality end-of-life care were identified. These units of text were underlined and descriptive notes were written in the margins of the transcripts, a process referred to as *coding*. Coded units were then labeled as specific end-of-life care issues. Many issues were not mutually exclusive, but issues that were conceptually different were given different descriptive labels. Labeled issues were then compared within

	Participants		
Characteristics	**Dialysis (n = 48)**	**HIV* (n = 40)**	**Long-term Care (n = 38)**
Sex, No.			
Male	30	35	13
Female	18	5	25
Race/ethnicity, No.			
White	30	37	35
African American	8	0	0
Hispanic	2	1	0
Asian	3	0	0
Other	5	2	3
Education, No.			
No high school	2	0	6
Some high school	4	3	12
High school graduate	13	3	9
Some college	7	17	3
College graduate	22	17	8
Age, mean (range), y	48.3(20-80)	39.6(25-54)	76.3(65-Š85)**

Table 2. Participant Characteristics

*HIV indicates human immunodificiency virus.
**In long-term care study, data were gathered by strata. Therefore, mean age was derived using an estimated and weighted calculation.

and between interviews. Similar issues were grouped together under 1 overarching domain label and the data were recoded by domain. The prevalence of each domain was recorded and descriptive statements about each were developed using the patients' words. Quotes that were selected for presentation in the article were good illustrations of the domain and provide data from the various patient populations. This process was conducted by 1 analyst (D.K.M.), who frequently consulted with a second analyst (P.A.S.) regarding excerpts of the primary transcript data and the clustering of the data into domains.

Several steps were taken to verify the results, a concept in qualitative research analogous to reliability and validity in quantitative research.[13,14] These included (1) use of 3 separate data sets to verify the conceptual domains, (2) general familiarity with the data sets by investigators (P.A.S. and M.K.) other than the primary analyst, (3) systematic checking of the developing conceptual domains against supporting quotations by a second analyst (P.A.S.), (4) review of the manuscript by an independent scholar studying quality end-of-life care (James Tulsky, MD), and (5) explicit comparison of our taxonomy

with 3 other taxonomies derived from a different methodological perspective.[3-5]

Sample Size

Sample size was not formally calculated. Instead, participants were enrolled until no new concepts arose during analysis of the successive interviews, a concept called *saturation* by qualitative researchers.

Research Ethics

All 3 studies were approved by the University of Toronto Committee on Research With Human Subjects, and written informed consent was obtained from all subjects.

RESULTS

Demographic characteristics of the 126 patients from the 3 data sets are shown in **TABLE 2**. As shown in **TABLE 3**, the analysis identified 5 domains of quality end-of-life care: receiving adequate pain and symptom management, avoiding inappropriate prolongation of dying, achieving a sense of control, relieving burden, and strengthening of relationships with loved ones. The next most prevalent theme was mentioned

by less than 5% of participants. We present a description of these domains with verbatim quotes from participants.

Receiving Adequate Pain and Symptom Management

Pain was a concern for many respondents. A few participants mentioned other symptoms such as vomiting, breathlessness, and diarrhea.

I've been adamant that I wanted treatment in sort of end stage to be minimal—pain reduction, but not life sustaining. I don't—if anyone could say they did—like being in pain and I don't find the idea of being incontinent or bowel-dysfunctional, not to mention mentally incompetent, remotely interesting.

I wouldn't want a lot of pain; it's one of the worst ways to go.

If I'm in pain, severe pain, and the doctors can do nothing, the pain persists and there's nothing to take the pain away, I don't think it's fair to let me suffer like that, or anybody. We don't let the animals suffer; why should we?

Table 3. Domains of End-of-Life Care from Patients' Perspectives*				
	Participants			
	Dialysis (n = 48)	**HIV/AIDS (n = 40)**	**Long-term Care (n = 38)**	**Total (N = 126)**
Receiving adequate pain and symptom management	3 (6.2)	10 (25.0)	15 (39.5)	28 (22.2)
Avoiding inappropriate prolongation of dying	23 (47.9)	29 (72.5)	25 (65.8)	77 (61.1)
Achieving a sense of control	9 (18.8)	21 (52.5)	18 (47.4)	48 (38.1)
Relieving burden	14 (29.2)	21 (52.5)	13 (34.2)	48 (38.1)
Strengthening relationships with loved ones	16 (33.3)	21 (52.5)	12 (31.6)	49 (38.9)

*Data are number (percentage). HIV indicates human immunodificiency virus; AIDS, acquired immunodeficiency syndrome.

Avoiding Inappropriate Prolongation of Dying

Participants were afraid of "lingering" and "being kept alive" after they no longer could enjoy their lives. Quality-of-life concerns seemed to fuel this fear; many were terrified of becoming a "vegetable" or living in a coma. These participants adamantly denounced "being kept alive by a machine." They wanted to be "allowed to die naturally" or "in peace."

I didn't want to be kept alive artificially forever just to die later on and suffer, you know, without need for an extra year. Let me go anyways. Get it done with the first time.

I wouldn't want life supports if I'm going to die anyway. There's no dignity in it. It's just a guinea pig thing.

I've always told my mother… if it ever comes down to being put on a life-support system, I wouldn't go for it unless there's a chance that I would come around and be normal again. But if there is chance of me being put on a life-support system and becoming a vegetable, I said forget it.

Achieving a Sense of Control

Participants were adamant that they wanted to retain control of their end-of-life care decisions while they were capable of doing so, and that they wanted the proxy of their choice to retain control if they became incapable.

I have very definite ideas of what I would want done and what I wouldn't want done, especially after watching various friends go through their deaths.

I want control, but it shouldn't be disruptive. It can be productive if it's thoughtful and if others are consulted.

That's my life. Nobody has any right to tell me that. I can't let a stranger talk me out of anything. That's what I want. They don't know how I live. It's very, very important to me now that I can make choices for myself.

Relieving Burden

The participants were greatly concerned about the burden that their dying would impose on loved ones. They identified 3 specific burdens: provision of physical care, witnessing their death, and substitute decision making for life-sustaining treatment.

I don't want them making the decisions for me without knowing how I would decide the same thing. It just makes life easier for everybody. They don't have to say, 'Well, what would he do in this situation?' if it's already written down. I know if I was incapacitated, it would be a stressful time for the people I've chosen as my proxy. It would be tough in some situations to make those decisions. So by doing it in advance I save them the bother…. I chose not to designate my parents as proxies. I felt that would probably be a little bit hard on them. I mean, I'm sure they'd be willing to do so, but I think from the standpoint of just saving their feelings as much as possible, I'd rather not have them make those decisions, if the time came that it was necessary.

I'd want to die here, not at home. I wouldn't want to put that burden on my family.

I hope to stop myself from becoming a burden to them [children]. Looking after somebody either takes a lot of money, in which case you may get somebody to baby-sit for you, or you have to do it yourself, and I do not wish my children to be

in the position of having to do that. Therefore, I would rather die faster than later.

Strengthening Relationships With Loved Ones

A majority of participants felt that considerations with respect to loved ones were integral to their dying experience. For the dying experience to be meaningful, participants desired the full involvement of loved ones in communication about their dying. At times, this meant overcoming resistance, their own and others', to engage with uncomfortable subject matter. But even so, participants felt that the need for communication with loved ones was of overwhelming importance. When this intimacy was achieved, participants found their relationships strengthened.

I've never told anyone in my family that I was HIV-positive. And so, in order to complete my living will, I had to tell him [brother] I was HIV-positive, which was really quite a challenge for me. And I did tell him, and everything has just worked out fine. He's a hundred percent supportive and it couldn't be better. Our relationship is even closer now; we were close before—we've always been a close family. But now we're really close.

It was one of the decisions we discussed and she [wife] says when I am in this situation she is capable to make decisions for me. She didn't want to leave it to me because I cannot make decisions when I, you know. It was nice because she was showing me this kind of love and this kind of sympathy; when I am in that situation, she will be able to continue assisting me. So I was very happy about that, really. She always tells me she is going to be there for me when I cannot make a decision.

It helped me get closer to my family, to get an idea how they feel about me. There were so many times I wanted to get their opinion on certain things, and when I discussed that with them they showed me that they are going to be there for me every time.

COMMENT

From these patients' perspectives, quality end-of-life care includes 5 domains: receiving adequate pain and symptom management, avoiding inappropriate prolongation of dying, achieving a sense of control, relieving burden on loved ones, and strengthening relationships with loved ones.

Comparison With Expert Models

Table 1 compares the patients' perspectives on quality end-of-life care with 3 models derived from an expert perspective. The similarities among the models support the validity of the conceptual domains with respect to all the models.

There are also important differences between patient- and expert-derived models. First, compared with taxonomies from an expert perspective, the patient-derived description of quality end-of-life care is simpler and more straightforward. For instance, it has the fewest domains of the 4 models. Second, the patient-derived taxonomy is more specific. For example, rather than using general labels such as "psychological," the patient perspective speaks of "achieving a sense of control"; rather than "social," it speaks of "relieving burden" and "strengthening relationships." Third, the patient-derived taxonomy is less bound by established concepts for which measurement scales are available (such as quality of life). This raises the question of whether the measurable has been driving out the important in the development of expert-derived taxonomies of quality end-of-life care. Fourth, the patient-derived model omits general and possibly vague concepts such as "global quality of life," "overall quality of life," and "patient perception of care." Fifth, the patient-derived taxonomy is more homogeneously focused on outcomes rather than processes of care (such as ACP or "provider continuity and skill") or periods of care (such as "bereavement"). Finally, the description is derived from the perspective of patients, giving it inherent authenticity. The patient's (and family's) concerns rightfully belong in the center of our focus because they are at the center of the dying experience. The following comments explore the individual domains from the patient's perspective with reference to existing knowledge.

Receiving Adequate Pain and Symptom Management

Although the issue of treating pain and other symptoms has been championed by the palliative care movement, it is still a problem for many dying patients. For instance, Lynn et al[15] found that 4 in 10 dying patients had severe pain most of the time. Greater attention to the attitudes and skills of health care workers with respect to pain and symptom control may be warranted. Clearer guidelines separating appropriate pain control from euthanasia may also help alleviate clinicians' fears with respect to pain management.

Avoiding Inappropriate Prolongation of Dying

Ahronheim et al[16] found that 47% of incurably ill patients with advanced dementia and metastatic cancer received nonpalliative treatments. Solomon et al[17] found that 78% of health care professionals surveyed reported that they sometimes felt the treatments they offered patients were overly burdensome. Hanson et al[18] found that a frequent recommendation of bereaved family members was to improve end-of-life care, emphasizing better communication. Based on their own observations and data from Tulsky et al,[19] which highlighted inadequacies in end-of-life communication, Hanson et al speculated that "discussions that focus on specific treatment decisions may not satisfy the real needs of dying patients and their families."[18] This is also the sense that one gets when reading the data from our study. The current approach of asking for consent to specific treatments may not meet the needs of dying patients and their families. Dying patients sometimes overestimate their survival probabilities, and these estimates may influence their treatment choices.[20] Specific treatment discussions may not adequately support the patient's hope and discourage false hope. Indeed, emphasizing consent for specific procedures may often be a way to avoid confronting the larger issue of death and discussing the patient's dying. Physicians may use informed consent discussions as a proxy for the more important communications about values and dying. Although such consent is legally required and, therefore, necessary, it is not sufficient. The primary focus of discussions about the use of life-sustaining treatment should be on the realistic and achievable goals of care.[21,22]

Achieving a Sense of Control

When participants said they wanted to achieve a sense of control, they seemed to have in mind a psychosocial outcome rather than a precise specification of what treatments would be received. Although the SUPPORT study[23] showed that incorporating patients' wishes into care may not affect the rate of use of life-sustaining treatments, this may not be the outcome patients have in mind, based on our data. Patients want a voice in their end-of-life care rather than specific control over each life-sustaining treatment decision. This finding further supports the notion discussed herein that our current approach to end-of-life communication, which focuses on the use of individual treatments, may be too specific to address patients' psychosocial needs in the face of death.

Relieving Burden and Strengthening Relationships With Loved Ones

Participants emphasized their desire to relieve burdens and strengthen relationships with their loved ones. These psychosocial outcomes were achieved through involving loved ones in decisions about end-of-life treatments. When dying patients had discussions with their loved ones, they seemed to feel less isolated in the face of death. The discussions also relieved their loved ones of the burden of having to make treatment decisions alone. These social and family considerations are not well captured in the current approach to end-of-life decision making in bioethics, which focuses on the patient's rights individually and not in his or her social and family context. Traditional approaches to bioethics may underestimate the importance of social and family ties.[24-27] As noted by Byock,[28] dying offers important opportunities for growth, intimacy, reconciliation, and closure in relationships. Although most commentators focus on end-of-life communication between physicians and patients,[29,30] these results suggest that communication between dying people and their loved ones is crucial.

Implications for Research and Practice

This taxonomy has implications for research and practice. Researchers are beginning to improve end-of-life care in "breakthrough" collaboratives of health care organizations. If the focus of these initiatives is primarily (or exclusively) on medical expert-derived domains of quality end-of-life care, it is likely that they will miss issues of concern to patients and families. This study underscores the importance of a patient perspective in these important quality improvement initiatives.

The domains of quality end-of-life care described here can be easily used by clinicians at the bedside to review the quality of care of dying patients, and to teach students principles of quality end-of-life care.[31] One of us (P.A.S.) has used this framework at the bedside of dying patients and found that it can clarify the goals of treatment for the health care team and provide a helpful conceptual framework for teaching the care of dying patients to medical students and residents. The domains we have identified from the patient perspective can be used by clinicians as a checklist for the adequacy of the end-of-life care they provide. Some questions clinicians can ask themselves are: Am I adequately treating pain and other symptoms? Am I appropriately prolonging dying? Am I helping patients achieve a sense of control, relieve burdens on their families, and strengthen relationships with loved ones?

Strengths and Limitations

Generalizability is both a strength and a limitation of this study. The patient perspective on quality end-of-life care was derived from 3 diverse populations: dialysis, HIV, and long-term care. Moreover, this study includes patients not traditionally studied; most of what we know about palliative care comes from studies of patients with cancer. However, the data should be generalized with caution beyond the specific patient populations studied. Also, our participants were predominantly white; culture and ethnicity influence perceptions of end-of-life care.

The main limitation of this study is that it represents a secondary analysis of data. The original purpose of the studies was to examine ACP (for the dialysis and HIV studies) and control at the end of life (for the long-term care studies). Thus, the data may overemphasize issues related to ACP and underemphasize other issues in end-of-life care. Three of the issues identified in this study (achieving a sense of control, relieving burden, and strengthening relationships with loved ones) were identified in the previous studies on ACP.[8,9] However, 2 other issues (avoiding inappropri-

ate prolongation of dying and receiving adequate pain and symptom control) were identified in this study alone. There may be other domains, such as spirituality or economic issues (identified in some of the expert taxonomies), that were overlooked. Moreover, this limitation may also have distorted the relative importance of the issues we identified to patients; we make no claim that the frequency with which these issues were mentioned indicates their priority to patients.

CONCLUSIONS

From a patient's perspective, quality end-of-life care includes 5 domains: receiving adequate pain and symptom management, avoiding inappropriate prolongation of dying, achieving a sense of control, relieving burden, and strengthening relationships with loved ones. These domains could form the conceptual foundation for research and practice with respect to quality end-of-life care.

Funding/Support: Dr Singer was supported by the National Health Research and Development Program, Ottawa, Ontario, through a National Health Research Scholar Award and is currently supported by a Scientist Award from the Medical Research Council of Canada, Ottawa. Dr Singer is Sun Life Chair in Bioethics at the University of Toronto, Toronto, Ontario. The work was also supported by the Physicians' Services Incorporated Foundation of Ontario.

Disclaimer: The views expressed herein are those of the authors and do not necessarily reflect those of the supporting groups.

Acknowledgment: We thank Edward E. Etchells, MD, Laura Purdy, PhD, James Tulsky, MD, Leigh Turner, PhD, and James G. Wright, MD, for reviewing an early version of the manuscript; Elaine C. Thiel, for serving as research coordinator of the dialysis and HIV studies; and reviewers for helpful comments.

References

1. Council on Scientific Affairs, American Medical Association. Good care of the dying. *JAMA*. 1996;275:474–478.
2. Feinstein AR. *Clinical Judgment*. Baltimore, Md: Williams & Wilkins; 1967.
3. Measuring quality of care at the end of life: a statement of principles. *J Am Geriatr Soc*. 1997;45:526–527.
4. Field MJ, Cassel CK, eds, for the Institute of Medicine. *Approaching Death: Improving Care at the End of Life*. Washington, DC: National Academy Press; 1997.
5. Emanuel EJ, Emanuel LL. The promise of a good death. *Lancet*. 1998;351(suppl 2):21–29.
6. Cleary PD, Edgeman-Levitan S. Health care quality: incorporating consumer perspectives. *JAMA*. 1997;278:608–612.
7. Manning PK, Cullum-Swan B. Narrative, content, and semiotic analysis. In: Denzin NK, Lincoln YS, eds. *Handbook of Qualitative Research*. Thousand Oaks, Calif: Sage Publications Inc; 1994:463–477.
8. Singer PA, Martin DK, Lavery JV, Thiel EC, Kelner M. Mendelssohn DC. Reconceptualizing advance care planning from the patient's perspective. Arch Intern Med. 1998;158:879–884.
9. Martin DK, Thiel EC, Singer PA. A new model of advance care planning: observations from people with HIV. Arch Intern Med. In press.
10. Kelner MJ. Activists and delegates: elderly patients' preferences about control at the end of life. *Soc Sci Med*. 1995;4:537–545.
11. Singer PA, Thiel EC, Naylor CD et al. Treatment preferences of dialysis patients: implications for advance directives. *J Am Soc Nephrol*. 1995;6:1410–1417.
12. Singer PA, Thiel EC, Salit I, Flanagan W, Naylor CD. The HIV-specific advance directive. *J Gen Intern Med*. 1997;12:729–735.
13. Strauss A, Corbin J. Grounded theory methodology: an overview. In: Denzin NK, Lincoln YS, eds. *Handbook of Qualitative Research*. Thousand Oaks, Calif: Sage Publications Inc; 1994:273–285.
14. Strauss A, Corbin J. *Basics of Qualitative Research: Grounded Theory Procedures and Techniques*. Thousand Oaks, Calif: Sage Publications Inc; 1990.
15. Lynn J, Teno JM, Phillips RS, et al. Perceptions by family members of the dying experience of older and seriously ill patients. *Ann Intern Med*. 1997;126:97–106.
16. Ahronheim JC, Morrison S, Baskin SA, Morris J, Meier DE. Treatment of the dying in the acute care hospital. *Arch Intern Med*. 1996;156:2094–2100.
17. Solomon MZ, O'Donnell L, Jennings B, et al. Decisions near the end of life: professional views on life-sustaining treat-

ments. *Am J Public Health*. 1993;83:14–23.

18. Hanson LC, Danis M, Garrett J. What is wrong with end-of-life care? opinions of bereaved family members. J Am Geriatr Soc. 1997;45:1339–1344.

19. Tulsky JA, Chesney MA, Lo B. How do medical residents discuss resuscitation with patients? J Gen Intern Med. 1995;10:436–442.

20. Weeks JC, Cook F, O'Day SJ, et al. Relationship between cancer patients' predictions of prognosis and their treatment preferences. *JAMA*. 1998;279:1709–1714.

21. Fischer GS, Alpert HR, Stoeckle JD, Emanuel LL. Can goals of care be used to predict intervention preferences in an advance directive? *Arch Intern Med*. 1997;157:801–807.

22. Pearlman RA, Cain KC, Patrick DL, et al. Insights pertaining to patient assessments of states worse than death: *J Clin Ethics*. 1993;4:33–41.

23. The SUPPORT Principal Investigators. A controlled trial to improve care for seriously ill hospitalized patients: the Study to Understand Prognoses and Preferences for Outcomes and Risks of Treatments (SUPPORT). *JAMA*. 1995:274: 1591–1598.

24. Lindemann Nelson H, Lindemann Nelson J. *The Patient in the Family*. New York, NY: Routledge; 1995.

25. Hardwig J. What about the family? *Hastings Cent Rep*. March/April 1990:5–10.

26. Blustein J. The family in medical decision making. *Hastings Cent Rep*. May/June 1993:6–13.

27. High DM. Families' roles in advance directives. *Hastings Cent Rep*. November/December 1994 (suppl):S16–S18.

28. Byock I. *Dying Well: Peace and Possibilities at the End of Life*. New York, NY: Riverhead Books; 1997.

29. Emanuel LL, Danis M, Pearlman RA, Singer PA. Advance care planning as a process: structuring the discussions in practice. J Am Geriatr Soc. 1995;43:440–446.

30. Virmani J, Schneiderman LJ, Kaplan RM. Relationship of advance directives to physician-patient communication. Arch Intern Med. 1994; 154:909–913.

31. Singer PA, MacDonald N. Bioethics for clinicians, 15: quality end of life care. *CMAJ*. 1998;159:159–162.

Author Affiliations: *Toronto Hospital and the Department of Medicine (Dr Singer), Joint Centre for Bioethics (Drs Singer and Martin), and the Institute of Human Development, Life Course, and Aging (Dr Kelner), University of Toronto, Toronto, Ontario.*

Corresponding Author and Reprints: *Peter A. Singer, MD, MPH, FRCPC, University of Toronto Joint Centre for Bioethics, 88 College St, Toronto, Ontario, Canada M5G 1L4 (e-mail: peter.singer@utoronto.ca).*

Hospice referral decisions: The role of physicians

Brenda S. Sanders, MS
Tracy L. Burkett, PhD
George E. Dickinson, PhD
Robert E. Tournier, PhD

In our study, we collected and evaluated the opinions of physicians in the Lowcountry of South Carolina (Berkeley, Charleston, and Dorchester counties) regarding their referrals to hospice programs and the extent of influence that their patients and families had on the decision. The research questionnaire was sent to 36.2 physicians who made referrals to hospice (53 percent response rate) and to 337 physicians who did not make referrals (40 percent response rate). Results revealed that medical doctors take the initiative in referrals. They felt that late referrals were due to reluctance on the part of the patient and the patient's family to admit that death was imminent. No differences were found in age, sex, medical specialty, percent of terminally ill patients per practice, or initiative taken. However, when the age and sex of physicians were evaluated, a statistically significant difference was found; females younger than 45 years of age were more likely to make referrals than younger males. Younger physicians were more likely to perceive that the family's reluctance to admit that death was near was a barrier to hospice referrals.

Introduction

Although it may seem obvious that an individual with a terminal prognosis would seek palliative care and want to enter a hospice program, hospice referrals often are not made until the last few days of life. The General Accounting Office[1] reports that 28 percent of all Medicare beneficiaries in a hospice program received hospice care for one week or less. Our study examines why these referrals are so late and investigates the part that physicians play in end-of-life decision making and hospice referrals.

Hopp and Duffy[2] note that there is a particular need for more information about the experiences of people and their family members facing end-of-life decision making. Accordingly, Johnson and Slaninka[3] cite a need for further research to investigate the factors that influence late access to hospice care.

In our study, we collected and evaluated the opinions of physicians in the Lowcountry of South Carolina (Berkeley, Charleston, and Dorchester counties) regarding their referrals to hospice programs and the extent of influence that their patients and families had on the decision. One of the major goals was to determine who takes the initiative and why referrals to hospice often come so late in the illness of many patients. We also wanted to develop a profile of referring doctors based on age, sex, medical specialty, and percentage of terminally ill patients.

Methods

A list of physicians who had made referrals to hospice between January 1, 1990 and September 30, 1999 was obtained from the oldest hospice program in our study region. This list included 526 physicians making referrals during this period. However, since 164 of these physicians had moved out of the area by the time of data gathering, the number of physicians included in the study was 362. To compare referring physicians to nonreferring ones, we obtained a list of all physicians (1,787) in the tri-county area, from the South Carolina Office of Research and Statistics in Columbia, South Carolina. From this list, we selected a random sample of 337, which excluded physicians making referrals to hospice. Although there was only one hospice in the tricounty area in 1990, there are currently seven. Because of this, there was a probability that some of the physicians who were not referring to the oldest hospice made referrals to other hospices. In such cases, these responding physicians were placed into the "referring physician" category. Since our focus was on hospice referrals overall versus nonhospice referrals, we were not concerned with the results of anyone individual hospice program.

The questionnaire, designed by the authors, was initially mailed to 27 physicians in the tricounty area. These physicians served as a panel, and their feedback helped to refine the questionnaire. Of this group, 19 (70 percent) returned the questionnaire in November of 1999. Based on the comments of the panel of physicians, questions were added and deleted, and the questionnaire was redesigned with more cafeteria-style questions and fewer open-ended questions. For example, we replaced open-ended questions asking for reasons why hospice referrals were late. We provided a list of reasons from which the respondents could choose. The panel was also helpful in making sure the right questions were asked to achieve our objectives. The one-page (legal size) questionnaire was enhanced by pretesting it on this panel of physicians. The revised questionnaire was then mailed to the 699 physicians in December of 1999, along with a cover letter and an addressed, stamped envelope.

The survey consisted of eight questions. The first four questions were the independent variables: medical specialty, age at last birthday, sex, and percent of patients with terminal illnesses. The other questions constituted the dependent variables: What percent of your terminally ill patients are referred to a hospice program? Who takes the initiative in hospice referrals? Does a hospice program ever refuse to take a patient? Why do you think hospice

referrals are sometimes late in the patient's illness? Several questions were followed by a request to explain the answer given.

Medical specialties in our samples were collapsed using Jerry Jacobs' breakdown.[4] Age was dichotomized with a breaking-point age of 45. This age was chosen because the Census Bureau uses this as the beginning age for people categorized as "middle-aged." This breakdown allowed analysis of physicians who were not yet middle-aged and those who were middle-aged and older.

Chi-square tests of significance were used to determine if differences existed between each of the independent and the dependent variables. All tests were carried out at the .05 significance level.

Results

Of the 699 surveys mailed, 328 were returned (47 percent). Of the 362 questionnaires mailed to doctors making referrals to the oldest hospice, 193 returned the survey (53 percent); a 40 percent return rate resulted from surveys mailed to physicians not making referrals to the oldest hospice (135 out of 337). However, 47 physicians from the nonreferral sample had made hospice referrals, obviously to some of the other hospice programs in the area. These physicians were added to the referrals group, bringing the total number of physicians making referrals to 240. The final count of physicians who did not make referrals was reduced to 88.

There were 253 males and 67 females in the study. Age distribution revealed that 157 physicians were younger than 45, and 166 were 45 or older. (Some totals do not match the total number of study participants, due to missing data). Overall, few statistically significant differences in the independent variables of specialty—age, sex, and percent of terminally ill patients, were found, when analyzed by each of the dependent variables.

Of the physicians making hospice referrals, 59.46 percent of terminally ill patients were referred to hospice, on average. On average, terminally ill patients represented 5.41 percent of the physician's patient load. When asked what underlies a decision not to refer a terminally ill patient to hospice, the most frequently cited reasons were: the refusal of family/patient, the family wants to care for the patient, and the patient ends up in the hospital anyway. A male neurologist, aged 36, summarizes his feelings about the patient ending up in a hospital:

> When the terminally ill patient is still up and going, hospice services are not desired by the patient, family, and doctor. Once the patient becomes truly ill and debilitated, the caregivers in the family do not feel they can handle the situation at home. Patients are admitted to the hospital and then transferred to a nursing home.

Another physician, a 38-year-old male neurosurgeon, explains, "Transition to hospice care is a very hard turn for many patients (i.e., going from putting up a fight to giving up and accepting failure and waiting for death)."

In 13 percent of physician referrals, a hospice program refused to take the patient. The most frequently cited reasons for such refusal were: difference in opinion regarding life expectancy, economic reasons, unstable/unsafe home, too much active treatment (e.g., radiation and chemotherapy), and no primary caregiver. The frustration of one 37-year-old male internal medicine physician is obvious in his comments regarding an admittance refusal, "Hospice said they had taken all the unfunded patients they could that month but would place the patient on a waiting list. I have never referred another patient to that hospice again."

The largest number of referrals to hospice were in internal medicine and general practice (Table 1). Since internal medicine includes oncology and general practice includes family medicine, these results were not surprising. From the sample of doctors

Table 1. Physician specialties by referral/nonreferral to hospice

Specialty	Refers to hospice		Does not refer to hospice		Total
	Frequency	Percent	Frequency	Percent	
Internal medicine	89	92	8	8	97
General surgery	15	88	2	12	17
Surgical specialties	9	60	6	40	15
Neurological surgery	6	100			6
Ophthalmology			5	100	5
Neurology	7	89	1	12	8
Radiology			6	100	6
0bstetrics/Gynecology	3	33	6	67	9
Pediatrics	8	44	10	56	18
Internal specialties	24	89	3	11	27
Psychiatry	6	33	12	67	18
Emergency medicine	7	54	6	46	13
General practice	56	95	3	5	59
Other	9	43	12	57	21
Total	239	75	80	25	319

Table 2. Age, sex, and referrals to hospice

Refers to hospice?			Female	Male	Total	Statistics
No	Age	< 45	15	17	32	chi-sq = 13.611
		> 45	5	43	48	P = .0000
	Total		20	60	80	
Yes	Age	< 45	34	88	122	chi-sq = 10.817
		> 45	13	105	118	P = .0001
	Total		47	193	240	

in the internal medicine category, only, 8 percent did not refer patients to hospice, and only 5 percent of general practice doctors did not. Specifically, of all the medical specialties, psychiatry and pediatrics had the largest numbers of nonreferrals (12 of 18, and 10 of 18, respectively). As

expected, the primary care physicians make most of the hospice referrals. The specialist refers the terminally ill patient to a primary care physician, who in turn makes the referral.

When age and sex were analyzed, statistically significant differences were found (Table 2). Women who were

younger than 45 were more likely to refer to hospice, whereas men younger than 45 were less likely to refer.

Physicians most frequently take the initiative in hospice referrals (Table 3), followed by family, and then "someone else" or the patient. In the "someone else" category, nurses

Table 3. Who takes initiative in making referrals?		Physician	Patient	Family	Other
Never	Frequency	1	36	9	31
	Percent		16	4	14
Rarely	Frequency	10	154	117	131
	Percent	4	67	51	44
Often	Frequency	186	38	101	58
	Percent	79	16	44	26
Always	Frequency	39	2	2	2
	Percent	17	1	1	1
Total		236	230	229	222

If other, who takes initiative?

	Frequency	Percent
Nurse	44	35
Social worker	22	18
Nursing home	7	6
Neighbor/friend	18	15
Home health	11	9
Discharge planner	13	11
Other	7	6
Total	125	100

have the highest rate of referral initiative (35 percent).

Although hospice referrals tend to be late in the patient's illness, hospice programs prefer earlier patient entry in order to provide palliative care. The most frequently cited reasons for late referrals by these physicians were: the family was reluctant to admit death was near (67 percent), the patient was reluctant to admit death was near (64 percent), and the physician was pursuing a cure (50 percent) (Table 4).

Reasons cited for later referrals were analyzed by age. The only variable that revealed a statistically significant difference was that phy-

sicians younger than 45 were more likely to perceive that the family was reluctant to admit that death was near (chi-square = .021). Of physicians younger than 45, 98 felt that the family was reluctant to admit death was near, whereas 59 physicians did not feel that way. Of physicians 45 years of age or older, 84 felt that the family was reluctant to admit death was near, whereas 82 did not feel that way. Though not statistically significant, physicians under age 45 were more likely (58 percent) to indicate that the physician pursuing a cure was the reason for late referral than were older doctors (41 percent). The younger doc-

tors seem less likely to "give in" to the death prognosis.

Discussion

Physicians in this study most frequently took the initiative in referrals, primarily those in internal medicine and general practice, followed in frequency by the patient's family. Although these data do not indicate the point in the patient's illness at which the physicians actually made referrals, it was found that physicians overwhelmingly initiate the referral, and that patients are less likely to initiate. These findings support the findings of Markson and colleagues[5] that most physicians feel

Table 4. Reasons for late referrals (N = 239)		
Why are referrals late?	Frequency	Percent
Physician waits until patient is bedridden	61	26
Physician pursues care	119	50
Medical rules do not allow treatment	62	26
Physician reluctant to admit death is near	76	32
Patient reluctant to admit death is near	152	64
Family reluctant to admit death is near	161	67
Difficulty in determining time for referral	16	7
Hospice-based restrictions	5	2
Financial factors	4	2
Hospice associated with death	5	2
Lack of knowledge of hospice	6	3
Referral restricts physician autonomy	2	1
Waiting for visible need	7	3
Other	8	3

they should take responsibility for initiating discussion of end-of-life preferences.

When asked why referrals to hospice were late, the physicians largely attributed it to the reluctance of the patient and the patient's family to admit that death was near. This supports findings by Ogle and colleagues[6] in studies of 131 primary care[6] and 264 physicians,[7] who identified patient and family readiness as the major barrier to earlier hospice referrals. Signing into a hospice program means that the patient knows that death is forthcoming, an acceptance that many do not wish to embrace. Johnson and Slaninka[3] also cited this fact as a reason for late referrals.

A statistically significant difference was found regarding physician age and the perception that late referrals were attributable to the reluctance of the patient and the patient's family to accept death as imminent. More physicians under the age of 45 felt this way. Perhaps the family's re-

luctance could be connected to their hesitation to believe or trust younger, less experienced doctors and their prognoses.

Another reason cited for late referrals was that the physician was pursuing a cure, indicating a reluctance on the part of the doctor to admit that the patient's death was imminent. This reason was cited more frequently by doctors under the age of 45. These doctors would have taken the Hippocratic Oath, in which they pledge to prolong life, more recently. Letting the patient die does not comply with that oath. This supports Johnson and Slaninka's finding that the desire on the part of physicians to consider active treatment is a barrier to hospice referrals.

Thus, physicians in this study were taking the initiative in hospice referrals, but they identified the patients and their families as the reason for the lateness of the referrals. Christakis and Escarce[8] found that late referrals to hospice reflect deci-

sions made by physicians rather than patients. In addition, sociologist and physician, Nicholas Christakis,[9] concluded that physicians usually avoid prognosticating, and when they do, they overestimate their patient's remaining days by a factor of two to five. Christakis does not find it surprising that in recent years the technological forces arrayed to treat serious illness, in an effort to control death by postponing it, have become focused on controlling death by managing and predicting it. When the physician discusses death, it is at a further point in the future than the patient may think, perhaps contributing to the delay in entering hospice.

No differences were found among doctors over 45 by sex. However, women under 45 years of age were more likely to refer to hospice than younger male physicians were. This finding supports Arnold, Martin, and Parker's[10] conclusion that female physicians seem better able to communicate sensitivity and caring to patients, they are more engaging in therapeutic listening and counseling, and they are more responsive to psychological needs. Better communication with patients may be the reason that these younger female physicians are more likely to refer terminally ill patients to hospice. Some male doctors may feel that in admitting there is nothing more they can do to save the patient, they are admitting failure, which might be difficult for them to accept.

Females show a higher degree of empathy and more emotional intensity than males in physician-patient relationships.[11] Referrals to hospice would support Dickinson and Tournier's[12] findings in the study of physicians immediately after graduating from medical school. This study showed female physicians were better able to relate to terminally ill patients and their families then male physicians. These findings were even more striking in a 10-year follow-up.[12] Thus, these "feminine characteristics" of gentleness, expressiveness, responsiveness, and kindness may help to explain the differences with regard to the young female physicians in our study.

Some doctors are simply not "programmed" toward hospice, as noted by one 42-year-old male surgeon in this study, "I forget about hospice until the patient is nearly dead. Should I refer sooner?" According to one 58-year-old male cardiologist, "I often simply don't think about it." Thus, a greater awareness of hospice might help increase referrals and encourage doctors to make them earlier in the illness. Johnson and Slaninka[3] noted a knowledge deficit about hospice among caregivers. In a survey of 1,013 family physicians, Miller and colleagues[13] reported that these doctors felt that they did not receive adequate education regarding death, dying, and hospice care. Accordingly, results of a study of family satisfaction with end-of-life care in seriously ill hospitalized adults suggeseted the need for improvement in end-of-life care, especially in communication and decision making.[14]

Many of these physicians were complementary of hospice. A 53-year-old female internal medicine physician said, "I am a big believer in hospice and the desirability of a peaceful, pain-free, dignified death—preferably outside of the hospital. I have learned much from the hospice nurses I have worked with." Likewise, a 29-year-old male internal medicine doctor said, "Overall, my dealings with hospice have been very impressive. I am thankful for their services."

In surveying 173 patients, Navari and Stocking[15] concluded that patients who chose hospice care indicated that their decision was influenced by their physician (88 percent), their caregiver (47 percent), and knowledge of hospice programs (44 percent). With these data suggesting that physicians play a pivotal role in initiating or encouraging hospice referrals, it would benefit hospice programs to increase physician awareness about the advantages of hospice early in their careers. A recent survey[16] suggests that although US medical schools are improving in this area, they are not up to the caliber of UK medical schools. Such awareness, followed by action early in the patient's terminal illness, would enhance the dying process for patients, their families, physicians, and other healthcare professionals.

Acknowledgment

This paper is a revision of a paper presented at the Southern Sociological Society Annual Meetings in New Orleans, LA, March 26-29, 2003.

Brenda S. Sanders, MS, *Department of Sociology and Anthropology, College of Charleston, Charleston, South Carolina.*

Tracy L. Burkett, PhD, *Department of Sociology and Anthropology, College of Charleston, Charleston, South Carolina.*

George E. Dickinson, PhD, *Department of Sociology and Anthropology, College of Charleston, Charleston, South Carolina.*

Robert E. Tournier, PhD, *Division of Social Science and Business, Pikeville College, Pikeville, Kentucky.*

References

1. Pear R: More patients in hospice care, but for far fewer final days. *NY Times.* 2000; September 18: A-23.

2. Hopp FP, Duffy SA: Racial variations in end-of-life care. *J Am Geriatr Soc.* 2000; 48: 658–663.

3. Johnson DB, Slaninka SC: Barriers to accessing hospice services before a late terminal stage. *Death Stud.* 1999; 23: 225–238.

4. Jacobs J: The specialty structure of the medical profession. Paper presented at the Eastern Sociological Society Annual Meetings, Baltimore, MD, March 17–19,1989.

5. Markson L, Clark J, Glantz L, et al.: The doctor's role in discussing advance preferences for end-of-life care: Perspectives of physicians in the VA. *J Am Geriatr Soc.* 1997; 45: 399–406.

6. Ogle K, Mavis B, Wang T: Hospice and primary care physicians: Attitudes, knowledge, and barriers. *Am J Hosp Palliat Care.* 2003; 20: 41–51.

7. Ogle K, Mavis B, Wyatt GK: Physicians and hospice care: Attitudes, knowledge, and referrals. *J Palliat Med.* 2002; 5: 85–92.

8. Christakis NA, Escarce JJ: Survival of medicare patients after enrolling in hospice programs. *N Engl J Med.* 1996; 335: 172–178.

9. Christakis, NA: *Death foretold: Prophecy and prognosis in medical care.* Chicago: University of Chicago Press; 1999.

10. Arnold RM, Martin SC, Parker RM: Taking care of patients: Does it matter whether the physician is a woman? Women in medicine (Special issue). *West J Med.* 1988; 149: 729–733.

11. Bylund CL, Makoul G: Empathic communication and gender in the physician-patient encounter. *Patient Educ Couns.* 2002; 48: 207–216.

12. Dickinson GE, Tournier RP: A longitudinal study of sex differences in how physicians relate to dying patients. *J Am Med Women s Assoc.* 1993; 48: 19–22.

13. Miller KE, Miller MM, Single N: Barriers to hospice care: Family physicians' perceptions. *Hosp J.* 1997; 12: 29–41.

14. Baker R, Wu AW, Teno JM, et al.: Family satisfaction with end-of-life care in seriously ill hospitalized adults. *J Am Geriatr Soc.* 2000; 48: 61–69.

15. Navari RM, Stocking CB: Preferences of patients with advanced cancer for hospice care. *JAMA.* 2000; 284: 2449.

16. Dickinson GE, Field D: Teaching end-of-life issues: Current status in United Kingdom and United States medical schools. *Am J Hosp & Palliat Care.* 2002; 19(3): 181–186.

A Commentary: The Role of Religion and Spirituality at the End of Life

Harold G. Koenig, MD, MHSc[1]

Most people cannot control the exact circumstances of their dying—when they die, where they die, how they die, how people treat them when they are dying, and so forth. They cannot be sure that they will die in "a sanctuary imbued with one's own order" (Kayser-Jones, 2001, p. 3). This is particularly true in the days ahead as limits on health care expenditures become more and more constraining. The fact is that doctors and nurses will be responsible for more and more patients and have less and less time with each patient. This trend is inevitable when one considers the future costs of financing health care and the changing U.S. population demographics up ahead.

Medicare expenditures will double in less than a decade ($220 billion/year in 1998 to more than $415 billion by 2007), even before a cohort of 75 million "baby boomers" reaches age 65 and begins to expand the current 35-million-member elderly population to more than 80 million by midcentury (Smith, Freeland, Heffler, McKusick, and Health Expenditures Projection Team, 1998). Moreover, after 2011, the need for health services will increase astronomically as the aging population grows and life expectancy increases with advances in medicine. Within the first half of this century, the ratio of the number of working persons ages 15–64 to the number of persons older than age 65 will drop from 5:1 in developed countries around the world in 1999 down to 2:1 (United Nations, 1999). This means that instead of five working persons for every one retired person, there will be only two working persons for every one person requiring support. What will our health care look like in the decades ahead?

The picture is not a pleasant one (Schneider, 1999). Acute care hospitals will be able to treat only the most severely ill patients (this trend is already occurring) and will come to look like today's intensive care units. After stabilization, sick patients will quickly be discharged to nursing homes, which will start to resemble acute care hospitals. Waiting lists to get into nursing homes will grow longer and longer, forcing the health care of aged and dying patients back into the community, back into people's homes—with most of the burden falling not on health care providers, but on family members. Lacking family members or the ability to pay for private care, many aging baby boomers could be forced to spend their last days "on city streets and in parks" (Schneider, 1999, p. 797). The bottom line is that dying patients will become less and less able to control the circumstances of their dying in the years ahead.

I agree with Kayser-Jones (2002) that we health care providers must do everything possible to learn about and train doctors, nurses, and family about how to enable and empower dying patients to control the circumstances of their death. However, we health care providers must also consider the changing health care system ahead and identify internal resources and community resources that could help them achieve a "good death," regardless of external circumstances over which they have no control.

Religion and Spirituality

Rather than desperately seek to control external circumstances, some persons have attitudes and viewpoints toward death and dying that make the need for such control less urgent. It is often religious faith and support from their spiritual community that give these people greater internal control over the dying process. (The example I use here, and the views I express throughout the article, are from a Judeo-Christian religious slant; examples from other traditional religious belief systems would work just as well, because all major religions provide solutions to the problem of death.) Rather than trying to control everything, faith allows them to give up the need for control and instead to trust that God will control their circumstances based on God's love, wisdom, and unique knowledge about their situations. They say, "It's all about letting go and letting God, not hanging on and holding tight to that which on this earthly plane is passing away."

These people are not trying to find a sense of home here on earth. Instead, they are looking forward to going *back* home, returning to their real home—to join loved ones who have already died and with the knowledge that loved ones still alive will soon join them. Dying is mainly about saying a temporary goodbye to loved ones and comforting them in their loss. It is a return to a place where they will no longer have pain or suffering, but rather have new bodies that will never become sick again. To those who believe, death is a time of true healing and wholeness like never before. For most of the rest of us, however, issues of controlling the external environment are more urgent and necessary, as is the need to create a home here on earth during the last remaining days of life.

The challenge, of course, is that most people do not have the kind of faith described herein. Instead, they have a combination of faith and lack of faith that make physical, psychological, social, and spiritual issues of great importance. Kayser-Jones (2002) has done a marvelous job of discussing the physical, psychological, and social aspects of dying. Spiritual struggles and needs also play a prominent role in the business of dying.

How common are religious or spiritual needs in older patients who are dying? Although few data are available, religious needs are widely prevalent even among nonterminal patients who are sick enough to be admitted to the hospital. Fitchett, Burton, and Sivan (1997) found that 76% of medical-surgical inpatients at a Chicago hospital had three or more religious needs (the figure was 88% for psychiatric inpatients). In another study of 330 consecutively admitted medical inpatients older than age 60, nearly 90% indicated they used religion to at least a moderate extent to help them cope, half of whom indicated that religion was the most important factor that kept them going (Koenig, 1998). Health care providers must provide dying patients with every opportunity to finish the psychological, social, and spiritual tasks of dying so that they and their families can ultimately experience a good death.

I now examine the physical, psychological, social, and spiritual needs of five groups: the dying person, the family, the health care provider, the nonreligious dying person, and the dying person without family.

The Dying Person

Relieving agonizing physical symptoms must be the first priority—otherwise, it will be impossible for the dying person to focus on the work that needs to be done. Although controlling physical pain is most important, I agree with Kayser-Jones (2002) that other physical symptoms need to be addressed as well: breathlessness, constipation, insomnia, and so forth. A second focus of care needs to be on enabling the patient to remain as alert and conscious as possible during those last days, while at the same time achieving physical comfort. A third focus needs to be on relieving depression, anxiety, or psychotic symptoms that may hinder the dying person from being fully conscious, and attending to relationships with others and with God. I agree again with Kayser-Jones (2002) that this should address feelings of loneliness, isolation, and abandonment, including spiritual abandonment.

A fourth focus of care, and one of the most important in this author's opinion, is on meeting spiritual needs—where spiritual needs are defined broadly in terms of both religious and nonre-

ligious spiritual needs. Religious needs involve making peace in one's relationship with God and with others and readying oneself for the life to come. Spiritual needs not restricted to religion involve finding purpose and meaning in one's remaining days, forgiving others and receiving forgiveness, accepting what one has accomplished and become during one's life, and saying goodbye. These are sometimes called the "tasks" of dying, whose successful completion leads to a good death.

Besides being supportive and life enhancing, as the vast majority of the literature suggests (Koenig, McCullough, and Larson, 2001), religious or spiritual beliefs may for some dying persons and their families create turmoil and distress (Franks, Templer, Cappelletty, and Kauffman, 1990–1991; Fry, 1990). Fearing judgment or punishment, and perhaps eternal damnation, these persons wrestle with their religious beliefs and relationship with God. We recently reported that hospitalized patients age 55 or older who experience religious turmoil have a significantly higher mortality rate during the 2 years after hospital discharge (Pargament, Koenig, Tarakeshwar, and Hahn, 2001). Although this religious struggle may somehow increase the risk of dying, another interpretation of the finding is that such struggle increases as patients approach nearer to death. Patients experiencing religious struggles were those who felt punished or abandoned by God, questioned God's love for them and power to help them, felt abandoned by their religious community, or believed the devil caused their illness. Regardless of direction of causation, such patients need help from religious professionals to help them work through the religious distress.

Finally, devoutly religious and concerned family members and sometimes even well-meaning health professionals may fear that the dying person is not "saved" and place pressure on him or her (who may be of a different religious faith) to get saved. How often does this occur? What are the negative (and positive) consequences of such interactions? What are sensitive ways that professionals can deal with such issues? These questions remain unanswered because of a void of research in this area.

The Family

What about families and their needs? The family needs education and direction on how to help the patient successfully complete the tasks of dying. The family needs emotional and spiritual support to enable them to meet the dying patient's needs, as well as physical support in terms of equipment and respite from the caregiver role. They also need support in letting go of the patient and coping with the grief of the expected loss and the guilt over imagined or real failings in their relationship with the patient. These unresolved psychological struggles can be a cause for a family's inability to accept the patient's poor prognosis or their becoming angry and requesting more technical treatment than is either indicated or the patient wants. It is perhaps also a cause for the inability of some family members to come physically and emotionally close to dying loved ones. Their guilt and grief serve as an insurmountable barrier between them and the person who is dying.

Does spirituality play a role in family members' ability to cope with the dying and death of loved ones? The research done thus far suggests it does. In a prospective study of a cohort of 62 family caregivers of persons with either endstage Alzheimer's disease or recurrent metastatic cancer, Rabins, Fitting, Eastham, and Zabora (1990) at Johns Hopkins examined baseline characteristics of family caregivers that predicted adaptation 2 years later. Nearly 30% of the variance in positive adaptation was explained by the number of social contacts and a further 13% by self-reported religious faith ($p < .0001$ for religious faith). Investigators concluded that a strong religious faith, along with frequent social contacts, were the two best predictors of positive adaptation in this group. At least three other studies have reported similar findings (Burgener, 1994; Keilman and Given, 1990; Wright, Pratt, and Schmall, 1985).

After the patient's death, the emotional and spiritual needs of family need to remain a focus—given the increasing morbidity for family members in the year after bereavement. This is where the religious community can assist health care providers. The religious community could be involved at every step along the way—supporting both the patient and the family during the dying process and afterward. The fact is that the religious community will be called on in the days ahead to take on more and more of the responsibility that formal health care providers now have for dying patients and families (not by choice, but by default because of reasons discussed previously).

Given that 80% of older Americans are church members, what is the religious community doing now that facilitates dying and death besides conducting funeral services? How might the religious community play a greater role in this process? What are some of the barriers that religious communities face in meeting the physical, emotional, and spiritual needs of dying members and their families? Again, the research is nonexistent.

The Health Care Provider

Providing a nurturing and caring environment for the dying is even more important for we the living than it is for those who are dying. It is important that pain and suffering in others should evoke in us a compassion and desire to meet the physical, emotional, and spiritual needs of those who are dying and of grieving families. What do we health care providers need to help those who are dying to complete the tasks of dying and achieve healing during those final days?

The emotional and spiritual needs of health care providers must be addressed so they are better able to meet the physical, spiritual, and emotional needs of dying patients and family members. It is difficult for health care providers to take care of those who are suffering and, regardless of what they do, will soon die. Health care providers who spend 24 hours a day, 7 days a week fighting disease and death may have a difficult time accepting when death is the necessary and preferred outcome. Instead, they see death as a reminder of their failure and inability to help the patient. Consequently, many feel guilty, and seeing the patient or family only increases that guilt. In addition, health care providers may have had negative experiences with

their own family members in terms of dying that influence their responses to patients. There may be a reluctance to become attached to dying patients, thereby exposing themselves to the emotional pain of separation when death occurs. Furthermore, lack of spiritual beliefs or spiritual conflicts on the part of health care providers can make it difficult to care for religious patients or meet their spiritual needs.

Thus, the unmet emotional or spiritual needs of health professionals will serve as barriers that prevent them from being fully present with the dying person and family. Such unmet needs may cause health professionals to abandon patients and families or reduce their willingness to interact with them and form bonds that are necessary for compassionate, meaningful care. Psychological and spiritual conflicts of providers will certainly prevent them from allowing dying patients to define their own dying experience.

Although it is almost silly to say this, it is important to remember that health professionals are human, too. They have many of the same vulnerabilities, neurotic needs, and unfulfilled hopes and dreams as patients who are dying. Some health professionals have strengths in dealing with dying patients, and others do not. Each will deal with dying patients in their own unique way. Those without strengths in this area will probably choose a specialty or specialized area that minimizes their contact with the dying. If forced into contact with dying persons and their families, they will put up emotional barriers to protect themselves and avoid becoming too attached or involved in the lives of such patients.

For some providers, such barriers are necessary to allow them to function; otherwise they would become emotionally overwhelmed from the pain that repeated contact with dying patients would evoke. Other health professionals with the type of personality and life experience that makes them feel comfortable with those who are dying will choose areas like oncology or hospice, in which their personal strengths and skills can be utilized. Because in the days ahead most health professionals will need to care for and address the needs of dying persons and their families, it is essential that health professionals receive counseling, training, and ongoing resources that will enable them to improve their competency in this area.

What role does the spirituality of health care providers play in helping them meet the physical, emotional, and spiritual needs of patients? Does spirituality enable providers to be more "present" with patients, because death is not as threatening or as final to them? Are there educational or training interventions that could be designed to help health care providers enhance their own spirituality in a way that would enable them to better meet the needs of dying patients? Almost no research has been done in this area.

The Nonreligious Dying Person

The nonreligious patient (about 10%–15% of Americans) is similar to the religious patient in needing physical symptoms controlled and consciousness preserved to do the work of dying. Again, however, little research exists on how nonreligious patients cope with death. Focus on emotional needs will probably have to be greater because of the absence of support from religious beliefs and absence of support from a religious community (30% of Americans are not members of religious communities). Attention to the needs of family members will also be greater both in education about delivering patient-centered care and in the meeting of emotional needs, particularly if the family is religious and the dying person is not. If the family is not religious, then other sources of community support besides the religious community will need to be sought. Thus, there is greater burden on the health care provider to meet the needs of both dying persons and their families to compensate for lack of religious resources.

Finally, whereas the dying person and/or family's lack of religious beliefs must be accepted, respected, and honored, spiritual needs (perhaps even spiritual struggles) arise in nonreligious persons just as they do in religious persons. Spiritual resources need to be made available to these persons in a nonthreatening way and at their own pace. The spiritual needs of patients who are not specifically religious include finding purpose and meaning, forgiving and receiving forgiveness, maintaining hope, saying goodbye, and coming to terms with whatever they perceive may occur after they die.

The Dying Person Without Family

The dying person without family will require more attention by health care providers in the emotional and spiritual areas, because there will be no one else to help the patient complete the tasks of dying. This is particularly true for the dying person who is not religious or does not have a spiritual community that can compensate for the lack of family. In these cases, health care providers may need to identify and mobilize the dying person's friends in the community to assist. Unfortunately, friends may be less reliable than family or the religious community (although not necessarily so, and this could be a topic for systematic study).

Conclusions

Patients who are dying and their families need to have physical, psychological, social, and spiritual needs comprehensively addressed during their final days of life. None of these areas should be neglected either in clinical care or in scientific research. When they are addressed in a compassionate, sensitive, and patient-centered way, this increases the likelihood that the dying process will be experienced as both comfortable and meaningful for patient, family, and health care providers. More research is needed to better understand the spiritual needs of dying persons, determine when religion contributes positively

and when it contributes negatively to the dying process, and decide what role the religious community can play in providing the kinds of support that patients and families need as they depend less and less on the formal health care system.

References

Burgener, S. C., (1994). Caregiver religiosity and well-being in dealing with Alzheimer's dementia. *Journal of Religion and Health 33*,175–189.

Fitchett, G., Burton, L. A., & Sivan, A. B., (1997). The religious needs and resources of psychiatric patients. *Journal of Nervous and Mental Disease 185*,320–326.

Franks, K., Templer, D. L., Cappelletty, G. G., & Kauffman I., (1990–1991). Exploration of death anxiety as a function of religious variables in gay men with and without AIDS. *OMEGA 22*, (1), 43–50.

Fry, P. S., 1990. A factor analytic investigation of homebound elderly individuals' concerns about death and dying, and their coping responses. *Journal of Clinical Psychology 46*:737–748.

Kayser-Jones, J. (2001, October 22–23). The experience of dying: How do older people view and experience end of life? Paper presented at the Integrative Conference on End-of-Life Research: Focus on Older Populations. Bethesda, MD: National Institutes of Health and National Institute of Nursing Research.

Kayser-Jones, J., (2002). The experience of dying: An ethnographic nursing home study. *The Gerontologist 42*, (Special Issue III), 11–19.

Keilman, L. J., Given, B. A., (1990). Spirituality: An untapped resource for hope and coping in family caregivers of individuals with cancer. *Oncology Nursing Forum 17*, 159

Koenig, H. G., (1998). Religious beliefs and practices of hospitalized medically ill older adults. *International Journal of Geriatric Psychiatry 13*, 213–224.

Koenig, H. G., McCullough, M., & Larson, D. B., (2001). *Handbook of religion and health: A century of research reviewed.* New York Oxford University Press.

Pargament, K. I., Koenig, H. G., Tarakeshwar, N., & Hahn, J., (2001). Religious struggle as a predictor of mortality among medically ill elderly patients: A two-year longitudinal study. *Archives of Internal Medicine 161*,1881–1885.

Rabins, P. V., Fitting, M. D., Eastham, J., & Zabora, J., (1990). Emotional adaptation over time in care-givers for chronically ill elderly people. *Age and Ageing 19*, 185–190.

Schneider, E. L., (1999). Aging in the third millennium. *Science 283*:796–797.

Smith, S., Freeland, M., Heffler, S., & McKusick, D., & The Health Expenditures Projection Team (1998). The next ten years of health spending: What does the future hold?. *Health Affairs 17*, 128–140.

United Nations, 1999. *Population ageing* 1999 (UN Publication No. ST/ESA/SER.A/179) New York Population Division, Department of Economic and Social Affairs, United Nations.

Wright, S. D., Pratt, C. C., & Schmall, V. L., 1985. Spiritual support for caregivers of dementia patients. *Journal of Religion and Health 24*, 31–38.

Address Correspondence to Harold G. Koenig, MD, MHSc, Duke University Medical Center, Box 3400, Durham, NC 27710. E-mail: koenig@geri.duke.edu
[1]Duke University Medical Center, Geriatric Research, Education and Clinical Center, Veterans Affairs Medical Center, Durham, NC.

UNIT 4
Ethical Issues of Dying, Death, and Suicide

Unit Selections

Key Points to Consider

- "What is a good death?" has been asked for centuries. What would constitute a good death in this time of high-tech medical care? Does the concept of a good death include the taking of a life? Defend your answer.

- Does the role of the health care provider include taking life or providing the means for others to do so? Why or why not?

- Are constraints required to prevent the killing of persons we do not consider worthwhile contributors to our society? Explain.

- Should limits be placed on the length of life as we consider the expenses involved in the care of the elderly and the infirm?

- For some individuals, suicide may seem to be the best solution to their situation. How might our society help such individuals "solve" their problems?

- Is the concept of "rational suicide" rational? Why or why not?

- Do you believe that high-risk-taking persons—such as heavy smokers, race-car drivers, overeating or under eating individuals, or persons mixing alcohol and drugs—are suicidal? Explain.

DUSHKIN ONLINE **Links: www.dushkin.com/online/**
These sites are annotated in the World Wide Web pages.

Articles on Euthanasia: Ethics
   http://ethics.acusd.edu/Applied/Euthanasia/
Kearl's Guide to the Sociology of Death: Moral Debates
   http://WWW.Trinity.Edu/~mkearl/death-5.html#eu
The Kevorkian Verdict
   http://www.pbs.org/wgbh/pages/frontline/kevorkian/
Euthanasia and Physician-Assisted Suicide
   http://www.religioustolerance.org/euthanas.htm
Living Wills (Advance Directive)
   http://www.mindspring.com/~scottr/will.html
Not Dead Yet
   http://www.notdeadyet.org/
Suicide Awareness: Voices of Education
   http://www.save.org
UNOS: United Network for Organ Sharing
   http://www.unos.org/
Youth Suicide League
   http://www.unicef.org/pon96/insuicid.htm

One of the concerns about dying and death pressing hard upon our consciences is the question of helping the dying to die sooner with the assistance of the physician. Public awareness of the horrors that can be visited upon us by artificial means of ventilation and other support measures in a high-tech hospital setting has produced a literature that debates the issue of euthanasia—a "good death." As individuals think through their plans for care when dying, there is a steady increase in the demand for control of that care.

Another controversial issue is physician-assisted suicide. Is it the function of the doctor to assist patients in their dying—to actually kill them at their request? The highly publicized suicides in Michigan, along with the jury decisions that found Dr. Kevorkian innocent of murder, as well as the popularity of the book *Final Exit*, make these issues prominent national and international concerns. Legislative action has been taken in some states to permit this, and the issue is pending in a number of others. We are in a time of intense consideration by the courts, by the legislatures, and by the medical and nursing professions of the legality and the morality of providing the means by which a person can be given the means to die. Is this the role of health care providers? The pro and contra positions are presented in several of the unit's articles. Although the issue is difficult and personally challenging, as a nation we are in the position of being required to make difficult choices. There are no "right" answers; the questions pose dilemmas that require choice based upon moral, spiritual, and legal foundations.

The word *suicide,* meaning "self" and "to kill," was first used in English in 1651. Early societies sometimes forced certain members into committing suicide for ritual purposes and occasionally expected such of widows and slaves. There is also a strong inheritance from Hellenic and Roman times of rational suicide when disease, dishonor, or failure were considered unbearable. Attitudes toward suicide changed when St. Augustine laid down rules against it that became basic Christian doctrine for centuries.

In recent years, suicide has attracted increasing interest and scrutiny by sociologists, psychologists, and others in efforts to reduce its incidence. Suicide is a major concern in the United States today, and understanding suicide is important so that warning signs in others can be recognized.

Just what constitutes suicide is not clear today. Risky behavior that leads to death may or may not be classified as suicide. We have differing attitudes toward suicide. Suicide rates are high in adolescents, the elderly, and males. A person with high vulnerability is an alcoholic, depressed male between the ages of 75 and 84. Suicidal persons often talk about the attempt prior to the act and display observable signs of potential suicide. Males are more likely to complete suicide than females because they use more lethal weapons. For suicidal persons, the act is an easy solution to their problems—a permanent answer to an often temporary set of problems. The public push for suicide prevention can also be a method of resolving the grief caused by a child taking his own life.

DEATH AND THE LAW

Lawrence Rudden

Evelyn was diagnosed with breast cancer in 1997. She spent the next four years dying.

At first she waged war on the cancer, attacking her own body with radiation and pills until she was left inhabiting something limp and unresponsive. Still, the cancer continued to grow inside her, replicating through her spine, shoulders, hips, pelvis, and liver.

She watched as her body began to fail her. There were awful waves of pain, violent coughing, constipation, abdominal cramps, convulsions, and humiliation. She had trouble breathing and walking. The sickness was overwhelming her. Evelyn was moved to an assisted living facility, where she was told she had less than six months to live. Plastic tubes were strung up, around and through her body. She lay on her hospital bed like a wax figure. There was nothing heroic about barely persisting.

Evelyn had seen her mother die a horrible, cringing death. She did not want that for herself. She wanted to die with dignity. On September 24, 2001, Evelyn asked the hospice nurse to help end her life. The nurse provided her with a number for Compassion in Dying, a nonprofit organization that supports the right of terminally ill patients to hasten their deaths. It agreed to help.

Richard Holmes, who suffered from terminal colon cancer, appeared in Portland, on November 7, 2001, to announce that he was upset with Attorney General Ashcroft's blocking of Oregon's assisted suicide law.

Evelyn thought about having her family and medical personnel with her as she ended her life. This made her happy. On November 27, 2001, she swallowed a glass of liquid medication, slipped immediately into a coma, and died fifteen minutes later, at the age of seventy-two. Two days earlier, she had written a letter: "On Thanksgiving, I hope everyone in my family will take time to feel thankful that I live in Oregon and have the means to escape this cancer before it gets any worse. I love you all."

Ashcroft declared that any doctor who prescribed lethal doses of painkilling medication with the specific intent of ending his patient's life would lose his license to prescribe medications and would serve a mandatory twenty-year sentence.

OREGON'S LAW

In 1997, Oregon passed the Death with Dignity Act, making it the only state to permit physician-assisted suicide. Since then, the act has survived an attempt by Congress to overturn it, court hearings on its constitutional validity, and two voter initiatives, in which Oregon residents approved the measure first by a slim margin in 1994, then overwhelmingly in 1997. To qualify for assistance, patients must make two oral requests and one written request at least two weeks apart, be terminally ill with less than six months to live, and be judged mentally competent to make the decision by two separate physicians. Patients are also required to administer the medication themselves. Court records indicate that ninety-one people—mostly cancer patients—have used the provision to end their lives.

"Oregon's law is written with safeguards that prevent patients from using the law prematurely or impulsively," says George Eighmey, executive director of the Oregon branch of the Compassion in Dying Federation. According to Eighmey, patients have sought to end their lives primarily to avoid the profound loss of bodily control and dignity that often accompanies the late stages of a terminal illness.

Can the federal government deny this opportunity to spend one's final months or days in a manner that one does not consider repulsive? According to Attorney General John Ashcroft, it not only can but should. The nation's highest lawyer has declared that assisted suicide is not a "legitimate medical purpose"; in between leading the war on terror, he has been hard at work attempting to punish Oregon doctors for prescribing medications intended to help terminally ill patients end their lives.

"For an oncologist to be unable to prescribe pain medication is incomprehensible." explains Oregon's Dr. Peter Rasmussen. "I would have to retire.... I want to continue to be a practicing physician.

In November 2001, Ashcroft declared that any doctor who prescribed lethal doses of painkilling medication with the specific intent of ending his patient's life would lose his license to prescribe medications and would serve a mandatory twenty-year sentence. He defended this ultimatum on the vague grounds that doctors prescribing lethal doses of painkilling medication were in violation of the federal Controlled Substances Act (CSA), a statute intended to punish illicit trafficking of pharmaceuticals.

Many of Oregon's dying and their family members are less enthusiastic about forcing terminal patients to die slowly, in pain and without dignity.

Supporters of the Ashcroft directive are fond of observing that it does not actually forbid doctors from helping patients end their lives. "Oregon's physicians could still practice assisted suicide, but they could not prescribe federally controlled substances for that purpose," explains Rita Marker, executive director of the International Task Force on Euthanasia and Assisted Suicide. In other words, doctors would still be free to prescribe, say, lethal doses of rat poison to Oregon's dying citizens. For obvious reasons—medical ethics, fear of lawsuits, the semblance of something resembling empathy and compassion—this will not happen. Nor, for that matter, would a doctor who had his license to prescribe drugs stripped under the Ashcroft directive be likely to remain a doctor for long. "For an oncologist to be unable to prescribe pain medication is incomprehensible," explains Oregon's Dr. Peter Rasmussen. "I would have to retire.... I want to continue to be a practicing physician. I would not be able to help my patients." So, despite some semantic zigzagging, the effect of the directive is really quite straightforward: to prevent states from experimenting with the practice of physician-assisted suicide.

Psychiatrist Greg Hamilton, of Portland's Physicians for Compassionate Care group, thinks this is plainly a good thing. "Helping a patient to die is to spend time with the patient and to treat his symptoms. It's not to overdose the patient. That's not helping a patient during his dying process. That's murdering the patient."

Many of Oregon's dying and their family members are less enthusiastic about forcing terminal patients to die slowly, in pain and without dignity. Linda Kilcrease watched as cancerous tumors wrapped around the blood vessels in her mother's neck, slowly constricting the flow of blood to and from the brain. "Her death was a race between her brain slowly exploding in one stroke after another when blood could not drain from her head, or her heart exploding trying to pump more blood into her head.... We watched as her head blew up like a balloon, forcing her eyes closed. When the blood first began to back up and could not drain, we watched as her heart began to beat so hard and fast, nearly ripping through her chest, trying to get blood into her head. The hospital staff gave us heartbeat and blood pressure monitors and we watched the wild fluctuations in vital statistics. We learned how to position Mom's head so her heart would calm down. We watched her change from a robust woman to a shriveled skeleton.... It was torture for everyone, but especially Mom.... Those who say pain medication and psychiatric help are all that is needed to help someone facing death have it all wrong. Neither would be of any use to my mother."

Denied the opportunity for physician-assisted suicide, some patients chose a more violent way of ending their lives. During the late stages of Emanuel McGeorge's cancer, he often found himself in a stupor from the morphine that was being pumped into his veins. A fiercely independent man, McGeorge worried that he was losing control over his life. "Mac did not want to be a sedated vegetable," recalls his wife, Patsy. And so one day he handed her a note, kissed her weathered cheek, then stumbled into the front yard, where he carefully lodged a shotgun in his mouth and pulled the trigger.

Personal ideology is an admittedly imprecise thing, and attempts by the government to dictate what is good for the character of the nation raise a more difficult question: to whose ideology should the law adhere?

By providing terminal patients with the opportunity to die peacefully, under medical care and with loved ones present, the Death with Dignity Act "has prevented more than fifty-seven people from committing violent suicides during the past five years," says Eighmey.

ASHCROFT DIGS IN HIS HEELS

Theoretically, the matter of physician-assisted suicide should be left to the states, as indicated by a 1997 Supreme Court ruling. "Throughout the nation," observed Chief Justice William Rehnquist in his majority opinion, "Americans are engaged in an earnest and profound debate about the morality, legality, and practicality of physician-assisted suicide. Our holding permits this debate to continue, as it should in a democratic society."

Having seemingly arrived at the principle that physician-assisted suicide is wrong, Ashcroft will be damned if he's going to allow the terminal patients of Oregon to exercise their legal right to end their unbearable suffering. Without so much as providing notice to Oregon officials or the general public, he has declared the practice "not medically legitimate," raising concerns that the country's top lawyer is being guided not by the nuances of law but rather by the moral certainties of personal ideology.

Of course, personal ideology is an admittedly imprecise thing, and attempts by the government to dictate what is good for the character of the nation raise a more difficult question: to whose ideology should the law adhere? Lacking a national religion or a single cultural custom, many legal issues take on a gray shade in America. Plainly, this is a good thing. History indicates that when the law and personal ideology get too close, the law often becomes a straightjacket to individual liberties. The Nazis maintained their power in part by using vague moral codes to destroy any threat to their power base. More recently, the Taliban used the law to punish all variety of sinners, from the heretics to the merely thoughtful. Early on, America's Puritan founders were also hard at work persecuting their neighbors for real and imagined shortcomings—a fact that continues to find expression in the numerous state codes regulating sexual conduct.

Though in general practice our society now tends to keep a proper distance between the law and personal ideology, this Puritan zeal for punishing what our leaders call sin may still rear its head from time to time. Exhibit A: Ashcroft's attempt to invalidate Oregon's Death with Dignity Act. Ashcroft carried the same tune while in Congress, where he twice supported legislation that would subject doctors to twenty years in prison if they prescribed federally regulated drugs to cause a patient's death. Both times the legislation failed.

Now, as attorney general, he is again insisting that physician-assisted suicide is "not a legitimate medical practice," an assessment he defends by observing that doctors are charged with helping patients live, not making them dead. Very good. Nevertheless, the Court has already allowed the administration of "risky pain relief," that is, doses of pain relief that are likely to hasten the death of a terminally ill patient. Is this procedure somehow more "legitimate" than assisted suicide? Is it medically legitimate to deny someone a right to die with dignity? Is such a right "fundamental" to patients whose condition is so severe that pain-relief medication is not sufficient to relieve their suffering? Is it somehow more medically legitimate to have politicians second-guessing doctors? And might strict federal oversight of doctors who prescribe pain medication actually have the broader effect of scaring them into undermedicating dying patients? These are all terribly complicated questions, though Ashcroft doesn't seem to mind ducking his head and smashing right through them.

Along the way, Ashcroft has set the stage for a classic battle of states' versus federal rights. Since Oregon doctors are prescribing federally controlled medications to help Oregon residents kill themselves, the Justice Department claims jurisdiction over the process. It argues that the CSA authorizes the attorney general to revoke a practitioner's license to prescribe medications, if he determines that the practitioner is acting in a manner that "threatens public health," regardless of state laws.

Advocates of states' rights maintain that Ashcroft is expanding the scope of the CSA beyond its original intent—regulating the illegal sale of pharmaceuticals. They also dispute that he has the authority to determine whether physician-assisted suicide constitutes "a legitimate medical practice" and quiver at the idea of an unelected, unaccountable government official dictating some of the most personal decisions of their lives. This intrusion, they maintain, is a violation of the spirit of the Constitution.

Round 1 went to the states' advocates. In his harshly critical rebuke of the Ashcroft directive, Oregon federal judge Robert Jones wrote that it would be "unprecedented and extraordinary" for Congress to assign the attorney general the authority to interpret what constitutes a legitimate medical practice. While Jones acknowledged that Ashcroft may be "fully justified, morally, ethically, religiously," in opposing assisted suicide, he emphasized that the attorney general's strong feelings alone do "not permit a federal statute to be manipulated from its true meaning, even to satisfy a worthy goal."

The Supreme Court emphasized that the right to physician-assisted suicide is a matter that should be decided by the states.

Intrepidly, the Justice Department carries on. On September 25, 2001, it filed an appeal with the Ninth U.S. Circuit Court of Appeals—the same court that previously ruled that the due process clause of the Fourteenth Amendment prevents the government from flatly banning physician-assisted suicide. The case will be heard in spring 2003, after which an appeal to the U.S. Supreme Court is expected.

SUPREME COURT PRECEDENCE AND INDIVIDUAL RIGHTS

In their 1997 ruling, the Supreme Court justices voted 9—0 that terminal patients do not have a generalized constitutional right to physician-assisted suicide. The ruling applied only to the cases before the Court and did not take into account the Oregon law. At the same time, the justices littered their opinions with enough qualifiers about specific constitutional rights and principles to effectively make a tangled mess of things. Justice Souter, for example, noted that a total ban on physician-assisted suicide could in fact be deemed unconstitutional if it violated certain basic and historically protected principles of personal autonomy. He added that there exist arguments of "increasing forcefulness for recognizing some right to a doctor's help in suicide."

Justice Breyer emphasized that forcing dying patients to live out their final days in great pain might violate a general right "to

WHY THE GOVERNMENT HAS AN INTEREST IN PRESERVING LIFE

Gerard V. Bradley

Attorney General Ashcroft wants to stop doctors who kill. He has good reason: doctors have a special responsibility to show by word and deed, in season and out, that intentionally killing another person is simply wrong. Yes, even if that person is, like Evelyn, terminally ill.

A doctor's calling is always to heal, never to harm. A doctor's calling is special, though not unique. None of us possesses a license, privilege, or permission to kill, but the healer who purposely kills puts into question, in a unique way, our culture's commitment to the sanctity of life. The scandal created by doctors who kill is great, much like that caused by lawyers who flout the law, or bishops—shepherds—who do not care about their flocks. Whenever someone whose profession centers upon a single good—healing or respect for law or caring for souls—tramples that good, the rest of us cannot help but wonder: is it a good after all? Maybe it is for some, but not for others? Who decides? Is all the talk of that good as supremely worthwhile idle chatter or, worse, cynical propaganda?

Do not intentionally kill. This is what it means—principally and essentially—to revere life. Making intentional killing of humans a serious crime is the earmark of society's respect for life. All our criminal laws against homicide (save for Oregon) make no exception—none whatsoever—for victims who say they want to die. Our law contains no case or category of "public service homicides," of people who should be dead. People hunting season is never open. Our laws against killing (except Oregon's) make no exception for those who suffer, even for those near death. None.

When someone commits the crime of murder, all we can say is that the victim's life was shortened. We know not by how much; the law does not ask, or care. After all, no one knows how much longer any of us shall live. Many persons who are the picture of health, in the bloom of youth, will die today in accidents, by another's hand, or of natural causes. Yes, we can say with confidence that someone's death, maybe Evelyn's, is near at hand. But so long as she draws breath, she has the same legal and moral right that you and I have not to be intentionally killed.

It is not that life is the only good thing which we, and our laws, strive to protect. Life is not always an overriding good; we accept certain risks to life. What is the alternative? Do nothing at all that creates some (even a small) chance of death? Would we get up in the morning? Drive our cars? Take medicine? Go swimming? Fly in airplanes? Some risk to life is acceptable where the risk is modest and the activities that engender it are worthwhile.

Sometimes the risk can be great and still worth accepting. We might instinctively step in front of a car, or jump into a freezing lake to save a loved one, or a stranger's wandering toddler. We might do the same upon reflection, but we do not want to die. We do not commit suicide.

Religious martyrs may face certain death, but they do not want to die. They submit to death as the side effect of their acts, whether these be described as witnessing to the truth, or, in the case of Saint Thomas More, avoiding false witness. The axman, the lion tamer, the firing squad—they kill. They intend death.

This distinction between intending and accepting death is not scholarly hairsplitting. This distinction is real, as real as space shuttles. The *Columbia* crew knew all along that they risked death by flying into space. That which they risked came to be, but they were not suicides.

Of course doctors may—even must— prescribe analgesics. Doctors should try to relieve the suffering of their terminal patients, up to and even including toxic doses. Not because they want to kill, any more than they want to kill patients in exploratory surgery. Doctors who prescribe strong painkillers want to help, even to heal. Given how ill some patients are, the risk of death is worth running, just as some very risky surgeries are a risk worth taking.

Evelyn wants to let go, and she needs help to do so. Yet, none of us walks into a doctor's office and demands a certain treatment. Doctors do not fetch medicines upon demand. They are not workmen at our services. Yes, doctors work toward our health in cooperation with us. They have no right to impose treatment we do not want. But we have no right to drugs, surgery, or anesthesia.

Or to lights out—even for Evelyn.

Why? Because autonomy, or self-rule, is not an all-consuming value. It is not a trump card. Evelyn honestly wishes to bring down the curtain. We may find her condition hideous, as she evidently does, but our feelings (of repulsion, sympathy, or whatever) are unreliable guides to sound choosing. Feelings certainly do not always, or even usually, mislead us. Often, though, they do.

Pause a moment and you will, if you try, think of something attractive and pleasing you did not choose today, because it would have been wrong, and something unappealing, even repulsive, you chose to do because it was right. For me, some days, it has to do with my mother, who suffers from advanced Alzheimer's. Enough said.

On what basis does a society and its governing authorities decide that life is a great common good? Because it is true: life is good. The law is a powerful teacher of right and wrong. Like it or not, what our laws permit is thought by many to be good, or at least unobjectionable. What the law forbids is believed to be, well, forbidden.

Why should our government take such an unyielding stand in favor of life? Because we are all safer where everyone's life is prized, not despised.

Gerard V. Bradley is professor of law at the University of Notre Dame

---

die with dignity." Justice Stevens wrote a separate opinion in which he plainly stated that if presented with an appropriate case, he would overrule a ban on physician-assisted suicide. In effect, Stevens recalled that our country does not have a national religion or culture. As our multicultural mélange of citizens may have very different moral, religious, or personal ideas about how they ought to spend their final days, terminal patients should have the freedom to pursue these convictions so long as their actions affect only their own morality. In other words, an individual should not be forced to spend his final days in excruciating pain simply because this is what his neighbor feels is right.

During a recent speech on Oregon's physician-assisted suicide law, Justice Scalia was even more straightforward: "You want the right to die," snorted Justice Scalia to his audience at the Northwestern School of Law of Lewis and Clark College. "That's right and that's fine. You don't hear me complaining about Oregon's law."

So, what to do? The Supreme Court emphasized that the right to physician-assisted suicide is a matter that should be decided by the states. Indeed, the democratization of this issue would have the beneficial effect of making real-world experience relevant to the law. Rather than freezing the law in accordance with the speculation of political or religious groups, we could learn from experience in a systematic fashion and thus make law adaptive to the individual needs of terminal patients.

Diagnosed with terminal ovarian cancer, Penny Schlueter of Pleasent Hill, Oregon, could no longer sit without pain and had to lie on her side. She planned to take advantage of the state's assisted suicide law when the time came.

For critics, experimentation with physician-assisted suicide would come at the unacceptable cost of making terminally ill patients vulnerable to increased pressure to end their lives—either by profit-oriented HMOs or out of implicit guilt for the financial and emotional burden they are exacting on relatives. "In an era of cost control and managed care, patients with lingering illnesses may be branded an economic liability, and decisions to encourage death can be driven by cost," says Cathy Cleaver of the U.S. Conference of Catholic Bishops. Cleaver points to the Netherlands, where physician-assisted suicide is legal and occurring at an alarming rate: "For years Dutch courts have allowed physicians to practice euthanasia and assisted suicide with impunity, supposedly only in cases where desperately ill patients have unbearable suffering. In a few years, however, Dutch policy and practice have expanded to allow the killing of people with disabilities or even physically healthy people with psychological distress; thousands of patients have been killed by their doctors without their request. The Dutch example teaches us that the 'slippery slope' is very real."

Even at this late date, some of our highest government officials remain dedicated to the idea of regulating the most intimate decisions of this country's citizens, even when the outcome affects only the morality of the actor.

In short, Cleaver worries that if we let doctors end the pointless suffering of terminal patients, the practice would quickly become the norm. Soon depressed people would be demanding a right to die, our palliative-care options would begin to lag behind the rest of the civilized world, and our doctors would be transformed into stalking butlers. An alarming thought, but just one thing: For years the Dutch had almost no formalized procedure in place to regulate the process. Physicians were expected to report themselves to a governing board, which would determine after the fact whether they had broken the law.

By contrast, Oregon's law requires extensive reporting requirements, and, after five years, "evidence points to 100 percent reporting compliance and no deviation from the rules in Oregon," says Barbara Coombs Lee, president of the Compassion in Dying Federation. In fact, a survey of Oregon physicians who have had experience with the Death with Dignity Act reports that some candidates are being screened out of the program. According to the study, only 29 (18 percent) of the 165 people who had requested medication under the act actually received a prescription.

For those who did receive one, control over their final few days, not access to healing options, was the point. It is unlikely that critics will pause long enough to acknowledge this rousing fact. Even at this late date, some of our highest government officials remain dedicated to the idea of regulating the most intimate decisions of this country's citizens, even when the outcome affects only the morality of the actor.

Truly, that is alarming.

Lawrence Rudden is director of research for the Graham Williams Group in Washington, D.C. He writes on politics and culture.

Why secular humanism is wrong: about assisted suicide

Wesley J. Smith

Secular humanist believers in assisted suicide euthanasia routinely dismiss opponents as religious zealots who are driven by a sectarian desire to impose Christianity on society. In this view, people like me care little about the right to personal autonomy and even less about human suffering. Rather, driven by religious fervor, we see ourselves on a "divine" mission to force the extension of each human life for as long as medically possible.

While this ridiculous stereotype might play well to those who see religious fundamentalists lurking under every rock, the most compelling arguments against assisted suicide are entirely secular. Moreover, many of the most effective opponents of the euthanasia agenda aren't religionists at all. These include medical and hospice professional organizations, advocates for the poor, and most especially the disability rights movement.

Why do so many secularists oppose assisted suicide? Books could be—and have been—written on the subject. But with space limited in this forum, I will focus briefly on just four: money, abuses, alternatives, and abandonment.

FOLLOW THE MONEY

It takes only about forty dollars for the drugs used in an assisted suicide. But it could take $40,000 (or more) to provide the medical care and mental health support necessary to alleviate an ill or disabled person's suicidal desire. In a health care world dominated by health maintenance organizations (HMOs), where profits come from cutting costs, assisted suicide would ultimately be about money.

Don't take my word for it. None other than Derek Humphry, founder of the Hemlock Society, argued in his most recent book, Freedom to Die, that "economic reality" is the answer to the oft-asked question about legalizing euthanasia, "Why now?" He writes that assisted suicide could result in the saving of "hundreds of billions of dollars" that "could benefit those patients who not only can be cured but who want to live."[1]

Taking that attitude even further, imagine how much more money could be saved—and thus profits made by HMOs—if euthanasia were made available (as many advocates want) to persons with disabilities, to the elderly who are "tired of life," and to those with permanent cognitive incapacities. Permit the killing of these folk as a "medical treatment," and Wall Street investors in HMOs would be dancing in the street!

And don't forget the pressures involving inheritance, life insurance, payment for nursing home care, and the like. Since our values often follow our pocketbooks, a right to die could quickly morph into a duty to end your life for the benefit of society and/or your family.

GUIDELINES DON'T PROTECT

Euthanasia proponents say that the answer to these and other concerns about abuses is for careful government regulation of assisted suicide. But experience in the Netherlands demonstrates clearly that "protective guidelines" don't protect against abuse. They merely give the illusion of control.

The Netherlands has permitted euthanasia since 1973 under supposedly rigorous guidelines, including requirements for repeated patient requests and an absence of alternative ways to relieve suffering. These so-called protections are violated with impunity. Indeed, since 1973, Dutch doctors have gone from killing terminally ill people who ask for it, to killing chronically ill people who ask for it, to killing physically well but depressed people who ask for it. (This later category of permissible killing resulted from a Dutch Supreme Court ruling that approved a psychiatrist's assisting the suicide of a healthy but grieving mother whose two children had died.)[2] Moreover, people who have not asked for euthanasia are routinely mercy-killed. According a paper published in the British medical journal The Lancet, doctors kill 8 percent of all infants who die in the Netherlands.[3] Repeated Dutch government studies have concluded that doctors there kill approximately one thousand patients each year who have not asked for euthanasia.[4] So much for protective guidelines.

What about Oregon, which has legalized assisted suicide? Not much is known about the actual practice of assisted suicide since it is practiced in darkest secrecy. But of the few cases that have come to public attention, almost all included abuses. For example, as reported by The Oregonian, one woman received assisted suicide from her HMO despite being diagnosed by two mental health professionals as having dementia and being under family pressure to end her life.[5]

EFFECTIVELY ALLEVIATING SUFFERING

The assisted suicide debate so dominates news coverage that many people are not even aware of the tremendous breakthroughs that have been made in treating pain and other distressing symptoms of illness and injury. The truth is that no one need ever die in agony. People still do, of course, but that is not because we don't know how to substantially alleviate suffering. It is because medical professionals just don't do a good enough job of it, and patients and their families are insufficiently educated about what can be done to demand better care.

This is a national scandal that demands concerted efforts to educate doctors and patients about the tremendous potential for pain control and relief of depression. And it requires laws to remove the chill doctors report feeling from the Drug Enforcement Agency when they prescribe aggressively for pain. Along these lines, when Rhode Island passed a law outlawing assisted suicide while explicitly authorizing the aggressive use of drugs for the treatment of pain, the medical use of morphine shot through the roof.[6]

COMPASSION OR ABANDONMENT?

People who support assisted suicide believe they are being compassionate. But are they really?

Imagine having a terminal illness and despairing about becoming a burden to your family, or of being forced to die in agony. You go to your doctors and suggest that perhaps the answer is assisted suicide. The doctor shrugs and says, "Well, it's your choice." Wouldn't that confirm your worst fears about the value of your life, your future prospects for suffering, your concern that you are now a burden on your family?

Assisted suicide is not an answer to the problems it seeks to address; it is to surrender to them. If we wish to remain a truly compassionate society that cares deeply for our ill, disabled, elderly, and dying, we will reject the siren song of killing and focus intently on improving care and suicide prevention to help the suicidal ill and disabled overcome the desire to end their lives.

Notes

1. Derek Humphry and Mary Clement, Freedom to Die: People, Polities and the Right-to-Die-Movement (New York: St. Martin's, 1998), pp. 333–34.
2. See for example, J. Remmelink et al., "Medical Decisions About the End of Life," in Report of the Committee to Study the Medical Practice concerning Euthanasia; The Study for the Committee on the Medical Practice concerning Euthanasia (2 vols., The Hague, 1991). For discussions of subsequent Dutch investigations of euthanasia, see Kathleen Foley and Herbert Hendin (eds.), The Case Against Assisted Suicide: For the Right to End-of-Life Care (Baltimore: John Hopkins, 2002).
3. Agnes van der Heide et al. "Medical End-of-Life Decisions Made for Neonates and Infants in the Netherlands," The Lancet 350 (July 26, 1997): 251–56.
4. Ibid.
5. Erin Hoover Barnett, "Is Mom Capable of Choosing to Die?" The Oregonian, October 17, 1999.
6. DEA published statistics of morphine use per capita.

Wesley J. Smith is a senior fellow at the Discovery Institute and an attorney and consultant to the International Task Force on Euthanasia and Assisted Suicide. His most recent book (co-authored with Eric M. Chevlen, M.D.) is Power Over Pain: How to Get the Pain Control You Need.

Doctor, I Want to Die. Will You Help Me?

Timothy E. Quill, MD

IT HAD been 18 months since a 67-year-old retired man whose main joy in life was his two grandchildren was diagnosed with inoperable lung cancer. An arduous course of chemotherapy helped him experience a relatively good year where he was able to remain independent, babysitting regularly for his grandchildren.

Recent tests revealed multiple new bony metastases. An additional round of chemotherapy and radiation provided little relief. By summer, pain and fatigue became unrelenting. He was no longer able to tolerate, much less care for, his grandchildren. His wife of 45 years devoted herself to his care and support. Nonetheless, his days felt empty and his nights were dominated by despair about the future. Though he was treated with modern pain control methods, his severe bone pain required daily choices between pain and sedation. Death was becoming less frightening than life itself.

A particularly severe thigh pain led to the roentgenogram that showed circumferential destruction of his femur. Attempting to preserve his ability to walk, he consented to the placement of a metal plate. Unfortunately, the bone was too brittle to support the plate. He would never walk again.

One evening in the hospital after his wife had just left, his physician sat down to talk. The pain was "about the same," and the new sleep medication "helped a little." He seemed quiet and distracted. When asked what was on his mind, he looked directly at his doctor and said, "Doctor, I want to die. Will you help me?"

Such requests are dreaded by physicians. There is a desperate directness that makes sidestepping the question very difficult, if not impossible. Often, we successfully avoid hearing about the inner turmoil faced by our terminally ill patients—what is happening to the person who has the disease. Yet, sometimes requests for help in dying still surface from patients with strong wills, or out of desperation when there is nowhere else to turn. Though comfort care (ie, medical care using a hospice philosophy) provides a humane alternative to traditional medical care of the dying,[1-7] it does not always provide guidance for how to approach those rare patients who continue to suffer terribly in spite of our best efforts.

See Box: "Compassion Needs Reason Too"

This article explores what dying patients might be experiencing when they make such requests and offers potential physician responses. Such discussions are by no means easy for clinicians, for they may become exposed to forms and depths of suffering with which they are unfamiliar and to which they do not know how to respond. They may also fear being asked to violate their own moral standards or having to turn down someone in desperate need. Open exploration of requests for physician-assisted death can be fundamental to the humane care of a dying person, because no matter how terrifying and unresolvable their suffering appears, at least they are no longer alone with it. It also frequently opens avenues of "help" that were not anticipated and that do not involve active assistance in dying.

"Doctor, I want to die" and "Will you help me?" constitute both a statement and a query that must each be independently understood and explored. The initial response, rather than a yes or no based on assumptions about the patient's intent and meaning, might be something like: "Of course, I will try to help you, but first I need to understand your wish and your suffering, and then we can explore how I can help." Rather than shying away from the depths of suffering, follow-up questions might include, "What is the worst part?" or "What is your biggest fear?"

THE WISH TO DIE

Transient yearnings for death as an escape from suffering are extremely common among patients with incurable, relentlessly progressive medical illnesses.[8-10] They are not necessarily signs of a major psychiatric disorder, nor are they likely to be fully considered requests for a physician-assisted death. Let us explore some of their potential meanings through a series of case vignettes.

Tired of Acute Medical Treatment

A 55-year-old woman with very aggressive breast cancer found her tumor to be repeatedly recurring over the last 6 months. The latest instance signaled another failure of chemotherapy. When her doctor was proposing a new round of experimental therapy, she said, "I wish I were dead." By exploring her statement, the physician learned that the patient felt strongly she was not going to get better and that she could not fathom the prospect of more chemotherapy with its attendant side effects. She wanted to spend what time she had left at home. He also learned that she did not want to die at that moment. A discussion about changing the goals of treatment from cure to comfort ensued, and a treatment plan was developed that exchanged chemotherapy for symptom-relieving treatments. The patient was relieved by this change in focus, and she was able to spend her last month at home with her family on a hospice program.

Comfort care can guide a caring and humane approach to the last phase of life by directing its energy to relieving the patients' suffering with the same intensity and creativity that traditional medical care usually devotes to treating the underlying disease.[1-7] When comprehensively applied, in either a hospice program or any other setting, comfort care can help ensure a dignified, individualized death for most patients.

Unrecognized or Undertreated Physical Symptoms

A stoical 85-year-old farmer with widely metastatic prostate cancer was cared for in his home with the help of a hospice program. Everyone marveled at his dry wit and engaging nature as he courageously faced death. He was taking very little medication and always said he was "fine." Everyone loved to visit with him, and his stories about life on the farm were legendary. As he became more withdrawn and caustic, people became concerned, but when he said he wished he were dead, there was a panic. All the guns on the farm were hidden and plans for a psychiatric hospitalization were entertained. When his "wish for death" was fully explored, it turned out that he was living with excruciating pain, but not telling anyone because he feared becoming "addicted" to narcotics. After a long discussion about pain-relieving principles, the patient agreed to try a regular, around-the-clock dosage of a long-acting narcotic with "as needed" doses as requested. In a short time, his pain was under better control, he again began to engage his family and visitors, and he no longer wanted to die. For the remainder of his life, the physical symptoms that developed were addressed in a timely way, and he died a relatively peaceful death surrounded by his family.

Though not all physical symptoms can be relieved by the creative application of comfort care, most can be improved or at least made tolerable. New palliative techniques have been developed that can ameliorate most types of physical pain, provided they are applied without unnecessary restraint. One must be sure that unrelieved symptoms are not the result of ignorance about or inadequate trials of available medical treatments, or the result of exaggerated patient or physician fears about addiction or about indirectly hastening death. Experts who can provide formal or informal consultation in pain control and in palliative care are available in most major cities and extensive literature is available.[11-14]

Emergent Psychosocial Problems

A 70-year-old retired woman with chronic leukemia that had become acute and had not responded to treatment was sent home on a home hospice program. She was prepared to die, and all of her physicians felt that she would "not last more than a few weeks." She had lived alone in the past, but her daughter took a leave of absence from work to care for her mother for her last few days or weeks. Ironically (though not necessarily surprisingly), the mother stabilized at home. Two months later, outwardly comfortable and symptom-free under the supportive watch of her daughter, she began to focus on wanting to die. When asked to elaborate, she initially discussed her fatigue and her lack of a meaningful future. She then confided that she hated being a burden on her daughter—that her daughter had children who needed her and a job that was beginning to cause serious strain. The daughter had done her best to protect her mother from these problems, but she became aware of them anyway. A family meeting where the problems were openly discussed resulted in a compromise where the mother was admitted to a nursing facility where comfort care was offered, and the daughter visited every other weekend. Though the mother ideally would have liked to stay at home, she accepted this solution and was transferred to an inpatient unit where she lived for 2 more months before dying with her daughter at her side.

Requests for help in dying can emanate from unrecognized or evolving psychosocial problems.[15] Sometimes these problems can be alleviated by having a family meeting, by arranging a temporary "respite" admission to a health care facility, or by consulting a social worker for some advice about finances and available services. Other psychosocial problems may be more intractable, for example, in a family that was not functioning well prior to the pa-

tient's illness or when a dominating family member tries to influence care in a direction that appears contrary to the patient's wishes or best interest. Many patients have no family and no financial resources. The current paucity of inpatient hospices and nursing facilities capable of providing comfort care and the inadequate access to health care in general in the United States often mean that dying patients who need the most help and support are forced to fend for themselves and often die by themselves. The health care reimbursement system is primarily geared toward acute medical care, but not terminal care, so the physician may be the only potential advocate and support that some dying patients have.

Spiritual Crisis

A 42-year-old woman who was living at home with advanced acquired immunodeficiency syndrome (AIDS) began saying that she wished she were dead. She was a fundamentalist Christian who at the time of her diagnosis wondered, "Why would God do this to me?" She eventually found meaning in the possibility that God was testing her strength, and that this was her "cross to bear." Though she continued to regularly participate in church activities over the 5 years after her initial diagnosis, she never confided in her minister or church friends about her diagnosis. Her statements about wishing she were dead frightened her family, and they forced her to visit her doctor. When asked to elaborate on her wish, she raged against her church, her preacher, and her God, stating she found her disease humiliating and did not want to be seen in the end stages of AIDS where everyone would know. She had felt more and more alone with these feelings, until they burst open. Once the feelings were acknowledged and understood, it was clear that they defied simple solution. She was clearly and legitimately angry, but not depressed. She had no real interest in taking her own life. She was eventually able to find a fundamentalist minister from a different church with an open mind about AIDS who helped her find some spiritual consolation.

The importance of the physician's role as witness and support cannot be overemphasized. Sharing feelings of spiritual betrayal and uncertainty with an empathetic listener can be the first step toward healing. At least isolation is taken out of the doubt and despair. The physician must listen and try to fully understand the problem before making any attempt to help the patient achieve spiritual resolution. Medically experienced clergy are available in many communities who can explore spiritual issues with dying patients of many faiths so that isolation can be further lessened and potential for reconnection with one's religious roots enhanced.

Clinical Depression

A 60-year-old man with a recently diagnosed recurrence of his non-Hodgkin's lymphoma became preoccupied with wanting to die. Though he had a long remission after his first course of chemotherapy, he had recently gone through a divorce and felt he could not face more treatment. In exploring his wishes, it was evident he was preoccupied with the death of his father, who experienced an agonizing death filled with severe pain and agitation. He had a strong premonition that the same thing would happen to him, and he was not sleeping because of this preoccupation. He appeared withdrawn and was not able to fully understand and integrate his options and the odds of treatment directed at his lymphoma, the likelihood that comfort care would prevent a death like his father's, or his doctor's promise to work with him to find acceptable solutions. Though he was thinking seriously of suicide, he did not have a plan and therefore was treated intensively as an outpatient by his internist and a psychotherapist. He accepted the idea that he was depressed, but also wanted assurances that all possibilities could be explored after a legitimate trial of treatment for depression. He responded well to a combination of psychotherapy and medication. He eventually underwent acute treatment directed at his lymphoma that unfortunately did not work. He then requested hospice care and seemed comfortable and engaged in his last months. As death was imminent, his symptoms remained relatively well controlled, and he was not overtly depressed. He died alone while his family was out of the house. Since his recently filled prescription bottles were all empty, it may have been a drug overdose (presumably to avoid an end like his father's), though no note or discussion accompanied the act.

Whenever a severely ill person begins to talk about wanting to die and begins to seriously consider taking his or her own life, the question of clinical depression appropriately arises.[16] This can be a complex and delicate determination because most patients who are near death with unrelenting suffering are very sad, if not clinically depressed. The epidemiologic literature associating terminal illness and suicide assumes that all such acts arise from unrecognized and/or untreated psychiatric disorders,[17-19] yet there is a growing clinical literature suggesting that some of these suicides may be rational.[2,16,20-25]

Two fundamental questions must be answered before suicide can be considered rational in such settings: (1) Is the patient able to fully understand his or her disease, prognosis, and treatment alternatives (ie, is the decision rational), and (2) is the patient's depression reversible, given the limitations imposed by his illness, in a way that would substantially alter the circumstances? It is vital not to overnormalize (eg, "anyone would be depressed under such circumstances") or to reflexively define the request as a sign of psychopathology. Each patient's dilemma must be fully explored. Consultation with an experienced psychiatrist can be helpful when there is doubt, as can a trial of grief counseling, crisis intervention, or antidepressant medications if a potentially reversible depression is present and the patient has time and strength to participate.

Unrelenting, Intolerable Suffering

The man with widely metastatic lung cancer described in the introduction felt that his life had become a living hell with no acceptable options. His doctors agreed that all effective medical options to treat his cancer had been exhausted. Physical activity and pride in his body had always been a central part of who he was. Now, with a pathologic fracture in his femur that could not be repaired, he would not even be able to walk independently. He also had to make daily trade-offs between pain, sedation, and other side effects. At the insistence of his doctor, he had several visits with a psychiatrist who found his judgment to be fully rational. Death did not appear imminent, and his condition could only get worse. Even on a hospice program, with experts doing their best to help address his medical, social, personal, and spiritual concerns, he felt trapped, yearning for death. He saw his life savings from 45 years of work rapidly depleting. His family offered additional personal and financial resources. They wanted him to live, but having witnessed the last months of progressive disability, loss, and pain, with no relief in sight other than death, they respected his wishes and slowly began to advocate on his behalf. "We appreciate your efforts to keep him comfortable, but for him this is not comfortable and it is not living. Will you help him?"

Physicians who have made a commitment to shepherd their patients through the dying process find themselves in a predicament. They can acknowledge that comfort care is sometimes far less than ideal, but it is the best that they can offer, or they can consider making an exception to the prohibition against physician-assisted death, with its inherent personal and professional risks. Compassionate physicians differ widely on their approach to this dilemma,[20-24, 26-29] though most would likely agree with an open discussion with a patient who raises the issue and an extensive search for alternatives.

Clinical criteria have been proposed to guide physicians who find assisted suicide a morally acceptable avenue of last resort[25]: (1) the patient must, of his or her own free will and at his or her own initiative, clearly and repeatedly request to die rather than continue suffering; (2) the patient's judgment must not be distorted; (3) the patient must have a condition that is incurable and associated with severe, unrelenting, intolerable suffering; (4) the physician must ensure that the patient's suffering and the request are not the result of inadequate comfort care; (5) physician-assisted suicide should only be carried out in the context of a meaningful doctor-patient relationship[22]; (6) consultation with another physician who is experienced in comfort care is required; and (7) clear documentation to support each condition above should be required (if and when such a process becomes openly sanctioned). It is not the purpose of this article to review the policy implications of formally accepting these criteria or of maintaining current prohibitions.[20-29] Instead, it is to encourage and guide clinicians on both sides of the issue to openly explore the potential meanings of a patient's request for help in dying and to search as broadly as possible for acceptable responses that are tailored to the individual patient.

THE REQUEST FOR HELP IN DYING

Dying patients need more than prescriptions for narcotics or referrals to hospice programs from their physicians. They need a personal guide and counselor through the dying process—someone who will unflinchingly help them face both the medical and the personal aspects of dying, whether it goes smoothly or it takes the physician into unfamiliar, untested ground. Dying patients do not have the luxury of choosing not to

COMPASSION NEEDS REASON TOO

A growing number of physicians today believe that it is morally permissible, perhaps even required, to assist certain of their patients in the act of suicide.[1-4] They take their inspiration from Quill's account of the way he assisted his young patient, Diane, to kill herself.[5] They are impressed by Quill's compassion and respect for his patient. Like him, they would limit the physician's participation in suicide to extreme cases in which suffering is unrelenting, unrelievable, and unbearable. Like him, they follow a flawed line of moral reasoning in which a compassionate response to a request for assisted suicide is deemed sufficient in itself to justify an ethically indefensible act.

In his article[6] in this issue of THE JOURNAL, Quill provides a more formal and systematic outline of what he believes the appropriate response of physicians should be to a request for suicide. He emphasizes that the reasons for the request must be identified and ameliorated (ie, pain and depression should be properly treated and psychosocial and spiritual crises resolved). To do these things properly, physicians themselves must listen and learn; accept their own mortality; be compassionate, honest, and "present" to their patients; and remain "open" to assisted suicide. If this approach fails to relieve suffering, Quill deems the case extreme enough to justify transgressing the ethical proscription against assisted suicide.

Most of Quill's recommendations are consistent with a physician's responsibility to provide comprehensive palliative care.[7] They would be equally binding on those opposed to assisted suicide. What is not acceptable is the faulty line of reasoning that underlies Quill's seemingly reasonable and moderate approach. That reasoning is marred by three ethical assumptions: (1) that compassion in decision making confers moral validity on the act of assisted suicide; (2) that Quill's decision-making process is, itself, morally sound; and (3) that, by itself, close analysis of cases is sufficient to establish the right and good thing to do in "extreme" cases.

To begin with, Quill begs the most important ethical question, namely, whether in certain cases assisted suicide can be ethically justified. This is the heart of a debate that is far from settled.[8] It cannot be settled here. Elsewhere,[9] I have tried to show that, like active euthanasia, assisted suicide is never morally permissible: both are acts of intentional killing; they are violent remedies in the name of beneficence; they seriously distort the healing purposes of medicine; they are based on erroneous notions of compassion, beneficence, and autonomy; and they divert attention from comprehensive palliative care.[10-12] Moreover, euthanasia and assisted suicide are socially disastrous. They are not containable by placing legal limits on their practice. Arguments to the contrary, the "slippery slope" is an inescapable logical, psychological, historical and empirical reality.

Quill's first implicit assumption is that assisted suicide can sometimes be justified, ie, a morally wrong act can be made morally right if the process used in deciding to perform it and the way it is performed are compassionate and beneficently motivated. The moral psychology of an act has a certain weight in assessing an agent's guilt, but not in changing the nature of the act itself.[10] Even a person's consent is insufficient to make suicide morally right. Nor is it justified by a gentle or genteel "approach" to the act. This, for example, is the stance of those who reject Jack Kevorkian's unseemly and preemptory use of his death machine, but commend

Quill's modulated approach.[3] To be sure, Kevorkian shows a shocking disregard for the most elementary responsibilities of a physician to a patient who becomes desperate enough to ask for assisted death.[13] But regardless of whether patients use Kevorkian's machine or Quill's compassionate prescription for sedatives, they are dead by premeditated intention. In either case, physicians, who are the necessary instruments of the patient's death, are as much a moral accomplice as if they had administered the dose themselves.

Even if we grant Quill's first assumption, we are left questioning the moral validity of Quill's recommended decision-making process. On the surface, Quill seems to place the initiative in the patient's hands and suggests that the physician merely be "open" to assisted suicide under the right circumstances. But, ultimately, the determination of the right circumstances is in the physician's hands. The physician controls the availability and timing of the means whereby the patient kills himself. Physician's assessment determines whether the patient is in the "extreme" category that, per se, justifies suicide assistance.

The opportunities for conscious or unconscious abuse of this power are easy to obscure, even for the best-intentioned physician. Physicians' valuation of life and its meaning, the value or nonvalue of suffering, the kind of life they would find bearable, and the point at which life becomes unbearable cannot fail to influence their decisions. These values will vary widely even among those who take assisted suicide to be morally licit. The physician might follow all of Quill's recommendations (eg, be honest and compassionate and listen to the patient), but find it virtually impossible to separate personal values from interaction with the patient.

Moreover, physicians must face their own frustrations, fatigue, and secret hopes for a way out of the burdens of caring for a suffering, terminally ill patient. The kind of intense emotional involvement Quill describes in Diane's case can induce emotional burnout in which the physician moves imperceptibly from awaiting the patient's decision and readiness, to subtle elicitation of a request for death. "Getting it over with" may not be only the patient's desire, but that of the physician, other health professionals, and family and friends.[14] Each will have his or her own reason for being open to assisting in suicide. Each reason is capable of being imputed to a vulnerable, exhausted, guilty, and alienated patient. When assisted suicide is legitimated, it places the patient at immense risk from the "compassion" of others. Misdirected compassion in the face of human suffering can be as dangerous as indifference.

Wesley's[15] astute analysis of Quill's treatment of his patient Diane[5] suggests that Quill himself was not totally immune to some of these psychodynamic dangers. The decision to respond to a request for assistance in suicide can be as much a danger to, as a safeguard of, the patient's right to self-determination. If it is known to be a viable option at the outset, it cannot fail to influence the patient, the physician, and everyone else involved in the patient's care. If it is not known at the outset, the patient is deprived of the clues needed to interpret her physician's actions. No matter how we examine it, Quill's "approach" is as morally dubious as the act to which it leads.

Finally, Quill's article implies that with an ever greater knowledge of the patient's circumstances, thoughts, and values and a sin

Box continued

Conpassion Needs Reason Too *Continued*

cere effort to understand them, we can reliably arrive at a point at which we move from the morally unacceptable to the morally acceptable. This is the "line of cases" approach that relies for its moral validity on the recently revived method of casuistry.[15] Casuistry is a useful method of case analysis rooted in legal procedure, but it is a dubious way to establish a moral norm.

Brody[1] recently used the casuistic method in a logically fallacious attempt to wipe out the distinction between killing and letting die. The problem with relying solely on the casuistic method of paradigm cases is that there must be something beyond the case by which to judge the case. This would be true even if we could encompass all the details of any case. We must still explicate why this case is a paradigm case that can be used in locating other cases along a moral spectrum. When we do, we discover that a normative principle has been at work. Behind every paradigm case, there is a moral system. Different moral systems judge paradigm cases differently. In the end, we must decide among moral systems, not cases.

It is important, therefore, to read through Quill's metaphorically elegant and compassionate story of Diane's death to the reasons underlying his actions. Clearly for Quill, the undeniably important affect of compassion takes on the status of an overriding moral principle. But compassion is a virtue, not a principle. Morally weighty as it is, compassion can become maleficent unless it is constrained by principle. In the world's history, too many injustices have been committed in the name of someone's judgment about what was compassionate for his neighbor. Compassion, too, must be subject to moral analysis, must have its reasons, and those reasons must also be cogent.

Edmund D. Pellegrino, MD

1. Brody H. Causing, intending and assisting death, *J Clin Ethics.* 1993; 4: 112–113.

2. Wanzer SH, Dyders DD, Edelstein SJ, et al. The physician's responsibility toward hopelessly ill patients, *N Engl J Med.* 1989; 320: 844–849.
3. Cassel CK, Meir DE. Morals and moralism in the debate over euthanasia and assisted suicide. *N Engl J Med.* 1990; 923: 750–752.
4. Ubel PA. Assisted suicide and the case of Dr Quill and Diane. *Issues Law Med.* 1993; 8: 487–502.
5. Quill TE. Death and dignity: a case of individualized decision making. *N Engl J Med.* 1991; 324: 691–694.
6. Quill TE. Doctor, I want to die, will you help me? *J.A.M.A.* 1993; 270: 870–873.
7. Lynn J. The health care professional's role when active euthanasia is sought. *J Palliat Care.* 1988; 4: 100–102.
8. Kass L. Neither for love nor money; why doctors must not kill. *Public Interest.* 1989; 94: 25–46.
9. Pellegrino ED. Doctors must not kill. *J Clin Ethics.* 1992; 8: 95–102.
10. Kamisar Y. Are laws against assisted suicide unconstitutional? *Hastings Cent Rep.* 1993; 23: 32–41.
11. Arkes H, Berke M, Doctor M, et al. Always to care, never to kill; a declaration on euthanasia. *First Things.* 1992; 20: 46.
12. Council on Ethical and Judicial Affairs, American Medical Association. Decisions near the end of life. *J.A.M.A.* 1991; 267: 2229–2233.
13. Kevorkian J. *Prescription Medicine; The Goodness of Planned Death.* Buffalo, NY: Prometheus Books; 1991.
14. It's over, Debbie. *J.A.M.A.* 1986; 259: 272. A Piece of My Mind.
15. Wesley P. Dying safety issues. *J Law Med.* 1993; 8: 467–485.
16. Jonsen AR. Casuistry as a methodology in clinical ethics. *Thsor Med.* 1991; 12: 295–307.

From the Georgetown University Medical Center, Washington, DC. Reprints not available.

undertake the journey, or of separating their person from their disease. Physicians' commitment not to abandon their patients is of paramount importance.

Requests for assistance in dying only rarely evolve into fully considered requests for physician-assisted suicide or euthanasia. As illustrated in the case vignettes, a thorough exploration and understanding of the patient's experience and the reason the request is occurring at a given moment in time often yield avenues of "help" that are acceptable to almost all physicians and ethicists. These clinical summaries have been oversimplified to illustrate distinct levels of meaning. More often, multiple levels exist simultaneously, yielding several avenues for potential intervention. Rather than making any assumptions about what kind of help is being requested, the physician may ask the patient to help clarify by asking, "How were you hoping I could help?" Exploring a patient's request or wish does not imply an obligation to accede, but rather to seriously listen and to consider with an open mind. Even if the physician cannot directly respond to a rational request for a physician-assisted death because of personal, moral, or legal constraints, exploring, understanding, and expressing empathy can often be therapeutic.[30,31] In addition, the physician and the patient may be able to find some creative middle ground that is acceptable to both.[32,33] Finding common ground that can enhance the patient's comfort, dignity, and personal choice at death without compromising the physician's personal and professional values can be creative, challenging, and satisfying work for physicians.

WHAT DO DYING PERSONS WANT MOST FROM THEIR PHYSICIANS?

Most patients clearly do not want to die, but if they must, they would like to do so while maintaining their physical and personal integrity.[34] When faced with a patient expressing a wish for death, and a request for help, physicians (and others) should consider the following.

Listen and Learn From the Patient Before Responding

Learning as much as possible about the patient's unique suffering and about exactly what is being requested is a vital first step. Physicians tend to be action oriented, yet these problems only infrequently yield simple resolutions. This is not to say they are insoluble, but the patient is the initial guide to defining the problem and the range of acceptable interventions.

Be Compassionate, Caring, and Creative

Comfort care is a far cry from "not doing anything." It is completely analogous to intensive medical care, only in this circumstance the care is directed toward the person and his or her suffering, not the disease. Dying patients need our commitment to creatively problem-solve and support them no matter where their illness may go. The rules and methods are not simple when applied to real persons, but the satisfaction and meaning of helping someone find his or her own path to a dignified death can be immeasurable.

Promise to Be There Until the End

Many people have personally witnessed or in some way encountered "bad deaths," though what this might mean to a specific patient is varied and unpredictable. Patients need our assurance that, if things get horrible, undignified, or intolerable, we will not abandon them, and we will continue to work with them to find acceptable solutions. Usually those solutions do not involve directly assisting death, but they may often involve the aggressive use of symptom-relieving measures that might indirectly hasten death.[3,35] We should be able to reassure all our patients that they will not die racked by physical pain, for it is now accepted practice to give increasing amounts of analgesic medicine until the pain is relieved even if it inadvertently shortens life. Many patients find this promise reassuring, for it both alleviates the fear of pain, and also makes concrete the physician's willingness to find creative, aggressive solutions.

If Asked, Be Honest About Your Openness to the Possibility of Assisted Suicide

Patients who want to explore the physician's willingness to provide a potentially lethal prescription often fear being out of control, physically dependent, or mentally incapacitated, rather than simply fearing physical pain.[36] For many, the possibility of a controlled death if things become intolerable is often more important than the reality. Those who secretly hold lethal prescriptions or who have a physician who will entertain the possibility of such treatment feel a sense of control and possibility that, if things became intolerable, there will be a potential escape. Other patients will be adequately reassured to know that we can acknowledge the problem, talk about death, and actively search for acceptable alternatives, even if we cannot directly assist them.

Try to Approach Intolerable End-of-Life Suffering With an Open Heart and an Open Mind

Though acceptable solutions can almost always be found through the aggressive application of comfort care principles, this is not a time for denial of the problem or for superficial solutions. If there are no good alternatives, what should the patient do? There is often a moment of truth for health care providers and families faced with a patient whom they care about who has no acceptable options. Physicians must not turn their backs, but continue to problem-solve, to be present, to help their patients find dignity in death.

Do Not Forget Your Own Support

Working intensively with dying patients can be both enriching and draining. It forces us to face our own mortality, our abilities, and our limitations. It is vital to have a place where we can openly share our own grief, doubts, and uncertainties, as well as take joy in our small victories.[37] For us to deepen our understanding of the human condition and to help humanize the dying process for our patients and ourselves, we must learn to give voice to and share our own private experience of working closely with dying patients.

The patients with whom we engage at this level often become indelibly imprinted on our identities as professionals. Much like the death of a family member, the process that they go through and our willingness and ability to be there and to be helpful are often replayed and rethought. The intensity of these relationships and our ability to make a difference are often without parallel. Because the road is traveled by us all, but the map is poorly described, it is often an adventure with extraordinary richness and unclear boundaries.

In memory of Arthur Schmale, MD, who taught me how to listen, learn, and take direction from the personal stories of dying patients.

References

1. Wanzer SH, Adelstein SJ, Cranford RE, et al. The physician's responsibility toward hopelessly ill patients. *N Engl J Med.* 1984; 310: 955–959.

2. Wanzer, SH, Federman, DO, Adelstein SJ, et al. The physician's responsibility toward hopelessly ill patients: a second look. *N Engl J Med.* 1989; 320: 844–849.

3. Council on Ethical and Judicial Affairs, American Medical Association. Decisions near the end of life. *JAMA.* 1992; 267: 2229–2233.

4. Rhymes J. Hospice care in America. *JAMA.* 1990; 264: 369–372.

5. Hastings Center Report. *Guidelines on the Termination of Life-Sustaining Treatment and the Care of the Dying.* New York, NY: The Hastings Center; 1987.

6. Zimmerman JM. *Hospice: Complete Care for the Terminally Ill.* Baltimore, Md: Urban & Schwarzenberg; 1981.

7. Quill T. *Death and Dignity: Making Choices and Taking Charge.* New York, NY: WW Norton & Co; 1993.

8. Aries P. *The Hour of Our Death.* New York, NY: Vintage Books; 1982.

9. Kubler-Ross E. *On Death and Dying.* New York, NY: Macmillan Publishing Co Inc; 1969.

10. Richman J. A rational approach to rational suicide. *Suicide Life Threat Behav.* 1992; 22: 130–141.

11. Foley KM. The treatment of cancer pain. *N Engl J Med.* 1989; 313: 84–95.

12. Kane RL, Bernstein L, Wales J, Rothenberg R. Hospice effectiveness in controlling pain. *JAMA.* 1985; 253: 2683–2686.

13. Twyeross RG, Lack SA. *Symptom Control in Far Advanced Cancer: Pain Relief.* London, England; Pitman Books Ltd; 1984.

14. Kerr IG, Some M, DeAngelis C, et al. Continuous narcotic infusion with patient-controlled analgesia for chronic cancer outpatients. *Ann Intern Med.* 1988; 108: 554–557.

15. Garfield C. *Psychosocial Care of the Dying Patient.* New York, NY: McGraw-Hill International Book Co; 1978.

16. Conwell Y, Caine ED. Rational suicide and the right to die: reality and myth. *N Engl J Med.* 1991; 325: 1100–1103.

17. Allenbeck P, Bolund C, Ringback G. Increased suicide rate in cancer patients. *J Clin Epidemiol.* 1989; 42: 611–616.

18. Breitbart W. Suicide in cancer patients. *Oncology.* 1989; 49–55.

19. MacKenzie TB, Popkin MK. Suicide in the medical patient. *Int J Psychiatry Med.* 1987; 17: 3–22.

20. Cassel CK, Meier DE. Morals and moralism in the debates on euthanasia and assisted suicide. *N Engl J Med.* 1990; 323: 750–752.

21. Quill TE. Death and dignity: a case of individualized decision making. *N Engl J Med.* 1991; 324: 691–694.

22. Jecker NS. Giving death a hand: when the dying and the doctor stand in a special

relationship. *J Am Geriatr Soc.* 1991; 39: 831–835.

23. Angell M. Euthanasia. *N Engl J Med.* 1988; 319: 1348–1350.

24. Brody H. Assisted death: a compassionate response to a medical failure. *N Engl J Med.* 1992; 327: 1384–1388.

25. Quill TE, Cassel CK, Meier DE. Care of the hopelessly ill: potential clinical criteria for physician-assisted suicide. *N Engl J Med.* 1992; 327: 1380–1384.

26. Singer PA, Siegler, M. Euthanasia: a critique. *N Engl J Med.* 1990; 322: 1881–1883.

27. Orentlicher D. Physician participation in assisted suicide. *JAMA.* 1989; 262: 1844–1845.

28. Gaylin WL, Kass R, Pellegrino ED, Siegler M. Doctors must not kill. *JAMA.* 1988; 259: 2139–2140.

29. Gomez CF. *Regulating Death: Euthanasia and the Case of the Netherlands.* New York, NY: Free Press; 1991.

30. Novack DH. Therapeutic aspects of the clinical encounter. *J Gen Intern Med.* 1987; 2: 346–355.

31. Suchman AL, Matthews DA. What makes the doctor-patient relationship therapeutic: exploring the connexional dimension of medical care. *Ann Intern Med.* 1988; 108: 125–130.

32. Quill TE. Partnerships in patient care: a contractual approach. *Ann Intern Med.* 1983; 98: 228–234.

33. Fisher R, Ury W. *Getting to Yes: Negotiating Agreement Without Giving In.* Boston, Mass: Houghton Mifflin Co; 1981.

34. Cassel EJ. The nature of suffering and the goals of medicine. *N Engl J Med.* 1982; 306: 639–645.

35. Meier DE, Cassel CK. Euthanasia in old age: a case study and ethical analysis. *J Am Geriatr Soc.* 1983; 31: 294–298.

36. van der Maas PJ, van Delden JJM, Pijnenborg L, Looman CWN. Euthanasia and other medical decisions concerning the end of life. *Lancet.* 1991; 338: 669–674.

37. Quill TE, Williams PR. Healthy approaches to physician stress. *Arch Intern Med.* 1990; 150: 1857–1861.

From the Program for Biopsychosocial Studies, School of Medicine, University of Rochester, and the Department of Medicine, The Genesee Hospital, Rochester, NY.

The views expressed in this article are those of the author and do not necessarily represent those of the University of Rochester or the Department of Medicine.

Reprint requests to the Department of Medicine, The Genesee Hospital, Rochester, NY 14607 (Dr Quill).

COMPETENT CARE FOR THE DYING INSTEAD OF PHYSICIAN-ASSISTED SUICIDE

WHILE the Supreme Court is reviewing the decisions by the Second and Ninth Circuit Courts of Appeals to reverse state bans on assisted suicide, there is a unique opportunity to engage the public, health care professionals, and the government in a national discussion of how American medicine and society should address the needs of dying patients and their families. Such a discussion is critical if we are to understand the process of dying from the point of view of patients and their families and to identify existing barriers to appropriate, humane, compassionate care at the end of life. Rational discourse must replace the polarized debate over physician-assisted suicide and euthanasia. Facts, not anecdotes, are necessary to establish a common ground and frame a system of health care for the terminally ill that provides the best possible quality of living while dying.

The biased language of the appeals courts evinces little respect for the vulnerability and dependency of the dying. Judge Stephen Reinhardt, writing for the Ninth Circuit Court, applied the liberty-interest clause of the Fourteenth Amendment, advocating a constitutional right to assisted suicide. He stated, "The competent terminally ill adult, having lived nearly the full measure of his life, has a strong interest in choosing a dignified and humane death, rather than being reduced to a state of helplessness, diapered, sedated, incompetent."[1] Judge Roger J. Miner, writing for the Second Circuit Court of Appeals, applied the equal-rights clause of the Fourteenth Amendment and went on to emphasize that the state "has no interest in prolonging a life that is ending."[2] This statement is more than legal jargon. It serves as a chilling reminder of the low priority given to the dying when it comes to state resources and protection.

The appeals courts' assertion of a constitutional right to assisted suicide is narrowly restricted to the terminally ill. The courts have decided that it is the patient's condition that justifies killing and that the terminally ill are special—so special that they deserve assistance in dying. This group alone can receive such assistance. The courts' response to the New York and Washington cases they reviewed is the dangerous form of affir-

mative action in the name of compassion. It runs the risk of further devaluing the lives of terminally ill patients and may provide the excuse for society to abrogate its responsibility for their care.

Both circuit courts went even further in asserting that physicians are already assisting in patients' deaths when they withdraw life-sustaining treatments such as respirators or administer high doses of pain medication that hasten death. The appeals courts argued that providing a lethal prescription to allow a terminally ill patient to commit suicide is essentially the same as withdrawing life-sustaining treatment or aggressively treating pain. Judicial reasoning that eliminates the distinction between letting a person die and killing runs counter to physicians' standards of palliative care.[3] The courts' purported goal in blurring these distinctions was to bring society's legal rules more closely in line with the moral value it places on the relief of suffering.[4]

In the real world in which physicians care for dying patients, withdrawing treatment and aggressively treating pain are acts that respect patients' autonomous decisions not to be battered by medical technology and to be relieved of their suffering. The physician's intent is to provide care, not death. Physicians do struggle with doubts about their own intentions.[5] The courts' arguments fuel their ambivalence about withdrawing life-sustaining treatments or using opioid or sedative infusions to treat intractable symptoms in dying patients. Physicians are trained and socialized to preserve life. Yet saying that physicians struggle with doubts about their intentions in performing these acts is not the same as saying that their intention is to kill. In palliative care, the goal is to relieve suffering, and the quality of life, not the quantity, is of utmost importance.

Whatever the courts say, specialists in palliative care do not think that they practice physician-assisted suicide or euthanasia.[6] Palliative medicine has developed guidelines for aggressive pharmacologic management of intractable symptoms in dying patients, including sedation for those near death.[3,7,8] The World Health Organization has endorsed palliative care as an integral component of a national health care policy and has strongly recommended to its member countries that they not consider legalizing physician-assisted suicide and euthanasia until they have addressed the needs of their citizens for pain relief and palliative care.[9] The courts have disregarded this formidable recommendation and, in fact, are indirectly suggesting that the World Health Organization supports assisted suicide.

Yet the courts' support of assisted suicide reflects the requests of the physicians who initiated the suits and parallels the numerous surveys demonstrating that a large proportion of physicians support the legalization of physician-assisted suicide.[10-15] A smaller proportion of physicians are willing to provide such assistance, and an even smaller proportion are willing to inject a lethal dose of medication with the intent of killing a patient (active voluntary euthanasia). These survey data reveal a gap between the attitudes and behavior of physicians; 20 to 70 percent of physicians favor the legalization of physician-assisted suicide, but only 2 to 4 percent favor active voluntary euthanasia, and only approximately 2 to 13 percent have actually aided patients in dying, by either providing a prescription or administering a lethal injection. The limitations of these surveys, which are legion, include inconsistent definitions of physician-assisted suicide and euthanasia, lack of information about nonrespondents, and provisions for maintaining confidentiality that have led to inaccurate reporting.[13,16] Since physicians' attitudes toward alternatives to assisted suicide have not been studied, there is a void in our knowledge about the priority that physicians place on physician-assisted suicide.

The willingness of physicians to assist patients in dying appears to be determined by numerous complex factors, including religious beliefs, personal values, medical specialty, age, practice setting, and perspective on the use of financial resources.[13,16-19] Studies of patients' preferences for care at the end of life demonstrate that physicians' preferences strongly influence those of their patients.[13] Making physician-assisted suicide a medical treatment when it is so strongly dependent on these physician-related variables would result in a regulatory impossibility.[19] Physicians would have to disclose their values and attitudes to patients to avoid potential conflict.[13] A survey by Ganzini et al. demonstrated that psychiatrists' responses to requests to evaluate patients were highly determined by their attitudes.[13] In a study by Emanuel et al., depressed patients with

cancer said they would view positively those physicians who acknowledged their willingness to assist in suicide. In contrast, patients with cancer who were suffering from pain would be suspicious of such physicians.[11]

In this controversy, physicians fall into one of three groups. Those who support physician-assisted suicide see it as a compassionate response to a medical need, a symbol of nonabandonment, and a means to reestablish patients' trust in doctors who have used technology excessively.[20] They argue that regulation of physician-assisted suicide is possible and, in fact, necessary to control the actions of physicians who are currently providing assistance surreptitiously.[21] The two remaining groups of physicians oppose legalization.[19,22-24] One group is morally opposed to physician-assisted suicide and emphasizes the need to preserve the professionalism of medicine and the commitment to "do no harm." These physicians view aiding a patient in dying as a form of abandonment, because a physician needs to walk the last mile with the patient, as a witness, not as an executioner. Legalization would endorse justified killing, according to these physicians, and guidelines would not be followed, even if they could be developed. Furthermore, these physicians are concerned that the conflation of assisted suicide with the withdrawal of life support or adequate treatment of pain would make it even harder for dying patients, because there would be a backlash against existing policies. The other group is not ethically opposed to physician-assisted suicide and, in fact, sees it as acceptable in exceptional cases, but these physicians believe that one cannot regulate the unregulatable.[19] On this basis, the New York State Task Force on Life and the Law, a 24-member committee with broad public and professional representation, voted unanimously against the legalization of physician-assisted suicide.[24] All three groups of physicians agree that a national effort is needed to improve the care of the dying. Yet it does seem that those in favor of legalizing physician-assisted suicide are disingenuous in their use of this issue as a wedge. If this form of assistance with dying is legalized, the courts will be forced to broaden the assistance to include active voluntary euthanasia and, eventually, assistance in response to requests from proxies.

One cannot easily categorize the patients who request physician-assisted suicide or euthanasia. Some surveys of physicians have attempted to determine retrospectively the prevalence and nature of these requests.[10] Pain, AIDS, and neurodegenerative disorders are the most common conditions in patients requesting assistance in dying. There is a wide range in the age of such patients, but many are younger persons with AIDS.[10] From the limited data available, the factors most commonly involved in requests for assistance are concern about future loss of control, being or becoming a burden to others, or being unable to care for oneself and fear of severe pain.[10] A small number of recent studies have directly asked terminally ill patients with cancer or AIDS about their desire for death.[25-27] All these studies show that the desire for death is closely associated with depression and that pain and lack of social support are contributing factors.

Do we know enough, on the basis of several legal cases, to develop a public policy that will profoundly change medicine's role in society?[1,2] Approximately 2.4 million Americans die each year. We have almost no information on how they die and only general information on where they die. Sixty-one percent die in hospitals, 17 percent in nursing homes, and the remainder at home, with approximately 10 to 14 percent of those at home receiving hospice care.

The available data suggest that physicians are inadequately trained to assess and manage the multifactorial symptoms commonly associated with patients' requests for physician-assisted suicide. According to the American Medical Association's report on medical education, only 5 of 126 medical schools in the United States require a separate course in the care of the dying.[28] Of 7048 residency programs, only 26 percent offer a course on the medical and legal aspects of care at the end of life as a regular part of the curriculum. According to a survey of 1068 accredited residency programs in family medicine, internal medicine, and pediatrics and fellowship programs in geriatrics, each resident or fellow coordinates the care of 10 or fewer dying patients annually.[28] Almost 15 percent of the programs offer no formal training in terminal care. Despite the availability of hospice programs, only 17 percent of the training programs offer a hospice rotation, and the rotation is required in only half of those programs; 9 percent of the programs have residents or fellows serving as members of hospice teams. In a recent survey of 55 residency programs and over 1400 residents, conducted by the American Board of Internal Medicine, the residents were asked to rate their perception of adequate training in care at the end of life. Seventy-two percent reported that they had received adequate training in managing pain and other symptoms; 62 percent, that they had received adequate training in telling patients that they are dying; 38 percent, in describing what the process will be like; and 32 percent, in talking to patients who request assistance in dying or a hastened death (Blank L: personal communication).

The lack of training in the care of the dying is evident in practice. Several studies have concluded that poor communication between physicians and patients, physicians' lack of knowledge about national guidelines for such care, and their lack of knowledge about the control of symptoms are barriers to the provision of good care at the end of life.[23,29,30]

Yet there is now a large body of data on the components of suffering in patients with advanced terminal disease, and these data provide the basis for treatment algorithms.[3] There are three major factors in suffering: pain and other physical symptoms, psychological distress, and existential distress (described as the experience of life without meaning). It is not only the patients who suffer but also their families and the health care professionals attending them. These experiences of suffering are often closely and inextricably related. Perceived distress in any one of the three groups amplifies distress in the others.[31,32]

Pain is the most common symptom in dying patients, and according to recent data from U.S. studies, 56 percent of outpatients with cancer, 82 percent of outpatients with AIDS, 50 percent of hospitalized patients with various diagnoses, and 36 percent of nursing home residents have inadequate management of pain during the course of their terminal illness.[33-36] Members of minority groups and women, both those with cancer and

those with AIDS, as well as the elderly, receive less pain treatment than other groups of patients. In a survey of 1177 physicians who had treated a total of more than 70,000 patients with cancer in the previous six months, 76 percent of the respondents cited lack of knowledge as a barrier to their ability to control pain.[37] Severe pain that is not adequately controlled interferes with the quality of life, including the activities of daily living, sleep, and social interactions.[36,38]

Other physical symptoms are also prevalent among the dying. Studies of patients with advanced cancer and of the elderly in the year before death show that they have numerous symptoms that worsen the quality of life, such as fatigue, dyspnea, delirium, nausea, and vomiting.[36,38]

Along with these physical symptoms, dying patients have a variety of well-described psychological symptoms, with a high prevalence of anxiety and depression in patients with cancer or AIDS and the elderly.[27,39] For example, more than 60 percent of patients with advanced cancer have psychiatric problems, with adjustment disorders, depression, anxiety, and delirium reported most frequently. Various factors that contribute to the prevalence and severity of psychological distress in the terminally ill have been identified.[39] The diagnosis of depression is difficult to make in medically ill patients[3,26,40]; 94 percent of the Oregon psychiatrists surveyed by Ganzini et al. were not confident that they could determine, in a single evaluation, whether a psychiatric disorder was impairing the judgment of a patient who requested assistance with suicide.[13]

Attention has recently been focused on the interaction between uncontrolled symptoms and vulnerability to suicide in patients with cancer or AIDS.[41] Data from studies of both groups of patients suggest that uncontrolled pain contributes to depression and that persistent pain interferes with patients' ability to receive support from their families and others. Patients with AIDS have a high risk of suicide that is independent of physical symptoms. Among New York City residents with AIDS, the relative risk of suicide in men between the ages of 20 and 59 years was 36 times higher than the risk among men without AIDS in the same age group and 66 times higher than the risk in the general population.[41] Patients with AIDS who committed suicide generally did so within nine months after receiving the diagnosis; 25 percent had made a previous suicide attempt, 50 percent had reported severe depression, and 40 percent had seen a psychiatrist within four days before committing suicide. As previously noted, the desire to die is most closely associated with the diagnosis of depression.[26,27] Suicide is the eighth leading cause of death in the United States, and the incidence of suicide is higher in patients with cancer or AIDS and in elderly men than in the general population. Conwell and Caine reported that depression was under-diagnosed by primary care physicians in a cohort of elderly patients who subsequently committed suicide; 75 percent of the patients had seen a primary care physician during the last month of life but had not received a diagnosis of depression.[22]

The relation between depression and the desire to hasten death may vary among subgroups of dying patients. We have no data, except for studies of a small number of patients with cancer or AIDS. The effect of treatment for depression on the desire to hasten death and on requests for assistance in doing so has not been examined in the medically ill population, except for a small study in which four of six patients who initially wished to hasten death changed their minds within two weeks.[26]

There is also the concern that certain patients, particularly members of minority groups that are estranged from the health care system, may be reluctant to receive treatment for their physical or psychological symptoms because of the fear that their physicians will, in fact, hasten death. There is now some evidence that the legalization of assisted suicide in the Northern Territory of Australia has undermined the Aborigines' trust in the medical care system[42]; this experience may serve as an example for the United States, with its multicultural population.

The multiple physical and psychological symptoms in the terminally ill and elderly are compounded by a substantial degree of existential distress. Reporting on their interviews with Washington State physicians whose patients had requested assistance in dying, Back et al. noted the physicians' lack of sophistication in assessing such nonphysical suffering.[10]

In summary, there are fundamental physician-related barriers to appropriate, humane, and compassionate care for the dying. These range from attitudinal and behavioral barriers to educational and economic barriers. Physicians do not know enough about their patients, themselves, or suffering to provide assistance with dying as a medical treatment for the relief of suffering. Physicians need to explore their own perspectives on the meaning of suffering in order to develop their own approaches to the care of the dying. They need insight into how the nature of the doctor-patient relationship influences their own decision making. If legalized, physician-assisted suicide will be a substitute for rational therapeutic, psychological, and social interventions that might otherwise enhance the quality of life for patients who are dying. The medical profession needs to take the lead in developing guidelines for good care of dying patients. Identifying the factors related to physicians, patients, and the health care system that pose barriers to appropriate care at the end of life should be the first step in a national dialogue to educate health care professionals and the public on the topic of death and dying. Death is an issue that society as a whole faces, and it requires a compassionate response. But we should not confuse compassion with competence in the care of terminally ill patients.

KATHLEEN M. FOLEY, M.D.
Memorial Sloan-Kettering Cancer Center
New York, NY 10021

REFERENCES

1. Reinhardt, Compassion in Dying v. State of Washington, 79 F. 3d 790 9th Cir. 1996.
2. Miner, Quill v. Vacco 80 F. 3d 716 2nd Cir. 1996.
3. Doyle D, Hanks GWC, MacDonald N. The Oxford textbook of palliative medicine. New York: Oxford University Press, 1993.
4. Orentlicher D. The legalization of physician-assisted suicide. N Engl J Med 1996; 335: 663–7.
5. Wilson WC, Smedira NG, Fink C, McDowell JA, Luce JM. Ordering and administration of sedatives and analgesics during the withholding and withdrawal of life support from critically ill patients. JAMA 1992; 267: 949–53.
6. Foley KM. The relationship of pain and symptom management to patient requests for physician-assisted suicide. J Pain Symptom Manage 1991; 6: 289–97.
7. Cherny NI, Coyle N, Foley KM. Guidelines in the care of the dying patient. Hematol Oncol Clin North Am 1996; 10: 261–86.
8. Cherny NI, Portenoy RK. Sedation in the management of refractory symptoms: guidelines for evaluation and treatment. J Palliat Care 1994; 10(2): 31–8.
9. Cancer pain relief and palliative care. Geneva: World Health Organization, 1989.
10. Back AL, Wallace JI, Starks HE, Pearlman RA. Physician-assisted suicide and euthanasia in Washington State: patient requests and physician responses. JAMA 1996; 275: 919–25.
11. Emanuel EJ, Fairclough DL, Daniels ER, Clarridge BR. Euthanasia and physician-assisted suicide: attitudes and experiences of oncology patients, oncologists, and the public. Lancet 1996; 347: 1805–10.
12. Lee MA, Nelson HD, Tilden VP, Ganzini L, Schmidt TA, Tolle SW. Legalizing assisted suicide—views of physicians in Oregon. N Engl J Med 1996; 334: 310–15.
13. Ganzini L, Fenn DS, Lee MA, Heintz RT, Bloom JD. Attitudes of Oregon psychiatrists toward physician-assisted suicide. Am J Psychiatry 1996; 153: 1469–75.
14. Cohen JS, Fihn SD, Boyko EJ, Jonsen AR, Wood RW. Attitudes toward assisted suicide and euthanasia among physicians in Washington State. N Engl J Med 1994; 331: 89–94.
15. Doukas DJ, Waterhouse D, Gorenflo DW, Seid J. Attitudes and behaviors on physician-assisted death: a study of Michigan oncologists. J Clin Oncol 1995; 13: 1055–61.
16. Morrison S, Meier D. Physician-assisted dying: fashioning public policy with an absence of data. Generations. Winter 1994: 48–53.
17. Portenoy RK, Coyle N, Kash K, et al. Determinants of the willingness to endorse assisted suicide: a survey of physicians, nurses, and social workers. Psychosomatics (in press).
18. Fins J. Physician-assisted suicide and the right to care. Cancer Control 1996; 3: 272–8.
19. Callahan D, White M. The legalization of physician-assisted suicide: creating a regulatory Potemkin Village. U Richmond Law Rev 1996; 30: 1–83.
20. Quill TE. Death and dignity—a case of individualized decision making. N Engl J Med 1991; 324: 691–4.
21. Quill TE, Cassel CK, Meier DE. Care of the hopelessly ill—proposed clinical criteria for physician-assisted suicide. N Engl J Med 1992; 327: 1380–4.
22. Conwell Y, Caine ED. Rational suicide and the right to die—reality and myth. N Engl J Med 1991; 325: 1100–3.
23. Foley KM. Pain, physician assisted suicide and euthanasia. Pain Forum 1995; 4: 163–78.
24. When death is sought: assisted suicide and euthanasia in the medical context. New York: New York State Task Force on Life and the Law, May 1994.
25. Brown JH, Henteleff P, Barakat S, Rowe CJ. Is it normal for terminally ill patients to desire death? Am J Psychiatry 1986; 143: 208–11.
26. Chochinov HM, Wilson KG, Enns M, et al. Desire for death in the terminally ill. Am J Psychiatry 1995; 152: 1185–91.
27. Breitbart W, Rosenfeld BD, Passik SD. Interest in physician-assisted suicide among ambulatory HIV-infected patients. Am J Psychiatry 1996; 153: 238–42.
28. Hill TP. Treating the dying patient: the challenge for medical education. Arch Intern Med 1995; 155: 1265–9.
29. Callahan D. Once again reality: now where do we go. Hastings Cent Rep 1995; 25 (6): Suppl: S33–S36.

30. Solomon MZ, O'Donnell L, Jennings B, et al. Decisions near the end of life: professional views on life-sustaining treatments. Am J Public Health 1993; 83: 14–23.

31. Cherny NI, Coyle N, Foley KM. Suffering in the advanced cancer patient: definition and taxonomy. J. Palliat Care 1994; 10 (2): 57–70.

32. Cassel EJ. The nature of suffering and the goals of medicine. N Engl J Med 1982; 306: 639–45.

33. Cleeland CS, Gonin R, Hatfield AK, et al. Pain and its treatment in outpatients with metastatic cancer. N Engl J Med 1994; 330: 592–6.

34. Breitbart W, Rosenfeld BD, Passik SD, McDonald MV, Thaler H, Portenoy RK. The undertreatment of pain in ambulatory AIDS patients. Pain 1996; 65: 243–9.

35. The SUPPORT Principal Investigators. A controlled trial to improve care for seriously ill hospitalized patients. JAMA 1995; 274: 1591–8.

36. Seale C, Cartwright A. The year before death. Hants, England: Avebury, 1994.

37. Von Roenn JH, Cleeland CS, Gonin R, Hatfield AK, Pandya KJ. Physician attitudes and practice in cancer pain management: a survey from the Eastern Cooperative Oncology Group. Ann Intern Med 1993; 119: 121–6.

38. Portenoy RK. Pain and quality of life: clinical issues and implications for research. Oncology 1990; 4: 172–8.

39. Breitbart W. Suicide risk and pain in cancer and AIDS patients. In: Chapman CR, Foley KM, eds. Current and emerging issues in cancer pain. New York: Raven Press, 1993.

40. Chochinov H, Wilson KG, Enns M, Lander S. Prevalence of depression in the terminally ill: effects of diagnostic criteria and symptom threshold judgments. Am J Psychiatry 1994; 151: 537–40.

41. Passik S, McDonald M, Rosenfeld B, Breitbart W. End of life issues in patients with AIDS: clinical and research considerations. J Pharm Care Pain Symptom Control 1995; 3: 91–111.

42. NT "success" in easing rural fear of euthanasia. The Age. August 31, 1996: A7.

Euthanasia: A need for reform

Summary

Recent high profile right-to-die cases have served to heighten the confusion surrounding euthanasia, particularly in relation to active and passive euthanasia. It is apparent that the underlying philosophical basis of the active-passive distinction has led to distortions in the law surrounding this issue, which further compounds the confusion. It is time for a more honest approach to assistance in dying. In the long-term, reform is inevitable and may involve reclassifying passive and active euthanasia as life-terminating acts. Nurses need to have an understanding of the ethical and legal basis of euthanasia to acknowledge and define their possible future role in relation to the provision of life-terminating acts.

Key Words * Euthanasia * Patients: rights * Right to die

These key words are based on subject headings from the British Nursing Index. This article has been subject to double-blind review.

Janis Moody

THE DEBATE surrounding euthanasia is a central issue in bioethics. High profile cases have increased public awareness about rights in relation to end-of-life decision-making and raised concerns regarding the overuse of life-sustaining medical technology. This has led to calls for the right to die with dignity and for the legalisation of physician-assisted suicide and/or voluntary active euthanasia (Battin et al 1998). Public perceptions of what euthanasia involves, however, tend to be confused and this is aggravated by the press, who, in seeking to dramatise 'right to die' cases, have created further confusion. A critical examination of the doctrines that inform the distinction between passive and active euthanasia is undertaken to demonstrate why this confusion exists. In the author's opinion, a more honest approach to death and dying will lead to much-needed clarity surrounding euthanasia. The nurse's role in relation to euthanasia is considered in the light of any proposed reform, as nurses have a key role to play.

Relevance to nursing

Many people view the doctor as having the main role with regard to involvement in end-of-life decision-making. However, the nurse's role is pivotal and, as such, the nursing profession needs to be ready to be actively involved in any debate on euthanasia. Because of the nature of their work and the amount of time spent with patients, nurses are in a unique position in relation to end-of-life decision-making. Nurses are involved in the dilemmas imposed by passive euthanasia and there is little acknowledgement of this or guidance to help them deal with it (Dines 1995). Furthermore, although it has yet to become a reality in the UK, were physician-assisted suicide to be legalised, the next step could be nurse-assisted suicide (Battin et al 1998). It is, therefore, increasingly important that nurses are aware of the ethical and legal issues surrounding assistance in dying.

Passive and active euthanasia

Two highly publicised cases demonstrate the confusion that exists in relation to euthanasia. These cases relate to Miss B and Diane Pretty (Ms B van NHS Trust Hospital [2002] and R (on the application of) Pretty v DPP [2002] 1 All ER 1). Miss B was paralysed from the neck down and requested that ventilatory support be withdrawn as she did not want to continue living under these circumstances. It is an established legal principle that a competent adult has an absolute right to refuse treatment. However, the healthcare team raised questions about Miss B's competency and were reluctant to withdraw treatment, knowing that it would result in Miss B's death. The case went to court and Miss B's right to have treatment withdrawn was upheld. The case of Diane Pretty, who had motor neurone disease, was different, in that she requested a declaration from the court that if her husband were to assist her to die, when she felt she could no longer continue to live, he would not be prosecuted for his part in her death. Her case went through the due process of the courts, including the European court, but her request was consistently refused. Although it is clear that these two cases are fundamentally different, both requests ultimately result in the individual's death. It is the difference in the means used to bring about death that results in much confusion.

The first case is classified as passive euthanasia, whereas the second is classified as active. It is the distinction between passive and active that is the crux of the matter, in that one form of assistance is acceptable and legal but the other is not. In many ways, however, the boundaries between active and passive euthanasia are becoming increasingly blurred, and the justifications for this distinction do not stand up to close scrutiny. For these reasons, there is a need for greater clarity in end-of-life decision-making as well as a more honest approach to death and dying.

A moral and legal analysis of the 'acts and omissions' involved in euthanasia has led to the categories of active and passive euthanasia. The Miss B and Diane Pretty cases provide examples of both sides of the active-passive distinction in euthanasia. Active euthanasia is classified as causing death by commission: that is, directly intervening to cause the death of the individual. In active euthanasia the death is the desirable end result that is foreseen and intended. Passive euthanasia is commonly classified as causing death by omission (Otlowski 1997). There are a number of activities associated with passive euthanasia, which include omissions such as the withholding and withdrawal of treatment and activities that have a side effect, but not the intention, of causing death (Beauchamp and Childress 1994). The doctrines relevant to maintaining the distinction between passive and active euthanasia are the acts and omissions doctrine and the doctrine of double effect (Begley 1998).

Acts and omission doctrine

The acts and omissions doctrine, which provides the underlying philosophical basis of the active-passive distinction, holds that there is a relevant moral difference between causing something bad to happen by means of an action, and allowing the same thing to happen by failing to act (Farsides 1992). Consequently, because an omission is viewed differently from an act, there is a moral difference between allowing a person to die through non-intervention and actively causing the person's death (Farsides 1992). At a common-sense level this distinction may have some appeal, in that it is generally accepted that doing something which results in certain consequences carries more responsibility than if the same consequences were to come about by not doing anything. On closer examination, however, it is apparent that omissions can be just as effective as actions in terms of bringing about change and, consequently, such importance should not be placed on the distinction between acts and omissions (Begley 1998). It is evident that an individual can kill someone by intentionally allowing that person to die, as killing can occur by omission as well as by commission (Beauchamp and Childress 1994).

It is widely accepted among healthcare professionals and the general public that it is permissible for doctors to allow patients to die by termination of life-sustaining treatment (classified as an omission), but that doctors and other healthcare professionals cannot kill their patients by active means such as a lethal injection (classified as an act) (Otlowski 1997). This distinction categorises killings as wrongful actions leading to death and, thus, killing is linked with an emotive connotation of moral wrongness and is prohibited (Brock 1993).

Rachels (1975) argues that the acts and omissions doctrine is based on a distinction between killing and letting die, which has no moral importance. He demonstrates that many arguments put forward to justify the distinction do not stand up to ethical scrutiny. He suggests that if the death of a person is viewed as beneficial and morally justifiable in a particular case, then the difference between killing the person and letting him or her die is not an issue.

Labelling an act as 'killing' or 'letting die' does not determine which is better or worse and does not provide justification for either. Nevertheless, it is clear that some instances of killing—for example, a vicious murder—may be worse than some instances of allowing to die—for example, discontinuing treatment in someone who is in a persistent vegetative state. However, establishing rightness or wrongness in a certain case depends on the justification on which the action is based, not on the type of action it is (Beauchamp and Childress 1994). Those who assume a difference between killing and letting die are considering moral categories other than the action itself. All incidences of killing and letting die must satisfy criteria independent of whether the method used is an act or an omission. Thus, it is not the difference between killing and allowing to die that is important; it is the presence of other morally important factors, most obviously the difference in motivation and intention (Brock 1993).

The law supports the view that there is a difference between acts and omissions. Criminal law adheres to a fairly rigid distinction between liability for acts that cause death and liability for omissions that cause death. Whereas the duty not to cause harm is virtually absolute, there is no general principle of liability for failure to act and prevent the occurrence of harm (Otlowski 1997). In the Bland case, the Law Lords held that the withdrawal of artificial nutrition and hydration (ANH) was an omission rather than an act, although there was some reluctance to adopt this position. In relation to the distinction between acts and omissions, Lord Mustill contended that: '… the current state of the law is unsatisfactory both morally and intellectually' (Airedale NHS Trust v Bland [1993] 1 All ER 821). The legitimate withdrawal of feeding and antibiotic therapy in this case was an omission to do something that the doctor was not legally required to do, that is, to continue with this treatment. It was, however, acknowledged that it was an omission with the intention to end the patient's life and this is what made this judgement so radical (Singer 1999).

As the Bland case demonstrates, there has been a tendency to avoid labelling medical conduct in such situations as criminal, which has had the consequence of causing significant distortions in the interpretation and application of the law (Otlowski 1997). Two primary rationales as to why withholding and withdrawing life-sustaining treatment should not be categorised as killing have been put forward by the courts, and these relate to causation and intention.

Causation

Causation is derived from the legal doctrine of proximate cause, which holds that to be a proximate or primary cause results in legal liability for the outcome. Legal judgements relating to causation and hence, liability, are often based on the obligation to treat. If a doctor is under an obligation to treat, it follows that omission to provide treatment breaches that obligation and, if death occurs, this would be an act of unjustified homicide. However, if there is no obligation to provide treatment, the underlying disease or injury serves as the proximate cause, and the doctor is not held liable (Beauchamp and Childress 1994). Proximate cause thus holds that in acts of foregoing treatment, an underlying disease or injury is already present, and medical technology is functioning to prevent the natural course of the disease or injury. When life-sustaining treatment is foregone the natural cause is released and a 'natural death' occurs (Beauchamp and Childress 1994).

Subtly but crucially evident in issues surrounding causation is a conceptual reliance on the distinction between the terms 'natural' and 'artificial'. The categorisation of death as natural has legal and moral effects, in that natural deaths are not killing and thus are neither illegal nor immoral, and do not confer responsibility or causation. As killing is implicated in the characterisation of medical practice as an intervention, it is generally held that, on killing a person, one is the direct causal agent of death; whereas in letting die, one merely allows the underlying physiological process to follow its natural course (Hop-

kins 1997). It should be borne in mind, however, that even if death is considered natural, the doctor can still be held culpable if he or she allows someone in his or her care to die, for example, a treatable underlying infection.

Proximate cause is a complicated concept which confuses the distinction between killing and allowing to die, as well as issues surrounding the cause of death (Beauchamp and Childress 1994). Legal protections for natural death can result in a more painful death in some cases, in that allowing someone to die by omitting life-sustaining medical treatment can be a long and onerous process. It has been suggested that a more humane approach would be to use active means, such as a lethal injection, which would produce the same result (Rachels 1975).

Intention

From the foregoing analysis it becomes increasingly clear why confusion exists and this is further compounded by the doctrine of double effect. This is based on the distinction between outcomes that are intended and those that are foreseen as unintended consequences of one's actions (Otlowski 1997). The doctrine of double effect aims to differentiate between prohibited and permissible actions by focusing on the intention of the healthcare professional. According to this doctrine, effects that would be morally wrong if caused intentionally are permissible if foreseen and unintended. The double effect doctrine is often used to provide a rationale as to why certain forms of treatment at the end of life that result in death are morally permissible and others are not (Quill et al 1997).

Four key conditions are identified in classic formulations of the doctrine of double effect. The first condition concerns the act itself, which must be good, or at least morally neutral. The second condition concerns the intention of the agent in that the good effect and not the bad effect must be intended. The bad effect, such as respiratory depression after the administration of pain-relieving medication, may be foreseen but is not the intended outcome. The third condition relates to the distinction between means and effects. For example, the bad effect, death, must not be a means to the good effect, relief of suffering. The fourth condition relates to the proportionality between the good and the bad effect. To meet this condition the good effect must outweigh the bad effect and the bad effect can be permitted only when there are proportionally good reasons for it (Quill et al 1997).

From a double effect perspective, giving high doses of narcotic analgesics to a dying patient to relieve pain and suffering is considered ethical even if it has the foreseen, but unintended consequence of hastening death. Conversely, in a situation where death is requested by a terminally ill patient with irreversible suffering, that same act would be considered unethical and a form of medical killing because the intention to kill the patient would be central to the action (Quill 1993). One of the main criticisms of the double effect doctrine is that it is almost impossible to establish the true intention of the agent and to distinguish between foreseen and intended actions, and intended and unintended side effects. This constitutes a serious challenge to this doctrine. For example, to claim that a doctor can withdraw ANH without intending the patient's death seems absurd: in withdrawing ANH, the patient's death is inevitable.

In addition, from a legal perspective problems abound with the use of the doctrine of double effect—for example, the distinction between intending and merely knowing that death will probably result from one's acts is a distinction that has never made a difference in criminal law. According to well-established legal principles, provided that the defendant subjectively knew that the administration of drugs would be life-threatening, criminal liability for homicide can theoretically be established even though the doctor's primary intention was to relieve the patient's suffering (Otlowski 1997).

Doctors are unique in their position, in that they can undertake acts, with a legally culpable state of mind, which result in the death of their patients, but they are exempt from the law of murder, when such acts by non-doctors would result in criminal liability (Sanai 1999). The prevailing assumptions regarding the legality of this practice are, however, irreconcilable with established criminal law principles, and the law is clearly being manipulated to sanction what is widely regarded as legitimate medical practice (Otlowski 1997).

Sanctity of life principle

It is important to recognise the justificatory basis of these doctrines, which is to maintain the illusion that the sanctity of life principle is still intact and to prevent further erosion of this principle. The sanctity of life principle is based on the premise that it is always wrong to end an innocent human life intentionally. The acts and omissions doctrine and the doctrine of double effect are used by those who wish to maintain an absolute prohibition against the intentional shortening of life and who adhere to the view that, irrespective of the consequences, a doctor should never actively and deliberately kill a patient (Tannsjo 2000). The sanctity of life principle is, however, facing ongoing erosion as it seems that it is no longer enough to have a life, but that life must be of a certain quality and be considered a worthwhile life (Keown 2000).

The erosion of the sanctity of life principle and the move to a quality of life ethic may ultimately make the acts and omission doctrine and the doctrine of double effect redundant. In the light of the foregoing discussions relating to these two doctrines, this may lead to much-needed clarity with regard to how end-of-life decisions are made. If one does not hold that there is an absolute prohibition against shortening life, then the acts and omissions doctrine and the doctrine of double effect with their attendant complexities are obsolete and not necessary in end-of-life situations. Those who prefer this position would state that the benefits of relieving distress may sometimes outweigh the harms of shortening life when the patient is terminally ill. The advantage of this view is that it avoids the complex arguments surrounding acts and omissions and the validity of distinctions between intending and foreseeing effects of one's acts, and it also seems to accord with the moral intuitions of most people (Randall and Downie 1996). This would lead to greater honesty and clarity in this area by overcoming existing discrepancies and anomalies.

It is understandable that the acts and omissions doctrine and the doctrine of double effect are invoked to help healthcare professionals deal with their involvement in death and to prevent killing being linked with healthcare interventions at the end of life. The influence of these theories has been enormous, particularly in trying to preserve the sanctity of life principle and categorical injunction against killing, but this comes at a price, in that many decisions concerning life and death are being made on unsound grounds (Otlowski 1997). This has led to serious philosophical and legal distortions. To maintain the myth that healthcare professionals are not helping patients to die, a smokescreen of dubious distinctions has been created to justify actions and inactions that result in death (Beauchamp and Childress 1994).

Adherence to these principles means that even if a patient is terminally ill, as in the case of Diane Pretty, no appeal to mercy on the basis of her suffering or the inhumanity of continuing life will at this time legally allow health professionals to intentionally help her to die by active means. Moral practice allows health professionals to kill patients in hopeless and painful situations by passive means, which is regarded by many as allowing nature to take its course and is thus more morally acceptable (Hopkins 1997). Patients are often under the illusion that natural death is in general a painless, dignified slipping away. However, it can take a long and unpredictable course. Administration of a lethal injection would provide a quick and painless death, whereas letting die may be neither quick nor painless (Kuhse 1999).

Perhaps it is time to admit that the ethical and legal distortions needed to maintain this illusion of the sanctity of life principle and protect healthcare workers is too high a price to pay. There are many ambiguities surrounding these complex doctrines which in the current climate surrounding end-of-life management makes them increasingly untenable. Thus, there is a need for a review of end-of-life decision-making and this entails acknowledging the ethical and legal inconsistencies inherent in these doctrines.

Reform

Fear of slippery slope predictions related to an ongoing moral decline with regard to sanctity of life contribute to maintenance of the status quo, even if this results in increasingly convoluted ethical and legal justifications for the way in which the end of life is managed. There is, however, an apparent inconsistency within law and ethics—this is if health professionals adhere to the right to autonomy in cases of refusing treatment and allow a person to die by this means, but then deny that same person the autonomous right to make arrangements by mutual consent with the doctor to bring about the patient's death by active means (Beauchamp and Childress 1994). The problem lies in developing a coherent policy that involves strict criteria and safeguards, but which is not so inflexible as to become unworkable. It is important to consider that almost any individual freedom involves some risk of abuse, but such abuse would be minimised by appropriate legal safeguards (Brogden 2001).

Reform in this area will involve a major philosophical shift but the time has come for health professionals to reconceptualise certain forms of assistance in dying as life-terminating acts, which are part of the responsibility of patient care. This will involve a review of traditional attitudes towards euthanasia and the policies that have resulted from the limitations imposed by the emphasis on the sanctity of life principle. To overcome these distortions, it needs to be recognised and acknowledged that intentionally letting die and helping to die by active means are morally and legally the same; they are both the intentional causation of death. Once this has been recognised, issues such as the circumstances in which health professionals could intentionally provide assistance to die in the medical context can be discussed (Beauchamp and Childress 1994).

Reconceptualisation would require that both omissions and acts be classified as life-terminating acts, for example, withdrawing and withholding life-sustaining interventions would be considered a life-terminating act, as would the provision of terminal sedation or a lethal injection in strictly monitored circumstances. Voluntariness would be central to any proposed reform and how people choose to die will be influenced by religious and other belief systems. Some people value the sanctity of life and believe that any form of active euthanasia is killing and therefore wrong. The law must protect people who believe that it would be wrong to be killed in this way (Uhlmann 1998). This does not mean that voluntary active euthanasia is morally wrong, but that because of strong moral beliefs this would not be an option for some people and would preclude the use of active euthanasia (Battin 1994). Other options for life-terminating treatment might fit better with their moral framework, and their right to self-determination in this matter should be respected.

Any changes in the law with regard to physicianassisted suicide and active euthanasia will undoubtedly have major consequences for the nursing profession; the ethical stance on this will affect the involvement of nurses in euthanasia and the decision-making process. Communication and co-operation between doctors and nurses is in the best interests of the patient in the context of end-of-life decisions, whether this involves passive or active means of procuring a peaceful death. Although nurses do not make end-of-life decisions, they often have to carry out such decisions. Therefore, they need to acknowledge and understand their role in this area to allow them to fully inform any debate on the extension of euthanasia to include more active means (Box 1).

Box 1. Recommendation for practice

- The law is distorted and misshapen, in that it allows human life to be terminated in certain circumstances but not in others
- In the long term, reform is inevitable and may involve reclassifying passive and active euthanasia as life-terminating acts
- Nurses are involved in decision-making and the practicalities relating to passive euthanasia, and the implications of this are often not acknowledged
- Nurses need to understand the ethical and legal basis of euthanasia to be fully involved in any debate which considers the extension of euthanasia to include more active means
- Nurses need to be ready to acknowledge and define their role in relation to the provision of life-terminating acts

---

Conclusion

The prevailing approach towards euthanasia has led to artificial and unsustainable distinctions, and a more honest approach to assistance in dying is required (Otlowski 1997). In the long term, reform is inevitable and may involve reclassifying passive and active euthanasia as life-terminating acts. Nurses often occupy a central role in the well-being of patients and, as such, any proposal to extend life-terminating acts to include active euthanasia will involve them. Nurses need to take part in this debate and be informed by relevant ethical and legal reasoning so that they are ready to acknowledge and define their role in the provision of life-terminating acts should this become a reality.

REFERENCES

Battin M (1994) The Least Worst Death: Essays in Bioethics at the End of Life. Oxford, Oxford University Press.

Battin M et al (Eds) (1998) Physician-assisted Suicide: Expanding the Debate. London, Routledge.

Beauchamp T, Childress J (1994) Principles of Biomedical Ethics. Fourth edition. Oxford, Oxford University Press.

Begley A (1998) Acts, omissions and motives: a philosophical examination of the moral distinction between killing and letting die. Journal of Advanced Nursing. 28, 4, 865–873.

Brock D (1993) Life and Death: Philosophical Essays in Biomedical Ethics. Cambridge, Cambridge University Press.

Brogden M (2001) Geronticide: Killing the Elderly. London, Jessica Kingsley Publishers.

Dines A (1995) Does the distinction between killing and letting die justify some forms of euthanasia? Journal of Advanced Nursing. 21, 5, 911–916.

Farsides C (1992) Active and passive euthanasia: is there a distinction? Care of the Critically Ill. 8, 3, 126–128.

Hopkins P (1997) Why does removing machines count as 'passive' euthanasia? Hastings Centre Report. 27, 3, 29–37.

Keown J (2000) Beyond Bland: a critique of the BMA guidance on withholding and withdrawing medical treatment Legal Studies. 20, 1, 66–84.

Kuhse H (1999) A modern myth: that letting die is not the intentional causation of death. In Kuhse H, Singer P (Eds) Bioethics: An Anthology. Oxford, Blackwell Publishers.

Otlowski M (1997) Voluntary Euthanasia and the Common Law. Oxford, Oxford University Press.

Quill T (1993) The ambiguity of clinical intentions. The New England Journal of Medicine. 329, 14, 1039–1040.

Quill T et al (1997) The rule of double effect: a critique of its role in end-of-life decision making. The New England Journal of Medicine. 337, 24, 1768–1771.

Rachels J (1975) Active and passive euthanasia. The New England Journal of Medicine. 292, 2, 78–80.

Randall F, Downie R (1996) Palliative Care Ethics: A Good Companion. Oxford, Oxford Medical Publications.

Sanai P (1999) The doctrine of double effect and the law of murder. Medico-Legal Journal. 67, 3, 106–120.

Singer P (1999) Is the sanctity of life ethic terminally ill? In Kuhse H, Singer P (Eds) Bioethics: An Anthology. Oxford, Blackwell Publishers.

Tannsjo T (2000) Terminal sedation: a possible compromise in the euthanasia debate? Bulletin of Medical Ethics. 163, 13–22.

Uhlmann M (Ed)(1998) Last Rights, Assisted Suicide and Euthanasia Debated. Washington DC, Ethics and Public Policy Center.

Janis Moody RGN, RMN, MA, MSc, is Lecturer, Napier University, School of Acute and Continuing Care Nursing, Edinburgh. Email: j.moody@napier.ac.uk.

From *Nursing Standard*, March 5, 2003, pp. 40-45. © 2003 by Royal College of Nursing Ltd. Reprinted by permission.

Colleen's **Choice**

When her fight against cancer became unbearable, a woman who savored life chose death as her only option. Now the U.S. government is challenging the law that helped her end the agony

By Barry Yeoman

THE NIGHT BEFORE COLLEEN Rice swallowed the medication that ended her life, she wanted to give her grandchildren one final, uncomplicated memory of their family matriarch. So with the kids out of sight, she hobbled upstairs to the bathroom, her daughter holding her steady and carrying the oxygen tank that helped her breathe through cancer-riddled lungs. She showered, put on her white housecoat, and returned to the family room of her daughter's home in Tigard, Oregon. Wanting quiet for her last night with her loved ones, Colleen removed her breathing apparatus—which she could live without for short periods of time—and with the turn of a switch, the room, usually filled with the whirring of the generator that supplied her oxygen, grew suddenly still. "I'm ready," she said.

The grandchildren were called in: 20-year-old Joshua, home from the Navy for Christmas; his 16-year-old sister, Ashley; and their 12-year-old cousin, Brendan, visiting with his father from Canada. They crowded around a small circular table—Colleen wanted them as close as possible—and brought out Tock, a French-Canadian game played with marbles, a deck of cards, and a red, white, and black wooden board with a circular center known as Heaven.

Everyone was in high spirits. As the marbles migrated around the Tock board, Joshua entertained the family with his Jim Carrey impersonations and showered his grandmother with kisses and tickles. Colleen laughed hard, even though the laughter attacked her chest with a stabbing pain. "Stop! Stop!" she protested, hating to stifle the merriment on which she thrived. Her daughter, Cathy Paul, knew what most of the kids did not: Their grandmother, whose debilitation and feeling of helplessness were worsening daily, would end her life in less than 12 hours. Cathy struggled to keep smiling as her relatives moved their marbles in and out of Heaven. At one point, Colleen pulled her daughter aside and whispered, "I'm coughing up blood."

THE SACRIFICE "Even if the law weren't available," says Colleen's husband, Scott, "she made me promise I would help her."

By 11 P.M., Colleen was worn out from the lack of oxygen. "Night, Grandma," the kids said casually, but Cathy stopped them before they wandered off. "No," she said. "Give Grandma a hug and a kiss good night." Inside, she wanted to scream, "Tell her how you feel! This is the last time you'll see your grandmother's smile."

The house quiet, Cathy turned to her mother. "You don't have to do this," she said.

"Yes, I do," the older woman answered. She offered no explanation, but Cathy understood why her mother planned to take a lethal prescription of barbiturates the next morning. The product of a strong Catholic family, Colleen had escaped a deadening first marriage and spent almost four de-cades on a spiritual and creative quest. The journey carried her to a metaphysics institute, where she studied spiritual issues; to the ends of the U.S. in a motor home, selling her waxwork paintings with her husband, Scott; and to the Atlantic coast of Ireland, where she researched a historical novel. Her work mostly complete at 67, she was now largely confined to the sofa and bed, her senses dulled by morphine, the space between her lungs and chest cavity filling with fluid from her tumor. Left to its own devices, her body would have quit within a couple of months, maybe less, but Colleen didn't want to experience the misery of suffocating as her lungs became unable to deliver oxygen to her body. Instead, she wanted a quiet, prayerful death, surrounded by her family.

"I'm going to bed now," she announced. Scott had retired earlier in the evening to be alert when Colleen needed his support in the morning.

"Why don't we just stay up a bit?" Cathy asked.

"I really need the sleep," Colleen said, heading toward her room. Tomorrow would be one of the most important days of her life. She needed to be ready.

THE LAW THAT would allow Colleen Rice to hasten her death will face a serious challenge this year in a federal appeals court. The Oregon Death With Dignity Act, which allows physicians to write lethal prescriptions for certain terminally ill patients, was used by only 91 Oregonians in its first four years on the books. Yet it has prompted a crusade by U.S. Attorney General John Ashcroft, who in November 2001 directed the Drug Enforcement Administration to prohibit doctors who prescribe fatal doses of medicine from writing prescriptions under the Controlled Substances Act. Ashcroft, a longtime opponent of physician-assisted suicide, claims the law violates the Act, which bars doctors from prescribing drugs for anything other than legitimate medical purposes. Though a federal judge blocked Ashcroft from enforcing his order, the issue will not be settled until all courts have weighed in. It seems inevitable that the case will go to the U.S. Supreme Court.

'People treat their dogs better,' Colleen had said of the American medical system. 'If I'm on life support, just pull the plug.'

The Oregon measure, unique in the nation, was approved twice by voters, despite heavy opposition from the Catholic Church. During those campaigns, critics charged that the law would trigger a "slippery slope"—from voluntary suicide to the Nazi-like extermination of undesirables.

In reality, the Death With Dignity Act is quite specific: It allows state residents with less than six months to live to request medication to end their lives "in a humane and dignified manner." The patient must ask three times over a period of 15 days or more, twice orally and once in writing. Two physicians must approve the petition, and they must refer the patient to counseling if there are signs of depression or other mental disorders. Finally, the patient has to be able to swallow the drugs without assistance. The physician is not allowed to intervene at the bedside.

In the five years since the law took effect, state officials say it has proceeded without medical complications. Those who have committed assisted suicide typically have been well-educated men and women with both health insurance and access to hospice care. "The critics have been terribly disappointed that the warnings they gave—that this would lead to euthanasia and selective killing of the elderly— have not come true," says Alan Bates, a

physician and state legislator from Ashland. Instead, he says, the law has restored a sense of control to dying Oregonians, even those who don't end up taking the drugs. "The choice gives them a sense of peace," he says. "They know that at the end they won't be in terrible pain."

Even when they don't choose assisted suicide, Oregon patients feel more empowered to orchestrate the final months of their lives than patients anywhere else in the nation. The Beaver State leads the U.S. in many of the indicators for top-quality end-of-life care. Oregon consistently shows the lowest rates of in-hospital deaths, and the state ranks first in the use of medical morphine, a key indicator of whether terminally ill patients are receiving adequate pain control. Oregon is also among the top states when it comes to the availability of hospice services.

Yet physician-assisted suicide remains the most controversial aspect of end-of-life care, both in the state and the country— similar measures have failed by close margins in Maine and Hawaii—and some Oregonians are publicly rooting for Ashcroft to prevail. Critics point to data showing that loss of independence, rather than physical pain, is why 94 percent of patients opt for suicide. "Dying makes us dependent on people, and we don't like that. We have to learn that it's okay to be cared for," says Father John Tuohey, an ethicist in Portland's Providence Health System who opposes the law. "Is this a good public policy to send out to people: When you become too burdensome, feel free to check out?"

THE DOUBT On the final night, Colleen's daughter, Cathy Paul, told her mother: "You don't have to do this."

Few people actually choose assisted suicide. In Oregon, 1 percent ask their doctors for prescriptions, and only .1 percent receive approval or follow through, says Susan Tolle, director of the Center for Ethics in Health Care at Oregon Health & Science University (OHSU). The ones who do hasten their deaths follow a pattern: They are generally self-reliant, accomplished individuals who personify Oregon's pioneer spirit. "This is a group of people whose life experiences make them value control," says Linda Ganzini, an OHSU psychiatry professor who has studied the issue. "They often associate being cared for by somebody as humiliating. They develop this fierce individualism. In Oregon, they're

admired for those characteristics." For people like this, the prospect of spending their last days in a morphine haze, soiling their bedsheets and being turned over by nurses, is worse than death itself. "It's not that their pain can't be controlled," says Katrina Hedberg, a medical epidemiologist for the Oregon Department of Human Services. "It's that to control it they give up what makes their life meaningful."

COLLEEN RICE NEVER imagined she'd be choosing between a pain-ridden life and a dignified death when she visited her doctor in September 2000. She was suffering from breathing trouble that had left her fatigued, and doctors suspected asthma. Then a CT scan showed a tumor on one lung. Follow-up tests confirmed the severity of her illness.

Colleen put on her makeup that morning. She wanteed to look good on her final day. There was a softness in the room, a feeling of warmth.

Scott, her husband, had accompanied Colleen on all her doctor visits, so he was prepared for the worst, doing most of his grieving in long phone calls to Colleen's sisters. But when Colleen calmly told her daughter the news—that she had only six months to live—Cathy collapsed. "My life got sucked out of me," remembers Cathy.

Colleen remained strong—a strength that had only grown throughout her life. One of six kids in an Irish Catholic family in Ottawa, she married a neighborhood boy at 20 and moved to a military base in a remote subarctic town in Manitoba, where she scrubbed the tile floors daily and kept the radio tuned to reports of polar-bear sightings. It was only after her divorce 10 years later, and her move back to Ottawa, that she began the inner journey she had long delayed, taking classes in religion and meditation. It was then that she met her future husband, Scott. She was 39. He was 22. "She was young for her age, and I was old for mine," he recalls three decades later. "She was loosening up and learning to play." They married in 1976 and eventually moved to Oregon, where they took an

Switching Sides

Why one of the biggest supporters of doctor-assisted suicide has changed her mind

In 1992, DIANE MEIER, M.D., CO-AUTHORED some of the first guidelines for doctor-assisted suicide. "My sense was that patients were the only ones who knew what was best for them," says Meier, director of the palliative care program at New York's Mount Sinai School of Medicine. "The medical profession's opposition to physician-assisted suicide seemed breathtakingly arrogant."

In the decade since, Meier has become one of the premier opponents of death-with-dignity laws. She now believes that existential despair, not physical pain, is what motivates many patients to end their lives—and that most doctors are not properly prepared to deal with the psychological components of serious illness.

Meier's about-face was spurred by a patient, an 87-year-old immigrant who lived alone and battled a series of chronic health problems: diabetes, high blood pressure, arthritis, loss of hearing and sight. The patient could barely walk. She was constantly irritable. Unable to live as she was accustomed, "her life frame was shrinking," Meier says. "Several times she said she just wanted me to give her a pill."

Since assisted suicide is not legal in New York—nor is it legal anywhere in the U.S. for patients without terminal illnesses—Meier resorted to a treatment that her colleagues frequently overlook. She listened to the woman's litany of problems: her guilt at having been a bad parent to her now-adult children, her anger at their rejection. With the patient's permission, Meier called the woman's adult children and encouraged them to set aside their old resentments. They heeded the doctor's words, taking turns visiting their mother. "By the end of her life, her relationships with her kids were healed," Meier says. "It wasn't until that happened that she allowed herself to die." One day she told Meier, "I'm going to die in five days and see my husband on the other side." And she did.

When a patient asks to die, "nine times out of ten it's an expression of despair and a communication to the physician to hear the despair," says Meier. Unfortunately, most doctors are either ill-equipped or too busy to explore these feelings. Allowing doctors with limited repertoires to prescribe lethal medicines, she believes, is dangerous public policy.—B. Y.

---

interest in an art form called CireCraft, which uses crayon wax, a travel iron, and a hot plate to create intricate landscapes. Before long they bought an orange-and-black Cabana motor home, christened it Pumpkin, and began a three-year road trip to show and sell their art. In 1985, Colleen started her last great adventure. She signed up for a *Writer's Digest* correspondence course and started a historical novel, which would occupy the rest of her life and involve three research trips to Ireland's rugged Atlantic coast.

As her health went downhill, and her book remained unpublished, Colleen kept a calm exterior. There were decisions to make. The doctors told her that chemotherapy might extend her life by months but would not cure the cancer. Colleen decided she had too much unfinished business to be crippled by chemo's side effects. Instead, she opted for palliative, or comfort, care. Hospice workers provided oxygen to help her breathe, along with morphine to ease the pain and relieve her sense of breathlessness. They treated the side effects of her medication and made available a 24-hour nurse who could be telephoned in emergencies. With her basic comfort provided for, Colleen used her final months—there were only three, it turned out—to complete the most important tasks of her life: healing some long-standing conflicts with Cathy and enlisting the family to help edit her novel.

She also began the process of requesting a lethal prescription. Colleen had been aware of the physician-assisted suicide issue for almost seven years and had supported it during the 1994 and 1997 referenda. "People treat their dogs better," she had said of the American medical system, which generally requires that doctors keep patients alive no matter what. She surely knew the profound, almost ironic effect the law has had on end-of-life care in Oregon. The more patients inquire about hastening their deaths, the more doctors search for alternatives to alleviate their suffering. Since the state's first death-with-dignity vote eight years ago, health care institutions have been scrambling to stay on the cutting edge of quality-of-life care for the terminally ill. In 1995, OHSU started building its own comfort-care team for dying patients in hospitals—a radical innovation in a profession that aims to cure rather than soothe the sick. Professional organizations are presenting more end-of-life care workshops. "People wouldn't go to those before the law," says Barbara Coombs Lee, president of the Compassion in Dying Federation. "Now it's standing room only."

The law has also pushed the state's news media to examine end-of-life issues, including pain management and hospice availability. In turn, Oregonians are increasingly insisting on top-notch care for terminal patients. "When I was in medical school, you'd never see a family walk up to a doctor and say, 'This is not what our mother would have wanted,'" says OHSU's Susan Tolle. "The Oregon vote was a wake-up call for medicine."

But critics such as Joanne Lynn, director of the Washington Home Center for Palliative Care Studies in Washington, D.C., warn against applying the lessons of one state to the rest of the country. Oregon has been successful, she says, because it's a forward-thinking, fairly affluent place that guarantees health care to its citizens. It had a strong infrastructure to care for the terminally ill. By contrast, Maine (where voters defeated a proposed death-with-dignity law in 2000) has one of the lowest uses of the Medicare hospice benefit of any state. It would need to guarantee universal hospice and palliative care if such a law were passed, says Ganzini, the OHSU psychiatrist. Allowing assisted suicide in Maine, she says, "seems like a pretty bad idea."

For the last months of her life, Colleen Rice lived at her daughter's house in a makeshift bedroom adorned with a miniature statue of an angel, a Lakota Indian prayer, and a rosary an ancestor had brought over during the Irish potato famine. At night Scott lay awake, listening to his wife's breathing in the hospital bed a foot away, and hearing Jasmine, their German shorthaired pointer, snoring on his other side. He synchronized his breathing with Colleen's. Sometimes, when her respiration slowed, he'd take two breaths for every one of hers. Other times Colleen would wake up, angry at still being alive, worried that if she waited too long she would no longer be able to swallow the medication by herself. If that happened, anyone who assisted her would be breaking the law.

On the final morning, at 5 A.M., there was a knock at the door. Standing outside was George Eighmey, executive director of Compassion in Dying of Oregon. Since the passage of the law, Eighmey and his volunteers have visited families, located sympathetic doctors and pharmacists, and stood at bedsides at the end when asked.

"Here's Mr. Death," Colleen said, deadpan, as he walked through the door, then broke into laughter.

Colleen had put on her makeup that morning. She wanted to look good on her final day. She took an anti-nausea medication to ensure that she wouldn't vomit the bitter-tasting barbiturates later in the morning. Eighmey explained the procedure to the family, then helped them crush the 90 barbiturates and mix their contents with orange juice to make swallowing easier.

Finally, after the anti-nausea drug had taken effect, the family gathered around. Outside, it was still black. "I remember walking into the bedroom," says Eighmey. "It might sound strange, but there was a softness in the air, a feeling of warmth. Colleen was such a warm, reassuring woman, she gave others permission to feel sad and to participate."

When the time came, Eighmey asked Colleen her wishes one last time. "Are you absolutely sure you want to do this?"

"Yep, let's do it," Colleen replied matter-of-factly.

"Colleen, it's not too late to back out," Eighmey said. "If you have any hesitation, we can dump this down the toilet."

"Nope," she responded. "I'm ready." After a quick toast, she lifted the glass and drank. Almost immediately she began to doze. Cathy started reciting the Lakota prayer that would fill the room for the next two hours:

"O Great Spirit,
whose voice I hear in the winds,
and whose breath gives
life to all the world, hear me!
I am small and weak.
I need your strength and wisdom."

Between each verse, her relatives chanted. "We let you go," they said. "Go to the light. We love you. Find the light." Then, one by one, her family recited the next verses, broken up by more chanting, until finally...

"Make me always ready
to come to you with clean hands
and straight eyes, so when life fades,
as the fading sunset, my spirit
will come to you without shame."

Within minutes Colleen had slipped into a coma. The dawn broke bright and warm, a startling contrast to the usual rain of December mornings. The family kept up their prayer, punctuated by exhortations: "We release you. Find the light."

Two hours after she took the medicine, Colleen Rice was gone. Everyone left the room except Cathy, who sat with her mother for a few minutes before waking her children. Eighmey dialed the hospice to report an "expected death." Colleen's primary-care doctor signed the death certificate, listing the cause as lung cancer.

Two years later, Cathy still breaks down when she recalls her mother's illness and hastened death. Sometimes she imagines what her mother would be doing if the cancer had gone away. Then she remembers the Ashcroft directive, and knows exactly what Colleen would be up to. "If she had been cured," Cathy says, "she would be standing on some steps in Washington, D.C., shouting, 'How dare you take away our right to die in dignity? You don't have that right.'"

Barry Yeoman previously wrote about prescription drugs for AARP Modern Maturity. *Colleen Rice's novel,* In the Midst of Darkness, *is available on Amazon.com.*

End-of-Life Care:

Forensic Medicine vs. Palliative Medicine

This article provides an understanding of how state laws, the office of the Attorney General (John Ashcroft), and issues related to end-of-life and assisted suicide are being resolved in cases related to palliative medicine and forensic medicine.

Joseph P. Pestaner

The increasing life expectancy of terminally-ill people has raised many public policy concerns about end-of-life care.[1] Due to increased longevity and the lack of cures for illnesses like cancer and heart disease, palliative care, particularly pain management, has become an important mode of medical therapy[2] Palliative care providers feel that "[h]ealth care professionals have a moral duty to provide adequate palliative care and pain relief, even if such care shortens the patient's life."[3] Practitioners of forensic medicine grapple with determining when to classify the death of a person formerly receiving palliative care as a non-natural death.[4] Such classification may be paramount in the enforcement of new statutes that aim at preventing assisted suicide or monitoring the quality of health care, but it potentially places forensic medicine and palliative medicine in adversarial roles. Now that multiple states have passed laws against assisted suicide[5] and U.S. Attorney General John Ashcroft has issued a new drug-enforcement policy[6] that undermines an Oregon's legalization of assisted suicide, it is important for healthcare workers in palliative care to know which actions may violate State and Federal laws.[7]

One effort to prohibit use of listed drugs for assisted suicide was the Pain Relief Promotion Act (PRPA), which passed the House in 1999 but stalled in the Senate in the fall of 2000 due to efforts by Senator Ron Wyden of Oregon.[8] The PRPA, which provides criminal punishment for physicians who cause or assist in causing a patient's death

through the use of controlled substances, would have pre-empted Oregon's physician-assisted suicide law.[9] "Under PRPA, physicians would violate the federal Controlled Substances Act if they administer opioids or other drugs to hasten a patient's death."[10] The PRPA would have created uncertainty for health-care providers as to what would be considered appropriate palliative therapy for pain[11] but perhaps even more uncertainty has been created by the Bush administration's efforts to ensure that debate over the Oregon law took place without the public's scrutiny.[12]

This comment examines the forensic medicine challenges in this new medicolegal environment where proper palliative care has become a priority, but there is a strong movement to criminalize efforts by health-care personnel to assist in suicide. Medical examiner cases for the State of Maryland demonstrate differences in medical opinion relating to forensic and palliative medicine; as the laws and regulations stand now, prosecutors in Maryland are charged with the very difficult task of prosecuting health-care personnel who purposefully assist in hastening another's death by administering medicine. Through these case studies, legal and medical issues arise when an individual's death was arguably hastened by the administration of narcotics. These cases reveal the practical difficulties involved in any attempt to use the law to protect patients from assisted suicide and overtreatment with pain medications. These difficulties are due in part to differences in the underlying viewpoints of practitioners of palliative care and forensic medicine, particularly with regard to the significance of postmortem toxicology levels. The legal bounds of physician conduct are explored for possible guidelines to assist health-care practitioners as well as for limitations a prosecutor may face in bringing murder charges against a health-care provider. The first part of this comment examines how death investigation is performed in the state, the second part will examine borderline palliative care cases that have been investigated by medical and legal representatives of the state, and the third part will examine potential problems the future holds for the enforcement of such regulations through a discussion of clear-cut cases of homicide at the end of life. Civil actions are not addressed.

I conclude that there is really no reason that a palliative care provider should have any concern about criminal prosecution or administrative sanction. In particular, the state will not take action if the medical records reflect care within the expected standard of care even if the treatment "hastens" another person's death. Even if treatment is not within the standard of care and reaches a grossly negligent level, successful criminal prosecution will rarely occur. As the laws and regulations stand now in Maryland, to criminally convict a palliative care provider of a homicidal act essentially requires an admission of guilt. I also argue that implementation of effective regulatory policy requires agreement on appropriate standards of care in the medical community before any just enforcement can be accomplished by the law.

DEATH INVESTIGATION, STATE OF MARYLAND

Generally, a person undergoing palliative pain treatment requires frequent contact with a physician for evaluation and review of treatment.[13] When death occurs and such an outcome is expected, the death certificate will typically be completed by the physician who oversees the care of the patient and generally no investigation of circumstances surrounding such a death will occur, particularly if death occurs within a health-care facility.[14] If death occurs outside of a health-care facility, then law enforcement officials or emergency medical personnel will generally be called to the scene to investigate the situation and initiate contact with the treating physician; if the treating physician signs the death certificate, the death investigation will usually stop at that point since the death was not unexpected.[15]

At the time of death, state officials will generally only undertake an investigation of the death of a patient undergoing palliative pain therapy if the treating physician refuses to sign the death certificate[16] or the law requires the involvement of the Office of the Chief Medical Examiner (OCME).[17] Maryland law provides that,

> [t]he State has a compelling interest to safeguard the peace, health, and good order of the community. To this end, it needs to know when a death results from a criminal act or when the cause of death is such that the health and well-being of others may be adversely affected. That it may obtain this knowledge is the purpose and the underlying basis of the statutes pertaining to postmortem examinations.[18]

In Maryland, part of the death investigation may include an autopsy so that the medical examiner may determine the cause and manner of death.[19]

The cause of death is the injury or disease process that resulted in death and the manner of death is classified as natural, suicide, accident, homicide or undetermined,[20] Determining the cause and manner of death are considered the duties of the medical examiner.[21] The conclusions of the medical examiner regarding the cause and manner of death are an important part of the death investigation and are admissible at trial.[22] The injuries and other pertinent anatomic findings, as well as toxicologic data, are documented through an autopsy report by a qualified forensic pathologist. The autopsy is just one step in the investigation to evaluate the appropriateness of care provided or other circumstances surrounding the death. In general, when the deceased had a physician attending to his or her care and death was an expected outcome, the OCME will not investigate.

To illustrate the issues that can arise in the investigation of the deaths of palliative care patients, I have reviewed the records of the Maryland OCME dating back 10 years. I examined deaths that raised challenging death certification questions related to palliative care and end-of-life issues.[23] The jurisdiction of the OCME encompasses all counties and municipalities, including the City of Baltimore, in the state of Maryland.[24] I reviewed each selected file, including the police and investigative reports and photos, for cause and manner of death, age, sex, location where initial incident and death occurred, and the circumstances surrounding the police involvement.[25] I reviewed autopsy reports completed by members of the OCME pathology staff in accordance with accepted forensic pathology standards including a complete autopsy examination, toxicologic studies, and a complete incident investigation.

The two cases I selected were ones that hugged the line separating natural from non-natural manners of death. Natural deaths are caused completely by disease; non-natural deaths include suicide, accident, and homicide.[26] A suicide is a violent death caused by the decedent, an accident is a violent death from an unforeseeable act, and a homicide is a violent death caused by another person.[27] The cases were brought to the attention of the OCME because the care provided appeared to be substandard and/or there were events surrounding the death that were considered suspicious. I examined two cases in which classification of the manner of death as natural was questionable because pain medication may have hastened the patient's death.[28]

Case 1[29]

The first case involved an elderly woman with progressive supranuclear palsy[30] who was being taken care of by her daughter at home. The woman was terminally ill and her death was expected. A palliative care nurse reported the patient to be in pain and morphine was prescribed by the attending physician though pain medication had not previously been needed. The daughter contacted her mother's physician because she was having difficulty getting the morphine prescription filled. The daughter told the physician that she possessed a single dose of methadone and asked if she could administer the methadone to her mother. The physician stated that a one-time dose of methadone would be adequate. The woman died within hours of the administration of methadone and the physician signed the death certificate. A social service worker who knew the daughter and was concerned by related events that occurred just prior to the mother's death contacted the police. After the police were notified, the OCME investigated the case and an autopsy was performed. At autopsy, there was an abscess and bronchopneumonia in the lung, as well as anatomic evidence of supranuclear palsy. The methadone level was 600 nanograms per milliliter (ng/ml). The OCME concluded that the cause of death was progressive supranuclear palsy and the manner of death was natural.

Case 2[31]

In the second case, an elderly woman with a history of Alzheimer's disease and breast cancer died at home where she was living with her daughter. Some family members alleged that their mother had been mistreated by caretakers including her daughter and wanted an autopsy; a private pathologist chose not to perform the autopsy because of possible future legal proceedings. The Sheriff of the local jurisdiction contacted OCME to assist in the investigation. An autopsy revealed Alzheimer's disease, bronchopneumonia and 7,000 ng/ml of morphine in the blood. No injuries were found and no residual breast cancer was found. The OCME initially concluded that the immediate cause of death was from lobar pneumonia and the manner of death was natural. After the OCME obtained the toxicology results and heard from other family members alleging mistreatment, it amended the cause of death to morphine intoxication due to pain management

related to Alzheimer's disease. Contributory causes of death were pneumonia and breast cancer, and the manner of death was unclassified.

Determining the Cause and Manner of Death

When the OCME is involved in determining the cause and manner of death, notification of deaths that have occurred is performed by law enforcement officials, licensed medical personnel or citizens of the state that have concerns about the circumstances surrounding the death.[32] The challenge and statutory duty of the medical examiner is to determine the cause and manner of death. To make such a determination in cases that are unclear generally requires a complete investigation by forensic investigators and law enforcement officers, a complete autopsy, and review of medical records and other available pertinent information.

Examination of these two cases offers insight into the difficulties and challenges of enforcing legislation regulating palliative care and the health-care providers who provide such care. In both cases, a complete autopsy was performed as well as forensic toxicologic drug testing. In medical examiner cases where a complete autopsy has been done, a forensic pathologist has to make a decision as to the cause and manner of death. This is the first step in a criminal investigation involving death. The conclusions of the medical examiner may determine how aggressively a case can be pursued by prosecutors due to limitations of the medical testimony available.

Case Discussion

In case 1, there is a clear temporal relation between the administration of pain medication and death.[33] Toxicologic results were consistent with a single administration of methadone.[34] Progressive supranuclear palsy is a disease that causes widespread loss of tissues that make up the brain; the immediate cause of death usually occurs from aspiration pneumonia.[35] In the case examined, there was clear evidence of aspiration pneumonia but certainly the methadone may have suppressed the respiratory drive, hastening death.[36] Making a conclusion about the toxicity of methadone without knowing any historical or clinical information is very difficult.[37] The report of events occurring prior to the death was verified by investigators and police; the doctor had indeed given verbal approval for the methadone administration, but no person was present when the woman became unresponsive.[38] Police asked the treating physician about his actions and he replied, "I would do it over again."[39] The main concern in this case was the manner in which a narcotic substance was dispensed.[40] The physician had never physically examined the patient and he allowed another patient's medication to be administered to his patient. The OCME considered methadone an appropriate treatment for a patient who needed pain therapy, and therefore methadone administration could not be considered a contributory cause of death to a reasonable degree of medical certainty, even though it may have hastened death.[41]

In case 2, the conclusions of the OCME were challenged pursuant to a Maryland statute.[42] Over the past 10 years, two cases have come before the administrative law judge to evaluate the opinions of the OCME.[43] At issue in case 2 was whether the pain medication, Roxanol (liquid morphine), prescribed to the elderly woman, had anything to do with the cause of death.[44] Based on the investigation completed by the OCME, the administrative law judge concluded that the pain medication was at a lethal level despite the fact that it was being provided for palliative care.[45]

Roxanol was the only drug prescribed during the last eighteen days of the patient's life for pain. Though the patient denied having pain, there were physical signs of pain in her arm and torso presumably from either metastatic breast cancer to bone or from degenerative bone disease.[46] No physician examined the decedent during the time that she was being treated with Roxanol, even though the amount of medication was increased steadily.[47] In a case where expert testimony was crucial, the administrative law judge gave little credibility to the OCME experts in writing her opinion: "[W]hile the State's experts offered credible information about morphine intoxication, I believe each of them had insufficient knowledge about the use of morphine as pain management therapy to conclude that the decedent had died of morphine intoxication."[48] In this regard, the administrative law judge thought the only credible testimony came from a nurse and physician who were experts in palliative medicine.[49] According to the palliative care experts, the level of morphine recovered did not have any meaning because patients develop pain tolerance and what mattered was controlling the pain.[50] Interestingly, chronic substance abusers with acute overdoses have levels that are significantly less than that seen in case 2. "The State's experts were in agreement that in all their years of experience, they had never seen such a high level of morphine, even in drug addicts."[51] The explanation that the administrative law judge and the palliative care experts provided to explain the drug level was tolerance; the decedent had developed such a high tolerance that the level was meaningless and could not have caused or contributed to her death.[52] Accordingly, the cause and manner of death were amended to "pneumonia" and "natural," respectively.[53] Such a conclusion has great meaning for the enforcement of new statutes pertaining to palliative care. Drug levels are frequently used not only to demonstrate causation but also to allow one to make inferences regarding intent. If drug levels at death have no meaning for palliative care patients, then other methods of investigation are necessary to enforce the new laws, even though drug levels are the most objective evidence to demonstrate "hastening" of death from medication.

Discrepancies in medical testimony will perhaps prompt some research into how to monitor patient safety during palliative therapy. As it stands now, the standard of care for palliative medicine does not address the meaning of drug levels as none are clinically obtained or indicated in monitoring pain management. On the other hand, much significance is placed on levels in determining the cause and manner of death. Only research can help settle this apparent conflict between palliative and forensic medicine.

ENFORCEMENT ISSUES

The challenge to forensic medicine when considering the events surrounding the death of someone who has been under the treatment of another physician is not just determining the cause and manner of death, but whether the care violated any regulations or health-care standards. When improper care has been alleged and an unbiased opinion is necessary to determine whether any non-natural process led to death, the OCME will investigate the circumstances around an individual's death.[54] As discussed above, the OCME generally does not get involved in cases where a palliative care recipient dies. In addition, in the only hearing in Maryland where sworn testimony has been given regarding end-of-life care, major differences were noted in the medical testimony of forensic medicine and palliative medicine experts. Where reliance on drug levels to determine if a person's death was hastened is not considered enough evidence, as in the Drummond Case 2 discussed above,[55] proving a case of intentionally hastening another's death would be difficult.

The cases discussed above are typical of palliative care cases that may be investigated by the OCME. In each case, there is clinical evidence of disease and many reasons for the patient to die, but circumstances surrounding the death are suspicious.[56] Considerations for death certification after administration of medical care include the foreseeability of potential therapeutic complications and whether any rules or regulations were violated that need to be reported to other government agencies. In both examples, a core issue concerns the quality of care that was provided and whether the prescribing practices were within the roles and regulations of the medical board. Negligent care that exceeds the foreseeable risks of the care provided would be considered non-natural. Comparable circumstances arise frequently at the OCME,[57] and the medical board is routinely notified about drug prescribing practices of concern.[58] In both cases, the medical board reviewed the case and found no irregularity and investigated no further.[59]

Deaths that are a result of negligent drug administration by a health-care provider are frequently classified as accidental[60] because administration of the wrong dose would not be considered a predictable complication of accepted therapy.[61] In general, death-related to therapy is classified as accidental, whereas natural deaths are the result of disease.[62] When administration of a drug causes death, the manner of death would be classified as homicide, which means that the death is the result of another's action.[63] In some jurisdictions in Canada, deaths that occur during surgery are classified as homicide because of the violent action of the surgeon resulting in death, though such convention is unusual.[64] As such, the difficulty in classifying deaths of people formerly receiving palliative care is evident and each case must be carefully investigated when allegations are made that improper care caused a patient's death.

Palliative Medicine

Palliative care is a critical component of end-of-life therapy where treatment options for cure do not exist and relief from unnecessary suffering is all that can be offered.[65] Pain management is an important facet of such care. Palliative medicine is based on an underlying premise that if, during the treatment of pain, pain medication hastens the patient's death, that is appropriate and acceptable.[66] The defense of such therapy is based on the doctrine of double effect.[67] Double effect is a "long-standing rule for evaluating the morality of clinical practice, particularly the care of the terminally-ill, [which] has been variously known as the Principle, or Doctrine, or Rule of Double Effect."[68] Even so, the doctrine is invoked only when a dilemma is reached in making a decision that has risks and benefits.[69] From a forensic medicine perspective, if a medication hastens another death then, by definition, that death cannot be classified as natural.[70] The challenge of forensic medicine becomes how one demonstrates that medication hastened the death of someone who has a terminal condition and is given large doses of pain medication.[71] In general, "[d]eaths due to diagnostic maneuvers or therapy represent acts of commission and can pose some difficulty in classification. By universal convention, deaths caused by physicians are classified as homicides only if there is demonstrable intent to kill or if there is gross and wanton disregard for the safety of the patient."[72] Typically, non-natural deaths that are a result of overmedication by health-care providers are classified as accidents; classifying a death as a homicide requires more evidence.[73] There is re-luctance to classify such cases as a homicide, but the law regarding assisted suicide is evolving to limit how aggressive such therapy can be used and is limiting what physicians can do in end-of-life care.[74] Yet in case 2, when the state's experts from the Forensic Medicine Center provided testimony about pain medication that was found at autopsy at an exceptionally high level, the administrative law judge discounted that observation and changed the cause of death to encompass only natural disease, remarking that the OCME experts were not knowledgeable about palliative care.[75] Evidence that is typically important for determining overdoses from medications include not only autopsy and clinical findings, but medication levels as well. If drug levels at death have no meaning for palliative care patients, then death investigators cannot demonstrate "hastening" of death from medication. As a result, the question of the intent of those who administer pain medication will not be reached, making new regulations such as the Pain Relief Promotion Act of 1999 ineffective.[76] Perhaps further guidance from the legislators as to what actions would be unacceptable would be necessary or use of a different standard, such as recklessness, rather than intent.[77] Recklessness has been described as the standard to which health-care providers should be held in determining the legality of their actions.[78] Such a framework transforms the issue from determination of specific intent to whether the health-care worker took a justifiable risk.[79]

A major concern for palliative care providers and pain experts is persistent problem of undertreatment of patients with chronic pain.[80] In fact, it has been found that:

> Sixty nine percent of patients would opt for suicide if they felt their pain could not be relieved. Fear of unacceptable pain was a major component of requests to physicians for assisted suicide. The increased awareness of the public in assisted suicide and the recent popularity of the book *Final Exit* give evidence to this well-founded concern. Undertreatment of acute and chronic cancer pain persists despite decades of efforts to provide clinicians with information about analgesics.[81]

One reason for the undertreatment of pain by physicians is the threat of criminal prosecution or reprimand for illegal prescription practices.[82] Further, though sanctions are not common, a recent law review article states that "[d]octors' fears of disciplinary action and criminal prosecution are justified."[83] Even so, accountability for undertreatment of pain is becoming an area of tort law that is just starting to be seen by the courts.[84] In fact, a physician was recently disciplined in Oregon for not providing adequate pain management[85] A newspaper article describing the case further states, "[w]e are again in a time of change. The health community is gradually adopting standards that recognize a right to pain management."[86]

Nevertheless, when end-of-life care issues arise, there is an uncertainty as to what is acceptable practice and what the laws mean to the practice of medicine. Enforcement of standards against undertreatment is left to plaintiffs lawyers, while state and federal criminal prosecutors enforce standards against overmedication. Maryland has gone further and its Board of Physician Quality Assurance has established a "Physician's Palliative Care Pain Hotline" to assist physicians in queries for pain management and have physicians available that are board certified in hospice and palliative care medicine.[87]

Criminal Prosecution

End-of-life decisions are challenging to prosecutors; they tend not to aggressively pursue prosecutions involving such decisions.[88] Two other cases in the State of Maryland that exemplify the reluctance of prosecutors also broaden the area of uncertainty when considering the medicolegal approaches to such deaths.[89] The first case involved an elderly woman who was administered an unauthorized bolus of morphine by a nurse. Her body had to be exhumed for autopsy.[90] The OCME determined that the cause of death was morphine intoxication and the manner of death was homicide.[91] At trial, the treating physician reportedly changed his position from stating that the morphine bolus was unauthorized to stating that it was authorized in an effort to protect other health-care workers and the murder charges were dropped.[92] In the second case, an elderly woman was found dead at home with a plastic bag secured around her head.[93] Initially, it was thought by police the woman secured the bag by herself and the death was a suicide, but investigation revealed that the plastic bag was secured by her son as her pain had become unbearable.[94] The OCME concluded that the cause of death was suffocation and the manner of death was homicide.[95] The State' Attorney's Office brought the case before a grand jury, which did not indict the son.[96] These two cases demonstrate the challenges prosecutors have when the victim is at the end of life. Borderline cases where the evidence is not as strong as in these two cases demonstrate that proof that a person's death was "hastened" will not meet the higher burden of proof beyond a reasonable doubt required in criminal law.

Double Effect

Health-care providers find justification for allowing pain medication that may cause or hasten death in the doctrine of double effect.[97] "The idea is that the physician intends only to relieve the patient's pain; while morphine will also kill the patient, this second effect is not intended, and the physician's act is therefore not wrong."[98] This double effect doctrine was first conceived by Roman Catholic theologians in considering the situation in which a foreseeable bad consequence may occur from one's action.[99] Though this approach may justify a physician's act, the statutes in Maryland clearly seek to protect patients at the end of life from care that is substandard and potentially criminal.[100] Some commentators have argued that the doctrine of double effect is applicable when the health-care provider has a tree dilemma because certain recommended therapy may cause harm.[101] Of course, all treatments have possible side-effects, but the doctrine of double effect should be used when no safe alternatives exist and death is a distinct possibility.[102]

Forensic pathologists attempt to render opinions based on a complete investigation that would include an autopsy and involve OCME investigators as well as law enforcement officers. Such investigations are without testimony under oath and conclusions are to a reasonable degree of medical certainty. Always of concern is that the system would not promptly identify physicians such as Dr. John Shaw, who was found guilty of killing fifteen elderly women by injecting them with diamorphine and given fifteen life sentences.[103] Based on the information reviewed, it seems clear how it would be easy for any death investigation system to overlook such cases until the evidence became overwhelming. Nobody would question that patients are entitled to pain management; such a right has been affirmed by the Supreme Court.[104] Yet, from a medicolegal perspective, it is when care provided falls below expected standards that the non-natural line has been reached.

How the law chooses to view such cases will certainly continue to evolve. The laws are such that physicians who intend to break the laws and regulations can do so unless the family complains and makes allegations forcing the state to investigate. Once the state investigates, aggressive legal prosecution would seem unlikely based on a review of cases from the past decade.

In Maryland, the doctrine of double effect is incorporated into our new assisted suicide law; the requirement of the assisted suicide law will not be met if a health-care professional administers, prescribes, or dispenses medications to relieve pain even if the medication or procedure hastens death.[105] The state only wants to address those cases where medication has intentionally been administered to hasten the death of another person, though such a case has never been prosecuted by the state. It appears that criminal prosecution of health-care workers who provide substandard palliative care is unlikely; even clear intent to assist in an individual's death through the administration of medication has rarely resulted in successful criminal prosecution.[106] Determining at what point prosecution of a palliative care case should be pursued by the State can be very difficult due to the subjectivity and philosophy of the prosecutor.[107] As Meisel et al. wrote, "[t]he criminal law is often perceived as a barrier to making end-of-life decisions. Whether criminal liability is a realistic concern depends heavily on the discretion of participants in the criminal justice system, and perhaps none more so than criminal prosecutors."[108] Based on a study of criminal prosecutors, it appears that the "personal beliefs predicted whether a prosecutor would prosecute" particularly when the attorneys "believed that the physicians' actions were morally correct."[109] Important in making such a determination will be examination of the facts on a case-by-case basis to determine exactly to what extent another's death was hastened.[110]

In less than a decade, the bright line distinction between actively and passively hastening death has begun to erode, and a new debate has emerged about whether and how to breach the barrier between the two. Whether a new consensus will form and how long it will take remains unclear, but there are many indications of movement in that direction. Despite US Supreme Court rulings that state laws criminalizing assisted suicide are constitutional, there are many reasons to believe that the movement for legalization of actively hastening death will continue and achieve at least limited recognition—not just in the United States, but worldwide—by legislation, by judicial decision or by a more informal legal mechanism.[111]

In Maryland, much progress has been made toward allowing individuals to make choices with respect to end-of-life decisions as evidenced by the Health Care Decisions Act of 1993.[112] It was within this legal framework that the Maryland Attorney General expressed his opinion that "[a]ssisted suicide, whether the assistance is rendered by a physician or someone else, is probably a common law crime in Maryland;"[113] the state has now made assisted suicide a statutory crime.[114] Such opinions and laws are considered by some to be bad policy because they create uncertainty among health-care workers.[115] Such concerns have been addressed by the Maryland Board of Quality Assurance, which assures Maryland physicians that Undertreatment of pain should not occur out of fear of adverse action from the Board.[116] The Board suggests "adequate documentation" to protect the physician from legal action.[117]

It appears that the ethical debate about what the law considers acceptable pain alleviation will continue. The forensic medicine perspective is clear in that if medication hastens another's death, then the death, in a pure sense, is not natural.[118] No cases of criminal prosecution for hastening another's death have occurred in the 1990's in Maryland. The death investigation begins with the medical examiner, and cases that require further attention are sent to the State's Attorneys for more investigation. Palliative cases are generally excluded as the deaths occur under another physician's care and are expected. Even when cases come to the system's attention, some cases are not clear-cut as to when a drug may have hastened another's death. Even when the evidence is clear, there is a reluctance among prosecutors to move forward with prosecution in some cases, as evidenced by the fact that there has never been a prosecuted case of assisted suicide against any health-care provider in the state of Maryland, though such occurrences may have happened but did not come to the attention of the authorities.[119] "It has been said that where the law criminalizes assisted suicide it is not enforced. District attorneys are not prosecuting, grand juries are not indicting, and when a rare case goes to trial, juries are acquitting."[120] The underlying difficulty is in proving the case even when the prosecutors believe them to be homicides.[121] The states need to consider alternative enforcement frameworks. One approach would be the recklessness framework,[122] but further definition of what would be considered reckless and appropriate by both palliative and forensic medicine experts still needs to be accomplished. So much is at stake. Making quality palliative pain care a priority has been difficult as state and federal governments have passed new laws to criminalize certain actions relating to end-of-life care. Proof that criminal homicide occurred in end-of-life cases will be rare but health-care providers do not understand the law and are intimidated by the possibility of prosecution. Thus, although successful criminal prosecution will be rare, undertreatment of pain may remain common, an unsatisfactory endpoint. More investigation needs to be undertaken so that appropriate pain care can be provided and encouraged while medical providers who breach well-defined standards are discouraged. Defining those standards will be of utmost importance to quality end-of-life care.

CONCLUSION

In the current medicolegal environment, practically speaking, palliative care providers should really not be concerned about adverse action for overtreatment, particularly if they renders care within the expected standards. Interestingly, the only testimony as to what measures can be used to examine "hastening" that has been credited is that provided by workers in palliative care. As it stands now, to criminally convict a health-care provider of homicide essentially requires an admission of guilt. Challenging forensic medicine questions will continue to arise as more laws and regulations at the state and federal level are enacted to regulate end-of-life care. Implementation of effective regulatory policies requires stability in medical knowledge and agreement within the medical community on standards of appropriate care before any just enforcement can be accomplished by the law. The clash between forensic medicine and palliative medicine is underway, and only once the conflicts between these fields are resolved can effective laws be implemented and enforced.

REFERENCES

1. See generally N.M. Gorsuch, "The Right to Assisted Suicide and Euthanasia," *Harvard Journal of Law & Public Policy, 23* (2000): 599-710; see also T. Finucane, "Thinking About Life-Sustaining Treatment Late in the Life of a Demented Person," *Georgia Law Review, 35* (2001): 691-705.

2. See generally D.C. Baldwin, Jr., "The Role of the Physician in End-of-Life Care: What More Can We Do?" *Journal of Health Care Law & Policy, 2* (1999): 258-267; see also R. Porter, "Failure to Treat Pain is Elder Abuse," *Trial, 37* (September 2001): 87.

3. See D.H. Smith and R.M. Veatch, eds., *Guidelines on the Termination of Life Sustaining Treatment and the Care of the Dying* (Bloomington, IN: Indiana University Press, 1987): at 129.

4. See B. Levine et al., "Palliative Pain Therapy at the End of Life & Forensic Medicine Issues," *The American Journal of Forensic Medicine and Pathology, 22* (2001): 62-64; see also W.U Spitz, ed., *Spitz and Fisher's Medicolegal Investigation of Death* (Springfield, Illinois: Charles C. Thomas, 1993): at 175 (stating that a natural death is caused exclusively by disease).

5. See N.M. Gorsuch, "The Right to Assisted Suicide and Euthanasia," *Harvard Journal of Law & Public Policy, 23* (2000): 599-710.

6. See J. Barnett and T. Detzel, "Ashcroft Acts to Undo Oregon's Suicide Law: The Order: The Policy Bars Lethal Doses of Federally Controlled Drugs," *Portland Oregonian,* November 7, 2001, at A-I.

7. "AMA Supports Laws Opposing Physician-Assisted Suicide, Regulating Drug Use," *Medical Malpractice Law & Strategy, 17,* no. 2 (1999): 12:

> Delegates to the American Medical Association's Dec. 5-8 convention in San Diego voted to support federal legislation that would prohibit physician-assisted suicide, while voting to support regulating the use of pain medication. The AMA is continuing to back the Pain Relief Promotion Act, which was passed by the House in October. The bill would require the Drag Enforcement Administration to revoke the medical license of and pursue criminal charges against any physician who prescribes controlled substances, such as morphine, to assist in the suicide of a terminally ill patient, regardless of state law. (The law would not be retroactive, so physicians who have assisted in suicides in Oregon would not be prosecuted.) The delegates concluded that their objection to physician-assisted suicide outweighed their concerns about excessive regulation proposed by the bill; a number of physicians had felt that the increased federal oversight would be an intrusion into state-regulated medicine.

See also Medical Board of California, Effective Pain Management—Legal Update, Action Report (October 2001), at 1.

8. See J. Barnett and T. Detzel, supra note 6.

9. See D. Orentlicher & A. Caplan, "The Pain Relief Act of 1999," *JAMA, 283* (2000) 255-258 (reviewing the potential problems that the Act may raise for palliative care).

10. Id.

11. See id.

12. See J. Barnett, "Bush Policy on Suicide is Cloaked in Secrecy," *Portland Oregonian,* November 11, 2001, at D-1.

13. See D. Doyle, G.W.C. Hanks, N. Macdonald, eds., *Oxford Textbook of Palliative Medicine* (New York, NY: Oxford University Press, 1993): at 187:

> The selection of an appropriate drug and the implementation of an optimal dosing regimen depend on a comprehensive assessment of the pain, medical condition, and the psychosocial status of the patient, followed by repeated evaluations during the course of therapy. The management of chronic pain with adjuvant analgesics, therefore must be viewed as a labour-intensive endeavor, in which frequent contact with the patient is necessary to ensure appropriate administration of the drug.

See also K. Eguchi, J Klastersky, R. Feld, eds., *Current Perspectives and Future Directions in Palliative Medicine* (Hong Kong: Springer, 1980).

14. Md. Code Ann., [Health-Gen.] [section] 4-212 (1995):

> A certificate of death regardless of age of decedent shall be filled out and signed by: The medical examiner, if the medical examiner takes charge of the body; or if the medical examiner does not take charge of the body, the physician who last attended the deceased. In the absence or inability of the attending physician or with the attending physician's approval, the certificate may be completed by: the attending physician's associate, the chief medical officer or designee of the institution in which death occurred, or the physician who performed an autopsy upon the decedent, provided the individual has access to the medical history of the case and death is due to natural causes. The person completing the cause of death and medical certification shall attest to the accuracy by signature or by an approved electronic process.

15. See id.

16. Id.:

> Each individual concerned with carrying out this subtitle promptly shall notify the medical examiner if the deceased was not under treatment by a physician during the terminal illness, the cause of death is unknown, or the individual considers any of the following conditions to be the cause of death or to have contributed to the death: an accident, homicide, suicide, alcoholism, criminal of suspected criminal abortion or another external cause.

17. Md. Code Ann., [Health-Gen.] [section] 5-309 (1999) ("Medical examiner's cases to be investigated include deaths by violence, by suicide, by casualty or if the deceased was in apparent good health or unattended by a physician and in any suspicious or unusual manner.").

18. *Snyder v. Holy Cross Hosp.,* 352 A.2d 334, 342 (Md. Ct. Spec. App. 1976) (holding that where cause of death could not be determined without an autopsy, the interest of the state in ascertaining the true cause of death outweighed the interest of a Jewish Orthodox

family that did not want an autopsy on the body of their son who died suddenly at age eighteen).

19. Md. Code Ann., [Health-Gen.] [section] 5-310 (2003):

When cause of death is established to a reasonable degree of medical certainty, the medical examiner who investigates the case shall file in the medical examiner's office a report on the cause of death within 30 days after notification of the case. If the medical examiner who investigates a medical examiner's case considers an autopsy necessary, the Chief Medical Examiner, the Deputy Chief Medical Examiner, an assistant medical examiner, or a pathologist authorized by the Chief Medical Examiner shall perform the autopsy.

20. *See Sippio v. State* 714 A.2d 864, 871(Md. 1998); see also *Schlossman v. State,* 659 A.2d 371,381 n.5 (Md. App. 1995).

21. See id.

22. See id.

23. The Office of the Chief Medical Examiner has a computerized system, AS 400, that allows for search and retrieval based on codes used by the Maryland Department of Health and Mental Hygiene.

24. See Records of the Office of the Chief Medical Examiner, State of Maryland (on file at the Office of the Chief Medical Examiner, accessible with the permission of the Chief Medical Examiner).

25. See id.

26. See Spitz, supra note 4, at 175.

27. See id.

28. See Records of the Office of the Chief Medical Examiner, supra note 24.

29. See id.

30. See I.H. Adams and L.W. Duchen, eds., *Greenfield's Neuropathology* (New York, NY: Oxford University Press, 1992): at 1001, 1345 (supranuclear palsy is a prototype subcortical dementia demonstrating diffuse symmetric neuronal loss).

31. See Records of the Office of the Chief Medical Examiner, supra note 24.

32. See notes supra 14-17.

33. See Records of the Office of the Chief Medical Examiner, supra note 24.

34. See id.

35. See Adams and Duchen, supra note 30; R.S. Cotran, et al., eds., *Robbins Pathologic Basis of Disease* (Philadelphia: W.B. Saunders, 1994): at 1333.

36. See S.B. Karch, *The Pathology of Drug Abuse* (Boca Raton, FL: CRC Press, 1993): at 266 (describing ten cases where death was attributed to methadone with findings consistent with respiratory arrest).

37. Id.

38. See Records of the Office of the Chief Medical Examiner, supra note 24. After giving her mother the methadone, the daughter successfully had the morphine prescription filled, after which she came home to find her mother unresponsive.

39. See id.

40. See id.; Md. Regs. Code tit. 10.07.02 [section] 15A (2003) ("Pharmaceutical services shall be provided in accordance with accepted professional principles and appropriate federal, State and local laws.")

41. See id.

42. See Md. Code Ann., [Health-Gen.] [section] 5-310 (1994) (detailing how the findings of the OCME are challenged):

Except in a case of a finding of homicide, a person in interest as defined in [section] 10-611(e) (3) of the State Government Article may request the medical examiner to correct findings and conclusions on the cause and manner of death recorded on a certificate of death under [section] 10-625 of the State Government Article within 60 days after the medical examiner files those findings and conclusions. (ii) If the Chief Medical Examiner denies the request of a person in interest to correct findings and conclusions on the cause of death, the person in interest may appeal the denial to the Secretary, who shall refer the matter to the Office of Administrative Hearings. A contested case hearing under this paragraph shall be a hearing both on the denial and on the establishment of the findings and conclusions on the cause of death. (iii) The administrative law judge shall submit findings of fact to the Secretary. (iv) After reviewing the findings of the administrative law judge, the Secretary, or the Secretary's designee, shall issue an order to: 1. Adopt the findings of the administrative law judge; or 2. Reject the findings of the administrative law judge, and affirm the findings of the medical examiner. (v) The appellant may appeal a rejection under subparagraph (iv) 2 to a circuit court of competent jurisdiction. (vi) If the final decision of the Secretary, of the Secretary's designee, or of a court of competent jurisdiction on appeal, establishes a different finding or conclusion on the cause or manner of death of a deceased than that recorded on the certificate of death, the medical examiner shall amend the certificate to reflect the different finding or conclusion under [section] 4-212 and [section] 4-214 of this article and [section] 10-625 of the State Government Article.

43. Personal communication from Laurie Bennett, Administrative Law Judge of the Maryland Office of Administrative Hearings, to author (November 17, 1999).

44. *See Patricia Drummond v. Office of the Chief Medical Examiner,* Maryland Office of Administrative Hearings, No. 93-DHMH-CME-96-039786.

45. See id at 15-16.

46. See id. at 10.

47. See id. "Her care providers prescribed Roxanol (i.e. liquid morphine), 5 ccs every six hours, on the reasonable assumption that she was in considerable pain." Additionally, the medication was increased and "As the appellant's pain intensified, Dr. Fieldson [the treating physician] increased the Roxanol prescription from 5 ccs every six hours to every four hours." Id. at 11. Dr. Fieldson increased the Roxanol to five cc every three hours just before her death. See id. at 11-12. See also D.I. Mostofsky and J. Lomranz, eds., *Handbook of Pain and Aging* (New York, NY: Plenum Press, 1997): at 89 (reporting few studies assessing pain in patients with dementia and stating, "As dementia progresses, direct assessment of the patient may become impossible").

48. See Drummond, supra note 44, at 20.

49. See id. at 23.

50. See Drummond, supra note 44, at 25.

51. Id.

52. See id.; M.A. Ashburn and L.J. Rice, eds., *The Management of Pain* (New York, NY: Churchill Livingstone, 1998): at 134 (contradicting the findings of the hearing and stating, "The development of tolerance is a slow process occurring over months to years. Studies in cancer patients have demonstrated that most patients reach a dose that remains constant for prolonged periods."); Letter from John E. Smialek, Chief Medical Examiner, State of Maryland, to Mr. Leonard Collins (September 28, 1999) (on file with author) (reviewing the toxicologic findings of Natalie D. Eddington, Associate Professor of Pharmaceutical Sciences and concludes that the level of mor-

phine "is not consistent with the accounts given by family members."); B. Levine et al., "Palliative Pain Therapy at the End of Life & Forensic Medicine Issues," *The American Journal of Forensic Medicine and Pathology, 22* (2001): 62-64 (reviewing the literature and finding that morphine levels as high as 1000 ng/ml have rarely been reported for cancer patients receiving palliative pain therapy). In Drummond, the free morphine concentration was several times higher than the highest free morphine reported in multiple studies.

53. See Drummond, supra note 44, at 29 (By a preponderance of the evidence ... the findings of the Chief Medical Examiner as to the cause and manner of death were incorrect.") See Records of the Office of the Chief Medical Examiner, supra note 24 (the Secretary of the Department of Health or designee may adopt or reject the findings in such a matter but the Secretary never reviewed the case to decide for himself how the Department should view the findings).

54. See id.

55. See Drummond, supra note 44, at 28.

56. See Records of the Office of the Chief Medical Examiner, supra note 24.

57. See id.; B. Levine et al., "An Unusual Morphine Fatality," *Forensic Science International, 65* (1994): 7-11 (reporting that, "Next to ethanol, morphine from heroin use is the most frequently encountered drug of abuse on cases investigated by the office of the Chief Medical Examiner, State of Maryland (OCME)").

58. See Records of the Office of the Chief Medical Examiner, State of Maryland.

59. See id.; see also G. Garland, "Differing Views on Discipline for Doctors: Legislative Report Recommends Changes to Streamline System," *Baltimore Sun,* December 5, 2001, at 4B.

60. See C.S. Hirsch & M. Flomenbaum, "Problem-Solving in Death Certification," *Check Sample, 8,* no. 1 (1995): 1-31, at 8.

61. See id. at 18.

62. See id. at 8.

63. See id. at 21.

64. See id. at 29.

65. See D. Doyle, G.W.C. Hanks, and N. Macdonald, eds., *Oxford Textbook of Palliative Medicine* (New York, NY: Oxford University Press, 1993): at 7.

66. See Smith and Veatch, supra note 3,

67. See B.A. Thompson, "Final Exit: Should the Double Effect Rule Regarding the Legality of Euthanasia in the United Kingdom Be Laid to Rest," *Vanderbilt Journal of Transnational Law, 33* (2000): 1035-1077.

68. D.P. Sulmasy, "Commentary: Double Effect—Intention is the Solution, Not the Problem," *Journal of Law, Medicine & Ethics, 28,* no. 1 (2000): 26-28.

69. See id.

70. See D. DiMaio and V.J.M. DiMaio, *Forensic Pathology* (Boca Raton, FL: CRC Press, 1993): at 4.

71. See Spitz, supra note 4, at 177; N.L. Cantor and G.C. Thomas, "The Legal Bounds of Physician Conduct Hastening Death," *Buffalo Law Review, 48* (2000): 83-173, at 111 ("When a terminal patient is given risky analgesics, causation is always an issue. It is very difficult to establish that analgesics hastened a dying process when critical natural pathologies were already afflicting the debilitated, terminally ill patient.").

72. Id.

73. See Hirsch & Flomenbaum, supra note 60.

74. See D. Orentlicher & A. Caplan, "The Pain Relief Act of 1999," *JAMA, 283* (2000): 255-58.

75. After the administrative hearing, staff members of the Forensic Medicine Center were required to attend an End of Life Seminar on Palliative Care and Pain Management on May 24, 1999.

76. See Orentlicher & Caplan, supra note 74.

77. See Cantor and Thomas, supra note 71.

78. See id.

79. See id.

80. See R.S. Weiner et al., eds., *Pain Management: A Practical Guide for Clinicians* (Boca Raton, FL: CRC Press, 1998): at 705.

81. Id.

82. H.J. Bourguignon & S.R. Martyn, "Physician-Assisted Suicide: The Supreme Court's Wary Rejection," *University of Toledo Law Review, 31* (2000): 253-72.

83. Id. at 264-65 (further describing the impact of the process as severe even if the investigation results in only a warning).

84. "Emerging Issues in Health Care," *Health Law, 12,* no. 2 (1999): 21-23, at 22.

85. See E. Goodman, "A Doctor Taken to Task for Under-Treating his Patients' Pain," *Baltimore Sun;* September 14, 1999, at A 17.

86. Id.; The American Board of Medical Specialties, at <http://www.abanes.org/certification/sub_req.html>(last visited September 9, 2003):

Pain management is the medical discipline concerned with the diagnosis and treatment of the entire range of painful disorders. Because of the vast scope of the field, pain management is often considered a multidisciplinary subspecialty. The expertise of several disciplines is brought together in an effort to provide the maximum benefit to each patient. Although the care of patients is heavily influenced by the primary specialty of physicians who specialize in pain management, each member of the pain treatment team understands the anatomical and physiological basis of pain perception....

87. See "Physicians Palliative Care Pain Hotline Update," Maryland Board of Physician Quality Assurance, 9, no. 3 (2001): at 4.

88. See A. Meisel, J.C. Jernigan, S.J. Youngner, "Prosecutors and End-of-Life Decision Making," *Archives of Internal Medicine, 159* (1999): 1089-95.

89. See Records of the Office of the Chief Medical Examiner, supra note 24,

90. See id.

91. See id.

92. See id.; Personal communication from Ann Dixon, former Deputy Chief Medical Examiner in Baltimore, Maryland, to author (February 25,2000).

93. See id.

94. See id.

95. See id.

96. See D.Q. Wilber & N.A. Youssef, "Son Spared Charges in ill Mother's Death," *Baltimore Sun,* March 5, 1999, at B-1.

97. See M.A. Hall et al., *Health Care Law and Ethics in a Nutshell* (St. Paul, MN: West Group Press, 1999): at 316.

98. Id.

99. See Thompson, supra note 67.

100. See Letter from Jack Schwartz, Assistant Attorney General and Director of Health Policy Development, State of Maryland to Ms. Becky Sutton of Hartley Hall Nursing Home (March 5, 1999) (on file with author).

101. See Sulmasy, supra note 68.

102. See id. at 28.

103. See B. Glauber, "Scarred by Evil, Haunted by What-Ifs," *Baltimore Sun,* February 6,2000, at A1.

104. See *Vacco v. Quill,* 521 U.S. 793,807 n.11 (1997).

105. See Md. Code Ann., [Crimes & Punishments] 27-416.

106. See A. Alpers, "Criminal Act or Palliative Care? Prosecutions Involving the Care of the Dying," *Journal of Law, Medicine & Ethics, 26,* no. 4 (1998): 308-26, at 309:

Eight years ago when the Minnesota cases were investigated, lawyers and ethicists assured physicians that "Nobody has gone to jail for administering too much morphine to a dying patient." That statement no longer holds true. In 1997, a Kansas jury found Dr. L. Stan Naramore guilty of attempted first-degree murder after he gave injections of fentanyl and Versed to a seventy-eight-year-old woman who was dying of cancer.

107. See Meisel, Jernigan, and Youngner, supra note 88.
108. See id.
109. See id. at 1094.
110. See id. at 1091.
111. See id. at 1091-92.
112. See J. Schwartz, "Symposium: Trends in Health Care Decision making," *Maryland Law Review, 53* (1994): 104143.
113. 78 Op. Att'y Gen. 109 (1993).
114. See Gorsuch, supra note 5.
115. See J.K. Rogers, "Punishing Assisted Suicide: Where Legislators Should Fear to Tread," *Ohio Northern University Law Review, 20* (1994): 647-58, at 651:

Although one can mount a tenable argument that anti-assisted suicide laws are unconstitutional, compelling public policy reasons are as important as constitutional concerns in rousing opposition to such bills. Upon examination, the bills do considerable damage to the doctor-patient relationship, and essentially 'throw to the wolves' people who seek relief from intense suffering. At the same time, they do not snare the intended culprit: renegade doctors (if such exist) who recklessly dispatch patients to a premature death.

116. See "Prescribing Controlled Drugs", *Maryland Board of Physician Quality Assurance, 4,* no. 1 (1996): 1-3.
117. See id. at 3.
118. See supra note 4.
119. See A.F. Siegel, "Judge Frees Teen Whose Girlfriend Killed Herself," *Baltimore Sun,* September 23, 2000, at B-1 (discussing the first case applying Maryland's law banning assisted suicide, in which the court rejected the argument of a teenager accused of providing a firearm to assist in his girlfriend's death that the assisted suicide law should apply only to health-care workers).
120. Rogers, supra note 115.
121. See Alpers, supra note 106, at 308 ("Although the county attorney [in a 1990 Minnesota case] determined the deaths were homicides, he believed that he had little chance of conviction because the elements of the crime could not be proved beyond a reasonable doubt.").
122. See Cantor and Thomas, supra note 71, at 117 ("A reckless state of mind is sufficiently culpable to prove murder or manslaughter under the MPC.... Under a recklessness framework, the issue shifts from the physician's specific intent to whether the risk created by the analgesics is justified.").

Joseph P. Pestaner, M.D., J.D., is a forensic pathologist for the Riverside County Sheriff's Department, Coroner Bureau, in Perris, California. Dr. Pestaner graduated from the University of Maryland School of Law in Baltimore, Maryland in May of 2002.

ELISABETH KÜBLER-ROSS'S FINAL PASSAGE

Internationally renowned author of the groundbreaking 1969 book *On Death and Dying* Elisabeth Kübler-Ross transformed American attitudes toward death. Now the increasingly controversial guru, whose autobiography appears this month, wants nothing more than her own

BY LESLIE BENNETTS

The rutted roads meandering off into the Arizona desert are unmarked, but it's not hard to find Elisabeth Kübler-Ross's house: it's the one with the towering burlap tepee and the carved wooden totem pole in its scorched front yard. Overhead the sky is vast and cloudless: the sun is so bright that you are momentarily blinded by the sudden Stygian gloom as you step inside.

The primary objects of her wrath are her spirit guides, or "my spooks," as she calls them

---

"Over here." The voice is weak, but it bristles with rage. It emanates from the darkest corner of an enormous, cluttered room, where the blinds are drawn and the only light is cast by a television flickering mutely. Crumpled in a reclining chair, buttoned up in a sweater despite the midday heat, Kübler-Ross regards her visitor with a baleful glare. How is she? "In constant pain," she snaps. How does she like Scottsdale? "I commute from here to the potty," she says, gesturing at the commode next to her chair. "For an active person like me to sit here 15 hours a day like a dummy—that's no pleasure. It's a useless existence. The only part of my body that functions is my brain." She has had several strokes in the last couples of years, and by now the 70-year-old Kübler-Ross is thoroughly fed up with her infirmities.

She fumbles for her Dunhills and lights a cigarette. "I tried to smoke myself to death, but it doesn't work," she says, scowling at me as if it were my fault.

I venture a question about why she sounds so mad. "Mad? That's not the word!" she exclaims. "I can't use a word that's strong enough. 'Frustrated' is too polite a word. 'Pissed' is a much better word. I'm *pissed!*"

A housekeeper offers me a cup of tea. "Just don't say to my health." Kübler-Ross warns. "To my quick transition—that's all I want."

Transition" is Kübler-Ross-speak for death, that final passage she has spent her entire professional life studying. For 30 years she has been internationally renowned as a pioneer in the field, the author of the groundbreaking 1969 book *On Death and Dying* and a slew of books that followed, the controversial guru who revolutionized the care of the terminally ill, who helped transform the medical profession's attitudes toward a once taboo subject, and who helped launch the hospice movement in America. She has shepherded thousands of patients through their transitions. But all she wants now is her own.

She knows exactly how it will be: the radiant light, the overwhelming feeling of peace and love, the spirit guides who will usher her into the next world, the transcendent knowledge. "I've been on the other side, and it's better than anything you can imagine," she says. "I don't have a shadow of a doubt."

"'Surrender' and 'resignation' don't exist in my vocabulary. Like the saints—they make me *sick!*"

With all that ahead of her, she is furious that she is being forced to wait. The primary objects of her wrath are her spirit guides, or "my spooks," as she calls them—those mysterious entities who guided her for so long. She won't even talk to them anymore.

"I'm on strike," she snarls. "They let me down. They're supposed to help you, and they don't help me. You're not supposed to know the time of your death; they keep it a top secret. I've asked about a thousand times, but they just don't answer it. All the languages I used to speak. I collected all the worst curse words, and I call them those names. Anybody who knows a language I don't know, I ask them for the strongest curse words. But it doesn't help.

I don't know what they have up their sleeve."

It's unwise to propose a more peaceful acceptance of her situation. "I'm not a person for resignation," she says ferociously. "'Surrender' and 'resignation' don't exist in my vocabulary. Not me! Like the saints—they make me *sick!*" She spits out the word as if it were a scorpion. "All this meek surrender—to me that's nauseating!"

Nor is suicide an option, since she believes in reincarnation. "The thought crossed my mind so many times, but if you end your life before the right time, you have to come back and learn all the lessons you didn't learn," she explains grumpily. "I'm not going to ruin my chance to be able to stay there. I don't have another life. I'm not coming back. That's it! I've asked my spooks many times. They said that I'm done with my work."

She stares into space, as if gazing at something I cannot see. Dark and unblinking, her eyes blaze fiercely in her leathery old face, fathomless as those of an ancient sea turtle. Is she really so unafraid of death?

"I'm looking forward to it," she says, her brusque tone softening. "Every night I think: Maybe tonight."

She tilts her face upward, as if to receive a blessing, or a caress. And for the briefest of moments, she smiles. She is not smiling at me.

It was the spooks that really did it. A tiny Swiss-born firebrand, Kübler-Ross had always been controversial; way back in the 1960s, when she started lecturing the medical profession about all the things it was doing wrong, the combination of her abrasive personality and her unwelcome message—that doctors and nurses were routinely failing their terminally ill patients by not helping them come to terms with death—meant that Kübler-Ross was not going to win any popularity contests.

But her work quickly earned her a worldwide reputation. Her books have sold millions of copies and have been translated into 20 languages, from Catalan to Serbo-Croatian; her most influential ideas have helped transform medicine. Kübler-Ross's description of the so-called stages of dying—the progression of a patient's coping mechanisms from denial and isolation through anger, bargaining with God, depression, and finally acceptance of the inevitable–provided a framework for treatment that endures to this day. Some researchers have questioned Kübler-Ross's model, troubled by how schematic and absolute it seems amid the messy human realities of living and dying, when emotions rarely conform so neatly to discrete categories. But until Kübler-Ross, no one was even talking about such issues, and even her critics acknowledge that her contribution in beginning the debate was invaluable.

Her personal style offended many. For her admirers, her certainty was inspirational and her charisma indisputable. "The room was packed, and within five minutes, this diminutive, tired-looking woman, with a heavy Germanic accent and a first appearance of extreme toughness, had transfixed the audience," reported a *Playboy* interviewer who heard Kübler-Ross speak 17 years ago. "What shone through her and hypnotized more than 500 people was her compassion, her deep vulnerability and her love of human beings. There was not a dry eye in the house, and my friend and I agreed that Elisabeth was the most powerful speaker we had ever heard."

But to her detractors, Kübler-Ross seemed arrogant if not downright insufferable. She didn't care; she was a woman with a mission, and she has never let anything—from philosophical opposition to actual attempts on her life—stand in her way.

For a long time Kübler-Ross—a physician, after all, an experienced psychiatrist with Establishment credentials—was accepted by the scientific community. Then she went public with her belief in the spirit world, and by the late 1970s she had started talking about her own spooks—the muscular, stoic-looking Indian who confirmed that she had lived a previous life as a Native American in the Southwest; "Salem," the tall figure in a turban and a flowing robe who took her back to the time of Jesus, when, he claimed, Kübler-Ross was a respected teacher named Isabel; "Pedro" and "Willie" and "Mario" and a host of others she described with great enthusiasm in her books and lectures.

Such startling assertions polarized opinion for good. The more conservative elements in the medical establishment dismissed her as a kook, while at the opposite end of the spectrum many New Age aficionados came to regard Kübler-Ross as a visionary. Go to any bookstore and check out the death-and-dying section; it will be full of books that invoke her name and credit her with inspiring a whole genre.

The debate is likely to resurface this month with the publication of Kübler-Ross's autobiography, *The Wheel of Life,* which is being billed as her final statement. To her acolytes, the story of her life is already familiar; key anecdotes have been repeated again and again. Until she was incapacitated, Kübler-Ross traveled more than 250,000 miles a year, leading workshops and speaking; her lectures drew 15,000 people a week, and she received a quarter of a million letters a year. But even her most faithful devotees will find some surprises: the book reveals a few juicy details Kübler-Ross kept private until now—such as the exact nature of the message her beloved ex-husband, a Jew who didn't believe in an afterlife, allegedly sent her from the spirit world after he died.

To Kübler-Ross, these events are a matter of course; when others question her claims, they receive only a dismissive shrug. "My mother has no doubt," says her son, Ken Ross, a photographer who lives in Phoenix. "That's what makes her a leader in her field."

She may be small, but she has always been formidable. Back in her native Switzerland, her very birth was cause for consternation. Her parents had been expecting a child, of course, but when the unprepossessing Elisabeth appeared, weighing scarcely two pounds, she was the firstborn of triplets. No one thought she would survive, let alone rebel.

I was supposed to have been a nice, churchgoing Swiss housewife," she remarks dryly at the beginning of her autobiography. But she dreamed of becoming a physician—a goal her tyrannical father, a bureaucrat at a Zurich office-supply company, refused to support. When she was in the sixth grade, he decreed her fate: "You will work in my office. I need an efficient and intelligent secretary."

Horrified, Elisabeth commenced her lifelong pattern of bucking authority whenever it got in the way of her plans. When she finished school and wouldn't go to work for her father, he threw her out of the house. She spent years working as a laboratory assistant before managing to get through medical school.

In the meantime, she had already begun her career as a humanitarian; when World War II ended, she took repeated leaves of absence from various jobs to do volunteer work throughout war-ravaged Europe. While working in Poland, she traveled to Maidanek, a Nazi concentration camp where hundreds of thousands of people had been murdered. In the barracks, prisoners had carved their names and drawings with their fingernails. Kübler saw one symbol repeated over and over: there were butterflies everywhere. It would be a quarter of a century before she understood why.

After she became a physician and married Emanuel Ross, an American neuropathologist, they moved to New York. Following two miscarriages, Elisabeth had her son, two more miscarriages, and then her daughter, Barbara. At the hospital where she worked, Kübler-Ross found herself increasingly appalled by the standard treatment of dying patients. "They were shunned and abused," she writes in her book. "Nobody was honest with them." Unlike her colleagues, she made it a point to sit with terminal patients, listening as they poured out their hearts to her.

At the University of Colorado, Kübler-Ross began giving lectures featuring dying patients who talked about what they were going through—thereby forcing other physicians and students to hear them. By the time the Rosses moved to Chicago, Elisabeth's lectures were attracting standing-room-only audiences. Many of the other doctors were furious, particularly after *On Death and Dying* made Kübler-Ross an international celebrity, but her determination never faltered. "My goal was to break through the layer of professional denial that prohibited the patients from airing their innermost concerns," she writes.

Kübler-Ross came to believe that people often clung to life long after they were "supposed" to die because they had unfinished business. When given the opportunity to make amends, to say the necessary good-byes, to make appropriate arrangements for survivors, they were able to relax and die a peaceful death, even a joyful one. While Kübler-Ross's prescriptions seem simple—listen to your patients, learn what their concerns are and help to address them—their impact was revolutionary. To her grateful patients and their families, she was revered as a virtual saint.

Having sat by the bedsides of thousands of dying men, women, and children, Kübler-Ross was also struck by how many of them saw visions of spirits who appeared to them in their final moments. Usually these were perceived as the spirits of departed loved ones who had come to help guide the dying person out of earthly life. These visions brought great peace to the dying, and some consolation to family members. Pondering the peculiar serenity of the dying, Kübler-Ross suddenly realized the meaning of the butterflies she had seen scratched into the walls at Maidanek so many years earlier. "Those prisoners were like my dying patients and aware of what was going to happen," she explains in *The Wheel of Life*. "Once dead, they would be out of that hellish place.... Soon they would leave their bodies like a butterfly leaves its cocoon. And I realized that was the message they wanted to leave for future generations. It also provided the imagery that I would use for the rest of my career to explain the process of death and dying."

A patient not only had come back to life but was able to repeat a joke one doctor had told while she was clinically dead.

Among Kübler-Ross's patients was a terminally ill woman named Mrs. Schwartz. She had been pronounced dead, but hours later, a nurse found that Mrs. Schwartz not only had come back to life but was able to repeat conversations and a joke one doctor had told while she was clinically dead. After Mrs. Schwartz spoke about this at a lecture, the students insisted the whole thing must have been a hallucination. Kübler-Ross wasn't so sure. "If I blew a dog whistle right now, none of us would hear it," she pointed out. "But every dog would. Does that mean it doesn't exist?"

Kübler-Ross began to interview patients who had been revived after the cessation of their vital signs. She also decided she was going to stop giving death-and-dying seminars, and to quit her job at the hospital where she was then working. As she prepared to resign, Mrs. Schwartz, who had finally died 10 months earlier, materialized to tell Kübler-Ross "not to give up your work on death and dying.... Do you hear me? Your work has just begun. We will help you." Even the unflappable Kübler-Ross was disconcerted, although she did manage to ask Mrs. Schwartz to scribble a note with earthly pen on paper before she vanished.

Kübler-Ross and her associates went on to interview 20,000 people about their near-death experiences. From Muslims to Eskimos, 2 years old to 99, they all seemed to report virtually the same thing. "Up till then I had absolutely no belief in an afterlife, but the data convinced me that these were not coincidences or hallucinations," Kübler-Ross reports in her book. "These remarkable findings led to an even more remarkable scientific conclusion that death did not exist—not in its traditional definition. I felt any new definition had to go beyond the death of the physical body."

Over the years, she too had several out-of-body experiences, including two near-death events (one because of a bowel obstruction and another due to cardiac fibrillation). "They were all good; they were all different," she tells me. "They have the same common denominator: the light, the peace, the love—more than anything you ever experienced in this lifetime. A totally different kind of love. What we call love is for the birds. 'I love you if you buy me a mink coat.' Pfffft." She waves her hand with eloquent contempt.

At least one of her otherworldly experiences was also terrifying. During one endless night of agony, she felt she was reliving the deaths of all her patients—but after re-experiencing their pain and fear, she emerged into what she calls cosmic consciousness, a state of grace that was temporary but life-altering. Such incidents persuaded her to reconsider her own attitude toward paranormal phenomena. "As I have learned since then, if you are not ready for mystical experiences, you will never believe them," she writes in her book. "But if you are open, then you not only have them, and believe in them; people can hang you by your thumbnails and you will know that they are absolutely real."

A spirit guide led Kübler-Ross back a couple of thousand years and she listened to Jesus preach

---

Unfortunately, Kübler-Ross's growing openness soon led her into the most ignominious chapter of her life. According to her book, in early 1976 she was contacted by a San Diego couple who promised to introduce her to spiritual entities. A high-school dropout and former sharecropper who had recently founded his own "Church of the Facet of Divinity," Jay Barham had developed a following based on his alleged ability to channel spirits. To

Kübler-Ross's delight, he proceeded to do so for her; during her very first session, a spirit guide led her back a couple of thousand years, and she spent a most enjoyable afternoon sitting on a hillside, listening to Jesus preach to a group of people.

Kübler-Ross's husband was appalled. "How can you believe that garbage?" Ross demanded. "Barham is taking advantage of you!"

When Ross abruptly asked for a divorce, on Father's Day, his wife was dumbfounded. They had been married 21 years, and she never got over his departure. But then Salem asked her to come out to San Diego and establish her own healing center on a mountain-top. Soon she was leading weeklong death-and-transition workshops at which Barham was the featured attraction. When visitors grew suspicious and challenged his ability to conjure up spirits, Barham issued a stern warning: If anyone turned on the lights while he was channeling, that person risked harming the spirits as well as Barham himself. (One woman, a friend of Kübler-Ross's, did so anyway—and there stood Barham, stark naked, wearing a turban.)

Ignoring a growing chorus of rumors about strange sexual goings-on, Kübler-Ross continued to describe Barham as "the greatest healer the world has ever known." Even after the San Diego district attorney's office launched an investigation of the alleged sexual abuse of a 10-year-old child by a "spirit entity" who may or may not have been Barham in disguise, setting off a firestorm of negative publicity, Kübler-Ross maintained her belief in his integrity. (No formal charges were ever filed.) Two years later, in a 1981 *Playboy* interview, she was still insisting that she had never witnessed any sexual activity and that the naysayers were trying to destroy Barham.

Kübler-Ross also vowed that if she were ever to discover that Barham was a phony she would have to commit suicide. The realization was apparently slow in dawning, and it failed to inspire such drastic action, but there is no question today that Kübler-Ross has reluctantly accepted the idea that she was deceived and exploited. She hates talking about Barham: "I don't want to give him any publicity!" But on the second day of my visit, she launches into a tirade about his alleged transgressions. "He was a dangerous man," she says grimly.

Barham moved to Honolulu in 1986, and he describes himself as retired. "I just play on the beach and enjoy the lovely bikinis," he tells me when I reach him by telephone. His wife is working as a marriage and family therapist, he adds. When I ask him about Kübler-Ross, Barham chuckles. "She's a great woman," he says. "Isabel—that's what I called her when I worked with her—she's real neat. She is a genius, and I enjoyed the five years I worked with her very much." As for Kübler-Ross's various accusations, he adds, "I have no need to defend myself. I have done nothing in my life that I regret, or that has ever harmed anybody—physically, verbally, or emotionally."

During one endless night of agony, Kübler-Ross felt she was reliving the deaths of all her patients. She emerged into what she calls cosmic consciousness, a state of grace.

Then his tone changes. He is not going to continue our conversation unless I give him a "whole lot of money," he says. "You get on a plane and bring $40,000 in cash, and we'll talk all you want." When I tell him that *Vanity Fair* doesn't pay for news or interviews, he says it's been nice talking with me. "You take care of yourself, now," he adds, a distinct note of menace in his voice. Then he hangs up. The next day he calls back, threatening to sue if *Vanity Fair* prints Kübler-Ross's charges against him.

When Kübler-Ross's San Diego house burned to the ground, investigators suspected arson; although no charges were ever filed. Kübler-Ross broke with Barham and has not been in touch with him since. Next, Kübler-Ross bought a 300-acre farm in the Shenandoah Valley, where she moved in 1984, hoping to set up a center for AIDS babies. Her plan set off a hysterical wave of local opposition that included not only protests, petitions, and town meetings to denounce Kübler-Ross but an escalating pattern of harassment, including burglaries and vandalism. Although she continued to live in Virginia for years, celebrating the official grand opening of the Elisabeth Kübler-Ross Center in 1990, eventually that chapter of her life ended in an eerie recapitulation of her experience in California. One night in 1994, as she was preparing to adopt 20 babies with AIDS, Kübler-Ross returned to Virginia from a trip to Baltimore and found her house in flames. All her possessions were destroyed, from family pictures and her father's diaries to hundreds of thousands of pages of research notes and documentation. Even her pet llama had been shot. Once again, arson was suspected, but no charges were ever filed—even though a local man was rumored to have bragged publicly about having incinerated Kübler-Ross's house. "My county would never have put him in jail," she says. "They were happy somebody did it."

At this point Kübler-Ross's son whisked her off to Arizona. "He was afraid they were going to shoot me next," she says. Safely ensconced in Scottsdale, she promptly had a massive stroke.

Kübler-Ross has achieved a bizarre equanimity about her horrendous losses. She has been betrayed; she shrugs. "Things always work out the way they have to." Two houses burned to the ground, everything she owned lost forever: no matter. "It was a blessing," she says. "I never even had to pack."

Many leaders are controversial, but only a few arouse passions violent enough to provoke attempted murder. Some people appear to thrive on conflict, even to relish it: but with Kübler-Ross it seems more an incidental by-product of her single-mindedness. When she wants to accomplish something, she simply has no interest in other people's objections.

When I ask if even her mistakes had meaning, she gives me a withering look. "Naturally," she says with contempt, as if I were a moron even to ask. "You have to be true to yourself, and that's one thing I have been all my life."

Even the Barham episode has been assimilated. "If I had it to do over again, I would still do it, because I learned a lot." Kübler-Ross says (although she later makes it clear to me that this enlightenment came through the spirits, not Barham).

Nowadays she spends most of her time alone, fending for herself; her housekeeper comes only three days a week. Although Ken lives in Phoenix, he travels constantly, and Barbara, a psychologist, lives in Seattle. But Kübler-Ross isn't quite as isolated as she seems: as her guest book attests. Shirley MacLaine had visited two days before I arrived, inscribing her entry in the book "To darling Elisabeth…" Kübler-Ross numbers a vast assortment of other notables among her acquaintances. When she dies, she wants to have 1,000 balloons with the image of E. T. imprinted on them released into the sky, to celebrate, (Why E. T.? "Because I loved him," she says.) When she was told she couldn't do that, because of copyright issues, she called up Steven Spielberg, she says, and got his permission. She spends her days surrounded by photographs of her family, a large picture of herself with Mother Teresa, and images of E. T. and angels and Jesus and the Virgin Mary; she seems to be on intimate speaking terms with all of them.

She wastes no time worrying about what history will make of her. The verdict is likely to be quite mixed. On one hand, Kübler-Ross is full of apocalyptic predictions, including one about an imminent natural cataclysm that will wipe out California and New York, among other places, and be followed by a period of enlightened earthly consciousness. On the other hand, even Kübler-Ross's harshest critics acknowledge her extraordinary legacy. A couple of years ago Dr. Samuel Klagsbrun, a clinical professor of psychiatry at Albert Einstein College of Medicine and one of the three physicians who brought a suit against New York State to decriminalize physician-assisted suicide, raised eyebrows by telling *The New York Times* that Kübler-Ross was destroying her life's work with her more outlandish proclamations. But he certainly doesn't deny her contribution.

"She is an enormously important pioneer in this area; I can't overemphasize how important," Klagsbrun tells me. "She put the subject on the map.... She identified the stages of dying in a way that made it less scary and more manageable. And she targeted the medical profession as having to change its approach and attitudes. Death became something you could talk about, anticipate, and deal with."

Kübler-Ross also played a crucial role in establishing alternatives to hospitals. "She had a tremendous influence on the hospice movement," says Florence Wald, a founding member of the Connecticut Hospice and former dean of the Yale University School of Nursing. "Doctors and nurses had been simply avoiding the problem of death, and focusing on patients who could get better. We have this tendency in medicine to be very academic, and to look at things as a scientist would. Elisabeth just took another path, which relied very much on her ability to capture an audience. She's almost a preacher."

To the less scientifically inclined, Kübler-Ross is practically a goddess. "She is a heroine of mine," says Betty Eadie, who credits Kübler-Ross with moving her

to write her own best-selling account of a near-death experience, *Embraced by the Light,* as well as her subsequent best-seller, *The Awakening Heart.*

"She gave me the strength to do what I knew I had to do. She's one of the leaders who were sent here on Earth to make a difference, who were developed by God for a purpose," Eadie explains.

When Kübler-Ross dies, she wants to have a thousand balloons with the image of E. T. imprinted on them released into the sky

---

While Kübler-Ross's more mystically oriented admirers see her as a courageous voyager into the beyond, other observers offer psychiatric explanations for her long drift toward the supernatural. Klagsbrun sees it as a result of the years Kübler-Ross spent at the bedsides of the dying, particularly those of thousands of doomed children. "It's not unknown for people who delve into this area to find themselves needing to soothe their losses by moving more and more toward a spiritual way of life," he observes. "Her psychological need to deny what she was experiencing, which was repeated losses, may have led her to escape those losses by turning to a denial of the losses. It's a way to undo the pain. She's an extreme example of burnout. I think that's sad. There are real consequences to not dealing with loss: you don't grow."

Dr. Sherwin Nuland, the surgeon whose best-seller, *How We Die,* won the 1994 National Book Award for nonfiction, views Kübler-Ross's philosophical evolution in terms of her own denial of death. "Like all the rest of us, she is having difficulty with the concept of the end of her consciousness," he suggests. "That's the reason we have invented the afterlife. We all clothe our thinking in philosophical terminology, but inside we're scared as hell and quaking in our shoes. She is no longer using the objectivity and rational thinking of a lifetime; she is creating a scenario that reassures her. I think she is guilty of magical thinking. I believe it's an extreme form of narcissistic self-absorption, where she finds it necessary to think she will be preserved. What she has done is create a belief system that defuses the terror of death."

When you ask doctors like Klagsbrun and Nuland how they explain near-death

experiences, they talk about physiological factors like oxygen deprivation to the brain. But those who have actually done clinical research claim that that explanation doesn't hold up. "A lot of medical professionals speak glibly, but don't really know what's in the literature," says Dr. Melvin Morse, a Seattle pediatrician whose own work prompted him to write the best-seller *Closer to the Light.* "There are dozens of studies of lack of oxygen to the brain that don't cause these kinds of experiences. People who are skeptical of near-death experiences are invariably people who are not keeping up. They don't know what's been published in the last 10 years."

Although Kübler-Ross's detractors often cite her own failure to publish her findings in scientific journals, Morse shrugs off such technicalities. "It's true that Kübler-Ross hasn't published a lot of rigorous scientific studies; she's just reached her own conclusions through thousands of interviews," he acknowledges. "But she's a giant in the field of near-death research. I might have been a little more scientific and systematic about it, but there's very little in my own research that she didn't anticipate. Fifty years from now, no one will know who her critics were, and Elisabeth Kübler-Ross will be a brighter light than ever."

Of course, from a purely objective standpoint, Kübler-Ross's belief in spirit guides is no more fantastical than a Hindu's belief in reincarnation, or a Christian's belief that Jesus was the son of God and was resurrected after his physical demise. At base, every belief system is predicated on faith, as is the scientific rationalist's conviction that there is no afterlife; since no one really knows for sure, even the nonbeliever is ultimately making a choice based on belief rather than verifiable empirical evidence. And as Kübler-Ross's friends point out, humankind has been grappling with such issues for millennia. "The real question at issue here is the mind-body problem," notes Dr. Raymond Moody, author of *Life After Life,* a pioneering study of near-death experiences. "After 2,500 years, Western civilization hasn't gotten any closer to the question of how consciousness is related to material substance. This is a chronically unresolvable controversy."

Kübler-Ross is well aware that her detractors think she's out of her mind; that's their problem. Puffing on her cigarette, she gives me a sly glance. "They'll know soon enough," she says calmly.

On my final visit to Kübler-Ross, I notice as I drive out into the desert that all the place names along the way are upbeat: from Paradise Road and Happy Valley to the Carefree Cactus Garden, they constitute a powerful testimonial to the relentless retirement-community optimism of Arizona. But farther out, the street signs dwindle, and when I come to Kübler-Ross's road, it is marked simply "No Outlet."

Her low adobe house is set in a broad, flat desert plain surrounded by barren mountains heaped with jumbles of bleached rock. From an airplane, the desiccated land looks monochromatic and cracked, driven everywhere with deep fissures. As I share another cup of tea with Kübler-Ross, I realize how much the landscape resembles her own sand-colored face: ravaged by time, carved into creases and canyons like the wrinkles of the earth's own skin, itself a silent testimonial to eons of upheaval.

Outside, in the gathering twilight, coyotes prowl through the underbrush, their eyes hungry and wolfish. The sun is setting, and the wind chimes stir, sending a faint tinkling music through the air, like cowbells from a faraway Alpine meadow. Once in a while a mountain lion materializes in the dusty driveway. This parched land seems a strange place for a Swiss girl to end her days, so far from the verdant valleys and flower-strewn mountain passes of her childhood. No matter; she will see them again soon enough. In her dreams her "transition" looks just like Switzerland.

She has all sorts of plans. She wants to chat with Jung, and Gandhi; it would be nice to visit with her childhood idol, Marie Curie, as well. And despite all her years of traveling around the world, she never made it to Nepal, Guatemala, or Peru. "I'll have to go after I make my transition," she says, as if this were merely a matter of speaking to her travel agent.

There may be other planets that need help, as well. "I think I had my share of Earth," she says with a distinct note of sourness.

And then there is Manny. She still considers him her husband: "I'm a one-man woman," she says, shrugging, as if his 10-year marriage to his second wife (whom Kübler-Ross refers to as "that lulu"), with whom he had a child, were an unfortunate momentary error. "I think once you get married, it's forever."

When Manny's heart began to fail, Kübler-Ross rented a condominium for him in Scottsdale; leaving his wife and child in Chicago, he moved to Arizona, where Ken and Elisabeth took care of him. The last time she saw him, Elisabeth made him promise that if she was right about life after death, he would send her some kind of signal from the beyond.

Manny died that afternoon. At the funeral in Chicago, it was snowing heavily, and Elisabeth noticed dozens of roses strewn in the snow around the grave site. She gathered them up and gave one to Barbara, who started to laugh—and then made a confession. When she was 10 years old, her father and mother had been arguing about Elisabeth's views on the afterlife, and Manny had promised Barbara that when he died, there would be red roses blooming in the snow if Elisabeth turned out to be right.

The night Manny died, Barbara had come home to find a dozen longstemmed roses on her doorstep. It had been snowing in Seattle for hours, and the roses were buried up to their buds in snow. Barbara knew instantly that her father was dead, but she didn't tell her mother about their agreement until the signal reappeared at the funeral in Chicago.

Elisabeth, of course, was ecstatic. Now she knows for sure that he is waiting for her. "I told Manny already: he better get ready for dancing in the galaxies. I'm going to drag him along," she reports, smiling as if she could already hear the music.

"I'm going to dance in all the galaxies," she says dreamily. "Just dance."

From *Vanity Fair*, June 1997, pp. 70, 75-77, 80, 82, 89. Copyright © 1997 with permission of the author, Leslie Bennetts.

Dr. Kübler-Ross, Who Changed Perspectives on Death, Dies at 78

By HOLCOMB B. NOBLE

Elisabeth Kübler-Ross, the psychiatrist whose pioneering work in counseling terminally ill patients helped to revolutionize the care of the dying, enabling people all over the world to die more peacefully and with greater dignity, died Tuesday at her home in Scottsdale, Ariz. She was 78.

Family members told *The Associated Press* she died of natural causes.

A series of strokes had debilitated her, but as she neared her own death she appeared to accept it, as she had tried to help so many others to do. She seemed ready to experience death, saying: "I'm going to dance in all the galaxies."

Dr. Kübler-Ross was credited with ending centuries-old taboos in Western culture against openly discussing and studying death. She set in motion techniques of care directed at making death less dehumanizing and psychologically painful for patients, for the professionals who attend them and the loved ones who survive them.

She accomplished this largely through her writings, especially the 1969 best-seller, "On Death and Dying," which is still in print around the world; through her lectures and tape recordings; her research into what she described as the five stages of death, based on thousands of interviews with patients and health-care professionals and through her own groundbreaking work in counseling dying patients.

She was a powerful intellectual force behind the creation of the hospice system in the United States through which special care is now provided for the terminally ill.

And she helped to turn thanatology, the study of physical, psychological and social problems associated with dying, into an accepted medical discipline.

"Dr. Elisabeth Kübler-Ross was a true pioneer in raising the awareness among the physician community and the general public about the important issues surrounding death, dying and bereavement," said Dr. Percy Wooten, president of the American Medical Association. He said much of her work was a basis for the A.M.A.'s attempts to encourage the medical profession to improve the care patients received at the end of life.

The A.M.A was one of her early supporters, though many of its members at first vigorously opposed her and attempted to ostracize her.

Florence Wald of the Yale School of Nursing said that before her research "doctors and nurses had been simply avoiding the problem of death and focusing on patients who could get better." She said, Dr. Kübler-Ross's "willingness and skill in getting patients to talk about their impending death in ways that helped them set a profoundly important example for nurses everywhere."

In the later part of her career, she embarked on research to verify the existence of life after death, conducting, with others, thousands of interviews with people who recounted near-death experiences, particularly those declared clinically dead by medical authorities but who were then revived. Her prestige generated widespread interest in such research and attracted followers who considered her a saint.

But this work aroused deep skepticism in medical and scientific circles and damaged her reputation. Her claims that she had evidence of an afterlife saddened many of her colleagues, some of whom believed that she had abandoned rigorous science and had succumbed to her own fears of death.

"For years I have been stalked by a bad reputation," she said in her 1997 autobiography "The Wheel of Life: A Memoir of Living and Dying." "Actually, I have been pursued by people who have regarded me as the Death and Dying Lady. They believe that having spent more than three decades in research into death and life after death qualifies me as an expert on the subject. I think they miss the point. The only incontrovertible fact of my work is the importance of life. I always say that death can be one of the greatest experiences ever. If you live each day of your life right, then you have nothing to fear."

Whatever scientists feel about her view of life after death, they continue to be influenced by her methods of caring for the terminally ill. Before "On Death and Dying," terminally ill patients were often left to face death in a miasma of loneliness and fear because doctors, nurses and families were generally poorly equipped to deal with death.

Dr. Kübler-Ross changed all that. By the 1980's, the study of the processes and treatment of dying became a routine part of medical and health-care education in the United States. "Death and Dying" became an indispensable manual, both for professionals and for family members. Many doctors and counselors have relied on it to learn to cope themselves with the loss of their patients, and face their own mortality.

Her early childhood may have been the "instigator," as she put it, in shaping her career. Weighing barely two pounds at birth, she was the first of triplets born to Ernst and Emma Villiger Kübler on July 8, 1926 in Zurich, Switzerland.

She might not have lived, she wrote, "If it had not been for the determination of my mother," who thought a sick child must be kept close to her parents in the intimate environment of the home, not at a hospital.

But there were moments in her childhood in a farm village when she saw death as both moving and frightening. A friend of her father who was dying after a fall from a tree invited neighbors into his home and, with no sign of fear as death approached, asked them to help his wife and children save their farm. "My last visit with him filled me with great pride and joy," she said.

Later, a schoolmate died of meningitis. Relatives or friends of the child were with her night and day, and when she died, her school was closed and half the village attended the funeral.

"There was a feeling of solidarity, of common tragedy shared," Dr. Kübler-Ross said. By contrast, when she was 5, she was "caged" in a hospital with pneumonia, allowed to see her parents only through a glass window, with "no familiar voice, touch, odor, not even a familiar toy." She believed that only her vivid dreams and fantasies enabled her to survive.

By the sixth grade, she wanted to be a physician. But her father, she said, saw only two possibilities in life: "his way and the wrong way." "Elisabeth," he said, "you will work in my office. I need an intelligent secretary."

"No thank you," she said, and her father's face flushed with anger.

"Then you can spend the rest of your life as a maid."

"That's all right with me," she replied.

When she finished school, she worked at various jobs and began her lifelong involvement with humanitarian causes. She volunteered at Zurich's largest hospital to help refugees from Nazi Germany. And when World War II ended, she hitchhiked through nine war-shattered countries, helping to open first-aid posts and working on reconstruction projects, as a cook, mason and roofer.

In Poland, her visit to the Majdanek concentration camp narrowed her professional goal: she would become a psychiatrist to help people cope with death.

Back in Switzerland, she enrolled at the University of Zurich medical school, receiving her degree in 1957. Within a year she had come to the United States; married Dr. Emanuel K. Ross, an American neuropathologist she met at the University of Zurich; begun her internship at Community Hospital in Glen Cove, N.Y., and become a research fellow at Manhattan State Hospital on Ward's Island in New York City.

There she was appalled by what she called routine treatment of dying patients: "They were shunned and abused," she wrote, "sometimes kept in hot tubs with water up to their necks and left for 24 hours at a time."

After badgering her supervisors, she was allowed to develop programs under which the patients were given individual care and counseling.

In 1962, she became a teaching fellow at the University of Colorado School of Medicine in Denver. A small woman, who spoke with a heavy German accent and was shy, despite extraordinary inner self-confidence, she was highly nervous when asked to fill in for a popular professor and master lecturer. She found the medical students rude, paying her scant attention and talking to one another as she spoke.

But the hall became noticeably quieter when she brought out a 16-year-old patient who was dying of leukemia, and asked the students to interview her. Now it was they who seemed nervous. When she prodded them, they would ask the patient about her blood counts, chemo-therapy or other clinical matters.

Finally, the teenager exploded in anger, and began posing her own questions: What was it like not to be able to dream about the high-school prom? Or going on a date? Or growing up? "Why," she demanded, "won't people tell you the truth?" When the lecture ended, many students had been moved to tears.

"Now you're acting like human beings, instead of scientists," Dr. Kübler-Ross said.

Her lectures began to draw standing-room-only audiences of medical and theology students, clergymen and social workers — but few doctors.

In 1965, she became an assistant professor in psychiatry at the University of Chicago Medical School, where a group of theology students approached her for help in studying death. She suggested a series of conversations with dying patients, who would be asked their thoughts and feelings; the patients would teach the professionals. At first, staff doctors objected.

Avoiding the subject entirely, particularly when treating the young, physicians and therapists would meet a dying child's questions with comments like, "Take your medicine, and you'll get well," Dr. Kübler-Ross said.

In "On Death and Dying," her account of the seminars on dying that she conducted at Chicago, she asked: What happens to a society when "its young medical student is admired for his research and laboratory work while he is at a loss for words when a patient asks him a simple question?"

She said children instinctively knew that the answers they received about their prognoses were lies and this made them feel punished and alone. Children were often better at coping with imminent death than adults, she said, and told of 9-year-old Jeff, who though weakened with leukemia asked to leave the hospital and go home and ride his bicycle one more time.

The boy's father, tears in his eyes, put the training wheels back on the bike at the boy's request, and his mother was kept by Dr. Kübler-Ross from helping him ride. Jeff came back after a spin around the block in final triumph, the psychiatrist said, and then gave the bicycle to his younger brother.

To bring public pressure for change in hospitals' treatment of the dying, she agreed to a request by *Life* magazine in 1965 to interview one of her seminar patients, Eva, who felt her doctors had treated her coldly and arrogantly. The *Life* article prompted one physician, encountering Dr. Kübler-Ross in a hospital corridor, to remark: "Are you looking for your next patient for publicity."

The hospital said it wanted not to be famous for its dying patients but rather for those it saved, and ordered its doctors not to cooperate further. The lecture hall for her next seminar was empty.

"Although humiliated," she said, "I knew they could not stop everything that had been put in motion by the press." The hospital switchboard was overwhelmed with calls in reaction to the *Life* article; mail piled up and she was invited to speak at other colleges and universities.

Not that this helped Eva much. Dr. Kübler-Ross said she looked in on her years later and found her lying naked on a hospital bed, unable to speak, with an overhead light glaring in her eyes. "She pressed my hand as a way of saying hello, and pointed her other hand up toward the ceiling. I turned the light off and asked a nurse to cover Eva. Unbelievably, the nurse hesitated, and asked, 'Why?' " Dr. Kübler-Ross covered the patient herself. Eva died the next day.

"The way she died, cold and alone, was something I could not tolerate," Dr. Kübler-Ross said. Gradually, the medical profession came to accept her new approaches to treating the terminally ill.

From her patient interviews, Dr. Kübler-Ross identified five stages many patients go through in confronting their own deaths. Often denial is the first stage, when the patient is unwilling or unable to face his predicament. As his condition worsens and denial is impossible, the patient displays anger — the "why me?" stage. This is followed by a bargaining period ("Yes, I'm going to die, but if I diet and exercise, can I do it later?"). When the patient sees that bargaining won't work, depression often sets in. The final stage is acceptance, a passive period in which the patient is ready to let go.

Not all dying patients follow the same progression, said Dr. Kübler-Ross, but most experience two or more of these stages. Moreover, she found, people who are experiencing traumatic change in their lives, such as a divorce, often experience similar stages.

Another conclusion she reached was that an untraumatic acceptance of death came easiest for those who could look back and feel they had lived honestly and felt they had not wasted their lives.

In later years, Dr. Kübler-Ross's insistence that she could prove the existence of a serene afterlife drew fire from scientists and many lecture appearances were canceled. The center she built in California in the late 1970's burned, and the police suspected arson. She set up another center in 1984 in Virginia to care for children with AIDS; that center also was burned, in 1994, and arson was again suspected. After the second fire, she moved to Scottsdale, Ariz., to be near her son, Kenneth, a freelance photographer.

That year, when Dr. Ross was dying, he moved to a condominium in Scottsdale near Dr. Kübler-Ross, even though they were divorced. She and their son, Kenneth, cared for him. In addition to the son, Dr. Kübler-Ross is survived by a daughter, Barbara Ross, a clinical psychologist, of Wausau, Wis.; her brother Ernst, of Surrey, England; and her triplet sisters, Erika and Eva of Basel, Switzerland.

As Dr. Kübler-Ross awaited her own death, in a darkened room at her home in Arizona, she acknowledged that she was in pain and ready for her life to end. But she said, "I know beyond a shadow of a doubt that there is no death the way we understood it. The body dies, but not the soul."

UNIT 5
Funerals and Burial Rites

Unit Selections

Key Points to Consider

- Describe how the funeralization process can assist in coping with grief and facilitate the bereavement process. Distinguish between grief, bereavement, and funeralization.

- Discuss the psychological, sociological, and theological/philosophical aspects of the funeralization process. How do each of these aspects facilitate the resolution of grief?

- Describe and compare each of the following processes: burial, cremation, cryonics, and body donation for medical research. What would be your choice for final disposition of your body? Why would you choose this method, and what effects might this choice have upon your survivors (if any)? Would you have the same or different preferences for a close loved one such as a spouse, child, or parent? Why or why not?

- Describe and compare the processes of dealing with human loss and loss of a companion animal.

 **Links: www.dushkin.com/online/**
These sites are annotated in the World Wide Web pages.

Cryonics, Cryogenics, and the Alcor Foundation
http://www.alcor.org

Funerals and Ripoffs
http://www.funerals-ripoffs.org/-5dProf1.htm/

The Internet Cremation Society
http://www.cremation.org

Funeral Consumers Alliance
http://www.funerals.org/

Decisions relating to the disposition of the body after death often involve feelings of ambivalence—on one hand, attachments to the deceased might cause one to be reluctant to dispose of the body, on the other hand, practical considerations make the disposal of the body necessary. Funerals or memorial services provide methods for disposing of a dead body, remembering the deceased, and helping survivors accept the reality of death. They are also public rites of passage that assist the bereaved in returning to routine patterns of social interaction. In contemporary America, 79 percent of deaths involve earth burial and 21 percent involve cremation. These public behaviors, along with the private process of grieving, comprise the two components of the bereavement process.

This unit on the contemporary American funeral begins with a general article on the nature and functions of public bereavement behavior by Michael Leming and George Dickinson. Leming and Dickinson provide an overview of the present practice of funeralization in American society, including traditional and alternative funeral arrangements. They also discuss the functions of funerals relative to the sociological, psychological, and theological needs of adults and children.

The next article by Davis gives an insider's view of the funeral process. The articles by Matson and Ficklen discuss issues related to cost and the planning of funerals. This unit concludes with two articles dealing with the loss of a pet or companion animal.

The Contemporary American Funeral

Michael R. Leming
St. Olaf College

George E. Dickinson
College of Charleston

Most people use the words *death, grief,* and *bereavement* imprecisely, which can lead to difficulty in communication. The words are closely interrelated, but each has a specific content or meaning. As discussed in chapter 1, death is that point in time when life ceases to exist. *Death* is an event. It can be attached to a certain day, hour, and minute. *Grief* is an emotion, a very powerful emotion. It is triggered or stimulated by death. Although one can have anticipatory grief prior to the death of a significant other, grief is an emotional response to death. *Bereavement* is the state of having lost a significant other to death. Alternative processes—such as denial, avoidance, and defiance—have been shown by psychologists and psychiatrists to be only aberrations of the grief process and, as such, are not viable means of grief resolution.

The decisions about ultimate method of final **disposition** of the body should be determined by the persons in bereavement. Those charged with these decisions will be guided by their personal values and by the norms of the culture in which they live.

With over three fourths of American deaths occurring in hospitals or other institutions for the care of the sick and infirm, the contemporary process of body disposition begins at the time of death when the body is removed from the institutional setting. Most frequently the body is taken to a funeral home. There, the body is bathed, embalmed, and dressed. It is then placed into a casket selected by the family. Typically, arrangements are made for the ceremony, assuming that a ceremony is to follow. The funeral director, in consultation with the family, will determine the type, time, place and day of the ceremony. In most instances, the ceremony will have a religious content (Pine, 1971). The procedure just described is followed in approximately 75 percent of funerals. Alternatives to this procedure will be examined later in this chapter.

Following this ceremony, final disposition of the body is made by either earth burial (79 percent) or cremation (21 percent). (These percentages are approximate national averages and will vary by region.) The bereavement process will then be followed by a period of postfuneral adjustment for the family.

HOW THE FUNERAL MEETS THE NEEDS OF THE BEREAVED

Paul Irion (1956) has described the following needs of the bereaved: reality, expression of grief, social support, and meaningful context for the death. For Irion, the funeral is an experience of significant personal value insofar as it meets the religious, social, and psychological needs of the mourners. Each of these must be met for bereaved individuals to return to everyday living and, in the process, resolve their grief.

The *psychological* focus of the funeral is based on the fact that grief is an emotion. Edgar Jackson (1963) has indicated that grief is the other side of the coin of love. He contends that if a person has never loved the deceased—never had an emotional investment of some type and degree—he or she will not grieve upon death. Evidence of this can easily be demonstrated by the number of deaths that we hear, see, or read about daily that do not have an impact on us unless we have some kind of emotional involvement with those deceased persons. We can read of 78 deaths in a plane crash and not grieve over any of them unless we personally knew the individuals killed. Exceptions to the preceding might include the death of a celebrity or other public figure, when people experience a sense of grief even though there has never been any personal contact.

In his original work on the symptomatology of grief, Erich Lindemann (1944) stressed this concept of grief and its importance as a step in the resolution of grief. He defines how the emotion of grief must support the reality and finality of death. As long as the finality of death is avoided, Lindemann believes, grief resolution is impeded. For this reason, he strongly recommends that the bereaved persons view the dead. When the living confront the dead, all of the intellectualization and avoidance techniques break down. When we can say, "He or she is dead, I am alone, and from this day forward my life will be forever different," we have broken through the devices of denial and avoidance and have accepted the reality of death. It is only at this point that we can begin to withdraw the emotional capital that we have invested in the deceased and seek to create new relationships with the living.

On the other hand, viewing the corpse can be very traumatic for some. Most people are not accustomed to seeing a cold body and a significant other stretched out with eyes closed. Indeed, for some this scene may remain in their memories for a lifetime. Thus, they remember the cold corpse, not the warm, responsive person. Whether or not to view the body is not a cut-and-dried decision. Many factors should be taken into account when this decision is made.

Grief resolution is especially important for family members, but others are affected also—the neighbors, the business community in some instances, the religious community in most instances, the health care community, and the circle of friends and associates (many of whom may be unknown to the family). All of these groups will grieve to some extent the death of their relationship with the deceased. Thus, many people are affected by the death. These affected persons will seek not only a means of expressing their grief over the death, but also a network of support to help cope with their grief.

Sociologically, the funeral is a social event that brings the chief mourners and the members of society into a confrontation with death. The funeral becomes a vehicle to bring persons of all walks of life and degrees of relationship to the deceased together for expression and support. It is for this reason that in our contemporary culture the funeral becomes an occasion to which no one is invited but to which all may come. This was not always the case, and some cultures make the funeral ceremony an "invitation only" experience. It is perhaps for this reason that private funerals (restricted to the family or a special list of persons) have all but disappeared in our culture. (The possible exception to this statement is a funeral for a celebrity—where participation by the public is limited to media coverage.)

At a time when emotions are strong, it is important that human interaction and social support become high priorities. A funeral can provide this atmosphere. To grieve alone can be devastating because it becomes necessary for that lone person to absorb all of the feelings into himself or herself. It has often been said that "joy shared is joy increased"; surely grief shared is grief diminished. People need each other at times when they have intense emotional experiences.

A funeral is in essence a onetime kind of "support group" to undergird and support those grieving persons. A funeral provides a conducive social environment for mourning. We may go to the funeral home either to visit with the bereaved or to work through our own grief. Most of us have had the experience of finding it difficult to discuss a death with a member of the family. We seek the proper atmosphere, time, and place. It is during the funeral, the wake, the shivah, or the visitation with the bereaved that we are provided with the opportunity to express our condolences and sympathy comfortably.

Anger and guilt are often deeply felt at the time of death and will surface in words and actions. They are permitted within the funeral atmosphere as honest and candid expressions of grief, whereas at other times they might bring criticism and reprimand. The funeral atmosphere says in essence, "You are okay, I am okay; we have some strong feelings, and now is the time to express and share them for the benefit of all." Silence, talking, feeling, touching, and all means of sharing can be expressed without the fear of their being inappropriate.

Another function of the funeral is to provide a *theological* or *philosophical* perspective to facilitate grieving and to provide a context of meaning in which to place one of life's most significant experiences. For the majority of Americans, the funeral is a religious rite or ceremony (Pine, 1971). Those grievers who do not possess a religious creed or orientation will define or express death in the context of the values that the deceased and the grievers find important. Theologically or philosophically, the funeral functions as an attempt to bring meaning to the death and life of the deceased individual. For the religiously oriented person, the belief system will perhaps bring an understanding of the afterlife. Others may see only the end of biological life and the beginning of symbolic immortality created by the effects of one's life on the lives of others. The funeral should be planned to give meaning to whichever value context is significant for the bereaved.

"Why?" is one of the most often asked questions upon the moment of death or upon being told that someone we know has died. Though the funeral cannot provide the final answer to this question, it can place death within a context of meaning that is significant to those who mourn. If it is religious in context, the theology, creed, and articles of faith confessed by the mourners will give them comfort and assurance as to the meaning of death. Others who have developed a personally meaningful philosophy of life and death will seek to place the death in that philosophical context.

Cultural expectations typically require that we dispose of the dead with ceremony and dignity. The funeral can also ascribe importance to the remains of the dead.

THE NEEDS OF CHILDREN AND THEIR ATTENDANCE AT FUNERALS

For children, as well as for their elders, the funeral ceremony can be an experience of value and significance. At a very early age, children are interested in any type of family reunion, party, or celebration. To be excluded from the funeral may create questions and doubts in the minds of children as to why they are not permitted to be a part of an important family activity.

Another question to be considered when denying the child an opportunity to participate in postdeath activities is what goes through the child's mind when such participation is denied. Children deal with other difficult situations in life, and when denied this opportunity, many will fantasize. Research suggests that these fantasies may be negative, destructive, and at times more traumatic than the situation from which the children are excluded.

Children also should not be excluded from activities prior to the funeral service. They should be permitted to attend the visitation, wake, or shivah. (In some situations it would be wise to permit children to confront the deceased prior to the public visitation.) It is obvious that children should not be forced into this type of confrontation, but, by the same token, children who are curious and desire to be involved should not be denied the opportunity.

Children will react at their own emotional levels, and the questions that they ask will usually be asked at their level of comprehension. Two important rules to follow: Never lie to the child, and do not overanswer the child's question.

At the time of the funeral, parents have two concerns about their child's behavior at funerals. The first concern is that the child will have difficulty observing the grief of others—particularly if the child has never seen an adult loved one cry. The second concern is that parents themselves become confused when the child's emotional reactions may be different than their own. If the child is told of a death and responds by saying, "Oh, can I go out and play?" the parents may interpret this as denial or as a suppressed negative reaction to the death. Such a reaction can increase emotional concern by the parents. However, if the child's response is viewed as only a first reaction, and if the child is provided with loving, caring, and supportive attention, the child will ordinarily progress into an emotional resolution of the death.

The final reasons for involving children in postdeath activities are related to the strength and support that children give other grievers. They often provide positive evidence of the fact that life goes on. In other instances, because they have been an important part of the life of the deceased, their presence is symbolic testimony to the immortality of the deceased. Furthermore, it is not at all unusual for children to change the atmosphere surrounding bereavement from one of depression and sadness to one of laughter, verbalization, and celebration. Many times children do this by their normal behavior, without any understanding of the kind of contribution being made.

SIX FEET UNDER

Thomas Lynch has buried 6,000 of his neighbors. He talks.

By Kristen Davis

I'd rather it be February...I want it cold. I want the gray to inhabit the air like wood does trees: as an essence not a coincidence...And a wind to make the cold more bitter. So that ever after it might be said, "It was a sad old day we did it after all." -The Undertaking

Few fathers leave counsel so poetic to their children. Thomas Lynch paints this vision for his own funeral in his book. He should know what he wants; he's held funerals for about 6,000 of his fellow townspeople as the undertaker in Milford, Mich., for nearly 30 years. Before that, Lynch's father, Edward, was an undertaker for more than 30 years. And five of his eight siblings own or work in one of the four Lynch & Sons funeral homes in the Detroit metro area.

Aside from his sideline as an accomplished writer, Lynch is typical of thousands of independent funeral-home directors in the U.S.—the ones, as he puts it, "who answer your call in the middle of the night, not the ones who telemarket you in the middle of dinner." They've faced challenges in the past 40 years: Jessica Mitford's savage best-selling expose of the industry, *The American Way of Death*, in 1963, the steady encroachment of cremation as an alternative to traditional funerals, and in the 1990s, the rise—and then the dramatic financial demise—of the corporate-owned chain funeral parlors run by the Loewen Group, Service Corp. International and Stewart Enterprises.

Today, the family-run funeral home is still the place—mostly unfamiliar—where most people turn when

there's a death in the family. We visited Milford to see how one insider views his work and his trade.

Wake me. Let those who want to come and look. They have their reasons. You'll have yours. And if someone says, "Doesn't he look natural!" take no offense. They've got it right. For this was always in my nature. It's in yours.

At the heart of muckraker Mitford's biting critique of the "American way of death" is the open-casket funeral, which she lampoons as both barbaric and excessively expensive. "If the undertaker is the stage manager of the fabulous production that is the modern American funeral, the stellar role is reserved for the occupant of the open casket," she writes. "It is to this end that a fantastic array of costly merchandise and services is pyramided to dazzle the mourners and facilitate the plunder of the next of kin."

The traditional American funeral is inarguably expensive. Holding a wake and memorializing a loved one at a funeral home in the U.S. cost an average of $6,130 last year, including a $2,330 casket and a $950 cemetery vault, according to the National Funeral Directors Association. A full traditional funeral with the same-priced merchandise at Lynch & Sons would cost $7,230. Lynch says his customers—many of whom choose something less than the full package of services—spend about $5,000. (These average costs don't include the cemetery plot, grave marker and fees for opening and closing the grave, which can add another $2,000 or more.)

"It's not unlike other consumer purchases," Lynch says matter-of-factly. "You can spend one-fifth the amount or five times the amount." What's important is not what you spend but what you do, he says, and he believes that includes the physical ritual of bearing away the body. "Ask any of the 3,000 families in New York who will not get their dead back," he says. "Ask them what they would pay to have a wake, and to have the body back to let it go again."

In his book he writes, "The presence and participation of the dead human body at its funeral is, as my father told it, every bit as important as the bride's being at her wedding, the baby at its baptism." In an interview in his large, second-floor office, with a portrait of his parents in his line of vision, he repeats the analogy, adopting it as his own.

If anyone tells you you haven't spent enough, tell them to go piss up a rope. Tell the same thing to anyone who says you spent too much. It's your money. Do what you want with it. But let me make one thing perfectly clear. You know the type who's always saying "When I'm dead, save your money, spend it on something really useful, do me cheaply"? I'm not one of them. Never was. I've always thought that funerals were useful. So do what suits you. It's yours to do. If a little upgrade in the pomp and circumstance makes you feel better, consider it money wisely spent.

Why does it cost $6,000-plus for a funeral? Lynch says it's not because the funeral business is wildly profitable. "Find me a vastly wealthy funeral-home director," he quips. He adds that in his career he's earned enough to afford "orthodontia but not boarding school" for his kids.

Basically, he says, it costs a lot to run a funeral home. Lynch says he takes in roughly $1 million a year in gross revenues. He spends about $350,000 a year on payroll, including his own salary of about $70,000 and pay for three other full-time and three part-time staffers. There's health insurance to buy and a retirement plan to fund. Maintaining the 11,000-square-foot Victorian that houses Lynch & Sons is the next-largest expense. Within the past two years, he's spent "$20,000 to recarpet, $60,000 on painting and refinishing furniture, $10,000 on doing the woodwork," aside from the cost of heating, lighting and computers. The funeral home also pays for Lynch's car, a late-model Cadillac that serves as a "family car" for funerals; plus two hearses (one a stately '39 Packard that was his father's) and a service van (the Dead Wagon, he calls it). After expenses and taxes, Lynch says he hopes to call 5%—or about $50,000 a year—profit.

He sets his fees by estimating costs for the year, adding a profit margin and dividing by the expected 200 or so funerals a year. Because customers pay the same amount whether there are 20 people or 200 at a funeral, the service fees ($3,950 for a "complete" funeral with two days of viewing, a ceremony at the funeral home or elsewhere, processional and committal) sometimes yield a profit and sometimes don't. The fees also subsidize a handful of funerals each year that pay little or nothing, such as welfare funerals and funerals for infants, for which Lynch charges the wholesale cost of the casket and no service fee.

Lynch says the bulk of his profits is in the markup on caskets, which runs about twice wholesale. (Back in the days before the Federal Trade Commission required funeral homes to break out service fees separately, all the profit and overhead was in the casket, which was marked up three to three and a half times the wholesale price or more.)

Lisa Carlson, executive director of Funeral Consumers Alliance and the author of *Caring for the Dead*, says funerals cost as much as they do because there are too many funeral homes. If every funeral home in Michigan had one funeral a day, she says, 334 would be needed to support the death rate there. The state has 805 funeral homes, according to her figures. When funeral homes have only one or two funerals a week, they need to charge a lot more to cover their overhead, she says.

While Lynch & Sons averages about four funerals a week, it can handle more. The week before we visited, the funeral home had 11; some weeks, there are none. In theory at least, funeral homes could probably handle more funerals, enjoy economies of scale, and charge less per funeral (or enjoy more profits, which is what the corporate funeral chains have failed to do so far).

But the critique is only valid, Lynch argues, "if we could be sure everyone died regionally appropriately and during business hours—and if people didn't care who buried whom." People want a funeral director who is local, he says, or "one who is religiously, ethnically or culturally like them."

I want a mess made in the snow so the earth looks wounded, forced open, an unwilling participant. Forgo the tent. Stand openly to the weather… After the words are finished, lower it… Stamp your *feet* in the cold, let your heads sink between your shoulders, keep looking down. That's where what is happening is happening.

In the earthy HBO TV series, *Six Feet* Under, funeral director David Fisher sits down with the young widow of a flashy entrepreneur (who turns out to have been a con man). He holds a three-ring binder with pictures of caskets.

"May I ask what kind of car your husband preferred?"

"He drives a BMW."

"Do you know what model?"

"The biggest, fastest one."

"I recommend the Titan series. Solid mahogany. Burlwood accents. The same wood used in luxury automobiles."

"Looks expensive."

"$9,000. It's more than just a casket. It's a tribute, really."

Tom Lynch does not sell caskets this way. His showroom holds about 22, ranging from a $79 cardboard box (for cremations) to a $12,000 mahogany casket Lynch says he's never sold. His spiel goes like this: "They are just boxes. There is nothing that gets you into heaven or keeps you out. No casket will make up for a lifetime of neglect, and you won't undo a life of honorable conduct by buying something cheap."

Most people, he says, take just five or ten minutes to choose a casket, and typically spend $2,000 to $3,000. That buys, say, a solid-oak casket, or one made of 18-gauge steel with a velvet, linen or crepe interior.

You can buy similar caskets for less online at a site such as Direct Casket (www.directcasket.com), but Lynch says almost no one does. "On the Internet you can spend $400 less for the same casket and you'll spend $600 for delivery," he says. (Next -day shipment from Direct Casket actually costs $200 to $400, and the savings appears to range from a few hundred to a thousand dollars or more, depending on the casket.) "If people stop buying caskets from funeral directors, this price will go up," Lynch says, pointing to his list of service fees, "and that price will go down," pointing to his casket price list. "So far it hasn't been a big issue here."

"When people are shown one casket marked $1,000, one marked $1,800 and one marked $2,500, which would you guess gets picked most often?" Carlson asks. "If a funeral home wants to make a bigger profit, there's a good chance that the first three caskets shown might be listed at $1,800, $2,500 and $3,200—and now the $2,500 casket will become the popular model."

Is that how it really works? we asked Lynch. "I'm not opposed to people spending money on a casket," he says. "I just don't feel like a casket retailer. That's not to say funeral directors aren't as savvy salespeople as anyone else. But if people feel they're dealing with a salesperson in the casket room, they won't come to you again."

Lynch's casket price list includes 14 wood models (aside from those designated "cremation" caskets); eight of them cost less than $3,000. The median price is about $2,750, and the least expensive, at $995, is the proverbial pine box. At nearby Elton Black & Son—a funeral home owned by Service Corp. International, the largest corporate-owned chain of funeral homes—the casket price list shows 16 wood caskets, only one priced below $3,000. The median price is about $4,300.

If you opt for burning, stand and watch. If you cannot watch it, perhaps you should reconsider. Stand in earshot of the sizzle and pop. Try to get a whiff of the goings on. Warm your hands to the fire. This might be a good time for a song. Bury the ashes, cinders and bones. The bits of the box that did not burn. Put them in something. Mark the spot.

As a way to hold down costs, Americans are choosing cremation over a traditional funeral. About 4% of bodies were cremated in the U.S. in the 1960s; the figure reached 25% in 2000 and is projected by the Cremation Association of North America to rise to 36% by 2010. "In many communities now, cremation is the tradition and the great formalities are the alternative," says Ron Hast, publisher of the trade publications *Mortuary Management* magazine and *Funeral Monitor*.

Lynch & Sons charges $1,450 to handle a "direct" cremation—-one in which the body is transported to a crematory and the funeral home is not involved in any services. That fee doesn't include a container for the body: You can provide your own (combustible) box, purchase a wood-bottomed cardboard box for $79, or even buy and burn a casket. The firm's casket price list includes cremation caskets ranging from a $395 utility case (cloth-covered fiberboard) to a $2,650 solid-cherry casket. The cost also doesn't include the crematory's fee of $160.

Costs are higher if you have a private family viewing (with embalming) or choose a full-fledged, full-priced funeral, followed by cremation. You can buy an urn to hold the ashes (Lynch & Sons' prices range from $200 to $500 for a selection of bronze, marble, ceramic and wood), or even "cremation jewelry," which allows several family members to keep—or wear—some of the ashes. (You can get a hollow heart- or cross-shaped pendant, for example, for $50 to $300.)

"With the increased cremation rate, mortuaries are scrambling to recover the income they would otherwise be making from what Jessica Mitford called 'the full fig funeral,'" according to Carlson. In SEC documents, SCI calls the "expansion of cremation marketing, merchandising and services" one of the "revenue-growth initiatives" it hopes will help turn around its miserable financials.

In his frequent writing for trade journals, Lynch is sharply critical of the hard sell. He scorns the "death-care salespeople" of Loewen and SCI who "put the sell before the service." And he scolds independent funeral directors who've reasoned that "if I don't sell out, I have to sell hard, too."

157

But whether it's soft sell or firm belief (and it appears to be the latter), Lynch is emphatic that having a direct cremation and then a memorial service ("to which the dead guy isn't invited because he has expenses attached to him") cheats the living of a meaningful experience. "Cremation could be a marvelous symbol and ritual," he says. "Too often it is just an exercise in convenience. It's the dead guy the funeral is about."

"Caring for your own dead is more to the point," Carlson says. In the first chapter of her book, she describes how, strapped for cash after her husband's death, she secured the necessary permits and drove the body to the crematory herself. To her surprise, she found it a comforting exercise: "I needed to be a part of John's death as I was of his life. If I had had money, I would have lost that—given that away—in a moment of grief and confusion." The bulk of the book advises others how to handle the details themselves.

The difference between Lisa Carlson and Jessica Mitford, says Lynch, "is that Lisa says to take care of your dead. Deal with them. Lisa understands that. Jessica never did. Jessica believed that if you got rid of the body cheaply, everything else would take care of itself." As for do-it-yourselfers, Lynch says, "Fine, I'm for it. If you don't want to do that, I answer around the clock and I have fees."

It's yours to do — my Funeral—not mine. The death is yours to live with once I'm dead. So here is a coupon good for Disregard. And here is another marked My Approval. Ignore, with my blessings, whatever I've said beyond Love One Another.

At the burial of *Six Feet* Under's Nathaniel Fisher—whose death in the first episode left the funeral home to his sons—a representative of a corporate funeral-home chain shows up to make a buyout offer. Later he threatens one of the sons: "In the death-care industry now, it's consolidate or die. Decide which, Nate, and give me a ring."

Lynch's corporate suitor was a fellow undertaker who came while he was watering impatiens outside the funeral home. "He had just sold his family firm to SCI; he said he thought it had made so many good changes for him." Lynch had no interest in consolidating—and it's the corporate chains that are now in peril. Loewen Group filed for bankruptcy in 2000. SCI has watched its profits—and share price—plunge. SCI stock peaked around $47 in 1998; it sold for $5 recently.

What the corporate chains tried to do was buy up independently owned homes, group them into local "clusters," and reap economies of scale by allowing a single embalming facility or fleet of cars to serve them all. "They have fallen on their faces, " says publisher Hast, in

part because they spent too much on acquisitions and in part because they raised prices and cut costs too aggressively.

"Their primary agenda is bottom-line profits rather than excellence in service," Hast says. "People have gone into this field because they feel a reward in comforting families, and all they hear is a constant hammering toward meeting sales goals."

Lynch says the hard-driving sales culture of the corporate funeral homes drives customers away—sometimes to his doorstep. Of Elton Black & Son, his SCI competitor in White Lake, Mich., he says: "I do more of their business than I used to, with people who wouldn't otherwise be our buyers geographically. I can only assume that it's something in the management style, or maybe just the prices."

Prices for services at Lynch & Sons and Elton Black are similar. Elton Black's service fee is lower, but it charges extra for things such as evening, holiday and weekend services and for dealing with an autopsied body. Lynch & Sons charges one price, period. The big difference is in the casket prices, and in the package deals and profit-padding extras.

Elton Black's price list shows three funeral packages (called Dignity Memorial Funeral Service Selections): one priced at $10,395 (including a choice of four $5,000 caskets), a second at $8,595 (with $3,500 to $3,700 caskets) and a third at $7,895 (with $3,000 to $3,400 caskets). Also in the package: a picture frame and leather keepsake presentation box to display the cards and other mementos, access to a "grief-management library," a "child/grandchild protection program" (which is insurance to pay for funerals for children and grandchildren), a one-hour phone card, a personal planning guide and the "Dignity Care Package." Sold separately for $585 and described as another "revenue initiative" to shareholders, the care package includes an after-care planner, an everlasting memorial (described as an "Internet Memorial/Archive") and a 24-hour "Compassion Helpline."

It isn't always easy to tell a corporate-owned funeral home from one that is family run, because after the buyout, the corporation often keeps the family name and hires the former owners as managers. But a price list like Elton Black's gives it away. By law, funeral homes are required to give you a general price list, plus price lists for caskets and outer burial containers, if you ask for them. Few families are in the mood for hardcore shopping when it comes to funerals, but getting all three price lists is the best way to gauge costs.

Lynch calls funerals at corporate-run homes McFunerals and says they cheapen the image of all funeral directors. "The damage done by SCI and Loewen and Stewart, both in their spectacular rise and precipitous fall, has been done to all of us," he writes in *The Director*, a trade magazine. "More and more we are hired to pick up and dispose of the dead and otherwise leave the living alone to sort things out with their clergy or therapist or pharmacist or bartender."

Like Mitford, the big-business approach focuses too much on the math, Lynch says. "McFunerals and Mitfunerals both miss the mark by a long shot.

How different religions pay their final respects

From mummies to cremation to drive-up wakes, funeral rituals reflect religious traditions going back thousands of years as well as up-to-the-minute fads.

William J. Whalen

Most people in the United States identify themselves as Protestants; thus, most funerals follow a similar form. Family and friends gather at the funeral home to console one another and pay their last respects. The next day a minister conducts the funeral service at the church or mortuary; typically the service includes hymns, prayers, a eulogy, and readings from the Bible. In 85 percent of the cases today, the body is buried after a short grave-side ceremony. Otherwise the body is cremated or donated to a medical school.

But what could be called the standard U.S. funeral turns out to be the funeral of choice for only a minority of the rest of the human race. Other people, even other Christians, bury their dead with more elaborate and, to outsiders, even exotic rites.

How your survivors will dispose of your body will in all likelihood be determined by the religious faith you practiced during your life because funeral customs reflect the theological beliefs of a particular faith community.

For example, the Parsi people of India neither bury nor cremate their dead. Parsis, most of whom live in or near Bombay, follow the ancient religion of Zoroastrianism. Outside Bombay, Parsis erected seven Towers of Silence in which they perform their burial rites. When someone dies, six bearers dressed in white bring the corpse to one of the towers. The Towers of Silence have no roofs; within an hour, waiting vultures pick the body clean. A few days later the bearers return and cast the remaining bones into a pit. Parsis believe that their method of disposal avoids contaminating the soil, the water, and the air.

Out of the ashes

The Parsis' millions of Hindu neighbors choose cremation as their usual burial practice. Hindus believe that as long as the physical body exists, the essence of the person will remain nearby; cremation allows the essence, or soul, of the person to continue its journey into another incarnation.

Hindus wash the body of the deceased and clothe it in a shroud decorated with flowers. They carry the body to a funeral pyre, where the nearest male relative lights the fire and walks around the burning body three times while reciting verses from Hindu sacred writings. Three days later someone collects and temporarily buries the ashes.

On the tenth day after the cremation, relatives deposit the ashes in the Ganges or some other sacred river. The funeral ceremony, called the *Shraddha*, is then held within 31 days of the cremation. Usually the deceased's son recites the prayers and the invocation of ancestors; that is one reason why every Hindu wants at least one son.

Prior to British rule in India, the practice of suttee was also common. Suttee is the act of a Hindu widow willingly being cremated on her husband's funeral pyre. Suttee was outlawed by the British in 1829, but occasionally widows still throw themselves into the flames.

Like the Hindus, the world's Buddhists, who live primarily in China, Japan, Sri Lanka, Myanmar, Vietnam, and Cambodia, usually choose cremation for disposing of a corpse. They believe cremation was favored by Buddha. A religious teacher may pray or recite mantras at the bedside of the dying person. These actions are believed to exert a wholesome effect on the next rebirth. Buddhists generally believe that the essence of a person remains in an intermediate state for no more than 49 days between death and rebirth.

While Hindus and Buddhists prescribe cremation, the world's 900 million Muslims forbid cremation. According to the Qu'ran, Muhammad taught that only Allah will use fire to punish the wicked.

If a Muslim is near death, someone is called in to read verses from the Qu'ran. After death, the body is ceremonially washed, clothed in three pieces of white cloth, and placed in a simple wooden coffin. Unless required by law, Muslims will not allow embalming. The body must be buried as soon as possible after death—usually within 24 hours. After a funeral service at a mosque or at the grave side, the body is removed from the coffin and buried with the head of the deceased turned toward Mecca. In some Muslim countries the women engage in loud wailing and lamentations during the burial.

Some Islamic grave sites are quite elaborate. The Mogul emperor Shah Jahan built the world-famous Taj Mahal as a mausoleum for his wife and himself. The Taj Mahal, which is one of the finest examples of Islamic architecture, was finished in 1654. It took 20,000 workers about 22 years to complete the project.

The Baha'i faith, which originated in Persia in the nineteenth century as an outgrowth of the Shi'ite branch of Islam, also forbids cremation and embalming and requires that the body not be transported more than an hour's journey from the place of death. Because Bahaism has no ordained clergy, the funeral may be conducted by any member of the family or the local assembly. All present at the funeral must stand during the recitation of the Prayer for the Dead composed by Baha'u'llah. Several million Baha'is live in Iran, India, the Middle East, and Africa; and an estimated 100,000 Baha'is live in the United States.

In Judaism, the faith of some 18 million people, the Old Testament only hints at belief in an afterlife; but later Jewish thought embraced beliefs in heaven, hell, resurrection, and final judgment. In general, Orthodox Jews accept the concept of a resurrection of the soul and the body while Conservative and Reform Jews prefer to speak only of the immortality of the soul.

Orthodox Judaism prescribes some of the most detailed funeral rites of any religion. As death approaches, family and friends must attend the dying person at all times. When death finally arrives, a son or the nearest relative closes the eyes and mouth of the deceased and binds the lower jaw before rigor mortis sets in. Relatives place the body on the floor and cover it with a sheet; they place a lighted candle near the head.

Judaism in its traditional form forbids embalming except where required by law. After a ritual washing, the body is covered with a white shroud and placed in a wooden coffin. At the funeral, mourners symbolize their grief by tearing a portion of an outer garment or wearing a torn black ribbon. The Orthodox discourage flowers and ostentation at the funeral.

The Jewish funeral service includes a reading of prayers and psalms, a eulogy, and the recitation of the Kaddish prayer for the dead in an Aramaic dialect. Like other Semitic people, Jews forbid cremation. Orthodox Jews observe a primary mourning period of seven days; Reform Jews reduce this period to three days. During the secondary yearlong mourning period, the Kaddish prayer is recited at every service in the synagogue.

Dearly beloved

Christianity, the world's largest religion, carries over Judaism's respect for the body and firmly acknowledges resurrection, judgment, and eternal reward or punishment.

These Christian beliefs permeate the liturgy of a Catholic funeral. Older Catholics remember the typical funeral of the 1940s and '50s: the recitation of the rosary at the wake, the black vestments, the Latin prayers. They probably recall the *"Dies Irae,"* a thirteenth-century dirge and standard musical piece at Catholic funerals prior to the liturgical changes of the Second Vatican Council in the 1960s.

Nowadays, those attending a Catholic wake may still say the rosary, but often there is a scripture service instead. The priest's vestments are likely to be white or violet rather than black. Prayers tend to emphasize the hope of resurrection rather than the terrors of the final judgment.

As death approaches, the dying person or the family may request the sacrament of the Anointing of the Sick. Once called Last Rites or Extreme Unction, this sacrament is no longer restricted to those in imminent danger of death; it is regularly administered to the sick and the elderly as an instrument of healing as well as a preparation for death.

Sacred remains

The Catholic Church raises no objections to embalming, flowers, or an open casket at a wake. At one time Catholics who wished to have a church funeral could not request cremation. In 1886 the Holy Office in Rome declared that "to introduce the practice (of cremation) into Christian society was un-Christian and Masonic in motivation." Today Catholics may choose the option of cremation over burial "unless," according to canon law, "it has been chosen for reasons that are contrary to Christian teaching."

The church used to deny an ecclesiastical burial to suicides, those killed in duels, Freemasons, and members of the ladies' auxiliaries of Masonic lodges. Today the church refuses burial only to "notorious apostates, heretics, and schismatics" and to "sinners whose funerals in church would scandalize the faithful." Catholics who join Masonic lodges no longer incur excommunication, although they still may not receive Communion.

The church has also softened its position on denying funeral rites to suicides. Modern pastoral practice is based on the understanding that anyone finding life so unbearable as to end it voluntarily probably was acting with a greatly diminished free will.

For Roman Catholics, the Mass is the principal celebration of the Christian funeral; and mourners are invited to receive the Eucharist. Most Protestant denominations, except for some Lutherans and Episcopalians, do not incorporate a communion service into their funeral liturgies. The Catholic ritual employs candles, holy water, and incense but does not allow non-Christian symbols, such as national flags or lodge emblems, to rest on or near the coffin during the funeral. In many parishes the pastor encourages the family members to participate where appropriate as eucharistic ministers, lectors, and singers. In the absence of a priest, a deacon can conduct the funeral service but cannot preside at a Mass of Christian burial.

The revised funeral liturgy of the Catholic Church is meant to stress God's faithfulness to people rather than God's wrath toward sinners. The Catholic Church declares that certain men and women who have lived lives of such heroic virtue that they are indeed in heaven are to be known as saints. The church also teaches that hell is a reality but has never declared that anyone, even Judas, has actually been condemned to eternal punishment.

Unlike Protestant churches, Catholicism also teaches the existence of a temporary state of purification, known as purgatory, for those destined for heaven but not yet totally free from the effects of sin and selfishness. At one time some theologians suggested that unbaptized babies spent eternity in a place of natural happiness known as limbo, but this was never church doctrine and is taught by few theologians today.

At the committal service at the grave site, the priest blesses the grave and leads the mourners in the Our Father and other prayers for the repose of the soul of the departed and the comfort of the survivors. Catholics are usually buried in Catholic cemeteries or in separate sections of other cemeteries.

Dressed for the occasion

The funeral rite in the Church of Jesus Christ of Latter-day Saints, which is the fastest growing church in the United States, resembles the standard Protestant funeral in some ways; but one significant difference is in the attire of the deceased. Devout Mormons receive the garments of the holy priesthood during their endowment ceremonies when they are teens. These sacred undergarments are to be worn day and night throughout a Mormon's life. When a Mormon dies, his or her body is then attired in these garments in the casket. At one time Mormon sacred garments resembled long johns, but they now have short sleeves and are cut off at the knees. The garments are embroidered with symbols on the right and left breasts, the navel, and the right knee, which remind the wearer of the oaths taken in the secret temple rites.

Mormons who reached their endowments are also clothed in their temple garb at death. For the men, this includes white pants, white shirt, tie, belt, socks, slippers, and an apron. Just before the casket is closed for the last time, a fellow Mormon puts a white temple cap on the corpse. If the deceased is a woman, a high priest puts a temple veil over her face; Mormons believe the veil will remain there until her husband calls her from the grave to resurrection. Mormons forbid cremation.

Freemasons conduct their own funeral rites for a deceased brother, and they insist that their ceremony be the last one before burial or cremation. Thus, a separate religious ceremony often precedes the Masonic rites. Lodge members will bury a fellow Mason only if he is a member in good standing and he or his family has requested the service.

All the pallbearers at the Masonic services must be Masons, and each wears a white apron, white gloves, a black band around his left arm, and a sprig of evergreen or acacia in his left lapel. The corpse is clothed in a white apron and other lodge regalia.

Masonry accepts the idea of the immortality of the soul but makes no reference to the Christian understanding of the resurrection of the soul and the body. The Masonic service speaks of the soul's translation from this life to that "perfect, glorious, and celestial lodge above" presided over by the Grand Architect of the Universe.

In memoriam

Other small religious groups have much less elaborate and formalized funeral services. Christian Scientists, for example, have no set funeral rite because their founder, Mary Baker Eddy, denied the reality of death. The family of a deceased Christian Scientist often invites a Christian Science reader to present a brief service at the funeral home.

Unitarian-Universalists enroll many members who would identify themselves as agnostics or atheists. Therefore, in a typical Unitarian Universalist funeral service, the minister and loved ones say little about any afterlife but extol the virtues and good works of the deceased.

Salvation Army officers are buried in their military uniforms, and a Salvationist blows taps at the grave side. In contrast, the Church of Christ, which allows no instrumental music during Sunday worship, allows no organs, pianos, or other musical instruments at its funerals.

The great variety of funeral customs through the ages and around the world would be hard to catalog. The Egyptians mummified the bodies of royalty and erected pyramids as colossal monuments. Viking kings were set adrift on blazing boats. The Soviets mummified the body of Lenin, and his tomb and corpse have become major icons in the U.S.S.R.

In a funeral home in California, a drive-up window is provided for mourners so that they can view the remains and sign the book without leaving their cars. In Japan, where land is scarce, one enterprising cemetery owner offers a time-share plan whereby corpses are displaced after brief burial to make room for the next occupant. Complying with the wishes of the deceased, one U.S. undertaker once dressed a corpse in pajamas and positioned it under the blankets in a bedroom for viewing.

The reverence and rituals surrounding the disposal of the body reflect religious traditions going back thousands of years as well as up-to-the-minute fads. All of the elements of the burial—the preparation of the body, the garments or shroud, the prayers, the method of disposal, the place and time of burial—become sacred acts by which a particular community of believers bids at least a temporary farewell to one of its own.

Reprinted with permission from *U.S. Catholic*, September 1990, pp. 29-35. © 1990 by U.S. Catholic, 205 West Monroe Street, Chicago, IL 60606.

The LAST THING you want to do

How to plan an economically sane funeral

Tim Matson

Guess what? You're going to die. Not today (with luck), not tomorrow (you hope), but some day. The Grim Reaper waits. Sure, you already knew that, and you try not to think about it. But before you flip the page, let me tell you the problem with death denial (those undertakers who happily profit on death fears can stop reading now). Ignorance may be bliss when it comes to mortality, but it's going to cost you.

A couple of years ago, hitting my mid-50s, I'd heard about enough overpriced funerals and unsatisfactory memorial services to take a stab at saving my relatives some money, and possibly unnecessary grief and confusion, by making my own funeral plan. I was also inspired by the story of a north-woods logger who built his own coffin and slept in it, "To get used to it," he said. Talk about confronting your demons.

I'd already spent plenty of time trying not to think about death. (My favorite ale was a dark brew called Courage.) But how long can you ignore the gray hairs, back aches, and general dilapidation? So I hit the road, dropping in on undertakers and coffin makers, stone carvers and grave diggers, looking for a simple exit strategy. In the process I gained a surprise dividend: emotional peace.

There was a bottom line rationale for my quest. As a tight fisted Vermonter, I don't like the notion of being fleeced by an undertaker when I'm in no position to fight back. Maybe you heard about the unidentified woman who froze to death under a car in Minnesota. In compliance with state law, an undertaker was appointed to handle her funeral arrangements. He planned to collect the usual nominal fee from the state, until it was discovered that the deceased had an impressive estate. The undertaker was able to raise his fee and, according to an attorney in mortuary law, "earn some extra income for a limited amount of work." A nasty preview of the surprisingly common fate many of us will share: Post-mortem larceny.

Strange, how little we're taught about one of life's big events. According to a recent study, 75 percent of hospice patients don't discuss death with their families. Marriage, sex, birth, growing tomatoes—we're up to the neck in life skills information. But death? Leave it to the experts.

There are 23,000 funeral homes in the United States, and they take in $25 billion every year (more than the airline industry and garbage collection). Not bad for a business that hardly existed 150 years ago, when deaths were handled by families, the church, or the local sawbones.

All that began to change with the industrial age. If you couldn't keep people down on the farm, the pursuit of happiness often ended with no one to dispose of the body.

Enter the undertaker (with help from a Civil War doctor who invented an embalming process that made it possible to preserve and transport bodies with one profitable stop at the funeral home). Back then it was called a mortuary, but funeral home had a much nicer ring to it, and the undertaker (make that funeral director) was catching on to a brilliant psychological insight. As Americans lost their intimate contact with death, they were just as happy to forget about the whole damned thing. It wasn't just industrial streamlining that inspired coffin makers to ditch the six-sided "toe pincher." A rectangular shape looked so much less like what it was. Changing the name to casket boosted the antiseptic effect even more.

The campaign continues today. Over the past decade or so, 10 to 15 percent of the funeral homes in the United States have been bought out by corporate chains whose names have been sanitized of any sepulchral trace, among the biggest is Service Corporation International (SCI). But they've made sure the Mom and Pop funeral parlors they acquired retain their trusted names. However, they have made big changes in mark-ups, often lure unwary customers into lucrative contracts, and occasionally even engage in deceptive deals with church organizations to corral customers. Coffin prices continue to be one of the worst over-charges, even after an FTC ruling in 1984 that allowed customers to buy their own coffins. Funeral directors still can charge as much as $1,000 for bring-your-own coffin "handling fees." (Virginia, Louisiana and Oklahoma still won't permit you to buy your own coffin.)

Before the stock market began its current meltdown, the death rush went bust. SCI is on the rocks. Financial analysts chalk it up to overpayment for acquisitions, but customers no doubt are also beginning to shy away from expensive services, especially of the last-minute, unplanned variety.

Consumer advocate Lisa Carlson, head of the Funeral Consumer's Alliance, suggests that an impromptu funeral is likely to cost much more than a planned event. "If you don't do your homework, it's like giving the funeral home a blank check," she warns. She points out that in the age of the internet, it's not difficult to research funeral options and costs on the web. Considering that funeral expenses average $6,000 in the United States, not including cemetery and monument costs (which bring the total up to $8,000, according to the American Association of Retired Persons), there's plenty of opportunity for savings.

So how exactly do you leave this world without being taken for a ride? Begin by asking yourself some basic questions. First, cremation or whole body burial? The funeral industry would prefer to put all of you 6 feet under because that's where the biggest profit lies. To bury a body usually involves treatment in a funeral home, often incurring hefty charges for cosmetology and embalming. Then there's the hearse, burial plot, headstone, and protective vault (to prevent the sod from collapsing on a rotting casket—sorry, in most cemeteries it's the law). Not to mention the coffin, which can cost thousands by itself, most of it in humongous funeral-home mark-ups. Throw in a memorial services, wake, and grave-side ceremony, and we're talking real, money. Oh, don't forget the flowers.

No wonder so many people are opting for cremation (25 percent now, and the number is rising dramatically). There's a new crematorium in my neighborhood that charges only $550, which includes pickup of the body and personal delivery of the remains. The young owner even throws in a composite granite urn, gratis. When local undertakers heard about this upstart, they tried to put him out of business for operating an unlicensed funeral home. He argued that he was simply operating a crematorium. Big difference, legally. The Vermont attorney general gave him a green light.

After reading about this no-frills rebel, I visited the crematorium (in an old coffin factory), checked out the retort (looks like a maple sap evaporator), and signed up. The average person requires about 40 pounds of gas to be cooked down to a five pound mound of gray ash. The ashes are scooped out of the oven into your choice of container: plain cardboard box, granite urn, or wooden cube, which costs extra.

Alas, the benefits of a quick, low budget cremation may be offset by a regrettable tendency to procrastinate when it comes to dealing with ash disposal. Did the deceased forget to leave instructions? Is the family itself scattered around the countryside, unable to gather for a timely sprinkling ceremony? Showing me around his funeral parlor, one undertaker opened the door into a room full of blue cardboard boxes—unclaimed ashes. If you don't want to wind up a trapped spirit in cosmic limbo, warn your family that you'll come back to haunt them if they ignore your wishes.

In fact, whatever your plans, a family discussion is essential. One bromide of the funeral trade still holds true: funerals are for the living. No sense inflicting unnecessary pain on the survivors.

If you do choose a whole body funeral, you're probably going to need the services of a funeral home. The body is usually transported from the place of death to the funeral establishment, where it is prepared for burial. However, unless the body can be buried within a few days, it may need to be embalmed. If a memorial service is planned with the deceased present, the body is placed in a coffin and transported to the church or synagogue. It's also usually possible to have a memorial service at the funeral home itself. Burial customarily follows the service.

If ever there were a time for planning, this is it. People are often so grief-stricken when a relative dies that rational choices are impossible, and some undertakers cash in on this pain. But remember, plan ahead doesn't mean pay ahead. Many undertakers will try to coax potential clients into signing up for a fixed fee funeral "whenever the time comes."

That may sound like a hedge against inflation, but they can't guarantee how long they'll be in business, or where you'll die. If you want to be sure the money will be there when it's needed, put it in a bank.

Fortunately, there are alternatives to expensive professional funerals. Most states allow people to handle funeral details without an undertaker. Options for do-it-yourself funerals include building the coffin, transporting the deceased, and even digging a backyard grave. In many states it's legal to bury a body on your own land, although there is usually some permitting required (including signed death certificate). In circumstances involving contagious diseases like hepatitis B and AIDS, special precautions have to be taken. Check with your state health department and town zoning administration first. The Funeral Consumer's Alliance can help, too. Home burials aren't for everyone, but a resourceful do-it-yourselfer can skip cremation entirely, build a coffin (or simply use a shroud), and dig the grave.

For those who bury their own dead, the motivation usually is less financial than spiritual. Again, the burial plot should be recorded in town documents. There's also a small but growing movement here and in England to "green burials," in specifically designated cemeteries, which dispense with coffins and vaults entirely.

Burial options aren't the only decisions you face. Advances in medical technology have made it possible to recycle various body parts, and many people feel ennobled by the idea of giving someone the gift of life when they die. Clearly, there's no lack of demand, with a national registry of potential recipients that outnumbers donors 3 to 1.

To avoid the potential for ethical abuses, financial rewards are not permitted for organ donation (although the hospital does pay the "harvesting" costs). Donating your body for medical research affords some financial benefits. The medical school usually pays for the cost of cremation, and may offer to bury the remains.

Most people prefer to arrange for the interment themselves. In fact, there's a trend of bringing the deceased home for burial (if he or she isn't there already). With ashes the process is relatively straightforward. The funeral director or crematory operator picks up the body and sends or delivers the ashes. In most states, no permit is needed to scatter ashes on your own property, or the ocean. It's often possible to create a small private cemetery, on your land.

Whether you build a coffin, bury a body or help plan a service, it's essential to play a part in funeral preparation to achieve a sense of closure. More than a year after her father's death, a friend still regrets being rushed through memorial preparations by the undertaker. "He handled everything," she said. "I don't feel like I was really involved, it happened so fast."

As for my plans, aside from the choice to be cremated, I'm leaving it up to my family to arrange a memorial service. Surprise me. But forget the cardboard box. I found a fallen maple tree limb and carved it into an urn. It's not big enough to sleep in, but it makes a great cookie jar, while I'm waiting.

Positive Trends

Kelly Smith is public relations director for the National Funeral Directors Association, in Brookfield, Wisconsin. He keeps an eye on surveys and trends connected to the funeral business, as well as updating his more than 13,000 members and the public on current issues.

Smith emphasized planning and said it's important to get the family involved in the process. Plans made in isolation may not jibe with family members' wishes, and they'll be the ones doing the work. If you plan to use a funeral home, decide how much you want to spend, and how the payment will be made. "Make sure the funeral home has provided all price information," he said. "Talk to the funeral director about payment. It can be tough to liquidate assets after a death. Make sure someone can get at the money."

Kelly said advancement payment contracts may be attractive to those who have no relatives or friends to take care of their wishes. "Advance payment can also be used to draw down assets for Medicaid purposes."

To choose a funeral home, "Visit some funeral homes and find out which one feels comfortable, which meets your family needs best." He suggested that one's children should be supportive of the plan.

A recent survey showed that people choose a funeral home based on location, reputation, and the family's previous experience. An AARP survey shows that 10 to 12 percent more of us now take the time to shop for a funeral home.

Perhaps the biggest trend of all, Kelly said, was a new emphasis on families looking for personal, individual services. "More people want a celebration," he said, "and less of the traditional mourning."

The Crusader

I first heard Lisa Carlson on a radio talk show about funerals. The show was produced in New Hampshire, where the Senate was considering a bill to grant family members and designated agents the right to handle funeral details such as death records, body transportation, and burial permits. The existing statute reserved those tasks for licensed undertakers, which Carlson argued denied people a traditional and often therapeutic involvement in family funerals, as well as creating unfair funeral costs.

She'd been invited to appear on the show as head of the Funeral and Memorial Society Association of America and as author of Caring for the Dead, about do-it-yourself funeral procedures. She appeared with the head of the New Hampshire

The $1,500 Bouquet

Though the actual costs of a funeral vary widely depending on where the services are purchased, average funeral costs break down this way (and, like a wedding, can easily get way out of hand):

- Casket: $2,000
- Vault: $1,000.
- Small Burial Plot: $1,000
- Headstone: $1,000
- Embalming: $500
- Cremation: $1,000
- Urn: $500
- Church or Synagogue Honorarium: $50–$500
- Flowers: $500 (country) $1,500 (city)
- AVERAGE COST: $7,050–$9,000

Undertakers and Embalmers Association, and it was a feisty debate, with Carlson making a persuasive case for the new law, and the funeral director making predictable pitches for the benefits of his services. The funeral industry declined to take an official position on the statute, and the law passed.

Carlson talked about being compelled to have a do-it-yourself funeral for her first husband to save money, and about finding that the emotional benefits were even more valuable than the financial ones. Subsequent family deaths had been followed with homemade funerals. Carlson is a believer.

I told her I was interested in understanding why we'd inherited such a schizophrenic culture about funeral practices: lots of violence and death in our entertainment, but little stomach for the real thing. I wondered where her organization fit in. There'd been a few deaths in my hometown recently, and I'd heard from several survivors who wished they'd taken a more hands-on approach. In the end, they'd left it up to the professionals and felt vaguely unfulfilled, even shortchanged.

"Memorial societies have been the world's best-kept secret for years," she said. "They started back in the late 1930s after the Depression. A radical Unitarian minister in Seattle was appalled at the high cost of dying, when the industry was pushing embalming and manufactured caskets. He represented a group of people who went to a funeral director and said, 'We don't think a funeral should cost more than such and such, we want a simple exit, no frills. If we send all our members to you, will you agree to honor this price?' That was how the first urban memorial society started. It was not inconsistent with some of the thoughts behind the old burial co-ops in the agrarian Midwest and South. Each one has a slightly different flavor, but a similar concern. How do we prepare for the end of life without spending a lot of money?"

To get to our current situation, she backtracks to pioneer America, when a group of women would come to the deceased's house and help with the laying out of the dead. Later, during the Victorian era, there would often be an elaborate laying out in the front parlor, with the body on display surrounded by fancy draperies. But as we became a more dispersed society, there wasn't room or time to lay Grandma out in the parlor anymore. We were spreading out, and the funeral moved from the family home to the undertaker's "home."

"But the public have been willing victims in this," Carlson points out. "There's a lot of superstitious thinking, 'If we talk about it, it might happen.' Or, 'I don't want to seem morbid.' I know my grandmother tried to talk to me about her funeral thoughts when I was in my 20s and I was very uncomfortable. I said, 'Oh Grammy, you're not going to die.' I wouldn't let her talk about it and she didn't insist. That was the sad thing. In hindsight I wish she had insisted."

In 1987, Lisa published her first book, Caring for Your Own Dead (followed 10 years later by Caring for the Dead: Your Final Act Of Love). Essentially a funeral "how-to" guide, it was inspired by a series of family deaths during the 1980s, beginning with the suicide of her husband. With two young children and next to nothing in the bank, she was forced to scrutinize every item in the funeral plan, and wound up putting together a homemade version, including transport of the body to the crematory. As she discovered, it wasn't the financial savings that proved most significant.

"That the total cost would now be under $200 had become secondary," she wrote. "I needed to be a part of John's death, as I was of his life. If I had had the money, I would have lost that—given that away—in a moment of grief and confusion."

The book presented detailed information on legal and hygienic requirements in every state, and an argument for getting involved in family funerals. People began calling her for help, not only survivors and self-planners, but also a chapter of the Funeral and Memorial Society of America (FAMSA, recently renamed the Funeral Consumer's Alliance). Carlson began by improving the visibility of the organization. She was profiled in a cover story in U.S. News and World Report headlined "Don't Die Before You Read This". She got mentions in Ann Landers, Dear Abby and appeared twice on Donahue. "After Dear Abby and Ann Landers, we got 30,000 pieces of mail. They had to pull in volunteers to handle it all."

Members of FCA pay a one-time $25 fee. "The active societies have done a funeral-price survey in their area and/or negotiated a discount for certain cooperating funeral homes. Definitely as a member you're going to get the cheapest funeral around. It saves hundreds of dollars. The societies have reciprocal arrangements, so if you die away from home there's a good chance you'll be eligible to use a cooperating funeral home wherever you are." The organization consists of 120 societies across the country, totaling about 500,000 members. Seattle has almost 100,000 members and a paid staff, whereas some local societies struggle with a volunteer staff, administered from someone's kitchen table.

"Anyone can get behind a consumer's right to choose," Lisa says, recalling a speech she gave to the alliance. "I told them, If the industry did not manipulate the grieving, did not hide the low-cost caskets, did not dominate the funeral boards with self-serving regulations, did not limit who could sell caskets or in what states you could care for your own dead, there would be

no need for our organization. But we have an obligation to protect the public at large, not just our members." The speech absolutely electrified the whole audience. "There was suddenly a new reason to do what we're doing."

"The conscientious, sensitive funeral director will help educate you," she says. "On the other hand, they will also very willingly let you turn it over to them, and they will plan a more expensive (funeral). The problem is that there are too many undertakers who expect full-time pay for part-time work. Years ago it was a sideline. Now they crank the prices up to charge you waiting-around-until-you-die time. The majority of funeral homes in Vermont are doing 50 calls a year. One a week. When you're a funeral home and you're sweating your mortgage, it's a situation that invites abuse."

She recounts several recent scandals in Vermont involving funeral directors convicted of fraud. One was discovered selling expensive caskets and then using cheap models for the burial; bodies were even piled up in his garage. Another coerced grieving survivors into buying unwanted services. Pre-need funds disappeared after one undertaker went bankrupt. "In any other business, when you've got too many suppliers the prices go down. In this business, they go up. Figure that."

Financial pressures have made many of the independent funeral homes easy picking for corporate buyouts, which triggers alarms for Carlson. "We know from reports that the manipulative sales tactics of these giant chains are pretty despicable. All they really care about is the stockholders, not the neighborhood family." She told me about a woman who belonged to a memorial society in the Midwest. After her death, it turned out that the cooperating funeral home had been bought out by SCI. They tried to add $250 to the previously contracted fee, and when the woman's son objected, they wouldn't release the ashes. The son called Carlson.

"He was rip-&S#@," she recalls. "He faxed me his material and I FedExed it to the FTC. Three days, and I got an opinion back. I never got an opinion so fast: It's illegal."

Despite these horror stories, Carlson foresees a positive future for consumers.

"Look at the generation that demanded we recycle. Many of them wrote their own wedding vows. They demanded the right to natural childbirth and home schooling. I think they are going to take charge of their funeral experience, just the way you're taking charge."

The phone rings and it's time for Carlson to do a talk show with a radio station in San Antonio. She's impressive, even awe-inspiring, this woman who's wrestling with life's biggest bummer. Some have criticized her for being hot-tempered, pushy, inflexible. But if that's what it takes to wake a culture in denial, so be it.

I thank her, feeling more resolute than when I arrived, but glad to be heading home.

Adapted from Round Trip to Deadsville, by Tim Matson. [C] 2000 Tim Matson, published in the U.S. by Chelsea Green Publishing Co., White River Junction, Vermont, or call MOTHER'S Bookshelf at (800) 888-9098.

TOMBSTONES, TOMBS & GOING CONCERNS

Your Final Act of Love ($29.95)
by Lisa Carlson
Upper Access, Inc.
PO Box 457
85 Upper Access Road
Hinesburg, VT 05461
802-482-2988
www.upperaccess.com
Comprehensive funeral information for the lay person. In addition to the do-it-yourself information, it covers cemetery and crematory laws and regulations and much more.

I Died Laughing ($8.75)
by Lisa Carlson
Upper Access, Inc. (see above address)
A genre bending approach to death that blends humor with useful information about everything from old age to living wills and cremation, and funeral rites and rights.

Dealing Creatively with Death ($14.95)
by Ernest Morgan
Upper Access, Inc. (see address above)
A small encyclopedia on death related problems, including death education, hospice, bereavement, simple burial and cremation.

Round Trip to Deadsville ($22.95)
by Tim Matson
Chelsea Green Publishing Company
PO Box 428
White River Junction, VT 05001
802-295-6300
www.chelseagreen.com
Tim Matson takes a wry, vaguely suspicious and whirlwind tour of the business of death.

FUNERAL CONSUMERS ALLIANCE
PO Box 10
Hinesburg, VT 05461
800-765-0107
www.funerals.org
A national advocacy organization with more than 120 local societies and alliances. All are nonsectarian nonprofit organizations.

AMERICAN ASSOCIATION FOR RETIRED PERSONS (AARP)
601 E Street, NW
Washington, DC 20049
800-424-3410
www.aarp.org
National organization offering free reports on many funeral related issues.

NATIONAL FUNERAL DIRECTORS ASSOCIATION
11121 W. Oklahoma Avenue
Milwaukee, WI 53227
414-541-2500
Leading trade organization, providing literature, materials, and speakers on many aspects of funeral planning.

GREENFIELD COFFINS (in England)
Producers of cardboard coffins
www.greenfieldcoffins.com

NATURAL DEATH CARE PROJECT
Sebastapol, California
A model project offering education for personal and legal rights concerning home or family directed funerals and final disposition.
www.naturaldeathcare.org

RAMSEY CREEK RESERVE
Ramsey Creek, South Carolina
They have a number of nature preserves where burial sites are located. An alternative to the traditional cemetery.
www.memorialecosystems.com

TRAPPIST CASKETS
Near Dubuque, Iowa
Sam Mulgrew, general manager
888-433-6934
The monastery is located on the second largest forest preserve in Iowa. The wood used in the production of the caskets is harvested from their own trees.
www.trappistcaskets.com

FANCY COFFINS TO MAKE YOURSELF
By Dale L. Power
Schiffer Publishing, Ltd.
ISBN: 0764312499
Detailed instructions and color photos provided to help guide you step by step toward crafting your own casket. One of the very few books of its kind.

An Unexpected Kind Of Family Foresight

When my father began to make plans for his own funeral,
my mother didn't object—she joined in.

By Ellen Ficklen

I know it sounds odd. But one of the most remarkable—and one of the kindest—gifts my father gave me was to plan the details of his own funeral service.

As a longtime Presbyterian minister, my father was a funeral expert of sorts. During his more than 35 years in the ministry he'd become well acquainted with death and with grieving survivors. He'd spent much of his professional time in hospitals, at funeral homes and services, and in houses that suddenly felt empty. Also, he'd had his own near-death experiences, having had a series of heart attacks.

Even so, his call to me at work was startling. He was phoning from home in northwest Washington, D.C., and asked if I could take off a couple of hours, go with him and my mother to a funeral home he'd selected and discuss plans for his funeral.

As a young man in a dark suit talked with my father, my mother and me at the funeral home, I was surprised to learn how many details my father had already thought about. He wanted the casket open before the service ("In case anyone wonders if I'm really in there")—but he wanted it closed once the service began. I always knew that he liked carnations, but when he said he wanted a "blanket of red carnations" draped over his closed casket, I was startled.

Who knew he had floral styling preferences?

The biggest surprise was that my father, the minister, didn't want his funeral held in a church. He wanted it in the funeral home's chapel: as an administrator for the Presbyterian churches in the region, he didn't want to seem to play favorites by singling out a specific church for his funeral. Considerate man that he was, he also wanted to make sure that there would be plenty of parking spaces—the generous parking lot was one of the reasons he'd chosen this funeral home.

My parents had always had a warm relationship, and spent the afternoon in a remarkably unsomber mood. My mom got the funeral-home rep loosened up and smiling—and she entered into the day's plan-ahead spirit, selecting her own funeral's details. When my dad picked the hymns he wanted sung at his service, my mom picked one for her own: "O God, Our Help in Ages Past." As a geologist and a teacher, she liked its imagery.

Then the rep led us into what I think of as the Casket Room. My parents had always said that when the time came, just put 'em in plain pine boxes and bury 'em. No problem, right? Ha! It seems that pine boxes aren't that common. Also, the rep explained, if a body is going to be transported to a distant cemetery (both

my parents wanted to be taken to the same country cemetery in New York's Hudson Valley, close to where my mom grew up), a simple box is considered a health risk.

So my father asked to see the least expensive casket instead. With a thoughtful expression, he reached inside it and gave the fabric lining a feel. "This feels chintzy—it's scratchy," he said. Fabric texture always had mattered to my dad, I realized. "What's the next one up in price?" He reached into casket No. 2 and felt its lining. "That's fine," he said. "I'll have the same," said Mom.

Wandering around this strange display room, I became fascinated by the top-of-the-line casket. It was a work of art, carved of rosewood and lined with silk—all destined, of course, to be buried under dirt. My father and mother joined me, and together we stared at this masterpiece.

"Who buys this kind of casket?" I asked.

"People who are very wealthy," our now-relaxed Casket Room guide responded. Then he added, "Or people who are feeling guilty. Buying this makes them feel less guilty. And I sell it to them."

A year later my dad had his final heart attack. Over the next few days my mom, my sisters and I came to appreciate his thoughtful planning. Late on the night he died I called the funeral home we'd visited. I told them that my dad's plan was on file, and the name of the hospital where they could pick up his body.

While the family was staggering around and generally trying to cope, the chapel was readied, the casket with the right lining (not, thank God, the chintzy, scratchy one) was prepared, a blanket of red carnations was ordered. My mom called my father's successor, who flew back from vacation to give the eulogy. Finally, and right on schedule, cars full of mourners began to fill the generous-size parking lot.

Years later, as my mother disappeared into the silence of Alzheimer's, we already knew what kind of funeral she wanted—the same one she'd planned the day my father planned his. In the country cemetery where my mother rejoined my father, family and friends gathered. It was windy. Thunderclouds scudded by overhead, and hawks swooped and circled. My mom's brother (also a minister) conducted the service. And then we sang the hymn she'd chosen so long ago—"O God, Our Help in Ages Past." We were doing exactly what we knew she wanted done.

Way to go, Mom and Dad. And thanks.

_____

FICKLEN *lives in Washington, D.C.*

Working With Death Was No Way to Live

I handled even the most morbid responsibilities with aplomb until the day I realized I could be next

BY LAURA BENNETT-KIMBLE.

When I was 24, I took a clerical job in a small-town funeral home. Adrift in unformed career aspirations, I thought working in an industry cloaked in mystery would be interesting and kind of cool. I liked the idea of helping people in such an intimate, dramatic situation. And because my role would be a professional one, I thought I would somehow be protected from feeling grief.

SIX FEET UNDER: I no longer gave any thought to hanging my coat in a closet half-filled with cardboard boxes holding unclaimed remains.

On my first day I took a call from a nursing home where a patient had expired. Nervously, I wrote down the details and paged the on-call funeral director. But as the days passed and I was drafted for an increasing number of bizarre chores, I realized I was going to function as much more than a secretary.

Most of my time was spent alone in that empty, quiet building, but when we were busy, I rushed around doing things I'd never imagined I could. I painted cold fingernails and lips a bright, cheerful pink. I helped embalmers dress bodies that flopped like rag dolls. After a few weeks I no longer gave any thought to hanging my coat in a closet half-filled with cardboard boxes holding unclaimed remains. I even got used to the peculiar smell of a funeral home, that oddly sweet combination of flowers, brewing coffee and embalming fluids.

Morbid? You bet. But as people remarked upon learning my occupation, "Well, I guess someone's got to do it." For a time I thought that someone was me. My family tree is filled with deeply caring yet reserved relatives. Thanks to this genetic taciturnity, I was well equipped to be a funeral-home worker. Honest sympathy and emotional distance are what keep you sane in that industry, and I had both. I learned how to harness that stoicism in order to get the job done, whether I was greeting dazed parents who'd just lost a baby or fastening a bra on the large, uncooperative body of an acquaintance's mother.

I never cried on the job, although the lone female funeral director in the company showed me it was all right to do so. She didn't seem to fear death or the emotions it evoked in bereaved survivors or in herself, and admitted to crying with the family of a girl who'd been killed when she swerved her car to miss a dog. "They need to cry," she noted as the family, smiling at her through their tears, left the building. "Scientific evidence shows tears release built-up toxins," she'd often say, "so cry your eyes out!"

Perhaps the toxins built up in me as the years progressed. I gradually became irritated when the funeral directors made golf plans and read People magazine in the office while real people grieved in the nearby chapel. But I developed a callous attitude myself. I swelled with frustration when a family tried to remember the spelling of their mother's sister's last name for an obituary. I became impatient with poky griev-ers. I wanted to shout, "Just get over it!" to people quite correctly dwell-ing on death.

In my young life, death had al-ways happened to someone else, and it seemed—dare I say it?—dramatic and exciting. But the more I saw how randomly death struck, the more I realized how vulnerable we all are.

One morning on the way to work I noticed flashing lights and rescue vehicles. As I drove past them, I saw the gnarled tangle of a sports car im-bedded in an overpass support. When I got to the office, I took the call from the hospital. The business-man's body, taken to the hospital morgue for inspection by the county medical examiner, was ready for re-moval. The subsequent funeral ser-vices weren't anything unusual, but I remember watching the new widow and her children with a pen-etrating eye. This man had been alive just minutes before I came along that highway, probably drink-ing coffee from a travel mug and mapping out his day on a cell phone. But suddenly his day's agenda was erased, and he'd become an inani-mate component in the funeral-home process.

My association with his transfor-mation scared me. I'd been involved with enough deaths by this time to have a certain level of comfort with the work at the funeral home, but I was not at all comfortable witness-ing the scene of death. The novelty of my job lost its appeal, and the satis-faction of assisting a family through one of its darkest moments disap-peared. I no longer felt like an out-sider, because now I knew I wasn't. I, too, could be snuffed out like a match. Sickened, I recoiled from the process of postmortem.

The local hardware-store owner once told me, "You've got to have a leather a—to do that kind of work." After three years, I finally accepted that I didn't. I needed to release my pent-up emotions and reclaim my humanity. I quit my job and spent the summer with friends and family before going back to college. Death, of course, didn't take a holiday. It had a job to do. But it was going to do it without my help.

BENNETT-KIMBLE lives in Grand Rap-ids, Mich.

Therapist Equates Owner Grief to Family Member Loss

Human-Animal Bond Impacts Physical, Mental Health: Experts Push Pet Bereavement Mainstream

This article compares human and companion-pet grief and gives practical suggestions help to deal with pet loss.

By Jennifer Fiala

Pet loss takes an emotional backseat to bereavement for a family member or friend.

While that's a typical stance among mental health professionals, it's often inaccurate, psychiatric forensic nurse Paul Clements claims.

The recent commentary "Support for Bereaved Owners of Pets" authored by Clements, Ph.D., RN, BC, Kathleen Benasuitti, MCAT, MPH, LPC, and Andy Carmone, MPH, RN, suggests that although society tends to trivialize bereavement of animals, grief surrounding pets missing or found dead often is severe. The article, published in *Perspectives of Psychiatric Care*, indicates pet-related grief is an area of mental healthcare the counseling profession and medical insurance companies largely ignore.

"My research comes from my work as a therapist dealing with sudden traumatic death and violent loss," Clements says. "The victims aren't always human. Grief is grief. I can say that how family members respond to missing children who are found dead and the responses of people dealing with the death of their animals are not much different."

Lack of literature

While it's clear owners and their pets have become increasingly attached, this fact has yet to be integrated into widespread protocols for grief and bereavement, the article says. The media, psychiatrists and veterinarians offer anecdotal reports of grief reactions following the death or disappearance of pets, yet there is a paucity of research on reactions related to pet deaths and even less literature on the topic, Clements says.

"Most of the literature we found came from the veterinary profession, not the therapeutic arena," he says. "This points directly to society's lack of understanding."

Flashback risks

If ignored, grief can become latent and re-emerge years after a pet's death when prompted by family member's death or other traumatic event, Clements says.

"I'm hearing about this from physicians and counselors," he says. "Children especially get disrupted when another traumatic situation arises and they start to bring up memories of pets that have died or were found dead. Child psychologists are seeing more and more of this."

Such flashbacks, he says, are signs of post-traumatic stress disorder brought on by unresolved feelings of depression and anxiety.

"Pets are a parallel for the issue of life or death for kids," Clements says. "Their deaths can be disturbing and prompt tremendous guilt."

The veterinarian's role

The first step to supporting bereaved owners is providing a foundation of acceptance for experiencing grief related to the loss of an animal. Much can be done to increase sensitivity when it comes to the death of a beloved pet, such as offering loss-related literature and a quiet room in the veterinary clinic for owners to grieve. This gives the bereaved license to explore the pet's emotional significance and the bond they shared, thereby starting some of the difficult work that comes with integrating a loss, Clements says.

Normalization is of utmost importance in establishing a therapeutic relationship with a bereaved pet owner, he adds. Minimizing the severity of the loss because the family member is an animal can be catastrophic and damaging, possibly derailing grief and adaptive coping, the commentary says.

Tips to accepting, adapting to pet loss

Practitioners can suggest a numberof ways clients can productively deal with grief, says Paul Clements, a psychiatric forensic nurse at the University of New Mexico.

- Obtain a wish list from a local animal shelter and throw a party asking friends and family to bring at least one item on the list. Donate these items to the shelter in memory of your pet.
- Plant a tree or flower garden in memory of the deceased pet as a living memorial to the animal.
- Write a letter expressing not only feelings related to the loss, but also the thoughts and feelings related to life with the beloved companion, including stories, moments the pet understood when no one else did, the times of sadness and pain, the times the pet simply sat quietly and lovingly by one's side, the times when the pet knew the owner was sick and nursed him/her back to health. This is also an opportunity to express gratitude for the pet.
- Write in stream-of-consciousness style about your life with the pet. Allow unedited, uncensored expression.
- Before going to sleep at night, admire a photograph of the pet and ask for a dream in which to say a proper farewell. Record your dreams until you've experienced one that is satisfying.
- If inclined toward group work, join a support group for humans coping with animal loss.
- Hold a memorial for the pet and invite the animal friends of the deceased. Feed them all special food to mark the occasion.
- Gather memories of the animal from other humans in the pet's life, and create a scrapbook with photos and stories.

Mourning the loss of a pet; coping strategies to help ease your grief and celebrate their memory

Arden Moore

For 21 years, Snickle, a tabby cat, shared her life with Diane and Dan Karella of Westminster, CA. A year ago, she suffered a stroke and hearing loss. When she began having trouble walking, acting confused, and being in pain, the Karellas had her euthanized by their veterinarian last September. "As hard as it was for us, we knew that the best thing we could do to ease her suffering was to have her put down," says Diane.

That didn't make saying goodbye any easier though. "We had Snickle since she was a 6-week-old kitten," says Diane. "Dan was so devastated when she died that he had to put her photo facedown on the bedroom dresser for about a month."

When a pet dies, whether suddenly or after a lingering illness, you may find yourself awkwardly apologizing to others for your sudden bursts of tears or unshakable blue moods. You may silently admonish yourself for not being able to save your beloved companion's life. You may vow to "never again get another dog or cat." After all, you reason, why endure another painful loss?

Time spent grieving isn't self-indulgent; it helps you heal.

All of these emotion-ridden actions and attitudes are part of the normal grief process, say pet-bereavement counselors. As more of us come to regard our dog, cat, or other pet as a valued member of the family, its death takes a greater personal toll on us.

Grief and Healing

"No matter how it happens, we are never ready emotionally for a beloved pet's death," says Wallace Sife, PhD, a clinical psychologist and founder of the Association for Pet Loss and Bereavement in New York City. "Many of us bond with our pets as if they were our children, but we can't protect them from illness or death. When Edel Meister, my miniature dachshund, died 14 years ago, I became an emotional basket case despite my professional training and experience. But then I perceived it as a potential turning point and soon became determined to ded-

icate my life to helping others go through the grieving and healing process."

The healthiest way to honor your pet's memory is to recognize that you need to grieve before you can heal, says Lorri Greene, PhD, a licensed psychologist who facilitates pet-loss support groups for the San Diego County Pet Bereavement Program in conjunction with the San Diego Humane Society. Dr. Greene says that most pet owners go through a grieving process that includes emotions ranging from denial to anger to depression and back again before an ultimate acceptance of their loss. "It may take you days, weeks, or even months to go through this process, and not everyone goes through it in a linear fashion," says Dr. Greene. "It is common to bounce back and forth from feeling anger to, say, feeling depressed."

And don't overlook the clout that guilt may deliver. "If you must euthanize your pet because you can't afford expensive treatments, or your dog slipped out your door and got hit and killed by a car, you may feel like a failure," says Dr. Greene.

10 Tips for Coping

Our experts offer these strategies to help you recover from the death of a pet.

1. Give yourself permission to grieve. Denying these natural emotions can elevate stress and physical fatigue and can even suppress healing.
2. Seek out friends and family members who share your compassion for animals. Focus more on their good intentions and not necessarily their words.
3. Dismiss and ignore comments from individuals who may trivialize your loss. "Those who have never had a pet are more likely to be judgmental or critical of your grieving," says Dr. Sife.
4. Recognize that your departed pet is one of a kind who can never be replaced. "When you are ready to have a new pet, embrace him for his uniqueness and avoid comparing him with previous pets," says Dr. Greene.
5. Treat yourself well. Eat nutritious meals, and get ample sleep and exercise.

6. Fight through blue moods by exercising. Physical activity helps to raise endorphins and other feel-good hormones in your body. Take longer walks, for example, in scenic areas.

7. Never say "Never again." Avoid declarations such as "I will never get another pet." These statements hinder healing.

8. Ritualize the pet's death through a ceremony or memorial service. "These are very therapeutic," says Dr. Sife. "But perhaps the greatest way to honor the memory of your pet is to learn how to become a better person as a result of having him in your life."

9. Spend time recalling happy memories of times that you shared with your pet. When the Karellas lost Snickle, they spent the rest of that day sitting on the back porch, a favorite place for Snickle, and sharing tearful embraces and fond memories of their long-living feline friend. Over the weeks that followed, sharing similar memories and moments helped the Karellas come to terms with the loss in a gentle and loving way.

10. Consider writing a letter to and from your departed pet. "The human brain can suppress and repress a lot of thoughts, and this letter-writing technique is a way to bring out creative thoughts. Seeing these words printed on a page can help in your bereavement process," says Dr. Greene.

Helping Others Heal

Don't forget the feelings of others affected by the pet's death, especially children and other pets. Say "died," not "put to sleep," when describing a pet's death to children under 14.

"A child may need an operation and hear the doctor tell him that he will 'put him to sleep,' and that may unduly frighten the child," says Dr. Greene. "Also, don't say 'God loved Fluffy so much that he brought him to heaven.' Avoid euphemisms; go with honesty."

If it's possible, let other pets sniff and inspect the body of the dead pet, says Dr. Sife, author of The Loss of a Pet (Howell Book House, 1998). "Animals view death as a natural process like birth; letting them sniff the body lets them know for sure what has happened," he says. "And keep their routines as normal as possible."

Saying goodbye to a loyal pet is one of life's hardest tasks, but Dr. Greene reminds us, "The definition of euthanize means a painless death to end physical suffering in an animal friend. It is truly the last gift we can give them."

For More Help

Check with your vet or animal shelter to find a pet-loss support group, or contact the Association of Pet Loss and Bereavement at (718) 382-0690. For a link to their Web site, go to www.prevention.com/links.

Pet expert Arden Moore is the award-winning author of The Kitten Owner's Manual and Real Food for Dogs (both Storey Books, 2001) and a graduate of The Humane Society of the United States's "Pets for Life" national companion-animal training program.

UNIT 6

Bereavement

Unit Selections

Key Points to Consider

- Discuss how the seven stages of grieving over death can also be applied to losses through divorce, moving from one place to another or the amputation of a limb (arm or leg). What is the relationship between time and the feelings of grief experienced within the bereavement process?

- Describe the four necessary tasks of mourning. What are some of the practical steps one can take in accomplishing each of these tasks? How can one assist friends in bereavement?

- What are the special problems encountered in the death of a child and in a prenatal death? How can one assist friends in this special type of bereavement?

- How can one know if one is experiencing "normal" bereavement or "abnormal" bereavement? What are some of the signs of aberrant bereavement? What could you do to assist people experiencing abnormal grief symptoms?

- Provide a list of "do's" and "don'ts" for dealing with children who have experienced a death.

DUSHKIN ONLINE **Links: www.dushkin.com/online/**
These sites are annotated in the World Wide Web pages.

Bereaved Families of Ontario Support Center
http://www.bereavedfamilies.net/
The Compassionate Friends
http://www.compassionatefriends.org
GriefNet
http://rivendell.org
Practical Grief Resources
http://www.indiana.edu/~famlygrf/sitemap.html
Widow Net
http://www.fortnet.org/WidowNet/

In American society many act as if the process of bereavement is completed with the culmination of public mourning related to the funeral or memorial service and the final disposition of the dead. For those in the process of grieving, the end of public mourning only serves to make the bereavement process a more individualized, subjective, and private experience. Private mourning of loss for most people, while more intense at its beginning, continues throughout their lifetime. The nature and intensity of this experience is influenced by the relationship of the mourner to the deceased, the age of the mourner, and the social context in which bereavement takes place.

This unit on bereavement begins with two general articles on the bereavement process. The first article, by Michael Leming and George Dickinson, describes and discusses the active coping strategies related to the bereavement process, disenfranchised grief, and the four tasks of bereavement. The second article, by Kenneth Doka, provides assistance for caregivers in dealing with the needs of bereaved survivors who cannot ac-

knowledge their grief publicly. Next, an article by Charles Corr enhances and broadens the concept of disenfranchised grief in significant ways and explains that there are aspects of most losses that are indeed disenfranchised, and the personal account by Mickie Mashburn gives an illustration of disenfranchised grief for a bereaved lesbian partner.

The article by Therese Rando ("The Increasing Prevalence of Complicated Mourning") illustrates the principles described by Leming and Dickinson by providing a critique of America's health care industry for its lack of involvement in the post-death grieving experience. These articles discuss many different types of death and the respective influences upon the bereaved while suggesting strategies for actively coping with grief. This article is followed by an article which attempts to help grievers through the dying process and at difficult holiday times. The remaining article of this unit focuses upon bereavement and coping strategies employed by a special population of grievers—children.

The Grieving Process

Michael R. Leming

St. Olaf College

George E. Dickinson

College of Charleston

Grief is a very powerful emotion that is often triggered or stimulated by death. Thomas Attig makes an important distinction between grief and the grieving process. Although grief is an emotion that engenders feelings of helplessness and passivity, the process of grieving is a more complex coping process that presents challenges and opportunities for the griever and requires energy to be invested, tasks to be undertaken, and choices to be made (Attig, 1991, p. 387).

Most people believe that grieving is a diseaselike and debilitating process that renders the individual passive and helpless. According to Attig (1991, p. 389):

> It is misleading and dangerous to mistake grief for the whole of the experience of the bereaved. It is misleading because the experience is far more complex, entailing diverse emotional, physical, intellectual, spiritual, and social impacts. It is dangerous because it is precisely this aspect of the experience of the bereaved that is potentially the most frustrating and debilitating.

Death ascribes to the griever a passive social position in the bereavement role. Grief is an emotion over which the individual has no control. However, understanding that grieving is an active coping process can restore to the griever a sense of autonomy in which the process is permeated with choice and there are many areas over which the griever does have some control....

Coping With Grief

The grieving process, like the dying process, is essentially a series of behaviors and attitudes related to coping with the stressful situation of changing the status of a relationship.... Many have attempted to understand coping with dying as a series of universal, mutually exclusive, and linear stages. However, because most will acknowledge that not all people will progress through the stages in the same manner, we will list a number of coping strategies used as people attempt to resolve the pain caused by the loss of a significant relationship.

Robert Kavanaugh (1972) identifies the following seven behaviors and feelings as part of the coping process: shock and denial, disorganization, volatile emotions, guilt, loss and loneliness, relief, and reestablishment. It is not difficult to see similarities between these behaviors and Kübler-Ross's five stages (denial, anger, bargaining, depression, and acceptance) of the dying process. According to Kavanaugh (1972, p. 23), "these seven stages do not subscribe to the logic of the head as much as to the irrational tugs of the heart—the logic of need and permission."

SHOCK AND DENIAL

Even when a significant other is expected to die, at the time of death there is often a sense in which the death is not real. For most of us our first response is, "No, this can't be true." With time our experience of shock diminishes, but we find new ways to deny the reality of death.

Some believe that denial is dysfunctional behavior for those in bereavement. However, denial not only is a common experience among the newly bereaved, but also serves positive functions in the process of adaptation. The main function of denial is to provide the bereaved with a "temporary safe place" from the ugly realities of a social world that offers only loneliness and pain.

With time the meaning of loss tends to expand, and it may be impossible for one to deal with all of the social meanings of death at once. For example, if my wife dies, not only do I lose my spouse, but also I lose my best friend, my sexual partner, the mother of my children, a source of income, the person who writes the Christmas cards, and so on. Denial can protect me from some of the magnitude of this social loss, which may be unbearable at one point in time. With denial, I can work through different aspects of my loss over time.

DISORGANIZATION

Disorganization is that stage in the bereavement process in which one may feel totally out of touch with the reality of everyday life. Some go through the 3-day time period just prior to the funeral as if on "automatic pilot" or "in a daze." Nothing normal "makes sense," and they may feel that life has no inherent meaning. For some, death is perceived as preferable to life, which appears to be devoid of meaning.

This emotional response is also a normal experience for the newly bereaved. Confusion is normal for those whose social world has been disorganized through death. When my father died, my mother lost not only all of those things that one loses with a death of a spouse, but also her caregiving role—a social role and master status that had defined her identity in the 5 years that my father lived with cancer. It is only natural to experience confusion and social disorganization when one's social identity has been destroyed.

VOLATILE REACTIONS

Whenever one's identity and social order face the possibility of destruction, there is a natural tendency to feel angry, frustrated, helpless, and/or hurt. The volatile reactions of terror, hatred, resentment, and jealousy are often experienced as emotional manifestations of these feelings. Grieving humans are sometimes more successful at masking their feelings in socially acceptable behaviors than other animals, whose instincts cause them to go into a fit of rage when their order is threatened by external forces. However apparently dissimilar, the internal emotional experience is similar.

In working with bereaved persons over the past 15 years, I have observed that the following become objects of volatile grief reactions: God, medical personnel, funeral directors, other family members, in-laws, friends who have not experienced death in their families, and/or even the person who has died. I have always found it interesting to watch mild-mannered individuals transformed into raging and resentful persons when grieving. Some of these people have experienced physical symptoms such as migraine headaches, ulcers, neuropathy, and colitis as a result of living with these intense emotions.

GUILT

Guilt is similar to the emotional reactions discussed earlier. Guilt is anger and resentment turned in on oneself and often results in self-deprecation and depression. It typically manifests itself in statements like "If only I had… ," "I should have… ,"

"I could have done it differently… ," and "Maybe I did the wrong thing." Guilt is a normal part of the bereavement process.

From a sociological perspective, guilt can become a social mechanism to resolve the **dissonance** that people feel when unable to explain why someone else's loved one has died. Rather than view death as something that can happen at any time to anyone, people can **blame the victim** of bereavement and believe that the victim of bereavement was in some way responsible for the death—"If he had been a better parent, the child might not have been hit by the car," or "If I had been married to him I might also have committed suicide," or "No wonder he died of a heart attack, her cooking would give anyone high cholesterol." Therefore, bereaved persons are sometimes encouraged to feel guilt because they are subtly sanctioned by others' reactions.

LOSS AND LONELINESS

As we discussed earlier, loss and loneliness are the other side of denial. Their full sense never becomes obvious at once; rather, each day without the deceased helps us to recognize how much we needed and depended upon those persons. Social situations in which we expected them always to be present seem different now that they are gone. Holiday celebrations are also diminished by their absence. In fact, for some, most of life takes on a "something's missing" feeling. This feeling was captured in the 1960s love song "End of the World."

> Why does the world go on turning?
> Why must the sea rush to shore?
> Don't they know it's the end of the world
> 'Cause you don't love me anymore?

Loss and loneliness are often transformed into depression and sadness fed by feelings of self-pity. According to Kavanaugh (1972, p. 118), this effect is magnified by the fact that the dead loved one grows out of focus in memory—"an elf becomes a giant, a sinner becomes a saint because the grieving heart needs giants and saints to fill an expanding void." Even a formerly undesirable spouse, such as an alcoholic, is missed in a way that few can understand unless their own hearts are involved. This is a time in the grieving process when anybody is better than nobody and being alone only adds to the curse of loss and loneliness (Kavanaugh, 1972, p. 118).

Those who try to escape this experience will either turn to denial in an attempt to reject their feelings of loss or try to find surrogates—new friends at a bar, a quick remarriage, or a new pet. This escape can never be permanent, however, because loss and loneliness are a necessary part of the bereavement experience. According to Kavanaugh (1972, p. 119), the "ultimate goal in conquering loneliness" is to build a new independence or to find a new and equally viable relationship.

RELIEF

The experience of relief in the midst of the bereavement process may seem odd for some and add to their feelings of guilt. My mother found relief in the fact that my father's battle with cancer had ended, even though this end provided her with new problems. I have observed a friend's relief 6 months after her husband died. This older friend of mine was the wife of a minister, and her whole life before he died was his ministry. With time, as she built a new world of social involvements and relationships of which he was not a part, she discovered a new independent person in herself whom she perceived was a better person than she had ever been.

Although relief can give rise to feelings of guilt, like denial, it can also be experienced as a "safe place" from the pain, loss, and loneliness that are endured when one is grieving. According to Kavanaugh (1972, p. 121):

> The feeling of relief does not imply any criticism for the love we lost. Instead, it is a reflection of our need for ever deeper love, our quest for someone or something always better, our search for the infinite, that best and perfect love religious people name as God.

REESTABLISHMENT

As one moves toward reestablishment of a life without the deceased, it is obvious that the process involves extensive adjustment and time, especially if the relationship was meaningful. It is likely that one may have feelings of loneliness, guilt, and disorganization at the same time and that just when one may experience a sense of relief something will happen to trigger a denial of the death. What facilitates bereavement and adjustment is fully experiencing each of these feelings as normal and realizing that it is hope (holding the grieving person together in fantasy at first) that will provide the promise of a new life filled with order, purpose, and meaning.

Reestablishment never occurs all at once. Rather, it is a goal that one realizes has been achieved long after it has occurred. In some ways it is similar to Dorothy's realization at the end of *The Wizard of Oz*—she had always possessed the magic that could return her to Kansas. And, like Dorothy, we have to experience our loss before we really appreciate the joy of investing our lives again in new relationships.

The Four Tasks of Mourning

In 1982 J. William Worden published *Grief Counseling and Grief Therapy*, which summarized the research conclusions of a National Institutes of Health study called the Omega Project (occasionally referred to as the Harvard Bereavement Study). Two of the more significant findings of this research, displaying the active nature of the grieving process, are that mourning is necessary for all persons who have experienced a loss through death and that four tasks of mourning must be accomplished before mourning can be completed and reestablishment can take place.

According to Worden (1982, p. 10), unfinished grief tasks can impair further growth and development of the individual. Furthermore, the necessity of these tasks suggests that those in bereavement must attend to "grief work" because successful

grief resolution is not automatic, as Kavanaugh's (1972) stages might imply. Each bereaved person must accomplish four necessary tasks: (a) accept the reality of the loss, (b) experience the pain of grief (c) adjust to an environment in which the deceased is missing, and (d) withdraw emotional energy and reinvest it in another relationship (Worden, 1982).

ACCEPT THE REALITY OF THE LOSS

Especially in situations when death is unexpected and/or the deceased lived far away, it is difficult to conceptualize the reality of the loss. The first task of mourning is to overcome the natural denial response and realize that the person is dead and will not return.

Bereaved persons can facilitate the actualization of death in many ways. The traditional ways are to view the body, attend the funeral and committal services, and visit the place of final disposition. The following is a partial list of additional activities that can assist in making death real for grieving persons.

1. View the body at the place of death before preparation by the funeral director.
2. Talk about the deceased and the circumstances surrounding the death.
3. View photographs and personal effects of the deceased.
4. Distribute the possessions of the deceased among relatives and friends.

EXPERIENCE THE PAIN OF GRIEF

Part of coming to grips with the reality of death is experiencing the emotional and physical pain caused by the loss. Many people in the denial stage of grieving attempt to avoid pain by choosing to reject the emotions and feelings that they are experiencing. Some do this by avoiding places and circumstances that remind them of the deceased. I know of one widow who quit playing golf and quit eating at a particular restaurant because these were activities that she had enjoyed with her husband. Another widow found it extremely painful to be with her dead husband's twin, even though he and her sister-in-law were her most supportive friends.

J. William Worden (1982, pp. 13–14) cites the following case study to illustrate the performance of this task of mourning:

> One young woman minimized her loss by believing her brother was out of his dark place and into a better place after his suicide. This might have been true, but it kept her from feeling her intense anger at him for leaving her. In treatment, when she first allowed herself to feel anger, she said, "I'm angry with his behavior and not him!" Finally she was able to acknowledge this anger directly.

The problem with the avoidance strategy is that people cannot escape the pain associated with mourning. According to Bowlby (cited by Worden, 1982, p. 14), "Sooner or later, some of those who avoid all conscious grieving, break down—usually with some form of depression." Tears can afford cleansing for wounds created by loss, and fully experiencing the pain ultimately provides wonderful relief to those who suffer while eliminating long-term chronic grief.

ADJUST TO AN ENVIRONMENT IN WHICH THE DECEASED IS MISSING

The third task, practical in nature, requires the griever to take on some of the social roles performed by the deceased, or to find others who will. According to Worden (1982, p. 15), to abort this task is to become helpless by refusing to develop the skills necessary in daily living and by ultimately withdrawing from life.

I knew a woman who refused to adjust to the social environment in which she found herself after the death of her husband. He was her business partner, as well as her best and only friend. After 30 years of marriage, they had no children, and she had no close relatives. She had never learned to drive a car. Her entire social world had been controlled by her former husband. Three weeks after his funeral she went into the basement and committed suicide.

The alternative to withdrawing is assuming new social roles by taking on additional responsibilities. Extended families who always gathered at Grandma's house for Thanksgiving will be tempted to have a number of small Thanksgiving dinners after her death. The members of this family may believe that "no one can take Grandma's place." Although this may be true, members of the extended family will grieve better if someone else is willing to do Grandma's work, enabling the entire family to come together for Thanksgiving. Not to do so will cause double pain—the family will not gather, and Grandma will still be missed.

The final task of mourning is a difficult one for many because they feel disloyal or unfaithful in withdrawing emotional energy from their dead loved one. One of my family members once said that she could never love another man after her husband died. My twice-widowed aunt responded, "I once felt like that, but I now consider myself to be fortunate to have been married to two of the best men in the world."

Other people find themselves unable to reinvest in new relationships because they are unwilling to experience again the pain caused by loss. [A] quotation from John Brantner... provides perspective on this problem: "Only people who avoid love can avoid grief. The point is to learn from it and remain vulnerable to love."

However, those who are able to withdraw emotional energy and reinvest it in other relationships find the possibility of a newly established social life. Kavanaugh (1972, pp. 122–123) depicts this situation well with the following description.

> At this point fantasies fade into constructive efforts to reach out and build anew. The phone is answered more quickly, the door as well, and meetings seem important, invitations are treasured and any social gathering becomes an opportunity rather than a curse. Mementos of the past are put away for occasional family gatherings. New clothes and new places promise dreams instead of only fears. Old friends are important for encouragement and permission to rebuild one's life. New friends can offer realistic opportunities for coming out from under the grieving mantle. With newly acquired friends, one is not a widow, widower, or survivor—just a person. Life begins again at the point of new friendships. All the rest is of yesterday, buried, unimportant to the now and tomorrow.

Disenfranchised Grief

KENNETH J. DOKA

Introduction

Ever since the publication of Lindemann's classic article, "Symptomatology and Management of Acute Grief," the literature on the nature of grief and bereavement has been growing. In the few decades following this seminal study, there have been comprehensive studies of grief reactions, detailed descriptions of atypical manifestations of grief, theoretical and clinical treatments of grief reactions, and considerable research considering the myriad variables that affect grief. But most of this literature has concentrated on grief reactions in socially recognized and sanctioned roles: those of the parent, spouse, or child.

There are circumstances, however, in which a person experiences a sense of loss but does not have a socially recognized right, role, or capacity to grieve. In these cases, the grief is disenfranchised. The person suffers a loss but has little or no opportunity to mourn publicly.

Up until now, there has been little research touching directly on the phenomenon of disenfranchised grief. In her comprehensive review of grief reactions, Raphael notes the phenomenon:

> There may be other dyadic partnership relationships in adult life that show patterns similar to the conjugal ones, among them, the young couple intensely, even secretly, in love; the defacto relationships; the extramarital relationship; and the homosexual couple.... Less intimate partnerships of close friends, working mates, and business associates, may have similar patterns of grief and mourning.

Focusing on the issues, reactions, and problems in particular populations, a number of studies have noted special difficulties that these populations have in grieving. For example, Kelly and Kimmel, in studies of aging homosexuals, have discussed the unique problems of grief in such relationships. Similarly, studies of the reactions of significant others of AIDS victims have considered bereavement. Other studies have considered the special problems of unacknowledged grief in prenatal death, [the death of] ex-spouses, therapists' reactions to a client's suicide, and pet loss. Finally, studies of families of Alzheimer's victims and mentally retarded adults also have noted distinct difficulties of these populations in encountering varied losses which are often unrecognized by others.

Others have tried to draw parallels between related unacknowledged losses. For example, in a personal account, Horn compared her loss of a heterosexual lover with a friend's loss of a homosexual partner. Doka discussed the particular problems of loss in nontraditional relationships, such as extramarital affairs, homosexual relationships, and cohabiting couples.

This article attempts to integrate the literature on such losses in order to explore the phenomenon of disenfranchised grief. It will consider both the nature of disenfranchised grief and its central paradoxical problem: the very nature of this type of grief exacerbates the problems of grief, but the usual sources of support may not be available or helpful.

The Nature of Disenfranchised Grief

Disenfranchised grief can be defined as the grief that persons experience when they incur a loss that is not or cannot be openly acknowledged, publicly mourned, or socially supported. The concept of disenfranchised grief recognizes that societies have sets of norms—in effect, "grieving rules"—that attempt to specify who, when, where, how, how long, and for whom people should grieve. These grieving rules may be codified in personnel policies. For example, a worker may be allowed a week off for the death of a spouse or child, three days for the loss of a parent or sibling. Such policies reflect the fact that each society defines who has a legitimate right to grieve, and these definitions of right correspond to relationships, primarily familial, that are socially recognized and sanctioned. In any given society these grieving rules may not correspond to the nature of attachments, the sense of loss, or the feelings of survivors. Hence the grief of these survivors is disenfranchised. In our society, this may occur for three reasons.

1. The Relationship Is Not Recognized

In our society, most attention is placed on kin-based relationships and roles. Grief may be disenfranchised in those situations in which the relationship between the bereaved and deceased is not based on recognizable kin ties. Here the closeness of other non-kin relationships may simply not be understood or appreciated. For example, Folta and Deck noted, "While all of these studies tell us that grief is a normal phenomenon, the intensity of which corresponds to the closeness of the relationship, they fail to take this (i.e., friendship) into account. The underlying assumption is that closeness of relationship exists only among spouses and/or immediate kin." The roles of lovers, friends, neighbors, foster parents, colleagues, in-laws, stepparents and stepchildren, caregivers, counselors, co-workers, and roommates (for example, in nursing homes) may be long-lasting and intensely interactive, but even though these relationships are recognized, mourners may not have full opportunity to publicly grieve a loss. At most, they might be expected to support and assist family members.

Then there are relationships that may not be publicly recognized or socially sanctioned. For example, nontraditional relationships, such as extramarital affairs, cohabitation, and homosexual relationships have tenuous public acceptance and limited legal standing, and they face negative sanctions within the larger community. Those involved in such relationships are touched by grief when the relationship is terminated by the death of the partner, but others in their world, such as children, may also experience grief that cannot be acknowledged or socially supported.

Even those whose relationships existed primarily in the past may experience grief. Ex-spouses, past lovers, or former friends may have limited contact, or they may not even engage in interaction in the present. Yet the death of that significant other can still cause a grief reaction because it brings finality to that earlier loss, ending any remaining contact or fantasy of reconciliation or reinvolvement. And again these grief feelings may be shared by others in their world such as parents and children. They too may mourn the loss of "what once was" and "what might have been." For example, in one case a twelve-year-old child of an unwed mother, never even acknowledged or seen by the father, still mourned the death of his father since it ended any possibility of a future liaison. But though loss is experienced, society as a whole may not perceive that the loss of a past relationship could or should cause any reaction.

2. The Loss Is Not Recognized

In other cases, the loss itself is not socially defined as significant. Perinatal deaths lead to strong grief reactions, yet research indicates that many significant others still perceive the loss to be relatively minor. Abortions too can constitute a serious loss, but the abortion can take place without the knowledge or sanctions of others, or even the recognition that a loss has occurred. It may very well be that the very ideologies of the abortion controversy can put the bereaved in a difficult position. Many who affirm a loss may not sanction the act of abortion, while some who sanction the act may minimize any sense of loss. Similarly, we are just becoming aware of the sense of loss that people experience in giving children up for adoption or foster care, and we have yet to be aware of the grief-related implications of surrogate motherhood.

Another loss that may not be perceived as significant is the loss of a pet. Nevertheless, the research shows strong ties between pets and humans, and profound reactions to loss.

Then there are cases in which the reality of the loss itself is not socially validated. Thanatologists have long recognized that significant losses can occur even when the object of the loss remains physically alive. Sudnow for example, discusses "social death," in which the person is alive but is treated as if dead. Examples may include those who are institutionalized or comatose. Similarly, "psychological death" has been defined as conditions in which the person lacks a consciousness of existence, such as someone who is "brain dead." One can also speak of "psychosocial death" in which the persona of someone has changed so significantly, through mental illness, organic brain syndromes, or even significant personal transformation (such as through addiction, conversion, and so forth), that significant others perceive the person as he or she previously existed as dead. In all of these cases, spouses and others may experience a profound sense of loss, but that loss cannot be publicly acknowledged for the person is still biologically alive.

3. The Griever Is Not Recognized

Finally, there are situations in which the characteristics of the bereaved in effect disenfranchise their grief. Here the person is not socially defined as capable of grief; therefore, there is little or no social recognition of his or her sense of loss or need to mourn. Despite evidence to the contrary, both the very old and the very young are typically perceived by others as having little comprehension of or reaction to the death of a significant other. Often, then, both young children and aged adults are excluded from both discussions and rituals.

Similarly, mentally disabled persons may also be disenfranchised in grief. Although studies affirm that the mentally retarded are able to understand the concept of death and, in fact, experience grief, these reactions may not be perceived by others. Because the person is retarded or otherwise mentally disabled, others in the family may ignore his or her need to grieve. Here a teacher of the mentally disabled describes two illustrative incidences:

> In the first situation, Susie was 17 years old and away at summer camp when her father died. The family felt she wouldn't understand and that it would be better for her not to come home for the funeral. In the other situation, Francine was with her mother when she got sick. The mother was taken away by ambulance. Nobody answered her questions or told her what happened. "After all," they responded, "she's retarded."

The Special Problems of Disenfranchised Grief

Though each of the types of grief mentioned earlier may create particular difficulties and different reactions, one can legitimately speak of the special problem shared in disenfranchised grief.

The problem of disenfranchised grief can be expressed in a paradox. The very nature of disenfranchised grief creates additional problems for grief, while removing or minimizing sources of support.

Disenfranchising grief may exacerbate the problem of bereavement in a number of ways. First, the situations mentioned tend to intensify emotional reactions. Many emotions are associated with normal grief. Bereaved persons frequently experience feelings of anger, guilt, sadness and depression, loneliness, hopelessness, and numbness. These emotional reactions can be complicated when grief is disenfranchised. Although each of the situations described is in its own way unique, the literature uniformly reports how each of these disenfranchising circumstances can intensify feelings of anger, guilt, or powerlessness.

Second, both ambivalent relationships and concurrent crises have been identified in the literature as conditions that complicate grief. These conditions can often exist in many types of disenfranchised grief. For example, studies have indicated the ambivalence that can exist in cases of abortion, among ex-spouses, significant others in nontraditional roles, and among families of Alzheimer's disease victims. Similarly, the literature documents the many kinds of concurrent crises that can trouble the disenfranchised griever. For example, in cases of cohabiting couples, either heterosexual or homosexual, studies have often found that survivors experience legal and financial problems regarding inheritance, ownership, credit, or leases. Likewise, the death of a parent may leave a mentally disabled person not only bereaved but also bereft of a viable support system.

Although grief is complicated, many of the factors that facilitate mourning are not present. The bereaved may be excluded from an active role in caring for the dying. Funeral rituals, normally helpful in resolving grief, may not help here. In some cases the bereaved may be excluded from attendance. In other cases they may have no role in planning those rituals or in deciding whether even to have them. Or in cases of divorce, separation, or psychosocial death, rituals may be lacking altogether.

In addition, the very nature of the disenfranchised grief precludes social support. Often there is no recognized role in which mourners can assert the right to mourn and thus receive such support. Grief may have to remain private. Though they may have experienced an intense loss, they may not be given time off from work, have the opportunity to verbalize the loss, or receive the expressions of sympathy and support characteristic in a death. Even traditional sources of solace, such as religion, are unavailable to those whose relationships (for example, extramarital, cohabiting, homosexual, divorced) or acts (such as abortion) are condemned within that tradition.

Naturally, there are many variables that will affect both the intensity of the reaction and the availability of support. All the variables—interpersonal, psychological, social, physiological—that normally influence grief will have an impact here as well. And while there are problems common to cases of disenfranchised grief, each relationship has to be individually considered in light of the unique combinations of factors that may facilitate or impair grief resolution.

Implications

Despite the shortage of research on and attention given to the issue of disenfranchised grief, it remains a significant issue. Millions of Americans are involved in losses in which grief is effectively disenfranchised. For example, there are more than 1 million couples presently cohabiting. There are estimates that 3 percent of males and 2–3 percent of females are exclusively homosexual, with similar percentages having mixed homosexual and heterosexual encounters. There are about a million abortions a year; even though many of the women involved may not experience grief reactions, some are clearly "at risk."

Disenfranchised grief is also a growing issue. There are higher percentages of divorced people in the cohorts now aging. The AIDS crisis means that more homosexuals will experience losses in significant relationships. Even as the disease spreads within the population of intravenous drug users, it is likely to create a new class of both potential victims and disenfranchised grievers among the victims' informal liaisons and nontraditional relationships. And as Americans continue to live longer, more will suffer from severe forms of chronic brain dysfunctions. As the developmentally disabled live longer, they too will experience the grief of parental and sibling loss. In short, the proportion of disenfranchised grievers in the general population will rise rapidly in the future.

It is likely that bereavement counselors will have increased exposure to cases of disenfranchised grief. In fact, the very nature of disenfranchised grief and the unavailability of informal support make it likely that those who experience such losses will seek formal supports. Thus there is a pressing need for research that will describe the particular and unique reactions of each of the different types of losses; compare reactions and problems associated with these losses; describe the important variables affecting disenfranchised grief reactions; assess possible interventions; and discover the atypical grief reactions, such as masked or delayed grief, that might be manifested in such cases. Also needed is education sensitizing students to the many kinds of relationships and subsequent losses that people can experience and affirming that where there is loss there is grief.

KEN DOKA, PH.D., is a professor of gerontology at the College of New Rochelle in New York. He became interested in the study of death and dying quite inadvertently. Scheduled to do a practicum in a facility that housed juvenile delinquents, he discovered that his supervisor had changed the assignment. Instead, Doka found himself counseling dying children and their families at Sloan-Kettering, a major cancer hospital in New York. This experience became the basis of two graduate theses, one in sociology entitled "The Social Organization of Terminal Care in Two Pediatric Hospitals," and the other in religious studies entitled "Pastoral Counseling to Dying Children and Their Families." (Both were later published.) His doctoral program pursued another longstanding interest: the sociology of aging. In 1983, Dr. Doka accepted his present position at the College of New Rochelle where he specializes in thanatology and gerontology.

Active in the Association for Death Education and Counseling since its beginnings, Dr. Doka was elected its president in 1993. In addition to articles in scholarly journals, he is the author of *Death and Spirituality* (with John Morgan, 1993), *Living with Life-Threatening Illness* (1993) and *Disenfranchised Grief: Recognizing Hidden Sorrow* (1989), from which the following selection is excerpted. His work on disenfranchised grief began in the classroom when a graduate student commented, "If you think widows have it rough, you ought to see what happens when your ex-spouse dies."

ENHANCING THE CONCEPT OF DISENFRANCHISED GRIEF

CHARLES A. CORR, PH.D.
Southern Illinois University at Edwardsville

Abstract

Doka (1989a, p. 4) defined disenfranchised grief as "the grief that persons experience when they incur a loss that is not or cannot be openly acknowledged, publicly mourned, or socially supported." He suggested that disenfranchisement can apply to unrecognized relationships, losses, or grievers, as well as to certain types of deaths.

This article contends that disenfranchisement in bereavement may have a potentially broader scope than has been hitherto recognized. That claim is defended by exploring further the implications of disenfranchisement and by suggesting ways in which certain understandings or misunderstandings of the dynamic qualities of grief, mourning, and their outcomes may be open to disenfranchisement or may participate in disenfranchisement.

The aims of this argument are to enhance the concept of disenfranchised grief in itself and to deepen appreciation of the full range of all that is or can be experienced in bereavement.

In 1989 Doka (1989a) first proposed the concept of "disenfranchised grief." His suggestion had an immediate appeal to many and the concept of disenfranchised grief has since been widely accepted by practitioners, educators, and researchers in the field of death, dying, and bereavement. In particular, it has been applied in ways that seek to elucidate and validate the experiences of a broad range of bereaved persons.

In his initial proposal, Doka described the concept of disenfranchised grief, identified those aspects of the grief experience that he understood to have been subject to disenfranchisement, provided examples of many ways in which disenfranchisement has occurred, and indicated why attention should be paid to the concept of disenfranchised grief. This article seeks to enhance understanding of the concept of disenfranchised grief and by so doing to deepen appreciation of the full range of all that is or can be experienced in bereavement. The present analysis begins with a review of Doka's original description of the concept of disenfranchised grief. Thereafter, the inquiry is guided by two primary questions: 1) What exactly is meant by the disenfranchisement of grief?; and 2) What is or can be disenfranchised in grief? Responding to these questions may help to enrich understanding of Doka's seminal concept in particular, and of bereavement in general. On that basis, it may also be possible for helpers to identify better ways in which to assist grievers of all types, especially those whose experiences have been disenfranchised.

Disenfranchised Grief: The Original Concept

In his original work, Doka (1989a, p. 4) defined "disenfranchised grief" as "the grief that persons experience when they incur a loss that is not or cannot be openly acknowledged, publicly mourned, or socially supported." In addition, he suggested that grief can be disenfranchised in three primary ways: 1) the relationship is not recognized; 2) the loss is not recognized; or 3) the griever is not recognized. Some comments on each of these three types of disenfranchisement may help to clarify Doka's original proposal.

Disenfranchised Relationships

Why don't you just stop crying and grieving for that person who died. He wasn't even close to you.

I just don't see why you should be so upset over the death of your ex-husband. He was a bum, you hated him, and you got rid of him years ago. Why cry over his being gone for good?

With respect to a *relationship* that is disenfranchised, Folta and Deck (1976, p. 235) have noted that "the underlying assumption is that the 'closeness of relationship' exists only among spouses and/or immediate kin." Unsuspected, past, or secret relationships may simply not be publicly recognized or socially sanctioned. Disenfranchised relationships can include associations which are well-accepted in theory but not appreciated in practice or in particular instances, such as those between friends, colleagues, in-laws, ex-spouses, or former lovers. Disenfranchised relationships may also include nontraditional liaisons such as those involving extra-marital affairs and homosexual relationships. In referring to these as instances of disenfranchised grief, the implication is that such relationships have often been or may be deemed by society to be an insufficient or inappropriate foundation for grief.

Disenfranchised Losses

Why do you keep on moaning over your miscarriage? It wasn't really a baby yet. And you already have four children. You could even have more if you want to.

Stop crying over that dead cat! He was just an animal. I bet that cat wouldn't have been upset if you had been the one to die. If you stop crying. I'll buy you a new kitten.

In the case of a *loss* which is disenfranchised, the focus of the disenfranchisement appears to arise from a failure or unwillingness on the part of society to recognize that certain types of events do involve real losses. For example, until quite recently and perhaps still today in many segments of society, perinatal deaths, losses associated with elective abortion, or losses of body parts have been disenfranchised. Similarly, the death of a pet is often unappreciated by those outside the relationship. And society is only beginning to learn about grief which occurs when dementia blots out an individual's personality in such a way or to such a degree that significant others perceive the person to be psychosocially dead, even though biological life continues. As one husband said of his spouse with advanced Alzheimer's disease, "I am medically separated from my wife—even though she is still alive and we are not divorced." To say that loss arising from a "medical separation" of this type is disenfranchised is to note that society does not acknowledge it to be sufficient to justify grief—or at least not sufficient to justify grief of the type that society associates with a physical death.

Disenfranchised Grievers

I don't know why that old guy in Room 203 keeps moaning and whimpering about the death of his loud-mouthed daughter who used to visit him every week.

With his poor memory and other mental problems, he hardly even knew when his daughter came to visit anyway.

I told Johnnie he should grow up, be a man, and stop whining about his grandfather's death. He's too young to really remember much about his grandfather or even to understand what death really means.

In the case of a disenfranchised *griever*, disenfranchisement mainly has to do with certain individuals to whom the socially-recognized status of griever is not attached. For example, it is often asserted or at least suggested that young children, the very old, and those who are mentally disabled are either incapable of grief or are individuals who do not have a need to grieve. In this case, disenfranchisement applies not to a relationship or to a loss, but to the individual survivor whose status as a leading actor or protagonist in the human drama of bereavement is not recognized or appreciated.

Disenfranchising Deaths

That teenager who killed himself must not have had all his marbles. His family is probably all screwed up, too. Don't be sorry for them. Just stay away from them.

It's just too bad that actor died of AIDS. God punished him for having all that sex. And now his boyfriends will probably wind up with all his money. They sure don't need us to feel sorry for them.

In his original concept, Doka (1989a) added that some types of deaths in themselves may be "disenfranchising." He offered as examples deaths involving suicide or AIDS. The point seems to have been that our society is repelled or turns away from certain types of death, mainly because their complexities are not well understood or because they are associated with a high degree of social stigma. As a result, the character of the death seems to disenfranchise what otherwise might have been expected to follow in its aftermath. But not all societies at all points in time would or have disenfranchised deaths associated with suicide or AIDS. In other words, what is disenfranchised in one social context may not be disenfranchised in another social context. This clearly recalls Doka's fundamental point that disenfranchised grief is always founded on a specific society's attitudes and values.

Why Pay Attention to Disenfranchised Grief?

The purpose of drawing attention to the meaning of disenfranchised grief and to the ways in which it can be implemented can be seen in Doka's (1989a, p. 7) observation that, "The very nature of disenfranchised grief creates additional problems of grief, while removing or minimizing sources of support." Additional problems arise that go beyond the usual difficulties in grief because disenfranchised grief typically involves intensified emotional reactions (for example, anger, guilt, or powerlessness), ambivalent relationships (as in some cases of abortion or some associations between ex-spouses), and concurrent crises (such as those involving legal and financial problems). In circumstances of disenfranchised grief there is an absence of customary sources of support because society's attitudes make unavailable factors that usually facilitate mourning (for instance, the existence of funeral rituals or possibilities for helping to take part in such rituals) and opportunities to obtain assistance from others (for example, by speaking about the loss, receiving expressions of sympathy, taking time off from work, or finding solace within a religious tradition).

Clearly, issues associated with disenfranchised grief deserve attention. They indicate that social outlooks often embody a judgmental element (whether explicitly articulated or not) and the short-term concerns of the group when dealing with some bereaved persons. That is, societies which disenfranchise grief appear to act on specific values or principles at the expense of an overarching interest in the welfare of all of their members. In these ways, disenfranchised grief can be seen to be an important phenomenon. It is also a phenomenon that is lived out in different ways in different societies, easily observed by those who pay attention to social practices, and hurtful to individual members of society if not to society itself. For all of these reasons, it is worth exploring further what is meant by saying that some grief is disenfranchised and what is or can be disenfranchised in grief.

What is Meant by Saying That Some Grief is Disenfranchised?

As has been noted, grief always occurs within a particular social or cultural context. The concept of disenfranchised grief recognizes that in various spoken and unspoken ways social and cultural communities may deny recognition, legitimation, or support to the grief experienced by individuals, families, and small groups.

It is important to recognize that the grief under discussion here is not merely silent, unnoticed, or forgotten. Any griever may keep silent about or decide not to reveal to the larger society the fact of his or her grief, or some of its specific aspects. Failing to disclose or communicate to others what one is experiencing in grief does not of itself mean that such grief is or would be disenfranchised. Society might be fully prepared to recognize, legitimize, and support grief that an individual, for whatever reason, holds in privacy and does not share.

Further, even when an individual is willing to share his or her grief, some grief experiences may still go unnoticed or be forgotten by society. Thus, Gyulay (1975) wrote of grandparents following the death of a grandchild as "forgotten grievers." She meant that all too often attention associated with the death of a child is focused on the child's parents or siblings to the exclusion of grandparents. In fact, however, bereaved grandparents often find themselves grieving both the death of their grandchild and the loss experienced by an adult who is simultaneously their own child (or son/daughter-in-law) and the child's parent (Hamilton, 1978). Typically, when this two-fold grief of grandparents is brought to the attention of members of society, it is not disenfranchised but acknowledged and respected.

In short, the concept of disenfranchised grief goes beyond the situation of mere unawareness of grief to suggest a more or less active process of disavowal, renunciation, and rejection. Not surprisingly, the word "disenfranchise" takes its origin from the term "enfranchise," which has two basic historical meanings: 1) "To admit to freedom, set free (a slave or serf)"; and 2) "To admit to municipal or political privileges" (*Oxford English Dictionary,* 1989, Vol. 5, p. 246). In the most familiar sense of this term, to enfranchise is to set an individual free from his or her prior condition by admitting that person to the electoral franchise or granting permission to vote for representatives in a government. Disenfranchisement applies to those who are not accorded a social franchise extended by society to individuals who are admitted to full participation in the community.

A more contemporary meaning of enfranchisement is to be granted a franchise or license to offer for sale locally some national or international product or service. For example, one might purchase or be awarded a franchise to sell a certain brand of fast food or automobile, or to advertise one's local motel as a member of a national chain of motels. Often one has to earn or somehow pay for the use of a franchise, and there may also be obligations to uphold certain service standards or to deliver a product of a certain type in a certain way. When the use of a franchise has not been earned or implemented properly, it may come into dispute or even be withdrawn by those in authority. In all of these examples, it is the permission to behave in a certain way (to vote, to act as a franchisee or agent of a franchise holder) that is central to both enfranchisement and disenfranchisement.

In the case of bereavement, enfranchisement applies in particular to those who are recognized by society as grievers. These are individuals who are free to acknowledge their losses openly, mourn those losses publicly, and receive support from others—at least within that society's accepted limits. Disenfranchised grief goes beyond the boundaries of what is regarded as socially-accepted grief. It is therefore denied the legitimacy and freedom that comes with social sanction and approval (Doka, 1989b; Pine et al., 1990).

What is or Can Be Disenfranchised in Grief?

Bereavement

Doka is clearly correct in recognizing that disenfranchisement can apply to relationships, losses, and grievers. These are, in fact, the three key *structural elements* that define the meaning of the term "bereavement." Thus, what Doka has really defined is "disenfranchised bereavement." For that reason, it may help to begin our exploration of how disenfranchisement applies to grief by reminding ourselves of how we understand the root concept of bereavement.

The word "bereavement" is widely understood to designate the objective situation of one who has experienced a significant loss. If there were no significant person or object to which an individual was attached, there would be no bereavement. For example, when a parent threatens to take away from a child a much-disliked serving of spinach as a "punishment" for the child's refusal to clean his or her plate at dinner, the child is not likely to experience a loss or to grieve. Further, if the object were a significant one to the child, but the child perceived (as a result of previous parental behavior patterns) that the threatened loss would not come about in fact, again there would be no bereavement or grief. Finally, if there were no individual to grieve a loss—as when someone threatens to or actually does take away a significant object, but the threat and the loss are not effectively communicated to the individual to whom they would presumably have been directed—again there is no bereavement or grief. A griever is effectively absent when the threat is merely an empty gesture made in his or her absence or when, for some other reason, there is no awareness or experience of a significant loss—as during the period between the death of a loved one in a far-off land and the communication of that fact to the survivor.

In short, the noun "bereavement" and the adjective "bereaved" only apply to situations and individuals in which there exists an experience such that one believes oneself to have been deprived of some important person or object. Both "bereavement" and "bereaved" (there is no present participial form, "bereaving," in standard English today) are words that derive from a verb not often used today in colloquial English. That word is "reave"; it means "to despoil, rob, or forcibly deprive" (*Oxford English Dictionary*, 1989, Vol. 13, p. 295). In short, a bereaved person is one who has been deprived, robbed, plundered, or stripped of something. This indicates that the stolen person or object was a valued one, and suggests that the deprivation has harmed or done violence to the bereaved person. In our society, all too many bereaved persons can testify that dismissal or minimization of the importance of their losses are familiar components of the experience of survivors, with or without added burdens arising from disenfranchisement.

We could explore further each of the central elements identified by Doka in describing his concept of disenfranchised grief. Such an exploration might produce: 1) a rich and varied portrait of the many types of *relationships* in which humans participate, including those fundamental relationships called "attachments" which serve to satisfy the basic needs of human beings; 2) a panorama of *losses* which may affect relationships involving human beings—some permanent, others temporary, some final, others reversible; and/or 3) a list of many different types of *grievers*. If we did this, it would become apparent (among other things) that loss by death is but one category of loss, and that certain types or modes of death are more likely to be disenfranchised than others. And we might also learn that while disenfranchising the bereaved involves costs of different types for individuals and societies themselves, enfranchising the disenfranchised might also involve costs of other types (Davidowitz & Myrick, 1984; Kamerman, 1993).

All of the above are ways to enrich appreciation of the concept of disenfranchised grief. Most involve simply accepting the conceptual scheme as it was originally proposed by Doka

and applying it to specific types of relationships, losses, and grievers. Applications of this type have been prominent in written reports and conference presentations in recent years (e.g., Becker, 1997; Kaczmarek & Backlund, 1991; Schwebach & Thornton, 1992; Thornton, Robertson, & Mlecko, 1991; Zupanick, 1994).

In this article, it seems more useful to try to enhance or enlarge the concept of disenfranchised grief by examining it critically in relationship to the *dynamic components* of the bereavement experience, especially as it is related to grief, mourning, and their outcomes.

Grief

> Stop feeling that way! You'll be better off if you just pack up all those bad feelings and throw them away with the garbage.

In reactions to being "reaved" or to perceiving themselves as having been "reaved," those who have suffered that experience typically react to what has happened to them. In normal circumstances, one would be surprised if they did not do so. Failure to react would seem to imply that the lost person or object was actually not much prized by the bereaved individual, that the survivor is unaware of his or her loss, or that other factors intervene. "Grief" is the reaction to loss. The term arises from the grave or heavy weight that presses on persons who are burdened by loss (*Oxford English Dictionary*, 1989, Vol. 6, pp. 834–835).

Reactions to loss are disenfranchised when they—in whole or in part; in themselves or in their expression—are not recognized, legitimated, or supported by society. How many times have grieving persons been told: "Don't feel that way"; "Try not to think those thoughts"; "Don't say those things (about God, or the doctor, or the person who caused the death)"; "You shouldn't act like that just because someone you loved died." Sometimes any reaction is judged to be inappropriate; in other circumstances, some reactions are accepted while others are rejected. In some cases, it is the existence of the reaction that is disenfranchised; in other examples, it is only the expression of the reaction that meets with disapproval. Through what amounts to a kind of "oppressive toleration" society often presses a griever to hold private his or her grief reaction in order not to trouble or disturb others by bringing it out into the open or expressing it in certain ways. The effect of any or all of these practices is to disenfranchise either some aspects of the grief or some modes in which they are manifested.

Grief as Emotions?

> I can understand why you're feeling upset about your mother's death. You can be sad if you want to. But you've got to start eating again and getting a good night's sleep.
>
> My co-worker used to be a such a great guy. But ever since his younger sister died, he comes to work and sometimes it's like he's wandering around in a fog and not concentrating on the job. I told him today that

he needs to pull himself together and get focused on his work again.

My friend was always such a cheery person at the Senior Citizen's Center. But ever since her grandchild died, she keeps asking all those difficult questions about why God let such a bad thing happen to an innocent child. I told her that it was OK to be sad, but she just had to accept God's will and stop questioning it.

In each of these examples, feelings of grief are legitimized but other aspects of the grief reaction are disenfranchised. One might also argue that something very much like this form of disenfranchisement can be found in much of the professional literature on bereavement. For example, quite often grief is described or defined as "the emotional reaction to loss." On its face, a definition of this type is at once both obvious and inadequate. Clearly, bereaved persons may or do react emotionally to loss; equally so, they may not or do not merely react emotionally to loss. Careless, unintentional, or deliberate restriction of the meaning of grief to its emotional components is an unrecognized form of disenfranchisement of the full grief experience.

In this connection, Elias (1991) reminded readers that, "Broadly speaking, emotions have three components, a somatic, a behavioral and a feeling component" (p. 177). As a result, "the term *emotion*, even in professional discussions, is used with two different meanings. It is used in a wider and in a narrower sense at the same time. In the wider sense the term *emotion* is applied to a reaction pattern which involves the whole organism in its somatic, its feeling and its behavioral aspects.... In its narrower sense the term *emotion* refers to the feeling component of the syndrome only" (Elias, 1991, p. 119).

The importance of feelings in the overall grief reaction to loss is undeniable. Equally undeniable is the importance of other aspects of the grief reaction. These include somatic or physical sensations and behaviors or behavioral disturbances, as Elias has indicated, as well as matters involving cognitive, social, and spiritual functioning. Establishing a comprehensive list of all of these aspects of the grief reaction to loss is not of primary importance here. What is central is the recognition that human beings may and indeed are likely to react to important losses in their lives with their whole selves, not just with some narrowly-defined aspect of their humanity. Failure to describe grief in a holistic way dismisses and devalues its richness and breadth.

Grief as Symptoms?

As a psychiatrist and her son-in-law, I tried to talk to your mother about your father's death. She refused and got upset after I told her that her unwillingness to discuss with me her reactions to the death was a classic symptom of pathological grief. She said she had talked to her sister and just didn't want to talk to you or me or her other children about it.

Sadness and crying are two of the main symptoms of grief. Whenever we identify them, we should refer the individual for therapy.

Another form of depicting or categorizing grief in a limiting and negative way involves the use of the language of *symptoms* to designate both complicated and uncomplicated grief. In principal, grief is a natural and healthy reaction to loss. There can be unhealthy reactions to loss. One of these would be a failure to react in any way to the loss of a significant person or object in our lives. However, most grief reactions are not complicated or unhealthy. They are appropriate reactions to the loss one has experienced. In cases of uncomplicated grief—which constitute the vast majority of all bereavement experiences—we ought to speak of signs, or manifestations, or expressions of grief. And we ought to avoid the term "symptoms" in relationship to grief, unless we consciously intend to use the language of illness to indicate some form of aberrant or unhealthy reaction to loss. When we use the language of symptoms to describe all expressions of grief, we have pathologized grief and invalidated or disenfranchised its fundamental soundness as the human reaction to loss.

Mourning

OK, we've had our grief ever since Kerri died. Now that the funeral is over, that's it. There's nothing more we can do and nothing more we need to do. So, let's just put all this behind us and forget it.

Many aspects of what is called grief in bereavement are essentially reactive. They seek to push away the hurt of the loss with denial, or turn back upon it with anger, or reply to its implacability with sadness. Much of this is like a defensive reflex. But there is more to most bereavement experiences than this. The other central element in a healthy bereavement experience is in the effort to find some way to live with the loss, with our grief reactions to that loss, and with the new challenges that are associated with the loss. As Weisman (1984, p. 36) observed, coping "is positive in approach; defending is negative." In brief, coping identifies the efforts that we make to manage perceived stressors in our lives (Lazarus & Folkman, 1984). In the vocabulary of bereavement, this is "mourning"—the attempt to manage or learn to live with one's bereavement. Through mourning grievers endeavor to incorporate their losses and grief into healthy ongoing living.

If we fail to distinguish between grief and mourning in appropriate ways, we run the risk of ignoring the differences between reacting and coping, between seeking to defend or push away our loss and grief, and attempting to embrace those experiences and incorporate them into our lives. This is another form of disenfranchisement insofar as it blurs distinctions between two central aspects of bereavement, misconceives what is involved in mourning an important loss, and refuses to acknowledge and support both grief and mourning.

At the simplest level, the efforts that one makes to cope with loss and grief in mourning are frequently not understood for what they are and thus are not valued by society. For example, a griever will be told not to go over the details of the accident again and again, as if such filling in of the stark outlines of a death is not an essential part of the process of *realization* or making real in one's internal, psychic world what is already real in the external, objective world (Parkes, 1996). Another familiar way of disenfranchising mourning occurs when a bereaved person is advised that the proper way to manage a loss is simply to "put it behind you" or "get beyond it." This assumes that one can simply hop over a stressful event in life, ignore the unwelcome interruption, and go on living without being affected by what has happened. Sometimes, bereaved survivors are even counseled to "forget" the deceased person as if he or she had not been a significant part of their lives. None of these are appropriate elements in constructive mourning.

Note that mourning is a present-tense, participial word. As such, it indicates action or activities of the type expressed by verbs. In the language of nouns, this is "grief work" (a phrase first coined by Lindemann in 1944). Lindemann understood "grief work" in a specific way, but the central point is that the grief work at the heart of mourning is an active, effortful attempt to manage what bereavement has brought into one's life (Attig, 1991, 1996).

Moreover, since the consequences of bereavement typically include both primary and secondary losses, as well as grief and new challenges, there is much to cope with in the whole of one's mourning. Indeed, contrasting loss and grief with the new challenges of bereavement could be said to require an oscillation between "loss-oriented" and "restoration-oriented" processes in mourning (Stroebe & Schut, 1995).

In other words, in his or her mourning a bereaved person is faced with the tasks of integrating into his or her life three major elements: 1) the primary and secondary losses that he or she has experienced, 2) the grief reactions provoked by those losses; and 3) the new challenges involved in living without the deceased person. For example, if my spouse should die I would be obliged to mourn or try to learn to live in healthy ways with her loss (the fact that she has been taken away from me constituting my primary loss), with the secondary losses associated with her death (e.g., being deprived of her company or being without her guidance in some practical matters), with my grief reactions to those losses (e.g., my anger over what has been done to me or my sadness at the apparent barrenness of the life that is now left to me), and with my new situation in life (e.g., after years of marriage I may be unclear how to function as a newfound single person). If any aspect of my losses, grief, or new challenges is disenfranchised, then my efforts to mourn or cope with those aspects of my bereavement will also be disenfranchised.

Mourning: Interpersonal and Intrapersonal Dimensions

Because each human being is both a particular individual and a social creature or a member of a community, mourning has two complementary forms or aspects. It is both an outward, public, or *interpersonal* process—the overt, visible, and characteristically shared, public efforts to cope with or manage loss and associated grief reactions—and an internal, private, or *intrapersonal* process—an individual's inward struggles to cope with or manage loss and the grief reactions to that loss. Each of these dimensions of mourning deserves recognition and respect.

Much of what has already been noted here about mourning applies to its intrapersonal dimensions, but disenfranchisement is also frequently associated with the interpersonal aspects of mourning.

Interpersonal Dimensions of Mourning

Don't keep on talking about how he died. It's not going to make any difference or bring him back. Nobody wants to be around you when you keep going on about it.

What's the point of having a funeral, anyhow? Couldn't they just bury their child privately and leave us out of it? I don't want to get dragged into it.

Many people in contemporary society are unwilling to take part in the public or *interpersonal* rituals of mourning. Some of this has to do with a certain weakness or shallowness in many interpersonal relationships in contemporary society and a loosening of the bonds that formerly bound together families, neighbors, church groups, and other small communities. But it also appears to be linked to a discomfort with public ritual and open expression of strong feelings. Good funeral and memorial rituals are essentially designed to assist human beings in their need to engage in three post-death tasks: 1) to dispose of dead bodies appropriately; 2) to make real the implications of death; and 3) to work toward social reintegration and healthful ongoing living (Corr, Nabe, & Corr, 1994). Without indicating how these tasks will otherwise be met, many act as if society and individuals should do away with all public expressions of mourning. Young people in our society frequently state that when they die no one should be sad and that money that would otherwise be spent for a funeral should only be used for a party. Thoughts like this disenfranchise full appreciation of grief and the needs of individuals to mourn their losses within communities of fellow grievers.

This disenfranchisement of the interpersonal dimensions of mourning is not typical of all individuals in our society and is unacceptable to many ethnic or religious groups. Similarly, it does not apply to rituals following the deaths of public figures (e.g., a president) or very prominent persons (e.g., certain celebrities). In these instances, as well as in the very formal rituals of the armed forces which mandate specific conduct and ceremonial practice in a context of death and bereavement, or the informal but growing practice of members of sports teams wearing black bands on their uniforms or dedicating a game to the memory of someone who has died, the interpersonal needs of a community cry out for expression and guidance in public mourning practices.

In fact, formal or informal rituals—which are a prominent example of the interpersonal dimension of mourning—have been created by human beings as a means of helping to bring order into their lives in times of disorder and social disruption. Thus, Margaret Mead (1973, pp. 89–90) wrote: "I know of no people for whom the fact of death is not critical, and who have no ritual by which to deal with it." Bereavement rituals are intended precisely to give social recognition, legitimation, and support in times of loss and grief. Specific rituals may fall out of favor and no longer serve these purposes for the society as a whole or for some of its members. But to assume that such rituals can simply be abandoned without replacement, that society can satisfactorily conduct its affairs and serve its members without any ritual whatsoever in times of death, is to misconceive the needs of human beings and expose the dangers involved in disenfranchising mourning. As Staples (1994, p. 255) suggested, "The rituals of grief and burial bear the dead away. Cheat those rituals and you risk keeping the dead with you always in forms that you mightn't like. Choose carefully the funerals you miss."

Intrapersonal Dimensions of Mourning

I was proud of her at the funeral. She was so brave and she never cried. But now she's always crying and sometimes she just seems to be preoccupied with her inner feelings. I think she's just chewing on her grief like some kind of undigested food and simply won't let go of it. Last week, I told her that there were times when we all understood it was appropriate to grieve. But she's got to get over it and she just can't keep on gnawing at it when she thinks she's alone.

Why does she keep going back to the cemetary on the anniversary of her husband's death? That's morbid for her to keep on stirring up those feelings over and over again. She doesn't talk much to anyone else about it, but I think she needs to get on with her life without this behavior.

Some authors (e.g., *Oxford English Dictionary,* 1989, Vol. 10, pp. 19–20) seem to restrict the use of the term "mourning" to the expression of sorrow or grief, especially those expressions involving ceremony or ritual. For example, there is a traditional language that uses phrases like "wearing mourning" to refer to dressing in certain ways (e.g., in black or dark-colored garments) as a public expression of one's status as a bereaved person. Despite its historical justification, limiting the term mourning in this way leaves us without a term for the *intrapersonal* processes of coping with loss and grief.

Other authors (e.g., Wolfelt, 1996) maintain and emphasize the distinction between the intrapersonal and interpersonal dimensions of bereavement by using the term "grieving" for the former and reserving the term "mourning" for the latter. Again, there is justification for some linguistic distinction between intrapersonal and interpersonal aspects of coping with loss and grief. But the central point for our purposes is that this last distinction is a linguistic effort to fill out what is involved in both the intrapersonal and interpersonal realms when bereaved persons strive to cope with loss and grief. In this way, linguistic distinctions between intrapersonal and interpersonal aspects of mourning work to expand or enhance what is involved in coping with loss and grief, not to restrict or disenfranchise selected aspects of that coping.

Mourning: Outcomes

It's been almost three weeks and she's still not finished with her grieving. I told her she had to forget him and get on with her new life.

We invited John to come on a blind date with us and Mary's cousin, but he refused. Mary told him that he's got to stop wallowing in tears. He needs to get over his first wife and start looking around for someone new. Six months is long enough to mourn.

A final arena for possible disenfranchisement in bereavement relates to assumptions about the *outcomes* of mourning. This has been touched on above. If mourning is a process of coping with loss and grief, we can rightly ask: What are the results which it strives to achieve? Many would say "recovery," "completion," or "resolution." Each of these terms appears to imply a fixed endpoint for mourning, a final closure after which there is no more grieving and mourning. "Recovery," is perhaps the least satisfactory of the three terms, because it also seems to suggest that grief is a bad situation like a disease or a wound from which one must rescue or reclaim oneself (Osterweis, Solomon, & Green, 1984; Rando, 1993). Recovery is often implied in metaphors of "healing" from grief; talking in this way may otherwise be quite helpful, but it tends to suggest a time at which one will be done with healing and after which one will apparently be back to one's former self essentially unchanged by the bereavement experience.

It has been argued earlier that it is not desirable to use symptom language to interpret grief and to impose disease models upon healthy experiences in bereavement. To that we can add here that there are no fixed endpoints in mourning. One can never simply go back to a pre-bereavement mode of living after a significant loss. In fact, there is ample evidence, for many at least, that mourning continues in some form for the remainder of one's life. Interpretations to the contrary disenfranchise processes related to loss and grief which take place after the assumed endpoint or completion of mourning. They also disenfranchise the life-changing power of significant losses and the ongoing need to continue to cope with loss, grief, and new challenges in life. The misconception that grief and mourning should be over in a short time or at some predefined point is what leads to the familiar experience of many bereaved persons that over time their grief appears to become disenfranchised (Lundberg, Thornton, & Robertson, 1987).

There are, in fact, different outcomes experienced by different individuals who are bereaved. That is not surprising. Individuals who live their lives in different ways may be expected to cope with loss and grief in different ways, and to come to different results in their coping work. Research by Martinson and her colleagues (McClowry, Davies, May, Kulenkamp, & Martinson, 1987) studied bereaved parents and other family members (mainly siblings) seven to nine years after the death of a child. Results suggested that different individuals and different families dealt with the "empty space" in their lives in different ways. Some worked diligently to "get over it," that is, to put the loss behind them and go on with their lives. Others sought to "fill the space" by turning their focus toward what they perceived as some constructive direction. This type of effort to find some positive meaning in an otherwise horrible event might be illustrated by those bereaved after automobile accidents associated with the use of alcoholic beverages who throw themselves into campaigns to prevent intoxicated drivers from driving motor vehicles or to take such drivers off the road when they have been identified. A third outcome identified in this research was that of "keeping the connection." This appeared in bereaved persons who struggled to maintain a place in their lives for the deceased individual, vividly illustrated by the mother who insists that she has two sons, despite her full awareness that one of them has died (e.g., Wagner, 1994).

The important point in this research is not to argue for one or the other of these three outcomes in mourning, or even to suggest that they are the only possible outcomes. The point is that mourning is a process of acknowledging the reality of a death, experiencing the grief associated with that loss, learning to live without the deceased, and restructuring one's relationship to the deceased in order that that relationship can continue to be honored even while the survivor goes on living in a healthy and productive way (Worden, 1991). This process can be carried out in different ways and it can be expected to have somewhat different results for different individuals. As one astute psychologist observed, it is not the time that one has to use but the use that one makes of the time that one has that makes all the difference in bereavement, grief, and mourning (S. J. Fleming, personal communication, 9/28/95).

Three widows in my own experience acted out their mourning in different ways. One removed her wedding ring after the death of her husband. She said, "I am no longer married to him." Another kept her wedding ring on the third finger of her left hand. She said, "We are still connected." A third removed her husband's wedding ring before his body was buried and had it refashioned along with her own wedding ring into a new ring which she wore on her right hand. She said, "I now have a new relationship with my deceased husband."

These and other possible variations identify alternative courses in bereavement and mourning. In each case, metaphors of healing or resolution are partly correct insofar as the survivor has found a constructive way in which to go forward with his or her life. The intensity of the bereaved person's grief may have abated, but many continue to experience grief and reoccurrences of mourning in some degree, in some forms, and at some times. Grief may no longer consume them as it seemed to do immediately after their loss. They have "gotten through" some difficult times in bereavement, but they are not simply "over" their grief. In fact, many bereaved persons report that their grief and mourning never completely end.

Outsiders must take care not to invalidate or disenfranchise the ongoing grief and mourning of the bereaved, as well as their healthy connectedness to the deceased, by speaking too facilely of closure and completion (Klass, Silverman, & Nickman, 1996; Silverman, Nickman, & Worden, 1992). Such language may speak not primarily about bereavement but about the time at which a helper judges that his or her role as a counselor or therapist is no longer required. Thus, when a bereaved child decides to leave one of the support groups at The Dougy Center in Portland, Oregon (because, as was once said, "he or she now has better things to do with his or her time"), he or she is given a drawstring pouch containing several small stones (Corr and the Staff of The Dougy Center, 1991). Most of the stones in the

pouch are polished and thus serve to symbolize what the child has achieved in coping with loss and grief; at least one is left in a rough state to represent the unfinished work that always remains in bereavement.

Conclusion

What have we learned from this reflection on the concept of disenfranchised grief? First, it is a concept with immediate appeal. It resonates with the experiences of many bereaved persons and of many clinicians and scholars who have sought to understand experiences of bereavement or tried to be of assistance to bereaved persons. Second, disenfranchisement involves more than merely overlooking or forgetting to take note of certain types of bereavement and grief. It is more active than that in its nature and more determined in its messages, even if they are often conveyed in subtle and unspoken ways. Whatever is disenfranchised in grief is not free to experience or to express itself. It is prohibited, tied down, not sanctioned, and not supported by society.

Third, as Doka (1989a) originally pointed out, disenfranchisement can apply to any or all of the key structural elements in bereavement—relationships, losses, and grievers—as well as to certain forms of death. However, as this article has made clear, disenfranchisement can also be associated with the full range of the various reactions to loss (grief) and their expression, the processes of coping with or striving to manage loss, grief, and the new challenges which they entail (mourning), both the intrapersonal and the interpersonal dimensions of those processes, and various ways of living out their implications. In the aftermath of a death, the possible scope of disenfranchisement is not confined merely to the structural elements of bereavement or to grief understood in a kind of global way; it can extend to every aspect or dimension of the experience of bereavement and be applied to all of the dynamics of grief and mourning.

Enhancing our understanding of the concept of disenfranchised grief can contribute to improved appreciation of its breadth and depth. This same effort also provides an added way of drawing out some of the implications of the underlying concepts of bereavement, grief, and mourning. Further, attention to the enhanced concept of disenfranchised grief reminds helpers of the sensitivities they need to keep in mind in order not to devalue or rule out of bounds important aspects of the experiences of bereaved persons.

A caring society ought not incorporate within its death system—either formally or informally—thoughts, attitudes, behaviors, or values that communicate to bereaved persons inappropriate or unjustified messages such as: "Your relationship with the deceased person did not count in our eyes"; "Your loss was not really a significant one"; "You are not a person who should be grieving this loss"; "We do not recognize some aspects of your grief" or "Your grief is not acceptable to us in some ways"; "Your grief is in itself a symptom of psychic disorder or lack of mental health;" "Your mourning has lasted too long"; "You are mourning in ways that are publicly or socially unacceptable"; "You should not continue to mourn inside your-self in these ways"; or "Your mourning should be finished and over with by now."

Rather than the perspectives described in the previous paragraph, a caring society ought to respect the complexities and the individuality of each bereavement experience. While remaining sensitive to the deficits and excesses that define complicated mourning in a relatively small percentage of bereavement experiences (Rando, 1993), a caring society and its members ought to appreciate that healthy grief honors cherished relationships and that constructive mourning is essential for those who are striving to live in productive and meaningful ways in the aftermath of loss. Consider how different our society would be if it listened to and acted on comments such as the following from Frank (1991), who wrote: "Professionals talk too much about adjustment. I want to emphasize mourning as affirmation.... To grieve well is to value what you have lost. When you value even the feeling of loss, you value life itself, and you begin to live again" (pp. 40–41).

REFERENCES

Attig, T. (1991). The importance of conceiving of grief as an active process. *Death Studies, 15,* 385–393.

Attig, T. (1996). *How we grieve: Relearning the world.* New York: Oxford University Press.

Becker, S. M. (1997, 26 June). *Disenfranchised grief and the experience of loss after environmental accidents.* Paper presented at the meeting of the Association for Death Education and Counseling and the 5th International Conference on Grief and Bereavement in Contemporary Society, Washington, DC.

Corr, C. A., and the Staff of The Dougy Center. (1991). Support for grieving children: The Dougy Center and the hospice philosophy. *The American Journal of Hospice and Palliative Care, 8*(4), 23–27.

Corr, C. A., Nabe, C. M., & Corr, D. M. (1994). A task-based approach for understanding and evaluating funeral practices. *Thanatos, 19*(2), 10–15.

Davidowitz, M., & Myrick, R. D. (1984). Responding to the bereaved: An analysis of "helping" statements. *Death Education, 8,* 1–10.

Doka, K. J. (1989a). Disenfranchised grief. In K. J. Doka (Ed.), *Disenfranchised grief: Recognizing hidden sorrow* (pp. 3–11). Lexington, MA: Lexington Books.

Doka, K. J. (Ed.) (1989b). *Disenfranchised grief: Recognizing hidden sorrow.* Lexington, MA: Lexington Books.

Elias, N. (1991). On human beings and their emotions: A process-sociological essay. In M. Featherstone, M. Hepworth, & B. S. Turner (Eds.), *The body: Social process and cultural theory* (pp. 103–125). London: Sage.

Folta, J. R., & Deck, E. S. (1976). Grief, the funeral, and the friend. In V. R. Pine, A. H. Kutscher, D. Peretz, R. C. Slater, R. DeBellis, R. J. Volk, & D. J. Cherico (Eds.), *Acute grief and the funeral* (pp. 231–240). Springfield, IL: Charles C. Thomas.

Frank, A. W. (1991). *At the will of the body: Reflections on illness.* Boston: Houghton Mifflin.

Gyulay, J. E. (1975). The forgotten grievers. *American Journal of Nursing, 75,* 1476–1479.

Hamilton, J. (1978). Grandparents as grievers. In O. J. Z. Sahler (Ed.), *The child and death* (pp. 219–225). St. Louis, MO: C. V. Mosby.

Kaczmarek, M. G., & Backlund, B. A. (1991). Disenfranchised grief: The loss of an adolescent romantic relationship. *Adolescence, 26,* 253–259.

Kamerman, J. (1993). Latent functions of enfranchising the disenfranchised griever. *Death Studies, 17,* 281–287.

Klass, D., Silverman, P. R., & Nickman, S. L. (Eds.) (1996). *Continuing bonds: New understanding of grief.* Washington, DC: Taylor & Francis.

Lazarus, R. S., & Folkman, S. (1984). *Stress, appraisal, and coping.* New York: Springer.

Lindemann, E. (1944). Symptomatology and management of acute grief. *American Journal of Psychiatry, 101,* 141–148.

Lundberg, K. J., Thornton, G., & Robertson, D. U. (1987). Personal and social rejection of the bereaved. In C. A. Corr & R. A. Pacholski (Eds.), *Death: Completion and discovery* (pp. 61–70). Lakewood, OH: Association for Death Education and Counseling.

McClowry, S. G., Davies, E. B., May, K. A., Kulenkamp, E. J., & Martinson, I. M. (1987). The empty space phenomenon: The process of grief in the bereaved family. *Death Studies, 11,* 361–374.

Mead, M. (1973). Ritual and social crisis. In J. D. Shaughnessy (Ed.), *The roots of ritual* (pp. 87–101). Grand Rapids, MI: Eerdmans.

Osterweis, M., Solomon, F., & Green, M. (Eds.) (1984). *Bereavement: Reactions, consequences, and care.* Washington, DC: National Academy Press.

The Oxford English Dictionary (1989). J. A. Simpson & E. S. C. Weiner (Eds.). 2nd ed.; 20 vols; Oxford: Clarendon Press.

Parkes, C. M. (1996). *Bereavement: Studies of grief in adult life* (3rd ed.). New York: Routledge.

Pine, V. R., Margolis, O. S., Doka, K., Kutscher, A. H., Schaefer, D. J., Siegel, M-E., & Cherico, D. J. (Eds.) (1990). *Unrecognized and unsanctioned grief: The nature and counseling of unacknowledged loss.* Springfield, IL: Charles C Thomas.

Rando, T. A. (1993). *Treatment of complicated mourning.* Champaign, IL: Research Press.

Schwebach, I., & Thornton, G. (1992, 6 March). *Disenfranchised grief in mentally retarded and mentally ill populations.* Paper presented at the meeting of the Association for Death Education and Counseling, Boston.

Silverman, P. R., Nickman, S., & Worden, J. W. (1992). Detachment revisited: The child's reconstruction of a dead parent. *American Journal of Orthopsychiatry, 62,* 494–503.

Staples, B. (1994). *Parallel time: Growing up in black and white.* New York: Pantheon.

Stroebe, M. S., & Schut, H. (1995, June 29). *The dual process model of coping with loss.* Paper presented at the meeting of the International Work Group on Death, Dying, and Bereavement, Oxford, England.

Thornton, G., Robertson, D. U., & Mlecko, M. L. (1991). Disenfranchised grief and evaluations of social support by college students. *Death Studies, 15,* 355–362.

Wagner, S. (1994). *The Andrew poems.* Lubbock, TX: Texas Tech University Press.

Weisman, A. D. (1984). *The coping capacity: On the nature of being mortal.* New York: Human Sciences Press.

Wolfelt, A. D. (1996). *Healing the bereaved child: Grief gardening, growth through grief and other touchstones for caregivers.* Fort Collins, CO: Companion Press.

Worden, J. W. (1991). *Grief counseling and grief therapy: A handbook for the mental health practitioner* (2nd ed.). New York: Springer.

Zupanick, C. E. (1994). Adult children of dysfunctional families: Treatment from a disenfranchised grief perspective. *Death Studies, 18,* 183–195.

Till death do us part

Mickie Mashburn

Lois Marrero and I met in 1986 while working at the Tampa police department. Lois had been an officer for four years, and I was a new recruit. Initially Lois and I were just friends. I admired her because she was so very passionate about life. Eventually she and I fell in love and realized we were soul mates. One day in 1990 I asked her, "Would you consider spending the rest of your life with me?" She told me, "I would like that very much." Lois moved in, and on May 25, 1991, we held a commitment ceremony at the Metropolitan Community Church in St. Petersburg. That was the happiest day of my life. I know she felt the same way.

For more than 10 years we were inseparable. Every morning I told Lois, "I love you more today than yesterday." She always replied, "Me too." We both loved sports, we worked out together daily, we volunteered at the Tampa AIDS Network. We went to as many spring training baseball games as we could. Lois loved Disney World and the Orlando Miracle, the women's basketball team. She often said, "Let's go to Orlando." I'd tell her, "You need to rest sometimes," but she'd answer, "When you die you can sleep."

Then came July 6, 2001.

Lois was so happy that summer morning, looking forward to a Miracle game we had tickets for after work. I phoned her at about 9 A.M. to see how her day was going. At 10:03 A.M. she sent a message to my beeper, like she often did—the numbers 45683968, for "I love you." Later we talked briefly, in what would be our last conversation. I heard the dispatcher on her police radio. Lois said, "I've got to hurry." I said, "Be careful, I love you." She replied, "I love you too."

For lunch a bunch of us bought sandwiches to eat at the station. Minutes later a lieutenant walked into the office. From the look on his face, we knew something terrible had happened. He glanced at me and then quickly looked away. My heart sank. He motioned for Betsy, another policewoman, to come outside. I said, "Something's happened to Lois." When Betsy returned, she knelt down in front of me. I said, "All I need to know is whether she's still alive." Betsy just started sobbing. I was devastated.

Lois was gunned down by a bank robbery suspect as she chased him into a parking lot. She was the first Tampa policewoman to be killed in the line of duty, just 40 years old. On her finger was the gold wedding ring we each wore, inscribed with the date of our ceremony and the words Forever Loved.

I was taken to the hospital where Lois's body was brought. Mayor Dick Greco, police chief Bennie Holder, and the top brass were there. They all knew about our relationship and wanted to help me any way they could. The department helped me make arrangements. Thousands of officers stood at attention outside her funeral. At the end Chief Holder took the American flag that had been draped over Lois's coffin and placed it, folded, in my lap; everyone treated me as the spouse.

But after the funeral, things changed with Lois's family. We had been close, but when I applied for Lois's pension as the surviving spouse—which would have been half Lois's salary for the rest of my life, probably about $500,000—the family opposed me and sought the benefits themselves.

In August the pension board unanimously turned me down, voting to award Lois's pension contributions, about $50,000, to her estate; since Lois and I never made a will, the money goes to her blood relatives. Her family also demanded that I turn over a lot of personal things: Lois's clothes, photo, albums, diplomas. They're even trying to claim the car she used, though we both helped buy it.

Other than making a will, Lois and I couldn't have done any more to make sure we were treated as spouses, because we weren't allowed to marry. I'm fighting the pension board's rejection of spousal benefits, and my appeal will be heard February 26. Lois was a fighter. If I had been killed instead, Lois would have demanded to be treated like any other spouse. She fought for justice. Now it's my turn.

As told to Peter Freiberg. Mashburn remains a police officer in Tampa, Fla.

THE INCREASING PREVALENCE OF COMPLICATED MOURNING: THE ONSLAUGHT IS JUST BEGINNING

Therese A. Rando, Ph.D.
Warwick, Rhode Island

ABSTRACT

In this article, complicated mourning is operationalized in relation to the six "R" processes of mourning and its seven high-risk factors are identified. The main thesis is that the prevalence of complicated mourning is increasing today due to a number of contemporary sociocultural and technological trends which have influenced 1) today's types of death; 2) the characteristics of personal relationships severed by today's deaths; and 3) the personality and resources of today's mourner. Additionally, specific problems in both the mental health profession and the field of thanatology further escalate complicated mourning by preventing or interfering with requisite treatment. Thus, complicated mourning is on the rise at the precise time when caregivers are unprepared and limited in their abilities to respond. New treatment policies and models are mandated as a consequence.

In the 1990s, the mental health profession (a term herein broadly used to encompass any caregiver whose work places him/her in the position of ministering to the mental health needs of another) and the thanatological community are at a crucial crossroads. Current sociocultural and technological trends in American society are directly increasing the prevalence of complicated mourning at the precise point in time at which the mental health profession is particularly both unprepared and limited in its abilities to respond to the needs created. Thanatology has a pivotal role to play in identifying this crisis, delineating the problems to be addressed, and advocating for the development of new policies, models, approaches, and treatments appropriate to today's grim realities. Failure of either profession to recognize these realities is bound to result not only in inadequate care for those who require it, but to place our society at greater risk for the serious sequelae known to emanate from untreated complicated mourning [1].

After a brief review of complicated mourning, this article will: 1) identify the high-risk factors for complicated mourning; 2) delineate the sociocultural and technological trends exacerbating these factors, which in turn increase the prevalence of complicated mourning; 3) indicate the problems inherent in the mental health profession that interfere with proper response to complicated mourning and to its escalation; and 4) point out the pitfalls for addressing complicated mourning that reside in the field of thanatology today. The focus on this article is restricted to raising awareness of the problem and discussing its determinants.

COMPLICATED MOURNING

Historically, there have been three main difficulties in defining complicated mourning. The first stems from the imprecise and inconsistent terminology employed. The very same grief and mourning phenomena have been described at various times and by various authors as "pathological," "neurotic," "maladaptive," "unresolved," "abnormal," "dysfunctional," or "deviant," just to name some of the designations used. Communication has been hampered by a lack of semantic agreement and consensual validation. This author's preference is for the term "complicated mourning." Such a term suggests that mourning is a series of processes which in some way have become complicated, with the implication being that what has become complicated can be uncomplicated. It avoids the pejorative tone of many of the other terms. Additionally, there is no insinuation of pathology in the mourner. Heretofore, complications typically have been construed to arise from the deficits of the person experiencing the bereavement. The term "complicated" avoids the assumption that the complications necessarily stem from the mourner him or herself. This is quite crucial because it is now well-documented that there are some circumstances of death and some postdeath variables that in and of themselves complicate mourning regardless of the premorbid psychological health of the mourner.

A second difficulty stems from the lack of objective criteria for what constitutes complicated mourning. Unlike the analogous medical situation in which the determination of pathology is more readily discerned and defined (e.g., the diagnosis of a broken bone usually can be easily agreed upon by several physicians following viewing of an x-ray), the phenomena in mourning tend not to be so concrete or unarguable. For instance, a woman hearing her deceased husband's voice in some circumstances is quite appropriate, whereas in others it reflects gross pathology.

The third and related difficulty is found because mourning is so highly idiosyncratic. It is determined by a constellation of thirty-three sets of factors circumscribing the loss and its circumstances, the mourner, and the social support received. No determination of abnormality technically ever can be made without taking into consideration the sets of factors known to influence any response to loss [2]. What may be an appropriate response in one circumstance for an individual mourner may be a highly pathological response for a different mourner in other circumstances. For this reason, it appears most helpful to look at complications in the mourning processes themselves rather than at particular symptomatology.

With this as a premise, complicated mourning can be said to be present when, taking into consideration the amount of time since the death, there is a compromise, distortion, or failure of one or more of the six "R" processes of mourning [1]. The six "R" processes of mourning necessary for healthy accommodation of any loss are:

1. Recognize the loss
   • Acknowledge the death
   • Understand the death
2. React to the separation
   • Experience the pain
   • Feel, identify, accept, and give some form of expression to all the psychological reactions to the loss
   • Identify and mourn secondary losses
3. Recollect and reexperience the deceased and the relationship
   • Review and remember realistically
   • Revive and reexperience the feelings
4. Relinquish the old attachments to the deceased and the old assumptive world
5. Readjust to move adaptively into the new world without forgetting the old
   • Revise the old assumptive world
   • Develop a new relationship with the deceased
   • Adopt new ways of being in the world
   • Form a new identity
6. Reinvest

In all forms of complicated mourning, there are attempts to do two things: 1) to deny, repress, or avoid aspects of the loss, its pain, and the full realization of its implications for the mourner; and 2) to hold onto, and avoid relinquishing, the lost loved one. These attempts, or some variation thereof, are what cause the complications in the "R" processes of mourning.

Complicated mourning may take any one or combination of four forms: symptoms, syndromes, mental or physical disorder, or death [1].

Complicated mourning symptoms refer to any psychological, behavioral, social, or physical symptom—alone or in combination—which in context reveals some dimension of compromise, distortion, or failure of one or more of the six "R" processes of mourning. They are of insufficient number, intensity, and duration, or of different type, than are required to meet the criteria for any of the other three forms of complicated mourning discussed below.

There are seven complicated mourning syndromes into which a constellation of complicated mourning symptoms may coalesce. They may occur independently or concurrently with one another. Only if the symptoms comprising them meet the criteria for the specific syndrome is there said to be a complicated mourning syndrome present. If only some of the symptoms are present, or there is a combination of symptoms from several of the syndromes but they fail to meet the criteria for a particular complicated mourning syndrome, then they are considered complicated mourning symptoms. The reader should be advised that a syndrome is not necessarily more pathological than a group of symptoms which clusters together but does not fit the description of one of the complicated mourning syndromes. Sometimes just a few complicated mourning symptoms—depending upon which they are—can be far more serious than the complicated mourning syndromes. With the exception of death, severity is not determined by the form of complicated mourning.

The seven syndromes of complicated mourning include three syndromes with problems in expression (i.e., absent mourning, delayed mourning and inhibited mourning); three syndromes with skewed aspects (i.e., distorted mourning of the extremely angry or guilty types, conflicted mourning, and unanticipated mourning); and the syndrome with a problem in ending (i.e., chronic mourning).

The third form that complicated mourning may take is of a diagnosable mental or physical disorder. This would include any DSM-III-R [3] diagnosis of a mental disorder or any recognized physical disorder that results from or is associated with a compromise, distortion, or failure of one or more of the six "R" processes of mourning. Death is the fourth form which complicated mourning may take. The death may be consciously chosen (i.e., suicide) or it may stem from the immediate results of a complicated mourning reaction (e.g., an automobile crash resulting from the complicated mourning symptom of driving at excessive speed) or the long-term results of a complicated mourning reaction (e.g., cirrhosis of the liver secondary to mourning-related alcoholism). The latter two types of death may or may not be subintentioned on the part of the mourner.

GENERIC HIGH-RISK FACTORS FOR COMPLICATED MOURNING

Clinical and empirical evidence reveals that there are seven generic high-risk factors which can predispose any individual to have complication in mourning [1]. These can be divided into two categories: factors associated with the specific death and factors associated with antecedent and subsequent variables.

Factors associated with the death which are known especially to complicate mourning include: 1) a sudden and unanticipated death, especially when it is traumatic, violent, mutilating, or random; 2) death from an overly-lengthy illness; 3) loss of a child; and 4) the mourner's perception of preventability. Antecedent and subsequent variables that tend to complicate mourning include: 1) premorbid relationship with the deceased which has been markedly angry or ambivalent or markedly dependent; 2) the mourner's prior or concurrent mental health problems and/or unaccommodated losses and stresses; and 3) the mourner's perceived lack of social support.

To the extent that any bereaved individual is characterized by one or more of these factors, that individual can be said to be at risk for the development of complications in one or more of the six "R" processes of mourning, and hence at risk for complicated mourning.

SOCIOCULTURAL AND TECHNOLOGICAL TRENDS EXACERBATING THE HIGH RISK FACTORS AND INCREASING THE PREVALENCE OF COMPLICATED MOURNING

Social change, medical advances, and shifting political realities have spawned the recent trends that have complicated healthy grief and mourning.

Social change, occurring at an increasingly rapid rate, encompasses such processes as urbanization; industrialization; increasing technicalization; secularization and deritualization (particularly the trend to omit funeral or memorial services and not to view the body); greater social mobility; social reorganization (specifically a decline in—if not a breakdown of—the nuclear family, increases in single parent and blended families, and the relative exclusion of the aged and dying); rising societal, interpersonal, and institutional violence (physical, sexual, and psychological); and unemployment, poverty, and economic problems. Consequences include social alienation; senses of personal helplessness and hopelessness; parental absence and neglect of children; larger societal discrepancies between the "haves" and the "have nots"; epidemic drug and alcohol abuse; physical and sexual abuse of children and those without power (e.g., women and the elderly); and availability of guns. All of these sequelae have tended to increase violence even more, to sever or severely damage the links between children and adults, and to expose individuals to more traumatic and unnatural deaths.

Medical advances have culminated in lengthier chronic illnesses, and increased age spans, altered mortality rates, and intensified bioethical dilemmas. These trends, plus those involving social change, accompany contemporary political realities of increasing incidence of terrorism, assassination, political torture, and genocide, which get played out against the ever-present possibility of ecological disaster, nuclear holocaust, and megadeath to impact dramatically and undeniably on today's mourner [4–6].

VIOLENCE: A PARTICULARLY MALIGNANT TREND

Any commentary on present-day trends would be negligent if it did not elaborate somewhat upon the phenomenon of violence in today's society. Violence contributes significantly to the increasing prevalence of complicated mourning, and is associated with most of its generic high-risk factors. One crime index offense occurs every two seconds in the United States, with one violent crime occurring every nineteen seconds [7]. Violent crime has risen to the extent that in April 1991 Attorney General Richard Thornburgh issued the statement that "a citizen of this country is today more likely to be the victim of a violent crime than of an automobile accident" [8]. The U.S. Department of Justice estimates that five out of six of today's twelve-year-olds will become victims of violent crime during their lifetimes [9], with estimates for the lifetime chance of becoming a victim of homicide in the United States ranging from one out of 133 to one out of 153 depending upon the source of the statistics [10]. One category of homicide—murder by juvenile—is increasing so rapidly that it is now being termed "epidemic" by psychologist and attorney Charles Ewing [11], an authority on child perpetrators of homicide.

Other types of crime and victimization are on the rise in the United States. The National Victim Center Overview of Crime and Victimization in America [12] provides some of the horrifying statistics:

- Wife-beating results in more injuries that require medical treatment than rape, auto accidents, and muggings combined.
- More than one out of every 200 senior citizens is the victim of a violent crime each year, making a total of 155,000 elderly Americans who are attacked, robbed, assaulted, and murdered every year—435 each day.
- New York City has reported an eighty percent increase in hate-motivated crimes since 1986, with seventy percent of them perpetrated by those under age nineteen.
- One in three women will be sexually assaulted during her lifetime.
- Every forty-seven seconds a child is abused or neglected.

Certainly, society not only condones, but escalates, violence. Books, movies, music videos, and songs perpetuate the belief that violence is not merely acceptable, but exciting. Books focusing on real-life serial killers; escalating movie violence associated with anatomically precise and sexually explicit images; and music portraying hostility against women, murder, and necrophilia are routine. According to Thomas Radecki, Research Director for the National Coalition on Television Violence, by the age of 18 the average American child will have seen 200,000 violent acts on television, including 40,000 murders [13]. Children's programming now averages twenty-five violent acts per hour, which is up fifty percent from that in the early 1980s [14]. The recently popular children's movie, *Teenage Mutant Ninja Turtles,* had a total of 194 acts of violence primarily committed by the "heroes" of the film, which was the most violent film ever to be given a "PG" rating [15]. In the week of March 11, 1990, *America's Funniest Home Videos* became the highest-rated series on television. Some of the stories on that program that viewers found particularly amusing included a child getting hit in the face with a shovel, seven women falling off a bench, a man getting hit by a glider, and a child bicycling into a tree [15]. All of this provides serious concerns given the twenty-year research of Leonard Eron and L. Rowell Huesmann, who found that children who watch significant amounts of TV violence at the age of eight were consistently more likely to commit violent crimes or engage in spouse abuse at age thirty [13]. These researchers determined that heavy exposure to media violence is one of the major causes of aggressive behavior, crime, and violence in society.

Other forms of violence are increasing as well. Reports of abused and neglected children continue to rise. They reached 2.5 million in 1990, an increase of 30.7 percent since 1986, and 117 percent in the past decade [16]. One out of three girls, and one out of seven boys, are sexually abused by the time they reach eighteen [17]. In the United States, when random studies are conducted without the inclusion of high-risk groups, one in eight husbands has been physically aggressive with his wife in the preceding twelve months [18]. At least 2,000,000 women are severely and aggressively assaulted by their partners in any twelve-month period [18]. It is a myth that what has been termed "intimate violence" is confined to mentally disturbed individuals. While ten percent of offenders do sustain some form of psychopathology, ninety percent of offenders do not look any different than the "normal" individual [19].

SEQUELAE OF THE TRENDS PREDISPOSING TO COMPLICATED MOURNING

As a result of all the aforementioned sociocultural and technological trends, there have been changes in three main areas which have significantly increased the prevalence of complicated mourning:

1. the types of death occurring today
2. the characteristics of personal relationships that are severed by today's deaths
3. the personality and resources of today's mourner.

Each of these adversely impacts in one or more ways upon one or more of the high-risk factors for complicated mourning, thereby increasing its prevalence.

TYPES OF DEATH OCCURRING TODAY

Contemporary American society is witnessing the increase in three types of death known to be at high risk for complicated mourning: 1) sudden and unanticipated deaths, especially if they are traumatic (i.e., characterized not only by suddenness

and lack of anticipation, but violence, mutilation, and destruction; preventability and/or randomness; multiple death; or the mourner's personal encounter with death [20]; 2) deaths that result from excessively lengthy chronic illnesses; and 3) deaths of children. Each of these deaths presents the survivors with issues known to compromise the "R" processes of mourning, hence each circumstance is a high-risk factor for complicated mourning.

Sudden and Unanticipated Traumatic Deaths

Sudden and unanticipated traumatic deaths stem primarily from four main causes: 1) accidents; 2) technological advances; 3) increasing rates of homicide and the escalating violence and pathology of perpetrators; and 4) higher suicide rates. Although mortality rates for children and youth in the United States have decreased since 1900, the large proportion of deaths from external causes—injuries, homicide, and suicide—distinguishes mortality at ages one to nineteen from that at other ages; with external causes of death accounting for about ten percent of the deaths of children and youth in 1900 and rising to 64 percent in 1985 [21].

Current trends reveal that "accidents"—a term covering most deaths from motor vehicle crashes, falls, poisoning, drowning, fire, suffocation, and firearms—are the leading cause of death among all persons aged one to thirty-seven and represent the fourth leading cause of death among persons of all ages [22]. On the average, there are eleven accidental deaths and approximately 1,030 disabling injuries every hour during the year [22]. Accidents are the single most common type of horrendous death for persons of any age, bringing deaths which are "premature, torturous, and without redeeming value" [23].

Technological advances simultaneously have both decreased the proportion of natural deaths that occur and increased the proportion of sudden and unanticipated traumatic deaths. For instance, substantial improvements in biomedical technology have culminated in higher survival rates from illnesses which previously would have been fatal. This leaves individuals alive longer to be susceptible to unnatural death. Additionally, the increase in unnatural death is due to greater current exposure to technology, machinery, motor vehicles, airplanes, chemicals, firearms, weapon systems, and so forth that put human beings at greater risk for unnatural death. For example, prior to the advent of the airplane, a crash of a horse and buggy could claim far fewer lives and be less mutilating to the bodies than the crash of a DC-10.

The third reason for the increase in sudden and unanticipated traumatic deaths stems from the increasing rates of homicide and the escalating violence and pathology of those who perpetrate these crimes upon others. The increase in actual homicide incidence; the rising percentage of serial killers; and the types of violence perpetrated before, during, and after the final homicidal act suggest that there are sicker individuals doing sicker things. More than ever before, homicide may be marked by cult or ritual killing, thrill killing, random killing, drive-by shootings, and accompanied by predeath torture and postdeath defilement. The increasing pathology of those who commit violent crimes may be seen as the result of the previously mentioned sociocultural trends, especially but not exclusively the individual's decreasing social connections and sense of power; fewer social prohibitions, and increasing societal violence. It reflects the increasing number of individuals with impaired psychological development, characterized often by an absent conscience, low frustration tolerance, poor impulse control, inability to delay gratification or modulate aggression, a sense of deprivation and entitlement, and notably poor attachment bonds and pathological patterns of relationships.

The fourth reason for the increase in sudden and unanticipated traumatic deaths follows from the higher suicide rates currently found in Western society. As above, these types of death appear to derive from all of the aforementioned trends contributing to complicated mourning in general.

The reader will note that most of the sudden and unanticipated traumatic deaths in this category also are preventable. Given that the perception of preventability is a high-risk factor predisposing to complicated mourning, to the extent that a mourner maintains this perception as an element in his or her mourning of the death, that individual sustains a greater chance for experiencing complications in the process.

Long-Term Chronic Illness Death

This type of death is increasing in frequency because of biomedical and technological advances that can combat disease and forestall cessation of life. Consequently, today's illnesses are longer in duration than ever before. However, it has been well-documented that there are significant problems for survivors when a loved one's terminal illness persists for too long [24]. These illnesses often present loved ones with inherent difficulties that eventually complicate their postdeath bereavement and expose them to situations and dilemmas previously unheard of when patients died sooner and/or without becoming the focus for bioethical debates around the use of machinery and the prolongation of life without quality. With the increase in the Human Immunodeficiency Virus (HIV) and Acquired Immunodeficiency Syndrome (AIDS), significant multidimensional stresses arise which engender those known to complicate mourning in anyone (e.g., anger, ambivalence, guilt, stigmatization, social disenfranchisement, problems obtaining required health care, and so forth). The fact that an individual may be positive for the HIV virus for an exceptionally long period of time prior to developing the often long-term, multiproblemic, and idiosyncratic course of their particular version of AIDS, with all of its vicissitudes, gives new meaning these days to the stresses of long-term chronic illness.

Parental Loss of a Child

In earlier years, by the time an adult child died, his or her parents would have been long deceased. Today, with increases in lifespan and advances in medical technology, parents are permitted to survive long enough to witness the deaths of the adult children they used to predecease. Clinically and empirically, it is well-known that significant problematic issues are associated with the parental loss of a child—issues which when compared to those generated by other losses appear to make this loss the most difficult with which to cope [25]. These problematic issues and complicated mourning are now visited upon older parents who remain alive to experience the death of their adult child. There is even some suggestion that additional stresses are added to the normal burdens of parental bereavement when the child is an adult in his or her own right [26]. It is a uniquely contemporary trend, therefore, that associated with all of today's deaths are a greater percentage of parents who, because of medical advancements, are alive to be placed in the high-risk situation for complicated mourning upon the death of their adult child. This is a population that can be expected to increase, and consequently swell the numbers of complicated mourners as well.

CHARACTERISTICS OF PERSONAL RELATIONSHIPS SEVERED BY TODAY'S DEATHS

As a consequence of societal trends, there has been an increase in conflicted and dependent relationships in our society. Both types are high-risk factors when they characterize the mourner's premorbid relationship with the deceased [1]. With more of these types of relationships than ever before, there is a relative increase in the prevalence of complicated mourning, which is predisposed to develop after the death of one with whom the mourner has had this type of bond.

In 1957, Edmond Volkart offered a classic discussion of why death in the American family tends to cause greater psychological impact than in other cultures, specifically causing the family to be uniquely vulnerable to bereavement [6]. The reasons he delineated are even more salient today, and are part of the trends already cited above. Among other trends, he noted that the limited range of interaction in the American family fosters unusually intense emotional involvement as compared to other societies, and that there is an exclusivity of relationships in the American family. Both trends breed overidentification and overdependence among family members, which in turn engender ambivalence, repressed hostility, and guilt that create greater potential for complications after the death. Adding fuel to this fire is the societal expectation that grief expression concentrates on feelings and expression of loss. There is a failure both to recognize and to provide channels for hostility, guilt, and ambivalence.

Problematic relationships are on the rise in our society for other reasons as well. Quite importantly, there is an overall increase in sexual and physical abuse of children, as well as other adults. Research repeatedly documents the malignant intrapsychic and interpersonal sequelae of abuse and victimization [27, 28]. This leaves the victim susceptible to complications in mourning not only because of the myriad symptomatology and biopsychosocial issues they caused, but typically with significant amounts of the anger, ambivalence, and/or dependence known to complicate any individual's mourning. In addition, the victimization may interfere with the mourner permitting him or herself to mourn the death of the perpetrator—an often necessary task that many victims resist because of inaccurate beliefs about mourning in general and/or misconstruals of what their specifically mourning the perpetrator's death may mean [1]. This only further victimizes the person through the consequences of incomplete mourning.

These forms of victimization are not the only experiences which give rise to the conflicted and dependent relationships identified as predisposing to complicated mourning. Individuals raised in families with one or more alcoholic parents or a parent who is an adult child of an alcoholic (ACOA), or with one or more parents who are psychologically impaired, rigid in beliefs, compulsive in behaviors, codependent, absent, neglectful, or chronically ill are vulnerable too. As sociocultural trends escalate these scenarios, relationships characterized by anger, ambivalence, and dependency will become prevalent, and complicated mourning will, in turn, become more frequent.

THE PERSONALITY AND RESOURCES OF TODAY'S MOURNER

Current trends suggest that the personality and resources of today's mourner leave that individual compromised in mourning for three reasons. First, given the trends previously discussed, the personalities and mental health of today's mourners are often more impaired. These impaired persons—who themselves frequently sustain poor attachment bonds with their own parents because of these trends—typically effect intergenerational transmission of these deficits via the inadequate parenting provided to their own children and the unhealthy experiences those children undergo. Clinically, one sees more often these days impaired superego development, lower level personality organization, narcissistic behavior, character disorder, and poor impulse control. Given that one's personality and previous and current states of mental health are critical factors influencing any mourner's ability to address mourning successfully, a trend towards relatively more impairment in this area has implications for greater numbers of people being added to the rolls of complicated mourners.

Another liability for a mourner is the existence of unaccommodated prior or concurrent losses or stresses. In this regard, a second reason for the increased prevalence of complicated mourning comes from the presence of more loss and stress in the life of today's mourner as compared to times in the past. To the extent that contemporary sociocultural trends bring relatively more losses and stresses for a person, both prior to a given death (e.g., parents' divorce) and concomitant with it (e.g., unemployment), today's mourner is relatively more disadvantaged given his or her increased exposure to these high-risk factors.

The third reason for increased complications in mourning arises from the compromise of the mourner's resources. Disenfranchised mourning [29] is on the rise, and the consequent perceived lack of social support it stimulates is a high-risk factor for complicated mourning. It is quite evident that conditions in contemporary American society promote all three of the main reasons for social disenfranchisement during mourning, i.e., in-

validation of the loss, the lost relationship, or the mourner [29]. Examples of unrecognized losses that are increasing in today's society include abortions, adoptions, the deaths of pets, and the inherent losses of those with Alzheimer's disease. Cases of the second type of disenfranchised loss that are on the increase include relationships that are not based on kin ties, or are not socially sanctioned (e.g., gay or lesbian relationships, extramarital affairs), or those that existed primarily in the past (e.g., former spouses or in-laws). Increasingly prevalent situations where the mourner is unrecognized can be found when the mourner is elderly, mentally handicapped, or a child. The more society creates, maintains, or permits individuals to be disenfranchised in their mourning, the more those individuals are at risk for complicated mourning given that disenfranchisement is so intimately linked with the high-risk factor of the mourner's perception of lack of social support.

PROBLEMS INHERENT IN THE MENTAL HEALTH PROFESSION WHICH INTERFERE WITH PROPER RESPONSE TO COMPLICATED MOURNING AND TO ITS ESCALATION

There are three serious problems inherent in mental health today that interfere with the profession's response to complicated mourning and its escalation. Each one contributes to increasing the prevalence of complicated mourning either by facilitating misdiagnosis and/or hampering requisite treatment. The three problems are: 1) lack of an appropriate diagnostic category in the DSM-III-R; 2) insufficient knowledge about grief, mourning, and bereavement in general; and 3) decreased funds for and increased restrictions upon contemporary mental health services.

In the DSM-III-R, there is the lack of a diagnostic category for anything but the most basic uncomplicated grief, with the criteria even for this being significantly unrealistic for duration and symptomatology in light of today's data on uncomplicated grief and mourning. If they want to treat a mourning individual, mental health clinicians are often forced to utilize other diagnoses, many of which have clinical implications that are unacceptable. Other diagnoses that clinicians employ to justify treatment and to incorporate more fully the symptomatology of the bereaved individual frequently include one of the depressive, anxiety, or adjustment disorders; brief reactive psychosis; or one of the V code diagnoses.

The second area of problems in the mental health profession is the shocking insufficiency of knowledge about grief and bereavement in general. Mental health professionals tend, as does the general public, to have inappropriate expectations and unrealistic attitudes about grief and mourning, and to believe in and promote the myths and stereotypes known to pervade society at large. These not only do not help, but actually harm bereaved individuals given that they are used to (a) set the standards against which the bereaved individual is evaluated, (b) determine the assistance and support provided and/or judged to be needed, and (c) support unwarranted diagnoses of failure and pathology [30]. Yet, the problem is not all in *mis*information.

Too many clinicians actually do not even know that they lack the requisite information they must possess if they want to treat a bereaved person successfully. Without a doubt, the majority of clinicians know an insufficient amount about uncomplicated grief and mourning; and of those who do know an adequate amount, only a fraction of them know enough about complicated mourning. Clinician lack of information and misinformation is the major cause of iatrogenesis in the treatment of grief and mourning.

An overall decrease in funds permitted and an increase in third-party payer insurance restrictions mark contemporary mental health services and constitute the third problem in the field adding to the prevalence of complicated mourning. These changes occur at a time when it not only is becoming more clearly documented that uncomplicated grief and mourning is more associated with psychiatric distress than previously recognized [31] and that it persists for longer duration [32], but precisely when the incidence of complicated mourning is increasing and demanding more extensive treatment for higher proportions of the bereaved. Consequently, at the exact point in time that the mental health community will have more bereaved individuals with greater complicated mourning requiring treatment for longer periods of time, mental health services will be increasingly subjected to limitations, preapprovals, third-party reviews by persons ignorant of the area, short-term models, and forced usage of inappropriate diagnostic classification. This scenario demands that the mental health professional working with the bereaved find new policies, models, approaches, and treatments which are appropriate to these serious realities. Failing to do so, the future is frightening as the current system simply is not equipped to respond to the coming onslaught of complicated mourners.

THE PITFALLS FOR ADDRESSING COMPLICATED MOURNING RESIDING IN THE FIELD OF THANATOLOGY TODAY

It is unfortunate, but true: Thanatologists are contributing to the rising prevalence of complicated mourning as are contemporary sociocultural and technological trends and the mental health profession. While it is not in the purview of this article to discuss at length the myriad problems inherent in our own field of thanatology that contribute to complicated mourning, it must be noted:

- A significant amount of caregivers lack adequate clinical information about uncomplicated grief and mourning, e.g., the "normal" psychiatric complications of uncomplicated grief and mourning.
- Many thanatologists, in their effort to promote the naturalness of grief and mourning and to depathologize the way they construe it to have been medicalized, maintain an insufficient understanding of complicated grief and mourning.
- There is nonexistent, or at the very least woefully insufficient, assessment conducted by caregivers who

assume that the grief and mourning they observe must be related exclusively to the particular death closest in time and who do not place the individual's responses within the context of his or her entire life prior to evaluating them.

- The phenomenon of "throwing the baby out with the bathwater" has occurred regarding medication in bereavement. Out of a concern that a mourner not be inappropriately medicated as had been done so often in the past, caregivers today often fail to send mourners for medication evaluations that are desperately needed, e.g., antianxiety medication following traumatic deaths.
- The research in the field has not been sufficiently longitudinal and has overfocused on certain populations (e.g., widows), leaving findings that are not generalizable over time for many types of mourners, especially complicated mourners.
- Caregivers do not always recognize that any work as a grief or mourning counselor or therapist must overlay a basic foundation of training in mental health intervention in general. While education in thanatology, good intentions, and/or previous experience with loss may be appropriate credentials for the individual facilitating uncomplicated grief and mourning (e.g., a facilitator of a mutual help group for the bereaved), this is not sufficient for that person offering counseling or therapy.
- Given that thanatology itself is a "specialty area," thanatologists often fail to recognize that the field encompasses a number of "subspecialty areas," each of which has its own data base and treatment requirements, i.e., all mourners are not alike and caregivers must recognize and respond to the differences inherent in different loss situations (e.g., loss of a child versus loss of a spouse or sudden and unanticipated death versus an expected chronic illness death).
- Clinicians working with the dying and the bereaved are subject to countertransference phenomena, stress reactions, codependency, "vicarious traumatization" [33], and burnout.

This constitutes a brief, and by no means exhaustive, listing of the types of pitfalls into which a thanatologist may fall. Each "fall" has the potential for compromising the mourning of the bereaved individual and in that regard has the potential for increasing the prevalence of complicated mourning today.

CONCLUSION

This article has discussed the causes and forms of complicated mourning, and has delineated the seven high-risk factors known to predispose to it. The purpose has been to illustrate how current sociocultural and technological trends are exacerbating these factors, thereby significantly increasing the prevalence of complicated mourning today. Problems both in the mental health profession and in the field of thanatology further contribute by preventing or interfering with requisite intervention. It is imperative that these grim realities be recognized in order that appropriate policies, models, approaches, and treatments be developed to respond to the individual and societal needs created by complicated mourning and its sequelae.

This article is adapted from a keynote address of the same name presented at the 13th Annual Conference of the Association for Death Education and Counseling, Duluth, Minnesota, April 26–28, 1991 and from the author's book, *Treatment of Complicated Mourning,* Research Press, Champaign, Illinois, 1993.

REFERENCES

1. T. Rando, *Treatment of Complicated Mourning,* Research Press, Champaign, Illinois, 1993.
2. T. Rando, *Grief, Dying, and Death: Clinical Interventions for Caregivers,* Research Press, Champaign, Illinois, 1984.
3. American Psychiatric Association, *Diagnostic and Statistical Manual of Mental Disorders,* (3rd ed. rev.), Washington, D.C., 1987.
4. H. Feifel, The Meaning of Death in American Society: Implications for Education, in *Death Education: Preparation for Living,* B. Green and D. Irish (eds.), Schenkman, Cambridge, Massachusetts, 1971.
5. R. Lifton, *Death in Life: Survivors of Hiroshima,* Random House, New York, 1968.
6. E. Volkart (with collaboration of S. Michael), Bereavement and Mental Health, in *Explorations in Social Psychiatry,* A. Leighton, J. Clausen, and R. Wilson (eds.), Basic Books, New York, 1957.
7. Federal Bureau of Investigation, U.S. Department of Justice, *Uniform Crime Reports for the United States,* U.S. Government Printing Office, Washington, D.C., 1990.
8. Violent Crimes up 10%, *Providence Journal,* pp. A1 and A6, April 29, 1991.
9. National Victim Center, *America Speaks Out: Citizens' Attitudes about Victims' Rights and Violence,* (Executive Summary), Fort Worth, Texas, 1991.
10. Bureau of Justice Statistics Special Report, *The Risk of Violent Crime,* (NCJ-97119), U.S. Department of Justice, Washington, D.C., May 1985.
11. Killing by Kids "Epidemic" Forecast, *APA Monitor,* pp. 1 and 31, April, 1991.
12. National Victim Center, *National Victim Center Overview of Crime and Victimization in America,* Fort Worth, Texas, 1991.
13. Violence in Our Culture, *Newsweek,* pp. 46–52, April 1, 1991.
14. J. Patterson and P. Kim, *The Day America Told the Truth,* Prentice Hall Press, New York, 1991.
15. National Victim Center, *Crime, Safety and You!,* 1:3, 1990.
16. Children's Defense Fund Memo on the Family Preservation Act, Washington, D.C., July 2, 1991.
17. E. Bass and L. Davis, *The Courage to Heal: A Guide for Women Survivors of Child Sexual Abuse,* Harper and Row Publishers, New York, 1988.
18. A. Brown, *"Women's Roles" and Responses to Violence by Intimates: Hard Choices for Women Living in a Violent Society,* paper presented at the conference on "Trauma and Victimization: Understanding and Healing Survivors" sponsored by the University of Connecticut Center for Professional Development, Vernon, Connecticut, September 27–28, 1991.
19. R. Gelles, *The Roots, Context, and Causes of Family Violence,* paper presented at the conference on "Trauma and Victimization: Understanding and Healing Survivors" sponsored by the University of Connecticut Center for Professional Development, Vernon, Connecticut, September 27–28, 1991.
20. T. Rando, Complications in Mourning Traumatic Death, in *Death, Dying and Bereavement,* I. Corless, B. Germino, and M. Pittman-Lindeman (eds.), Jones and Bartlett Publishers, Inc., Boston, (in press).
21. L. Fingerhut and J. Kleinman, Mortality Among Children and Youth, *American Journal of Public Health, 79,* pp. 899–901, 1989.
22. National Safety Council, *Accident Facts, 1991 Edition,* Chicago, 1991.
23. M. Dixon and H. Clearwater, Accidents, in *Horrendous Death, Health, and Well-Being,* D. Leviton (ed.), Hemisphere Publishing Corporation, New York, 1991.
24. T. Rando (ed.) *Loss and Anticipatory Grief,* Lexington Books, Lexington, Massachusetts, 1986.
25. T. Rando (ed.), *Parental Loss of a Child,* Research Press, Champaign, Illinois, 1986.
26. T. Rando, Death of an Adult Child, in *Parental Loss of a Child,* T. Rando, (ed.), Research Press, Champaign, Illinois, 1986.
27. C. Courtois, *Healing the Incest Wound: Adult Survivors in Therapy,* Norton, New York, 1988.
28. F. Ochberg (ed.), *Post-Traumatic Therapy and Victims of Violence,* Brunner/Mazel, New York, 1988.
29. K. Doka (ed.), *Disenfranchised Grief: Recognizing Hidden Sorrow,* Lexington Books, Lexington, Massachusetts, 1989.
30. T. Rando, *Grieving: How To Go On Living When Someone You Love Dies,* Lexington Books, Lexington, Massachusetts, 1988.
31. S. Jacobs and K. Kim, Psychiatric Complications of Bereavement, *Psychiatric Annals, 20,* pp. 314–317, 1990.
32. S. Zisook and S. Shuchter, Time Course of Spousal Bereavement, *General Hospital Psychiatry, 7,* pp. 95–100, 1985.
33. I. McCann and L. Pearlman, Vicarious Traumatization: A Framework for Understanding the Psychological Effects of Working with Victims, *Journal of Traumatic Stress, 3,* pp. 131–149, 1990.

From *Omega,* Vol. 26, No. 1, 1992–1993, pp. 43-59. © 1992 by Baywood Publishing Company, Inc. Reprinted by permission.

Article 41

Listening

Gerald Kamens

JUST AFTER I LEAVE the church and step into the sparkling sunlight on the way to my car, a woman I hadn't noticed before comes up to me. A recent widow, she speaks, at first hesitantly, about her faith not helping her when she needs it most. It has been a year since her husband died, and she finds things are getting worse, not better. She had to listen just last week to one well-meaning church member who had told her with assurance it was God's will, and that her husband was better off now, at last out of his pain.

I have had this experience many times now, over the year, mostly in Protestant and Catholic churches around Washington, D.C., where I talk about preparing for death as the last stage of our lives—so often, in fact, that several people in my hospice, where I have volunteered for 25 years, call me "Churchman." Usually I meet with the social action committee or the missions board or the community outreach women's guild. Sometimes it is the church powers-that-be. This Sunday morning, as happens very occasionally, I give the sermon in a Presbyterian church.

My topic is hospice as a special way of providing palliative care for those who can no longer be helped by the miracles of modern medicine. With these listeners, I can talk as well about the spiritual aspects of death and dying. It is a largely captive audience, but I regret that there is no

opportunity from the pulpit for the kind of give-and-take I need to find out what people are really concerned about. Afterward, the minister introduces me around at the coffee hour. We engage in pleasant chit-chat, mostly on subjects other than death.

I used to imagine it was a lot easier for a church congregation to digest my message than for a secular group. The written and spoken credos of Christian churches usually proclaim that there is a better place you go to after death, a sure and certain salvation and, at the end, eternal peace, rest and joy.

So what do I tell the woman in the parking lot, who must assume I am some sort of authority—obviously, since I was just up there speaking from the pulpit? I try to come up with something useful to say. But I think to myself that I'm not the right person, even though I was the sermon-deliverer for today, to talk to her about the importance of religious faith—at least not in the traditional definition of that word. I am here today, however—as a guest on other people's turf—not to discuss our respective theologies, but to try to be of service. And after 10 minutes of quiet conversation in the parking lot—actually, just a few words of comfort from me framing some attentive listening to her doubts and fears, she says she feels a little better, thanks me and seems to be smiling (or is that my wishful thinking?) as she walks away.

More often, I make bereavement calls, a different kind of one-on-one ministry. I phone the survivors, who daily face their recent losses with varying degrees of numbness, emotional pain and fear. Most tell me they're doing okay, as well as can be expected. Usually, after probing a bit to see what's behind the brave words, I wish them well on their journey.

But sometimes after death, after the condolences and casseroles have come and gone, mourners want to talk further with me. Perhaps the rest of the world expects them to get on with life too soon. Even their friends and family members may not want to dwell on their grief, or on the death that caused it—perhaps because of fears about their own mortality.

I am not supposed to offer advice. I'm given just phone numbers and a few other facts about people who are grieving "normally." Hospice social workers are charged with counseling the rest; or, in cases of prolonged or particularly unresolved grieving, they may refer the mourners to outside professionals.

Rather, I am supposed to listen, one hopes with care, compassion and intelligence, to those thoughts and fears the bereaved person may be reluctant to share with most others; about anger, doubts and "if onlys." About denial, depression, changes in eating and sleeping patterns. Once in a while, about suicidal thoughts—to which I immediately alert the social worker; or, if need be, I call 911.

But usually there is nothing that dramatic. Instead, just listening more than talking, with occasional gentle feedback for the bereaved—for a year or so after the patient's death—to help them get through the first anniversary of that memorable date. To help them get to a place where they can think of the spouse, parent or child who died, with thoughts not completely of pain. To assist them in their task of incorporating in their hearts and brains the whole memory, the sum of all the sadness and joys, of that person.

Sometimes I steer grievers to our structured support groups. But many prefer to continue one-on-one anonymous phone talks with me. A spouse frets that her husband's casket was left closed before the funeral service. Or left open. A 70-year-old man asks my advice on whether he should take up his daughter's invitation to move in with her and her husband in Texas. Or go to a retirement community. Or just stay put for a while. I summarize the options I'm hearing, and feed them back so he can mull them over. I suggest he not make a decision too quickly.

A friend of mine once asked me what qualified me for this work. Her tone of voice suggested some doubts as to my suitability—whether I'd really be a sympathetic ear. I imagine her concerns were little allayed by the description of my training courses and my readings, about my supervision by a professional social worker with appropriate degrees, and particularly by my possibly glib-sounding suggestion that my main qualification for bereavement listening was the sum of my life's experience.

I too have wondered what makes me feel qualified to sit, almost as in a confessional, lacking the right academic degrees, and hear the secret fears and concerns of those in bereavement. Of those who worry about things they or someone else might have done better, or faster. Of those uncertain about the purpose of their lives, often not ready to move on with those lives at the pace suggested by friends and relatives—who sincerely counsel them, for their own good, not to wallow in grief, not to dwell unduly on the past. Of those who feel guilt today about the relief initially felt when their loved one's pain and suffering was finally lifted by death.

And I have wondered why I persevere in listening to talk of death, and of the great losses people have suffered. I am aware of my need to be a do-gooder, a helper, my need for a spiritual vocation, for ego satisfaction—in part because I decided long ago to be a manager in a big organization and not, unlike my wife, a professional caregiver.

But there is more to it than that. More questions. Will listening to the concerns and fears of mourners better prepare me to acknowledge and feel my griefs over deaths in my own family? To face better the great unknown? The faint glimmers, at best, of what really happens at the end of our physical life, our mortal consciousness?

And, of course, to grieve as well over life's lesser events—time's ravages on my wife and me, our aging parents, disappointment over some of our earlier hopes for our five children and numerous other normal events of life. Can I can learn better how to deal with these happenings from those who open a part of their soul to me?

Each of us has, I believe, buried in our being a deep dark hole, which we try to fill, or conceal from ourselves, with things and people. Or firm or not-so-firm securities about heaven and the hereafter. Perhaps that hole is really our essential loneliness. That loneliness may indeed be the human condition—relieved, if we're fortunate, by God's grace. Does our loneliness and isolation become more real and visible in our last days on earth?

Perhaps I still work for my hospice because I have more to learn there, things that will ease my own inevitable fear of pain and of letting go. More to learn from those whose grief and concerns I try to assuage. More to appreciate in those sudden and fleeting communions that sometimes come to pass between us. I doubt I will ever know why for certain. But I plan to keep on listening.

Gerald Kamens, a volunteer for Hospice of Northern Virginia, also works for Search for Common Ground, an international conflict-resolution organization based in Washington, D.C.

Grief takes no holiday

For people who have lost loved ones, the holidays may elicit dread and apprehension. Here are some ideas that may help, now and year-round.

Grief will be with many of us this holiday season. If you're over age 40, there's a 1-in-3 chance that a close relative or friend of yours died in the last year. Or you may be among the 1 million Americans who lost a spouse. Still, in an era when the media seem to tout the wisdom of "closure" within days of any tragedy, it's easy to feel abnormal when confronted with the long, painful, and messy process of adapting to a death.

What is normal? In 1969, the psychiatrist Elisabeth Kübler-Ross introduced the idea that people go through five stages of grief: denial, anger, bargaining, depression, and acceptance. Her account helped legitimize the wide variety of emotions that grieving people experience. Unfortunately, it was popularized as a prescription for proper grief and may have given some people the idea that they must move through all the stages, in succession, to grieve "correctly" or completely.

Today, we have a greater appreciation for the very individual, lifelong process of coping with loss, and there are new ideas about how loved ones and professionals can help.

The face of grief

Healthy grieving can be a slow, difficult process that lasts for months or years. And although a person may gradually be able to refocus her life, she'll probably never "get over it" or stop thinking about the person who died.

Initially, a person may feel shock and numbness as the reality of the death sinks in. Yet during that time, she may seem to be handling things well and may be quite competent in managing the funeral and legal matters. Later, feelings of sadness, distress, anger, and guilt may become more prominent.

To others, a grieving person may seem irritable, disorganized, or restless. Rather than "moving on," she often feels worse and less able to function several months after a death than she did during the first weeks. That's one reason ongoing practical help and emotional support from friends is so important (see "How can I help?" below).

When grieving becomes complicated

If a person feels stuck and months go by with no improvement, however slow or painful, it could be a sign of complicated grief. Complicated grief is not a mental illness; it's the term mental health professionals use when grieving has proved to be particularly difficult and the bereaved person could benefit from professional attention (see box, "When to seek help").

Signs of complicated grief include an inability to accept that death has occurred; frequent nightmares and intrusive memories; withdrawal from social contact; and constant yearning for the deceased. Complicated grief is more common after a suicide or other traumatic death.

It's important to distinguish feeling down or depressed (who wouldn't feel sad after losing someone important?) from true clinical depression that requires treatment. In making this determination, a professional will assess whether someone is unable to cope with everyday activities and is showing symptoms not explained by grief. These include constant feelings of worthlessness and hopelessness, continual thoughts of death, suicidal thoughts, uncontrolled crying, delusions, and slowed thinking and physical responses.

In the year after a spouse's death, 50% of widows develop depression. Treatment may involve medication, psychotherapy, or both. Medication does not take away grief, but rather helps a grieving person preserve the emotional energy she needs to cope with her feelings.

A controlled study published in the American Journal of Psychiatry found that 16 weeks of treatment with an antidepressant led to recovery in people who had become depressed after losing a spouse or significant other. The medication reduced the symptoms of depression in more than half the participants, all over age 50, but it didn't change the intensity of their grief. Psychotherapy, at least in the short term, didn't reduce depression as dramatically as medication did. Participants receiving both were the most likely to complete their treatment.

The need to talk

For many of the bereaved, recognizing and expressing the strong emotions associated with grief is an integral part of healing. To that end, they may want to write about their feelings, talk to friends or a spiritual adviser, see a therapist, or join a support group. Under Medicare hospice programs, bereavement counseling is available for up to a year after the death.

• Group support. Relatives and friends often can't understand what a grieving person is going through. As the novelist Iris Murdoch said, "Bereavement is a darkness impenetrable to the imagination of the unbereaved." That's why people often find uniquely helpful support in discussing their loss with others in a similar situation.

Bereavement support groups may be general or may focus on a particular disease or type of relationship. They're not meant to be psychotherapy, although some are led by professionals. Some are ongoing; others are time-limited. A local hospice, hospital, or community organization may be able to guide you to a group that is capably led and seems like a good fit.

• Individual therapy. You may not be comfortable speaking in a group setting. Perhaps your relationship with the deceased was troubled, and you have difficulty talking about it. Or you wish to address unresolved issues from your past that a recent death has brought to the fore. In that case, working with a therapist one-on-one may be easier.

At the same time, new research suggests that people who find it difficult to disclose their feelings shouldn't be pressured to do so. In two European studies that followed widows and widowers for two years, neither talking nor writing about the loss reduced distress (Journal of Consulting and Clinical Psychology, February 2002).

The grieving body

Grief is physical as well as emotional. After a death, you may lose your appetite or have trouble sleeping. Other symptoms include abdominal or chest pain, headache, fatigue, heart palpitations, dizziness, and muscle tension.

Bereavement can also have subtler effects on health. Recently widowed women show reduced activity of natural killer cells (cells that attack viruses and tumors) and higher levels of the stress hormone cortisol compared with women whose husbands are still alive. Persistently elevated levels of stress hormones can reduce immunity, raise blood pressure and cholesterol, and induce abnormal heart rhythms.

In addition, some people are too upset to follow their usual diet, exercise, and medication regimens in the months following a death. All this can lead to a decline in health and an increased risk of death—particularly from heart disease—in the year or two following a loss.

If you think you're experiencing grief-related physical symptoms, your clinician can help determine whether a medical workup is warranted and may be able to help you find emotional as well as medical support. She or he may prescribe medication for insomnia or anxiety and will monitor its use to prevent drug tolerance or dependency.

Manner of death matters

After a death, we often imagine that we wouldn't feel quite as bad if circumstances had been different. If a death was sudden, we may have regrets about the lack of time for preparation or

---

> "BEREAVEMENT IS A DARKNESS IMPENETRABLE TO THE IMAGINATION OF THE UNBEREAVED."
>
> Iris Murdoch
> *The Sacred and Profane Love Machine*

How can I help?

Harvard psychiatrists offer the following advice for those trying to help grieving friends and family members.

Let someone talk. Ask about the deceased, even if you didn't know the person well. Don't avoid mentioning her or him at holidays or other usual occasions for reminiscing.

Don't try to make it better. Statements like "Cheer up," "It was God's will," and "You'll get over it" are not helpful.

Hang in there. However pained and helpless you feel when confronted with someone's sadness and misery, your willingness just to be there is an enormous gift, even if your time together is difficult. Company is especially helpful in the weeks and months after the funeral, when friends and relatives return to their regular lives.

Lend a hand. People who are grieving may be unable to say what they need. Offer to do something specific, such as chores or errands, even if you're not sure it's the right thing.

Don't break promises. Grieving people feel abandoned if you don't follow through on pledges to call, visit, or ask them over.

Don't judge or dictate how someone grieves. People grieve in their own ways, and their shifting needs (whether or not to discuss the deceased, for example) may seem inconsistent. Take your cue from them.

Be open to holiday changes. Someone who is grieving may wish to alter certain holiday traditions or withdraw from full participation.

---

goodbyes. And after a prolonged death, we may lament the time a loved one suffered. Some "if only" thinking is just part of coming to grips with a loss, but survivors are now being given more consideration in discussions of appropriate end-of-life care.

Recently, researchers interviewed people during the months following the death of a spouse or close relative. They found that those who felt unprepared or perceived the death as more violent than peaceful were more likely to be diagnosed with major depression, complicated grief, or both (American Journal of Geriatric Psychiatry, July–August, 2002). Another recent study found that women were far more likely to remain depressed or anxious two years after they became widows if they recalled their husbands having unrelieved anxiety prior to death from prostate or bladder cancer (British Journal of Cancer, May 20, 2002).

Persistently focusing on the circumstances of a death is one indication that a person might benefit from professional support. She might also find it helpful to visit the physician who treated her loved one. The doctor can review what occurred and answer questions about the final illness or death, including decisions about pursuing or withdrawing treatment.

Help for the holidays

Some people who are grieving find it reassuring to participate in holiday activities as usual. Others may find it too painful to do so. Here are a few ideas to help you through the holiday season, however you choose to observe it.

Build on tradition. For the holiday meal, place a lighted candle on the table in honor of the deceased; include one of his or her favorite foods. Create a memorial ornament or decoration. If the person who has died always played a special role in holiday festivities, formally ask another family member to carry on the tradition.

If tradition is too painful, change the way you celebrate. Instead of putting up a Christmas tree indoors, decorate an outdoor tree with lights and food items for the birds. Go out for dinner with friends or family instead of trying to have a crowd in for a holiday meal. Instead of staying at home, where memories may be strongest, take a holiday trip.

Do something for others. Volunteer to help others, through your place of worship or a charity. Invite someone who is alone during the holiday to join you and your family for a meal, a religious service, or an activity such as a concert. Make a donation to a favorite cause in memory of the deceased.

Help yourself adjust. Let others know that you might not participate in all the usual festivities. For example, you may feel like attending a religious service, but not the gathering that follows. Feel free to change plans at the last minute. Cry if you need to. Let others know if it's OK for them to share their memories of the deceased with you.

When to seek help

When trying to adjust to a loss, it can be difficult to reach out for help or even to recognize the need for it. Seek professional assistance if you notice the following:

- an increase in depression (or a history of depression)
- unwillingness of family or friends to continue talking about the loss
- suicidal thoughts
- persistent feelings of anxiety or jumpiness
- increased use of tobacco, alcohol, or controlled substances
- extreme difficulty moving forward (however slowly or painfully) in the grieving process
- multiple losses (for example, loss of a friend, job loss, and a health problem)
- continuing sleep problems
- significant weight loss or gain
- not feeling better after a year

Selected Resources

ARP Grief and Loss Programs 601 E St. NW, Washington, DC 20049 www.aarp.org/griefandloss/
Griefnet P.O. Box 3272, Ann Arbor, MI 48106 www.griefnet.org
Hospice Foundation of America 2002 S St. NW, Washington, DC 20009 (800) 854-3402 www.hospicefoundation.org/grief/

Discussing tragedy with your child

Jay Reeve

One of the most difficult tasks a parent has to face is that of talking about tragedy with their children. This can range from the death of a family member, to the death of a pet, all the way to local or national tragedies.

Although there is no way to make this task easy, there are some basic guidelines that may help parents organize the discussion in a way that is helpful to their children.

1) Remember to consider the developmental level of your child.

Children under the age of 8 or 9 may not understand abstract concepts like death or divorce. When speaking with younger children, remember to emphasize that they are safe and cared for. Be sure to include facts in a simple way, even if that seems hard for the child to hear (e.g., "We won't see Grandma anymore"). Couch these facts in as warm and supportive a framework as you can, for instances with reassurances that you are going to be there for them. With older children, it is appropriate to give more information.

2) Invite questions.

Even if your children seem to understand what happened, remind them that they can ask you questions any time. Many times, children take some time to process tragic events, and will not ask about them until later. Remind them that questions are okay.

3) Expect regression.

In the wake of loss or tragic events, many children will regress to earlier behaviors, particularly ones that are associated with comfort, such as seeking favorite toys, or wanting to sleep in the same room with their parents. These behaviors are normal coping mechanisms in the face of tragedy, and are no cause for alarm. Most children will return to more age appropriate behaviors in one to two months after the event, and often much more rapidly. However, if these behaviors continue beyond this general time frame, consult a professional. Particular attention should be paid to regressive behaviors that interfere with your child's functioning, such as excessive school refusal, sleep, or appetite disturbance.

4) Children express grief differently than adults.

Often times, children show their grief through anger and disobedience. If you see this happening, it helps to sit down with your child and let them know that feeling upset about the tragedy is okay. Many times, children don't know why they're upset—they need adults to help give them the words to express their feelings.

5) Structure helps.

One of the things that most help children through tragic loss is a continuity of family structure and tradition. If at all possible, keep up the things your family usually does—whether these are mealtimes, special games, or involvement in religious or cultural groups. While children need to have the tragedy acknowledged, they also need to know that the world will go on.

6) Remember your own grief.

Often times, parents will try to repress their own feelings in order to stay strong for their children. While it may not be helpful to grieve extensively in front of your child, it is very important to take care of yourself and your own feelings of loss. Children can easily sense when a parent is tense or anxious, and it is important to acknowledge your own pain and loss, and to get whatever help you need.

Finally, remember that tragedy is a part of every life—the job of parents is not to shield their children from tragedy, but to help their children become resilient enough to survive it. This is not often a job that anyone can do alone, and if you need help, ask for it, from friends, family, clergy, or helping professionals.

Written by Jay Reeve, Ph.D., staff psychologist, Children's Program, Bradley Hospital, Providence, Rhode Island

Counseling With Children in Contemporary Society

This article examines elements related to children's developmental understandings of death, ways to talk to children about death, a broad understanding of the nature of children's grief and bereavement, recognition of the common characteristics of grieving children, and useful interventions for the bereaved child by mental health counselors.

By Linda Goldman

This article examines elements related to children's developmental understandings of death, ways to talk to children about death, a broad understanding of the nature of children's grief and bereavement, recognition of the common characteristics of grieving children, and useful interventions. The research related to the child grief process and the intrinsic value of therapeutic and educational supports in working with grieving children are discussed through case studies, the professional literature, and practical interventions that support the process of grief therapy for mental health counselors and the bereaved child.

Grief counseling with children in contemporary society is a complex enterprise for mental health counselors (MHCs). Today's children are bombarded with loss in a way that many adults did not experience growing up. Common childhood losses are amplified by a world filled with terrorism, war, bullying, drugs, violence, sexuality, gender issues, and fear of nuclear or biological annihilation. Grief counseling with children benefits from the creation of a community grief team, whereby the parent or guardian, the school system, and the mental health counselor are part of an integral group that nurtures and supports the grieving child in an often confusing and unpredictable world. The purpose of this article is to address children's grief, focusing on their developmental understandings of death, ways to talk to children about death, the nature of children's bereavement, and the implications for mental health counselors. The research related to the child's grief process and the intrinsic value of supports through counseling and edu-

cation in working with bereaved children is woven into this material. This information is presented through case studies, research, and intellectual understandings to support the process of grief therapy for mental health professionals and their clients.

BEREAVED CHILDREN

It is essential when working with children who have experienced the death of someone close to them to be aware of the many childhood losses incurred. Often there are secondary losses for bereaved children. The death of a loved one can be the catalyst creating many secondary losses including loss of friends, home, schools, neighborhoods, self-esteem, and routines. Angela was a 7-year-old in a single parent home. She rarely saw her dad after her parent's divorce. Mom had died in a plane crash. Within a week she moved to another state to live with her dad and a stepmother and stepbrother she barely new. Angela began to do poorly in school and said she "couldn't concentrate." She told her dad that she had no energy to play soccer anymore. She felt different now that her mom had died, and she "didn't want to talk about it with anyone." Within a short time she had lost her mom, her home, her school, her friends, her neighborhood, her ability to learn, and her day-to-day life as she knew it. These are multiple childhood losses that can occur due to the death of a parent.

MHCs' awareness of the following common losses experienced by children (Goldman, 2000b) can give insight into the complexities of children's grieving process. In addition to the types of losses that come easily to mind, like the loss of a family member or friend, children experience more subtle or less obvious losses. Other relationship losses include the absence of teacher or a parent being unavailable due to substance abuse, imprisonment, or divorce. Children experience loss of external objects through robbery or favorite toys or objects being misplaced. Self-related losses include loss of a physical part of the body or loss of self-esteem perhaps through physical, sexual, emotional, or derivational abuse. Many children live with loss in their environment including fire, floods, hurricanes, and other natural disasters. A primary death can often create the secondary loss of a move, change of school, change in the family structure, or family separation. Other childhood losses are loss of routines and habits and loss of skills and abilities after the death of a close loved one. Lastly, the loss of a future and the protection of the adult world are common experiences for the grieving child, causing them sometimes to exhibit a lack of motivation and an inclination to choose violence as a way of solving problems.

Children's Developmental Understanding of Death

A child's understanding of death changes as he or she develops, as explained by Piaget's (Ginsberg, & Opper, 1969) cognitive stages of development. Gaining insight into children's developmental stages allows the MHC to predict and understand age-appropriate responses. During the pre-operational stage, usually ages 2-7, magical thinking, egocentricity, reversibility, and causality characterize children's thinking. Young children developmentally live in an egocentric world, filled with the notion that their words and thoughts can magically cause a person to die. Children often feel they have caused and are responsible for everything (Ginsberg, & Opper). For instance, 5-year-old Sam screamed at his older brother, "I hate you, and I wish you were dead!" He was haunted with the idea that his words created his brother's murder the following day. Due to Sam's age-appropriate egocentrism and magical perception, he saw himself as the center of the universe, capable of creating and destroying at will the world around him. Reversibility also characterizes children's grieving. For example, Jack, a 5-year-old first grader, was very sad after his dad died in a plane crash. Age-appropriately, he perceived death as reversible and told his friends and family that his dad was coming back. Jack even wrote his dad a letter and waited and waited for the mailman to bring back a response. Alice, age 7 years, who told me that she killed her mother, exemplifies the common childhood notion of causality in the following story. She was 4 years old when her mom died. When I asked how she killed her, she responded, "My mom picked me up on the night she had her heart attack. If she hadn't picked me up, she wouldn't have died; so I killed her."

Piaget's next stage of development, concrete operations, usually includes ages 7-12 years (Ginsberg, & Opper, 1969). During this stage the child, in relation to death, is very curious and realistic and seeks information. Mary, at age 10, wanted to know everything about her mother's death. She stated that she had heard so many stories about her mom's fatal car crash that she wanted to look up the story in the newspaper to find out the facts. Jason, age 11, wondered about his friend who was killed in a sudden plane crash. "What was he thinking before the crash, was he scared, and did he suffer?" Tom age-appropriately wondered at age 9 if there was an after-life and exactly where his dad was after his sudden fatal heart attack. These examples illustrate that, at this stage of development, children commonly express logical thoughts and fears about death, can conceptualize that all body functions stop, and begin to internalize the universality and permanence of death. They may ponder the facts about how the terrorists got the plane to crash, wanting to know every detail. When working with this age group, it is important to ask, "What are the facts that you would like to know?" and to assist children in finding answers through family, friends, media, and experts.

Adolescents' (age 13 and up) concept of death is often characterized in accord with Piaget's prepositional operations, implications, and logic stage of development (Ginsberg, & Opper, 1969). Many teenagers, being self-absorbed at this age, see mortality and death as a natural process that is very remote from their day-to-day life and something they cannot control.

Teenagers are often preoccupied with shaping their own life and deny the possibility of their own death. Malcolm, 16 years old, expressed age-appropriate thoughts when he proclaimed, "I won't let those terrorists control my life. I'll visit the mall in Washington whenever I want. They can't hurt me!"

Children can misinterpret language at different developmental stages. The young child can misunderstand clichés associated with grieving, and these clichés can actually block the grieving process. Sammy, at age 6, began having nightmares and exhibited a fear of going to sleep after he was told that his dog Elmo died because "the vet put him to sleep." Alice was told it was "God's will" that her grandmother died because "God loved her so much." Alice questioned, "Why would God take Grandma away from me, doesn't God love me, and will God take me too?" Tom, age 9 years, continually heard the message that dad was watching over him. One day he asked the mental health clinician, "Do you really think my dad is watching over me all of the time? That would be very embarrassing."

Talking to Children About Death

Sudden or traumatic deaths, divorce and abandonment, the death of a grandparent, and the loss of a pet are a few of the many grief issues that children face (Goldman, 2000b). These losses shatter the emotional and physical equilibrium and stability a child may have had. The terror, isolation, and loneliness experienced by too many of today's children after a death leave them living in a world without a future, without protection, and without role models. Children normally and naturally assume the adult world will care for them, support them, and nurture them. When Grandpa has a sudden fatal heart attack, Dad dies in a car crash, Mom dies of suicide, or sister Mary overdoses on drugs, a child's world is shattered. "How could this have happened to me?" is the first question.

Children need to know the age-appropriate truth about a death (Goldman, 2000b). They often have a conscious or unconscious knowing of when they are being lied to, and this knowing can create a secondary loss of the trust of their emotional environment. In talking with children, mental health counselors, parents, and teachers can define death as "when the body stops working." In today's world we need to provide specific definitions for children for different kinds of death. Suicide is when "someone chooses to make his or her body stop working," and homicide is "when someone chooses to make someone else's body stop working." MHCs can say, "Sometimes people die when they are very, very, very old or very, very, very sick; or they are so, so, so injured that the doctors and nurses can't make their bodies work any more." It is important to know that children ask questions such as "Will I die too?" The common questions that children ask about death and grieving give the MHC an insight into their process. The questions serve as a mirror to reflect the child's inner thoughts and feelings that might be otherwise hidden. By responding to questions like the following, the mental health professional or other adult can create an openness to grieve: (a) Who will take care of me if you die too?, (b) Will you and daddy die too?, (c) What is heaven?, (d) Can I die if I go to sleep?, (e) Where did grandpa go?, (f) Will it ever stop hurting?, (g) Why did God kill my mom?, (h) Will Grandpa come back?, (i) Will I forget my person?, (j) Did my person suffer?, and (k) Was it my fault?

Understanding the Nature of Children's Bereavement

Fox (1988) explained that one useful way to help bereaved children and monitor their ongoing emotional needs is to "conceptualize what they must do in order to stay psychologically healthy" (p. 8). Fox emphasized that, in order to assure children's grief will be good grief, they must accomplish four tasks: understanding, grieving, commemorating, and going on. Each child's unique nature and age-appropriate level of experience can influence how he or she works through these tasks. The specific cause of death can also influence the way a child accomplishes these tasks. A dad's death by suicide may create significantly different issues than an anticipated grandfather's death from pneumonia.

Bereaved children may not process grief in a linear way (Goldman, 2000b). The tasks may surface and resurface in varying order, intensity, and duration. Grief work can be "messy," with waves of feelings and thoughts flowing through children when they least expect it to come. Children can be unsuspectingly hit with these "grief bullets" in the car, listening to a song or the news, seeing or hearing an airplane overhead, reading a story in school, or watching the news about a terrorist attack. A fireman's siren, a jet fighter, a soldier in uniform, a postal letter, or a balloon bursting can trigger sudden and intense feelings without any warning, and often without any conscious connection to their grief and loss issue.

Common characteristics of grieving children. Children in the 21st century experience grief-related issues involving safety and protection that many adults may not have had as children. Whether children ever really enjoyed the protection of the adults in their lives is a debatable question, but the perception of that safety seems to have existed in previous generations. Although grief-related issues have always existed through time, today's children are exposed to an extraordinary visual and auditory barrage of input. The news, the World Wide Web, music, and videos are constantly bombarding children with sounds and images of school shootings, killings, violence, and abuse. Children are left with feelings of vulnerability and defenselessness. Either by real circumstances or vicariously through media reports, young people are inundated with issues such as murder, suicide, AIDS, abuse, violence, terrorism, and bullying that often hinder their natural grief processes. This disruption is an overlay for other interactive components that may affect a child's grief process.

Three categories of interactive components can be examined in assessing the grieving child (Webb, 2002):

- Individual factors
- Death-related factors
- Support system factors

The flowing and overlapping of these components create a complex world for the grieving child. Individual factors include cognitive and developmental age; personality components; past coping mechanisms in the home, school, and community environments; medical history; and past experience with death. Death-related factors involve the type of death, contact with the deceased such as being present at death, viewing the dead body, attending funerals and gravesite, expressions of "goodbye," and grief reactions. The third group of variables concerns the child's support system including grief reactions of the nuclear family and extended family; school, peer, and religious recognition and support of the grief process; and cultural affiliation including typical beliefs about death and the extent of a child's inclusion. Other factors related to a death that may increase complications for the grief process include suddenness and lack of anticipation, violence, mutilation, and destruction, preventability and/or randomness, multiple death, and personal encounter of the mourner such as a threat or shocking confrontation.

As noted by Webb (2002), "although virtually any death may be perceived by the mourner as personally traumatic because of the internal subjective feeling involved...circumstances that are objectively traumatic are associated with five factors known to increase complications for mourners" (p. 368). Learning to recognize the signs of grieving and traumatized children is essential to normalizing their experience of grief and trauma. A mental health counselor needs to be educated in these common signs in order to reinforce for bereaved children, families, and educators that these thoughts, feelings, and actions are natural consequences in the child's grief process. This reassurance helps to reduce anxiety and fear.

Children may experience the following physical, emotional, cognitive, and behavioral symptoms common in the grieving process: The child (a) continually re-tells events about his or her loved one and their death; (b) feels the loved one is present in some way and speaks of him or her in the present tense; (c) dreams about the loved one and longs to be with him or her; (d) experiences nightmares and sleeplessness; (e) cannot concentrate on schoolwork, becomes disorganized, and/or cannot complete homework; (f) finds it difficult to follow directions or becomes overly talkative; (g) appears at times to feel nothing; (h) is pre-occupied with death and worries excessively about health issues; (i) is afraid to be left alone; (j) often cries at unexpected times; (k) wets the bed or loses his or her appetite; (1) shows regressive behaviors (e.g., is clingy or babyish); (m) idealizes or imitates the loved one and assumes his or her mannerisms; (n) creates his or her own spiritual belief system; (o) becomes a class bully or a class clown; (p) shows reckless physical action; (q) has headaches and stomach aches; and (r) rejects old friends, withdraws, or acts out.

Complications in children's grief. In addition, children's grief can be complicated, and common signs include withdrawal, sleep disorders, anxiety, difficulty in concentration, and regression. The common signs associated with children's bereavement may become heightened by their intensity, frequency, and duration. The term disenfranchised grief is used by Doka (1989) to refer to losses that cannot be openly acknowledged, socially sanctioned, or publicly mourned. Five categories of situations may create complications for the bereaved child (adapted with permission from Goldman, 2001). These categories are:

- Sudden or traumatic death
- Social stigma and shame
- Multiple losses
- Past relationship with the deceased
- The grief process of the surviving parent or caretaker

They explain circumstances that can create complications leading to obstructions in the child's grief process.

Awareness of the commonality of feelings and thoughts surrounding these situations can aid the mental health counselor in normalizing what may seem so unfamiliar for the children.

Sudden or traumatic death can include murder, suicide, a fatal accident, or sudden fatal illness. With a sudden or traumatic death, an unstable environment is immediately created in the child's home. Children feel confusion over these kinds of death. A desire for revenge often is experienced after a murder or fatal accident. Rage or guilt, or both, emerge against the person who has committed suicide. A terror of violence and death unfolds, and the child feels shock and disbelief that suddenly this death has occurred.

Social stigma and shame frequently accompany deaths related to AIDS, suicide, homicide, terrorist attacks, or school shootings. Children as well as adults often feel too embarrassed to speak of these issues. They remain silent out of fear of being ridiculed or ostracized. These suppressed feelings get projected outward in the form of rage or inward in the form of self-hatred. Often times these children feel lonely and isolated. They cannot grieve normally because they have not separated the loss of the deceased from the way the deceased died.

Multiple losses can produce a deep fear of abandonment and self-doubt in children. The death of a single parent without a partner is a good example of a multiple loss. When the only parent of a child dies, the child can be forced to move from his or her home, the rest of his or her family and friends, the school, and the community. The child is shocked at this sudden and complete change of lifestyle and surroundings, and may withdraw or become terrified of future abandonment. Nightmares and/or bed-wetting could appear.

The past relationship to the deceased can greatly impact the grieving child. When a child has been abused, neglected, or abandoned by a loved one, there are often ambivalent feelings when the loved one's death occurs. A 5-year-old girl whose alcoholic father sexually abused her may feel great conflict when that parent dies. Part of her may feel relieved, even glad, to be rid of the abuse yet ashamed to say those feelings out loud. She may carry the secret of the abuse and become locked into that memory and be unable to grieve. Children often feel guilt, fear, abandoned, or depressed if grief for a loved one is complicated by an unresolved past relationship.

The grief process of the surviving parent or caretaker greatly affects children. If the surviving parent is not able to mourn, there is no role model for the child. A closed environment stops the grief process. Many times the surviving parent finds it too difficult to watch his or her child grieve. The parent may be unable to grieve him or herself or may be unwilling to recognize the child's pain. Feelings become denied and the expression of these feelings is withheld. The surviving parent may well become an absentee parent because of his or her own overwhelming grief, producing more feelings of abandonment and isolation in the child. Children often fear something will happen to this parent or to himself or herself and, as a result, become overprotective of the parent and other loved ones (Goldman, 2001).

IMPLICATIONS FOR MENTAL HEALTH COUNSELORS

There are important general purposes for the MHC when working with grieving children. A major purpose is allowing children freedom to express emotion. This expression of emotion is an integral component of counseling and includes interventions with writing, drawing, poetry, projective techniques, and dream work. Support groups for children enhance the expression of emotions with peers who are working through similar situations. Allowing children to connect to and maintain memories serves as another important purpose for the MHC professional. Through remembering and sharing with others, the bereaved child can maintain a continuing bond with the person who died. Educating grieving children and the adults around them underscores another purpose for the mental health counselor: To create common thoughts and practices that harmoniously integrate the network of support surrounding the bereaved child.

Identifying At-Risk Children

Grieving children wonder if the pain will ever stop hurting. As Celotta, Jacobs and Keys (1987) identified, two questions that at-risk children respond to 100% of the time are: "Do you feel hopeless?" and "Do you feel sad?" These responses were part of a checklist given to elementary school children to identify depression. Mental health counselors can create simple tools to help target children who are traumatized and may be at-risk. Asking them to write or draw in response to questions such as "What makes you the most sad?," "What makes you the angriest?," or "What makes you feel the loneliest?" can provide useful information. Jin, a 10-year-old student from China, explained his picture showing a boy with his soul next to him. His older brother had recently died of suicide. Jim explained, "This is me, and this is my soul. Sometimes I feel like killing myself so I won't feel all of the pain. Sometimes I wish I would just disappear." This simple intervention created the identification of an at-risk child and pointed out the need for further exploration and evaluation.

Interventions for Individual Counseling

"The goal of helping children of all ages to cope with death is to promote their competence, facilitate their ability to cope, and recognize that children are active participants in their lives" (Silverman, 2000, p. 42). Mental health counselors need to be prepared to respond to children's questions. Grieving children are becoming a larger and larger, growing segment of our youth; and their grief issues arise at younger and younger ages. Not that long ago, parents were advised to exclude their children from memorials and not talk to them about death or about feelings about their loved one. Today, mental health professionals can emphasize the importance of seeing children as recognized mourners and as an integral part of the family system's bereavement process. Mental health counselors can speak, share, and create a space for young people to freely participate in the family's mourning. The MHC's goal is to allow safe expression of children's grief responses in a respectful environment. Grief-resolution techniques are important to create and stimulate discussion and exploration of thoughts and feelings, because bereaved children cannot always integrate their emotions and their intellect. While the MHC is building a relationship of trust, children also experience support and affirmation in an atmosphere that honors and respects them. The following techniques allow them to spontaneously and safely work through difficult spaces at their own comfort level. Healing is promoted when children put their feelings outside of themselves (Goldman, 1998a).

Expression of feelings. There are several interventions that are useful for helping children to express themselves. Worry lists, letter writing, reality checks, worry and safe boxes, drawing, and poetry are all valuable interventions with children. Projective techniques and dream work are interventions that allow release of thoughts and feelings in verbal and nonverbal ways.

One of the common signs of grieving children is that they worry excessively about their health and the health of the surviving parent or guardian. Roxanne, 10 years old, had multiple deaths in her family and worked in grief therapy for many months. In one counseling session, she seemed worried and agitated. When asked to list her five greatest worries, her first was a concern she had never mentioned until that moment: "I'm so scared my dad will die too! He smokes and I want him to stop." She burst into tears. Roxanne decided to write her dad a letter to express her feelings; and after being given the choice to send it or not, she decided to give it to him. Her anger and frustration are obvious in the letter:

> Dear Dad, You know how I feel about you smoking right now. You know how many losses I've had already…I don't want you to go next. I really worry about you; so please stop smoking. I feel like ripping your head off to make you stop. Think before you buy so many cigarettes. Love, Roxanne P.S. Write me back. (Goldman, 2000b, p. 69)

Seven-year-old Brian's dad died in a sudden car crash. He confided during one session, "I'm worried my mom will die too. I think about it at school and before I go to bed." An intervention Brian found comforting was a reality check at mom's doctor. She had a complete check up and asked the doctor to write a note to Brian to reassure him that mom seemed healthy. This note provided a concrete and tangible linking object that comforted his worry about his mom's health. The letter read, "Dear Brian, I wanted to let you know that your mom had a complete physical exam and she seems to be very healthy. Dr. Jones."

Margie's dad was killed in the Pentagon attack. She began having nightmares and had great difficulty sleeping. She decided to create a safe box, with objects inside that made her feel safe and peaceful. She decorated her box in grief therapy, using magazines and stickers, to create images that were calming to her. Inside her box, she put a favorite stuffed animal; her dad's medal from the military; a picture of her dog, Snuffy; and a bracelet her best friend Tanya had given her. Margie put her safe box on her dresser in her bedroom where it made her feel better whenever she went to it.

Adam, a 13 year old, witnessed his brother being killed in a ride-by shooting. He was bombarded with stimuli that re-triggered his panic about the violent way his brother died. Loud noises, sirens, and even the burst of a balloon could immediately begin difficult feelings of panic and anxiety for him. One intervention that he found soothing was the creation of a worry or fear box in which he could place his fears. Adam drew pictures and found slogans that illustrated things that made him scared. Drugs, guns, and terrorists were a major theme. He cut a hole in the top of his box and began placing little notes, his own private fears, inside. Sometimes he shared them, but other times he did not. Writing down his fears was a first step for Adam to begin to identify and cope with them.

Writing, drawing, and poetry are useful interventions for expression of feelings for the bereaved child. They serve to allow safe release of often hidden feelings. Writing was useful for 8-year-old Julia whose best friend, Zoe, and Zoe's family died in the terrorist attack. The following is a part of a poem she created as a tribute to her friend in her memory book. "Julia. Remembers by memories and hearing her name. Who wishes for peace and unity. Strong" (Goldman, 2003, p.146). Tyler's best friend Juan was killed in a car crash. He drew a picture of one of his favorite memories with his friend Juan. They were playing soccer at the park and fell, and they both burst into laughter. Tyler said that, when he looked at his picture, he felt happy. Andrew was 16 years old when his grandfather and his favorite aunt died. His grief was coupled with his sadness as he watched family members grieve too. He expressed his grief through poetry in the following way: "Tears flow—As time passes—The relatives grieve—In love for the deceased" (Andrew Burt, personal communication, December 11, 2001).

Middle and high school students may successfully respond to writing in locked diaries. Melissa was a teenager who came to counseling after the suicide of her older brother Joey. The shame she felt about the way her brother Joey died made it difficult to discuss complex feelings openly. She mentioned in session that she loved her diary, and kept it under her bed locked, safe, and private. She wrote her "sacred" thoughts and feelings in her diary. She used her diary not only as a safe receptacle for feelings, but also as an avenue for expression she could choose to use according to her readiness.

Projective play and dream work are grief interventions that allow children to use their unconscious mind and their imagination to safely express thoughts and feelings (Goldman, 2001). Young children learn through play, and they also grieve through play. Role-playing, puppets, artwork, clay, and sand table work are a few of the many ways that they can imagine, pretend, and engage in meaningful activities that allow them to act out or project their grief feelings without having to directly verbalize them. Play therapy is especially useful with bereaved children. Children have a limited verbal ability for describing their feelings and a limited emotional capacity to tolerate the pain of loss, and they communicate their feelings, wishes, fears, and attempted resolutions to their problems through play (Webb, 2002). Projective play allows many young children to work through difficult times. Having props such as helping figures, puppets, costumes, and building blocks allows children to recreate their experience and role-play what happened and ways to work with what happened. Bereaved children feel empowered when they can imagine alternatives and possible solutions, release feelings, and create dialogue through projective play.

Sometimes, what may appear as a frivolous play activity can be an extremely meaningful outlet for children to recreate an event and safely express conflicting ideas. For example, 6-year-old Jared was very sad in a beginning grief therapy session. He missed his dad, who was killed in a car accident. He walked around the office, talking about how much he missed Dad and that he wished he could talk to him. Jared picked up a toy telephone and followed the mental health professional's suggestion that he call and tell him how he feels. Jared sat down on the floor, dialed the number, and began an ongoing, very present conversation with his dad including "Hi Dad. I love you and miss you so much. Are you ok? Do you miss me? I hope heaven is fun and you can play baseball there. Let me tell you about my day." Children may commonly reach out to initiate a connection to their deceased parent. Through projective play, Jared was able to feel he could communicate in a satisfying way with his father. Alex, who was bereaved in the Sept. 11th terrorist attack, spontaneously built towers of blocks to represent the Twin Towers, and then knocked them down with an airplane. When replaying the attack and the falling of the towers, Alex explained, "Airplanes make buildings go BOOM!" Allyson, a kindergartner, suffered the tragic death of her mom at the Pentagon. She created a cemetery out of blocks and explained what was bothering her through the use of toy figures. She reported, "When me and Daddy visit the cemetery I wonder about Mommy. There was no coffin or body at the cemetery. I wonder where my

Mommy's body is now." Play allowed the expression of deep concern about her mom's body and opened communication about this in the therapeutic environment. Allyson agreed to share her block cemetery and questions about mom with dad, as a way to begin to answer them. Michael, age 5 years, recreated the disaster setting of his dad's death. Dad was inside his office when a tragic fire took his life. Using toy doctors, nurses, fireman, and policeman as props, he pretended to be a rescue worker and saved his dad. Then he put on a fire hat and gloves and shouted, "Don't worry I'll save you. Run for your life."

Puppets and stuffed animals are also a safe way for children to speak of the trauma through projecting thoughts and feelings onto props, and dream work is another tool allowing children to process difficult feelings. For example, the MHC might inquire of a bereaved child, "I wonder what Bart (the dog puppet) would say about the trauma. Let's allow Bart to tell us about his story." In addition, children often feel survivor guilt after a sudden death (Worden, 1991). In dreams, sadness and depressing thoughts and feelings surface, accompanied by guilt that the child has survived, another person has died, and the child did not or could not help the deceased. Justin, a 10-year-old, explained a common theme in his dream. Justin continually revisited a nightmare after Uncle Max suddenly died during his military deployment. He shared his dream with his mental health professional and drew a picture showing his uncle calling out for help and Justin being unable to reach him.

Connecting to and maintaining memories. Silverman, Nickman, & Worden (1992) found that it was normal for children "to maintain a presence and connection with the deceased and that this presence is not static" (p. 495). The bereaved child constructs the deceased through an ongoing cognitive process of establishing memories, feelings, and actions connected to the child's development level. This inner representation leads to a continuing bond to the deceased, creating a relationship that changes as the child matures and his or her grief lessens. There are five strategies of connection to a deceased parent: (a) making an effort to locate the deceased, (b) actually experiencing the deceased in some way, (c) reaching out to initiate a connection, (d) remembering, and (e) keeping something that belonged to the deceased.

Those MHCs who work with bereaved children "may need to focus on how to transform connections and place the relationship in a new perspective, rather than on how to separate from the deceased" (Silverman et al., 1992, p. 503). In locating the deceased, many children may place their loved one in a place called "heaven" (p. 497). Michelle was 7 years old when she began in counseling. Her mom had died in a sudden car crash. One day Michelle asked in session, "What do you think heaven is?" Reflecting Michelle's question, the mental health professional asked, "What do you think it is?" Both began to draw a picture of their image of heaven. This intervention helped Michelle reflect on her own question, and she was able to

remember her mother by sharing the place where she thought Mom was. It was also a way to honor Mom, express things about Mom, and symbolically again tell Mom how much she loved her. In addition, Michelle wrote the follow story about heaven:

> What is heaven? This is what heaven is to me. It's a beautiful place. Everyone is waiting for a new person, so they can be friends. They are also waiting for their family. They are still having fun. They get to meet all the people they always wanted to meet (like Elvis). There are lots of castle where only the great live, like my Mom. There's all the food you want and all the stuff to do—There's also dancing places, disco. My mom loved to dance. I think she's dancing in heaven. Animals are always welcome. (My Mom loved animals.) Ask her how Trixie is. That's her dog that died. Tell her I love her. (Goldman, 2000b, pp. 79-80).

Memory books, memories boxes, and memory picture albums can all be used to address bereaved children's questions of "Will I forget my person?" Memory work is an important part of the therapeutic process. Children often fear thsy will forget their person who died, and memory work can provide a helpful tool to safely process the events of their grief and trauma. Memory books store pictures and writings about loved ones; memory boxes hold cherished objects belonging to a special person; and memory picture albums hold favorite photographs. Mental health counselors can ask children the following questions as a foundation for discussion and processing memories after a death: (a) Where were you when your person died?, (b) What was your first thought?, (c) What are the facts about how your person died?, (d) What makes you sad, happy, angry, frustrated?, (e) What sticks with you now?, (f) Did you do anything wrong?, (g) What is it you still want to know?, (h) What scares you the most?, (i) What makes you feel peaceful?, and (j) What can you do to feel better?

Memory books are extremely useful tools to allow children to express feelings and complete unfinished business, including feelings and thoughts that boys and girls were unable to communicate at the time of their person's death. Inside a memory book, grieving children can use stars, stickers, photographs, and other decorations to expand their own writings and drawings about their person. These are a few suggestions about various themes for memory book work: (a) The most important thing I learned from my person is…, (b) What was life like before your person died?, (c) What is life like now?, (d) My funniest memory is…, (e) My most special memory is…, (f) If I could tell my loved one just one more thing, I would say …, and (g) If I could say one thing I was sorry for it would be… (Goldman, 2000b). For example, Alfred, age 10, made a memory book page illustrating the events of September 11, 2001. It was his attempt to make sense of his world after the disaster. His memory page was a picture that helped him release feelings, tell stories, and express worries and concerns. The picture he drew showed where he was and what was happening at his New York school situated so close to ground zero. His only message was "Run for your life." With this memory book page, Alfred was able to begin to release some of the terror he felt that day at being so close to the Twin Towers as he also told his story.

Memory boxes are an excellent craft project for grieving children. They can be used to hold special articles, linking objects that are comforting because of belonging to or being reminders of the person who died. These objects can be put in a shoebox and decorated by the child as a valuable treasure of memories, which is also a tool for stimulating conversation. Memory boxes serve as a linking object by holding something that belonged to the deceased. These linking objects help the child maintain his or her connection or link to his or her loved one (Silverman et al., 1992). For instance, Tanya, an 8-year-old, made a memory box with pictures and special objects that reminded her of her friend Angie who died in a sudden plane crash. Tanya included pictures, stuffed animals, a list of her top favorite memories, and a bracelet her friend had given her. She explained that it made her "feel good" whenever she held it and she loved to share it with her friends and family. The memory box created a place where Tanya could "be with her friend Angie."

Creating memory picture albums with children titled "My Life" is often an extremely useful tool in creating dialogue and sharing feelings. Henry's dad died of cancer when he was 11. Henry created his memory album by choosing pictures he loved to make an album about his life before and after dad died. He placed each picture in his book and wrote a sentence telling about it.

Children love to express memories through artwork. Memory murals and memory collages are examples of memory projects that are helpful therapeutic interventions for grieving children. Children can creatively express feelings and thoughts about their loved ones. Fifteen-year-old Megan prepared a collage of magazine pictures that reminded her of her best friend, Ashley, who had recently died of cancer. She included Ashley's favorite foods, favorite clothes, favorite music, and favorite movie stars. Zack, age 9 years, was a best friend to Andrew, who had died when he was 6. Zack drew a picture for the cover of Andrew's third memorial booklet, "On the Occasion of Andrew's Third Anniversary." He explained that his drawing showed Andrew "shooting hoops in heaven." He felt in the few years since Andrew's death, he had been playing basketball, and assumed Andrew was doing the same in heaven. By participating in the memorial booklet, and being given a voice to explain his work, Zack was able to continue to actively remember his friend and participate in ongoing involvement with memory work.

Memory e-mails are a creative example of memory work and computer use. After 14-year-old Donald's classmate Ethan got killed in a car crash, Donald and his classmates decided to create a chat room only for e-mail memories about Ethan. They also created a memory video of Ethan, using a popular rock group as a background for a montage of pictures of Ethan from birth until he died, including friends, pets, and family.

Using children's grief and loss resources is an excellent technique to allow discussion and expression of sometimes hidden feelings. It's often reassuring to bereaved children to read words that speak of the loss they have experienced and the many new feelings they have associated with grief. Children's resources can become a helpful tool for parents. These books create meaningful discussion and often allow adults to dialogue about their common loss issues (Goldman, 2000b). A few examples of useful books for children on grief are: When dinosaurs die (Brown & Brown, 1996), When someone very special dies (Heegaard, 1988), Bart speaks out: Breaking the silence on suicide (Goldman, 1998a), Honoring our loved ones: Going to a funeral (Carney, 1999), and After a murder: A workbook for kids (The Dougy Center, 2002). Suggestions for useful books for grieving teens include: Death is hard to live with (Bode, 1993), When a friend dies (Gootman, 1994), Facing change (O'Toole, 1995), and Fire in my heart, Ice in my veins (Traisman, 1992). Readers can contact the author for a more complete list.

Support Groups

Many bereaved children feel alone and find peers and family members so often want them to move on and stop talking or even thinking about their person (Goldman, 2000b). They wonder who they can really talk with about their mom or dad or sister who has died. Often they feel different and choose not to share. Grief support groups can provide a safe haven for them to explore their overwhelming and often confusing feelings with others that understand because they are going through a grief process also. Becoming a member of an age-appropriate grief support group allows children and teens a safe place to share with others and create friendships.

Education

If mental health counselors can join together with parents, educators, therapists, and other caring professionals to create a cohesive unit, sharing similar thought forms, supports, resources, and information, a child's grieving experience becomes more congruent. Usually when children grieve, their world feels fragmented. The more consistency MHCs can create within children's lives, the more solid and secure their world will become. The role of mental health counselors as liaisons to parents, educators, and community members is an important aspect of children's grief therapy. Educating caring adults provides a united multiple support system for the grieving child.

Mental health professionals can educate surviving parents and guardians on common signs of grieving children and coach the adults on how to reduce the children's fear and anxiety about new thoughts and feelings. This education helps adults reduce their own anxieties that can unconsciously be projected onto their children. MHCs can provide age-appropriate words to help family members create open dialogue and identify their own unresolved grief and the impact of their grieving process on their children. For example, 15-year-old Mark lived with his grandmother after his mom's death. Grandma often told the mental health professional that she was concerned because Mark "doesn't seem to be grieving." One day in a seemingly unrelated conversation, she mentioned that Mark takes a nap every day on his mother's bed. Grandma was unaware that grieving teens commonly reach out to initiate a connection with their person who died (Silverman et al., 1992). That connection may well be taking a daily nap on mom's bed.

The MHC can also be an advocate for the grieving child in the school system. This advocacy can offer suggestions to educators, who are working with bereaved children, as a support after their person's death. Because children are sometimes flooded with feelings and are not immediately able to verbalize them, MHCs can work with educators in developing strategies for children to follow when they feel upset. In doing so, MHCs can emphasize the importance of the child being part of the decision-making process in choosing appropriate people or places they are comfortable with to be used to implement these strategies. These ideas can be implemented throughout the school year and continued for the next year if necessary. Suggestions include any or all of the following (Goldman, 1998b). The child (a) has permission to leave the room, if needed, without explanation, (b) can choose a designated adult or location within the school as a safe space, or (c) can call home if needed. Amy, who worried about Mom after Dad died, provides an example of how this might occur. She thought about her Mom a lot in the mornings and chose to call home at that time to make sure she was all right. Other strategies include the child's having (a) permission to visit the school nurse if needing a reality check, (b) a class helper, (c) private teacher time, (d) some modified work assignments, and (e) school personnel inform faculty, PTA, parents, and children of the loss. In addition, it may be useful to give the child more academic progress reports such as was done for Henry who had a hard time concentrating after his brother Sam died (Goldman, 2000a). Henry could not remember as well and found his test scores declined. Having frequent progress reports helped him keep his studies on track.

The MHC serves as a liaison to the school system to inform those involved that there is a grieving child in the school. Presenting a loss inventory (Goldman, 2000a) that can be shared with educators is a helpful tool for communication within the school. All too often school systems do not communicate to their entire staff that a child has experienced the death of a close loved one. This lack of knowledge can create trauma and an added layer of sadness for students. Liam was a fifth grader who was star athlete for the soccer game. Many parents and friends had gathered to watch the team in their tournament finals. Coach McGuire approached Liam before the game and asked, "Is your dad here today?" "No," Liam grumbled. "He had to work." Liam played his worst game. Coach McGuire was unaware that Liam's dad had died recently; there was no written record to communicate this within the school. If this school system had an established practice of using a loss inventory, this lapse in communication and its devastating impact on Liam may not have occurred.

A grief therapy homework assignment, which can be used even in educational or advocacy situations, can help children and teens identify their individual support systems. Children can be asked to create a "circle of trust," placing a picture of themselves in the center and three trusted people with their phone numbers that they can call for support. They can create a second circle for people they would call next. They may even create a third circle for people they know they cannot trust. Their circle of trust can stimulate dialogue in therapy as well as serve as a tool for recognition of those they can and cannot count on for support during their present loss (Goldman & Rosenthal, 2001).

Childhood Commemoration

Children become recognized mourners when adults create ways for bereaved children to ask questions and share thoughts and feelings about death. Adults can also prepare and invite children to participate in funerals, memorials, and other rituals. When children can attend a memorial service they gain a great gift, the gift of inner strength (Goldman, 1996). It assists their grief process to be included in the funeral and other rituals associated with the death of a loved one (Rando, 1991). Knowing they could participate and be present with adults in a community remembrance of a friend or family member gives them awareness of how people honor a life, come together for each other as a community, and say goodbye. Honoring a life gives children a way to value and respect their own lives. They become identified mourners and an ever present and integral part of the grief process. Research indicates that children who were allowed to attend the funeral of a loved one later expressed positive feelings about going and about the meaning they attached to their attendance (Silverman & Worden, 1992). Children in the study felt "it was important to them that they had attended. Attendance helped them to acknowledge the death, provided an occasion for honoring their deceased parent, and made it possible for them to receive support and comfort" (p. 319). This nurturing environment supports their emotional and spiritual growth as human beings. So often caring adults are too uncomfortable talking to children about death. They may not have the words to use, may feel powerless when children are sad or cry, and ultimately may inhibit tears and stop the grief process.

Bereaved children can actively commemorate their loss by participating in safe and comfortable processes that allow for the expression of grief (Goldman, 1996). The following are age-appropriate ways children and teens can give meaning to their many thoughts and feelings. They can plant a flower or tree, send a balloon, blow bubbles, or say a prayer. Bereaved children might light a candle or write a poem, story, or song about their loved one and share it. Some boys and girls find talking into a tape recorder or creating a video of memories is helpful. Others enjoy (a) making cookies or cakes and bringing them to the family of the person who has died, (b) creating a mural or collage about the life of the person who has died, or (c) drawing a picture or making a memory book. Christina and Christy were two young children who were prepared, invited, and given choices about joining in a memorial service for their friend, Andrew. They were an active part of the service, sitting with family members, blowing bubbles, sharing, listening, and drawing pictures for their friend.

CONCLUSION AND RECOMMENDATIONS

Research suggests that certain mental health outcomes may emerge for grieving children (Lutzke, Ayers, Sandier, & Barr, 1997). Bereaved children may show (a) more depression, withdrawal, and anxiety; (b) lower self-esteem; and (c) less hope for the future than non-bereaved children. Adults who were bereaved children tend to exhibit higher degrees of suicide ideation and depression and are more at risk for panic disorders and anxiety. Support for bereaved children is essential in helping to reduce negative outcomes related to unresolved or unexplored grief during childhood. The findings suggest that, although trauma associated with death-related situations could not always predict later symptom formation, therapeutic intervention at the time of the death may help to reduce or extinguish future anxiety that could escalate without intervention.

A key debilitating factor creating ongoing trauma for grieving children is often a sense of loss of control in their lives. Early interventions through counseling and grief support groups can help boys and girls regain their sense of control and reduce the stress associated with the death of a friend or family member. Early interventions may also support children in their grief by providing a meaningful relationship with at least one caring adult (e.g., the MHC). Mishara (1999) reported that children with strong social supports have a reduced presence of suicide ideation. Another study (U.S. Secret Service, 2002) clearly in-

dicates "the importance of giving attention to students who are having a difficult coping with major losses ... particularly when feelings of desperation and hopelessness are involved" (p. 14). The report suggests that an important aspect in prevention may be to allow young people the opportunity to talk and connect with caring adults.

The MHC needs to view him or herself not only as a therapist, but also as an advocate for bereaved children. MHCs' role as an ally and friend creates a link to the child's larger community that extends to parents, clergy, educators, physicians, and other health care professionals. Educating members of these supportive networking systems in the common signs of bereaved children and suggesting age-appropriate interventions can extend the boundaries of mental health services into the child's home, school, and community. MHCs are trained to see the child in the present and to view changes in behaviors as a cry for help. Using therapeutic interventions such as projective techniques, sharing, and listening allows children to work through their grief. Active involvement in commemoration, rituals, and support groups facilitates the healing process of the bereaved child. Giving boys and girls the opportunity to release their emotions within a safe haven is the underlying thread inherent in counseling grieving children.

REFERENCES

Bode, J. (1993). *Death is hard to live with.* New York: Dell.

Brown, L., & Brown, M. (1996). *When dinosaurs die.* New York: Little, Brown.

Carney, K. L. (1999). *Honoring our loved ones: Going to a funeral.* Wethersfield, CT: Dragonfly.

Celotta, B., Jacobs, O., & Keys, S. (1987). Searching for suicidal precursors in the elementary school child. *American Mental Health Counselors Association Journal, 9,* 38-48.

Doka, K. J. (Ed.). (1989). *Disenfranchised grief: Recognizing hidden sorrow.* New York: Lexington Books.

Dougy Center. (2002). *After a murder: A workbook for kids.* Portland, OR: Author.

Fox, S. S. (1988). *Good grief: Helping groups of children when a friend dies.* Boston, MA: The New England Association for the Education of Young Children.

Ginsberg, H., & Opper, S. (1969). *Piaget's theory of intellectual development.* Englewood, NJ: Prentice Hall.

Goldman, L. E. (1996). *We can help children grieve: A child-oriented model for memorializing. Young Children: The National Association for the Education of Young Children, 51,* 69-73.

Goldman, L. E. (1998a). *Bart speaks out: Breaking the silence on suicide.* Los Angeles, CA: Western Psychological Services.

Goldman, L. E. (1998b). *Helping the grieving child in the school. Healing Magazine, 3,* 15-24.

Goldman, L. E. (2000a). *Helping the grieving child in the school.* Bloomington, IN: Phi Delta Kappa International.

Goldman, L. E. (2000b). *Life and loss: A guide to help grieving children* (2nd ed.). New York: Taylor & Francis.

Goldman, L. E. (2001). *Breaking the silence: A guide to help children with complicated grief suicide, homicide, AIDS, violence and abuse* (2nd ed.). New York: Taylor & Francis.

Goldman, L. E. (2003). Talking to children about terrorism. In M. E. Eicht & K. J. Doka (Eds.), *Living with grief, coping with public tragedy* (pp. 139-149). Washington, D.C. Hospice Foundation of America.

Goldman, L. E. (2001). *Circle of trust: Support for grief.* In H. G. Rosenthal (Ed.), *Favorite counseling and therapy homework assignments* (pp. 108-110). New York: Taylor & Francis.

Gootman, M. (1994). *When a friend dies.* Minneapolis, MN: Free Spirit.

Heegaard, M. (1988). *When someone very special dies.* Minneapolis, MN: Woodland.

Lutzke, J. R., Ayers, T. S., Sandler, N. S., & Barr, A. (1997). *Risk and interventions for the parentally bereaved child.* In N. Sandier. & S. Wolchik (Eds.), *Handbook of children's coping: Linking theory and intervention* (pp. 215-242). New York: Plenum.

Mishara, B. (1999). *Conceptions of death and suicide in children ages 6-12 and their implications for suicide prevention. Suicide and Life-Threatening Behavior, 29,* 105-118.

O'Toole, D. (1995). *Facing change.* Burnsville, NC: Compassion Books.

Rando, T. (1991). *How to go on living when someone you love dies.* New York: Bantam.

Silverman, P. (2000). *Never to young to know: Death in children's lives.* NY: Oxford University.

Silverman, P., Nickman, S., & Worden, J. W. (1992). Detachment revisited: The child's reconstruction of a dead parent. *American Journal of Orthopsychiatry, 62,* 494-503.

Silverman, P., & Worden, J. W. (1992). *Children's understanding of funeral ritual.* Omega, 25, 319-331.

Traisman, P. S. (1992). *Fire in my heart: Ice in my veins.* Omaha, NE: Centering.

U.S. Secret Service. (2002). Preventing school shootings: A summary of U. S. Secret Service Safety school initiative. *National Institute of Justice Journal, 248,* 10-15.

Webb, N. B. (Ed.). (2002). *Helping bereaved children: A handbook for practitioners* (2nd ed.). New York: Guilford.

Worden, J. W. (1991). *Grief counseling and grief therapy: A handbook for the mental health practitioner.* New York: Springer.

Linda Goldman, CLPC, CT, is a grief therapist, author, and adjunct faculty at John Hopkins University, Baltimore, MD. E-mail: lgold@erols.com

Test Your Knowledge Form

We encourage you to photocopy and use this page as a tool to assess how the articles in *Annual Editions* expand on the information in your textbook. By reflecting on the articles you will gain enhanced text information. You can also access this useful form on a product's book support Web site at *http://www.dushkin.com/online/*.

NAME: DATE:

_____

TITLE AND NUMBER OF ARTICLE:

_____

BRIEFLY STATE THE MAIN IDEA OF THIS ARTICLE:

_____

LIST THREE IMPORTANT FACTS THAT THE AUTHOR USES TO SUPPORT THE MAIN IDEA:

_____

WHAT INFORMATION OR IDEAS DISCUSSED IN THIS ARTICLE ARE ALSO DISCUSSED IN YOUR TEXTBOOK OR OTHER READINGS THAT YOU HAVE DONE? LIST THE TEXTBOOK CHAPTERS AND PAGE NUMBERS:

_____

LIST ANY EXAMPLES OF BIAS OR FAULTY REASONING THAT YOU FOUND IN THE ARTICLE:

_____

LIST ANY NEW TERMS/CONCEPTS THAT WERE DISCUSSED IN THE ARTICLE, AND WRITE A SHORT DEFINITION:

We Want Your Advice

ANNUAL EDITIONS revisions depend on two major opinion sources: one is our Advisory Board, listed in the front of this volume, which works with us in scanning the thousands of articles published in the public press each year; the other is you—the person actually using the book. Please help us and the users of the next edition by completing the prepaid article rating form on this page and returning it to us. Thank you for your help!

ANNUAL EDITIONS: Dying, Death, and Bereavement 05/06

ARTICLE RATING FORM

Here is an opportunity for you to have direct input into the next revision of this volume.
We would like you to rate each of the articles listed below, using the following scale:

1. **Excellent: should definitely be retained**
2. **Above average: should probably be retained**
3. **Below average: should probably be deleted**
4. **Poor: should definitely be deleted**

Your ratings will play a vital part in the next revision.
Please mail this prepaid form to us as soon as possible.
Thanks for your help!

RATING	ARTICLE	RATING	ARTICLE
	1. Technology and Death Policy: Redefining Death		24. Colleen's Choice
	2. The Unsettled Question of Brain Death		25. End-of-Life Care: Forensic Medicine vs. Palliative Medicine
	3. Anatomy Lessons, A Vanishing Rite for Young Doctors		26. Elisabeth Kübler-Ross's Final Passage
	4. In Science's Name, Lucrative Trade in Body Parts		27. Kübler-Ross, Who Changed Perspectives on Death, Dies at 78
	5. Deaths Go Unexamined and the Living Pay the Price		28. The Contemporary American Funeral
	6. Teaching End-of-Life Issues: Current Status in United Kingdom and United States Medical Schools		29. Six Feet Under: Thomas Lynch Has Buried 6,000 Of His Neighbors. He Talks About the Business of Death.
	7. Communication Among Children, Parents, and Funeral Directors		30. How Different Religions Pay Their Final Respects
	8. Children, Death, and Fairy Tales		31. The Last Thing You Want to Do
	9. Terrorism, Trauma, and Children: What Can We Do?		32. An Unexpected Kind of Family Foresight
	10. Helping Teenagers Cope With Grief		33. Working With Death Was No Way to Live
	11. Trends in Causes of Death Among the Elderly		34. Therapist Equates Owner Grief to Family Member Loss: Human-Animal Bond Impacts Physical, Mental Health: Experts Push Pet Bereavement Mainstream
	12. Placing Religion and Spirituality in End-of-Life Care		35. Mourning the Loss of a Pet: Coping Strategies to Help Ease Your Grief and Celebrate Their Memory
	13. Dying Words: How Should Doctors Deliver Bad News?		36. The Grieving Process
	14. Patients Whose Final Wishes Go Unsaid Put Doctors in a Bind		37. Disenfranchised Grief
	15. Start the Conversation		38. Enhancing the Concept of Disenfranchised Grief
	16. Quality End-of-Life Care		39. Till Death Do Us Part
	17. Hospice Referral Decisions: The Role of Physicians		40. The Increasing Prevalence of Complicated Mourning: The Onslaught Is Just Beginning
	18. A Commentary: The Role of Religion and Spirituality at the End of Life		41. Listening
	19. Death and the Law		42. Grief Takes No Holiday
	20. Why Secular Humanism is Wrong: About Assisted Suicide		43. Discussing Tragedy With Your Child
	21. Doctor, I Want to Die. Will You Help Me?		44. Counseling With Children in Contemporary Society
	22. Competent Care for the Dying Instead of Physician-Assisted Suicide		
	23. Euthanasia: A Need for Reform		

(Continued on next page)

BUSINESS REPLY MAIL
FIRST CLASS MAIL PERMIT NO. 551 DUBUQUE IA

POSTAGE WILL BE PAID BY ADDRESEE

McGraw-Hill/Dushkin
2460 KERPER BLVD
DUBUQUE, IA 52001-9902

NO POSTAGE
NECESSARY
IF MAILED
IN THE
UNITED STATES

l.l.l....l.lll....ll.....lll.l.l.l.l.l....l.l.l.l.ll

- -

ABOUT YOU

Name   Date
_____

Are you a teacher? ☐ A student? ☐
Your school's name
_____

Department
_____

Address   City   State   Zip
_____

School telephone #
_____

YOUR COMMENTS ARE IMPORTANT TO US!

Please fill in the following information:
For which course did you use this book?
_____

Did you use a text with this ANNUAL EDITION? ☐ yes ☐ no
What was the title of the text?
_____

What are your general reactions to the *Annual Editions* concept?
_____

Have you read any pertinent articles recently that you think should be included in the next edition? Explain.
_____

Are there any articles that you feel should be replaced in the next edition? Why?
_____

Are there any World Wide Web sites that you feel should be included in the next edition? Please annotate.
_____

May we contact you for editorial input? ☐ yes ☐ no
May we quote your comments? ☐ yes ☐ no